Vegetables
How to Select, Grow and Enjoy

by
Derek Fell

Illustrations by
Joan Frain

HPBooks

Publishers
Bill and Helen Fisher

Executive Editor
Rick Bailey

Editorial Director
Randy Summerlin

Editor
Scott Millard

Art Director
Don Burton

Book Design
Dana Martin

About the Author

Derek Fell is an avid vegetable gardener and widely published garden writer and photographer. He took all the photos in this book. His gardening experience includes more than 15 years of working with vegetable seed companies. He has appeared as a guest gardening expert on ABC-TV's *Good Morning America,* and helped plan the White House vegetable garden. Fell continues to test new vegetable varieties and growing techniques on his two-acre farm in Bucks County, Pennsylvania.

About the Cover

The cover photo shows a sample harvest from the author's garden. At left, 'Supersteak VF' hybrid tomatoes; at right, 'Square' tomatoes. In the foreground in baskets are 'Burpee Hybrid' cantaloupe and Vegetable Spaghetti. At lower left in basket are 'Supersonic VF' and 'Yellow Perfection' tomatoes. At lower right are 'Jersey Golden' acorn squash and 'Fordhook Hybrid' watermelon. Center basket features 'Silver Queen' sweet corn, 'Giant Walla Walla' onion and 'Dusky' hybrid eggplant.

Acknowledgments

Eric A. Johnson, Horticulturist, Palm Springs, CA
Dr. Norman Oebker, Professor of Horticulture, Dept. of Plant Sciences, University of Arizona
Family Food Garden, for use of Automatic Vegetable Garden illustration, Del Erickson, artist

Published by HPBooks, P.O. Box 5367
Tucson, AZ 85703 602/888-2150
ISBN: 0-89586-106-2
Library of Congress Catalog Card Number: 81-82132
©1982 Fisher Publishing Inc. Printed in U.S.A

Contents

1

Pleasures of
Vegetable Gardening 5

2

Planning Your
Garden 9
Sample Garden Layouts 12
Automatic Vegetable Garden 14

3

Soil, Compost and
Fertilizer 19
Sample Soil Test 21
Compost 24
Fertilizer 26

4

Seed Starting and
Planting 31
Seed Catalogs 33
Starting with Seed 35
Planting 41
Climate and Planting Dates 44
Planting Chart 48

5

Water, Weed and
Mulch 53
Weeding 56
Mulching 58

6

Pests and
Diseases 61
Pest Control
for Common Insect Pests 65
Disease Control 68

7

Containers and
Small Spaces 71

8

Harvesting and
Storage 77
Storage and Preservation 79

9

Gallery of Garden
Vegetables 83

10

Edible Herbs 177

Index 191

Pleasures of Vegetable Gardening

No matter how vegetable gardening is described—hobby, pastime, hedge against inflation—it is blessed with benefits. Few experiences in life are more pleasurable and satisfying than planting seeds, being responsible for their growth and reaping a bountiful harvest. Consider the following:

☐ Vegetable gardening teaches self-help and instills a sense of accomplishment. The Chinese have a saying: *To be happy all your life, become a gardener.*

☐ Vegetable gardening is a pleasant escape from everyday stress and anxiety. Problems seem to dissipate as soon as you get your hands in the soil.

☐ Vegetable gardening teaches children responsibility and provides an opportunity for families to do something together. Exercise and learning derived from gardening stimulate the body and the mind.

☐ Vegetable gardening requires no expensive investment. Seeds are among the biggest bargains today, capable of returning a value more than 100 times their initial cost.

☐ Growing vegetables reduces your food bill. Don't expect to get rich from the savings, but a garden can fulfill the fresh-vegetable requirements of your family during the summer months. If you are lucky to live in a mild climate, you may be able to grow fresh vegetables year-round. In addition, many vegetables can be stored or preserved for use out of season.

☐ Garden-fresh vegetables are one of the best sources of vitamins. No other food group—milk, meat, eggs or fish—can match the balanced nutrition vegetables bring to a diet.

☐ The flavor of home-grown vegetables is reason enough to have a garden. Compare the taste of tomatoes from the supermarket produce counter to those picked at peak freshness from your own back yard. What a difference!

Just as there are many reasons to grow vegetables, there are many ways to grow them. As you read this book and talk with other gardeners, you'll receive an assortment of advice, some of it conflicting. Don't become confused trying to follow every expert's "fool-proof" techniques. Growing vegetables is not a pure science, and there are no exact formulas for success. Popular methods such as *mulch gardening, organic gardening, raised-bed gardening, French-intensive gardening, wide-row planting* and *square-foot gardening* are not applicable for all people and situations. The best way to garden is to borrow a little from each to suit you, the location and the vegetables you are growing.

Keep in mind that a vegetable garden can take on many forms. For example, many gardeners integrate vegetables into their landscape. Vegetables can be part of a foundation planting on one side of the house. They can be planted in terraces along a slope, or in a raised bed of railroad ties. Clusters of tomatoes, peppers and eggplant in containers along a redwood deck are attractive and productive. Or plant vegetables in graceful,

---

Left: Vegetable gardens are not limited in design to rectangular lots—this one is part of a backyard landscape. The hand-carved sign in the background sums up the feelings of its keeper. **Above:** Probably the greatest pleasure of growing vegetables is the payoff—a wheelbarrow brimming with a day's harvest.

Many gardeners want a garden that is low maintenance yet high yielding. Plans for an "Automatic Vegetable Garden" are given on page 15.

The author with a midsummer bounty of squash, cabbage and beans. Squash varieties include vegetable spaghetti, golden acorn, yellow zucchini and pear-shaped 'Kuta'.

Left: You can almost taste the crispness of these freshly pulled radishes. Planting more than one variety results in a colorful, varied harvest.

Far left: Planting in single rows is only one way to lay out your garden. This site is part of the kitchen gardens in Mt. Vernon, Virginia, at the home of George Washington.

free-form beds bordering a lawn or patio area. Many vegetables double as decorative vines. A simple trellis against a wall can be an ideal spot for a luxurious vine of vegetable spaghetti. It first covers the trellis with cool greenery, then produces numerous, dazzling yellow flowers. The payoff is armloads of tasty fruit.

ABOUT THIS BOOK
This book is intended to provide a complete guide to growing vegetables successfully. Emphasis has been placed on 10 important areas:

1. Selection of a good location.
Sunlight is one of the most important factors for a successful location. Vegetables need about seven hours of sunlight per day to grow properly. If you have no choice and some areas of the garden are in shade part of the day, plant leaf crops such as lettuce, chard, parsley and kale. See page 9.

2. Garden layout and design.
You have several options when it comes to the size and shape of your garden. Sample plans for small, medium and large gardens are shown on pages 12 and 13. How to plant a high-yield, "Automatic Vegetable Garden" is shown on page 15.

3. Recommended varieties.
The Gallery of Garden Vegetables, pages 82 to 175, lists favorite, generally adapted varieties for nearly every vegetable. Consider *hybrid* varieties for extra vigor and generally higher yields compared to *standard* varieties. See page 31.

4. Seeds, supplies and tools.
After you have invested time, materials and effort in preparing your garden for planting, it pays to plant quality seeds. Avoid low-priced specials. Such seeds may be out of date or inferior in quality. Purchase seeds from a reputable seed company, either from a seed rack or through a mail order catalog. See page 33 for a list of mail order sources.

Few tools are required for vegetable gardening. A spade, hoe, rake and trowel are considered essentials. The equipment you buy will depend on the size of your plot and how you like to garden. Other tools and supplies that ease or speed up garden maintenance are described on page 17.

5. Soil preparation.
The importance of having good garden soil cannot be overstated. Depending on the soil conditions in your region, it may be helpful to test your soil. See page 21. In most instances, addition of organic matter

Tina Fell prepares to harvest a pair of blemish-free 'Big Apple' cabbages.

Part of Hety Brost's daily garden treasure hunt includes a search for cucumbers to include in the evening salad.

Right: What could taste better than sun-ripened tomatoes from your own vines? These are 'Supersteak VFN'.

Far right: A-frame trellis saves garden space. Some vegetables such as cucumbers grow straighter fruit when trained vertically.

such as compost, peat moss, bark products or decomposed manure will be necessary. Step-by-step instructions on soil preparation are given on page 22.

6. When and how to plant.
Vegetables can be grouped into two general categories—cool season and warm season. Planting dates for each are different. The climate map and planting chart on pages 46 to 51 will tell you when and how to plant in your area.

7. Irrigation.
Vegetable plants demand steady amounts of water in their root zone. Don't wait until plants demonstrate need by wilting—it may be too late. Without continuous growth, flavor is affected or plants will not set fruit. The different ways to water are described on page 54.

Soil quality has a lot to do with how you water. Sandy soils drain quickly so they require more frequent watering. Clay soils drain slowly and become waterlogged. Drip irrigation systems can provide water in proper amounts. For more on drip irrigation, see page 55.

8. Weed control.
Weeds can destroy your enthusiasm for gardening faster than anything. The best advice is, don't let them get ahead. Careful soil preparation and using a *mulch,* a covering over the soil, will help control them. See page 58.

9. Pest and disease control.
Prevention is an important word when it comes to pest and disease control. Keeping the garden clean eliminates potential breeding grounds for insects and disease organisms. Checking your

vegetable plants frequently for signs of pest damage is also important. Spotting colonies of pests before they are established makes control much easier. See pages 61 to 69.

10. Harvesting.
Mouth-watering flavor is one of the reasons many gardeners grow vegetables. Picking vegetables when they have their best flavor is important. The listings on pages 77 to 79 tell the proper times to pick popular vegetables. It also helps to know how to store and preserve your harvests. Methods are described on page 79.

To be successful at growing vegetables, you need only understand the principles of how vegetable plants grow, and apply these principles to your particular gardening situation. The variables of nature often intrude, but they are part of the challenge.

Planning Your Garden

The time to begin thinking about which vegetables to plant is when the mail order seed and nursery catalogs become available. In parts of the South and West, this can be as early as September. In other parts of the United States, the catalogs are normally available in January. These colorful dream books, filled with beautiful pictures, try to seduce us into ordering dozens of seed packets and plants. But it is essential to *plan* your garden before you send in your order for plants and seeds. Without thinking ahead, you may buy too much of one vegetable and not enough of another. Or you may completely forget one of your favorites.

WHERE TO PLANT?
The first step to planning your garden is choosing a good location. Important considerations include:
Sunlight. Sunlight is the most important factor for a successful garden location. As a general rule, vegetables require a minimum of seven hours of full sun to produce worthwhile crops.

Most fruit-producing vegetables—tomatoes, squash, peppers—need almost a full day of sun. Root crops and leaf crops can get by with less. Sunlight is essential because vegetables obtain a good part of their food supply through a process known as *photosynthesis*. Photosynthesis occurs when sunlight shines on leaf cells containing water and *chlorophyll*—the green you see in a leaf. Photosynthesis allows the leaf to produce carbohydrates, which the plant uses to make sugars and starches, essential for its survival.

If you have no choice and must plant in an area that receives less-than-ideal sunlight, try growing early maturing varieties. They generally produce with less sun and lower temperatures.

When considering garden placement, note the shadows of nearby walls, trees and buildings. Also keep the seasonal patterns of the sun in mind. In midsummer when the sun is high, shade from a tall object may not be cast on the garden. But in the latter

part of the growing season the sun appears lower in the sky. Shadows lengthen and reach your garden. The reduced sunlight can bring production to an abrupt halt, even though many more weeks of frost-free growing conditions may remain.

Avoid a garden site that is shaded during noonday hours, when sunlight is brightest. If shadows from a building or a tree shade the garden during midday, it will significantly reduce crop yields. Years ago I planted a vegetable garden in a sunny spot, but a tall cherry tree cast shade over the garden for about an hour at noon. Although the garden received an average of seven hours sunlight each day, loss of the bright noon light prevented success with melons and other fruiting vegetables. Another location—an open meadow area—was prepared to grow these vegetables. Leaf vegetables, which generally require less sunlight, grow in the shaded garden.

Plant your garden so rows run north to south rather than east to west. This way, plants receive more

Left: A well-planned garden makes best use of available space. Dual rows of pole beans will soon cover this twine trellis. Above: 12x20' plot features wide, raised planting beds. Pine-needle mulch prevents most weed growth.

even exposure to the sun. Place taller plants and trellises to the north so they will not shade shorter plants.

Reflected light and heat. If a location has insufficient heat or light because it is shaded, you may be able to correct it by reflecting heat and light toward plants. For example, painting a dark wall white increases the amount of reflected light and heat onto plants. Clear plastic or aluminum foil spread over the soil also reflects light and heat onto plants. Actually, it is light *intensity* rather than direct sunlight that affects the growth of plants. In desert areas, you might want to *avoid* reflected heat so vegetable plants will not be overheated.

Soil drainage. Vegetables, like most plants, require good soil drainage. Both air and water are necessary in the root zone for plant growth. How well the soil drains depends on its composition. Clay soils have a tendency to drain slowly; sandy soils drain rapidly. Both can be improved with the addition of large quantities of peat moss, ground bark, compost or other organic material. Preparing the soil is discussed on page 22.

Low spots tend to retain water. Ditches lined with drainage tile can be installed to channel excess water away. If this is too costly or can't be done, plant your garden elsewhere, or build a raised planting bed.

Shelter and protection. Vegetables exposed to the drying effects of summer winds can suffer from serious moisture loss. Exposure to cool winds can create problems for warm-season crops such as melons, tomatoes and peppers. If your vegetable garden is exposed to such winds, consider planting a windbreak. A row of shrubs or trees is more effective than a solid fence or wall. When wind hits a solid barrier, it flows over and down with severe force. A windbreak of evergreens, shrubs or trees filters the force of the wind and dissipates it.

A special consideration is protection from animal pests. You may have to build a sturdy fence around your garden to keep rabbits, raccoons, deer and other animals out. Ways to control animal pests are discussed on page 64.

Proximity to the house. Try to locate the garden near the house. This makes it convenient to slip out the door at mealtime to gather a few crisp parsley leaves for a garnish, or some salad fixings. Locating your garden close to the house also means that it will be near a water faucet.

Toxic trees. Certain plants can be harmful to vegetable plants located nearby. Black-walnut trees give off a toxin through their roots that can poison the soil and prevent growth of many vegetables, particularly tomatoes. For this reason, do not add black-walnut leaves to compost or use them as a mulch.

Although not as toxic as black walnuts, pine trees can also inhibit growth of other plants, oozing a sticky resin from branches, cones and roots. Fallen, dried pine needles, however, are generally safe to use as a mulch.

Sunflower roots produce a growth inhibitor that effectively reduces competition from weeds. This inhibitor can also slow the growth of nearby vegetables.

SIZE OF GARDEN: SMALL, MEDIUM OR LARGE?

The size of your garden is often dictated by the amount of available land. Many modern homes are built on small lots so there is often little choice. Surprisingly, a common mistake for beginners is planting a garden that is *too big*. It is fairly simple to plant a large area, but maintaining it is another matter. Seeds and plants start out small, but before long you can be overwhelmed with weeding, watering, fertilizing and harvesting. If you fall behind in any of these tasks, especially weeding, the garden is headed for disaster.

When deciding garden size, realistically consider how much time you are willing to spend and the resources you have available. A small, well-cared-for garden yields much more than a large, neglected garden. If you have a friend or spouse who is willing to share some of the responsibilities, you can plant a larger area. Your partner will be more help if you involve him or her in deciding which vegetables to grow and how much to plant!

When planning garden space, you should have some idea of potential yields. Generally, seed packets are based on planting a 15-foot row. In most situations, a 15-foot row will supply enough fresh vegetables to feed a family of three. This is true of peas, beans, carrots, beets, onions, tomatoes, cucumbers, melons, peppers, cabbage, lettuce and most other popular vegetables.

Herbs such as parsley, garlic and thyme need much less space because a little goes a long way. If herbs are used mostly for kitchen flavorings, a 5-foot row is plenty.

At the other extreme, sweet corn and asparagus require a lot of space. To feed a family of three adequately, you will need to plant a 15-foot row for each person—a total of 45 feet.

Landscaped garden produces an abundant crop of vegetables and is an attractive, pleasant place to spend some time. Its owner, Mrs. Harriet Heaney of Philadelphia, uses a net to capture cabbage white butterflies *before* they lay their eggs.

The planting chart on pages 48 to 51 supplies guidelines as to the amount of plants needed per person.

Length of row also depends on whether you want quantities for canning or freezing. If you plan to store vegetables in these ways, add approximately 15 more feet of row. These recommendations are based on planting a single row. By growing a wide, matted row or a wide, block planting, a shorter row may be in order.

PLAN ON PAPER

After you have decided on the location of your garden, mark down the dimensions of the area you wish to plant. Graph paper is especially good for this purpose. You can lay out your plan using each square to equal a given unit of measurement. A common ratio is one square equals one foot of space. Mark off the plan into planting rows using the *straight-row system, wide-row system, block-planting system* or a combination of all three. For descriptions of these methods, see page 41. Your plan will give you a good idea of how many vegetables you have room for. Refer to the planting chart on pages 48 to 51 and the individual vegetable descriptions for information on row and plant spacing.

Review the vegetables you want to grow. Decide which crops you want to start from seed and which you prefer to buy as ready-grown transplants. Separate vegetables into annuals and perennials, allocating permanent locations for perennials such as asparagus, rhubarb and horseradish. Separate the vegetables again into cold-hardy varieties and cold-tender varieties. Divide your garden into two parts—one to plant early in the season with cold-hardy vegetables, and the other to plant later in the season with cold-tender crops.

In deciding where to plant varieties, place tall kinds such as pole beans, corn and tomatoes at the north end of the garden. This way they will not shade lower-growing vegetables such as bush beans and lettuce.

The following two pages show sample plans of small, medium and large garden layouts. Each makes use of traditional, rectangular plots and single, straight planting rows. Popular vegetables are included in the samples, but simply substitute your own choices where desired.

Large-scale garden at Longwood Gardens in Pennsylvania features vegetables in traditional single rows. Wide spacing between rows allows room for a power tiller for cultivation and weed control.

Raised beds—planting beds with soil above ground level—make efficient small gardens. All of the soil area can be planted and the garden is neat and easy to care for.

Sample Garden Layouts

Small garden. When planting a small garden—15x26' or smaller—your goal should be to produce maximum yields from minimum space. A limited amount of garden room forces you to be selective in the amount and kinds of vegetables grown. Avoid the temptation to grow corn or melons—they take up too much room.

The easiest-to-grow, most productive vegetables are illustrated in this sample. Bush-type cucumbers could be substituted in place of peppers. Among summer squash varieties, zucchini types are the most productive. Yellow crookneck varieties are also popular. A 15-foot row of tomatoes—5 or 6 plants—can produce up to 150 pounds of fruit. Supporting them with stakes or wire cages saves space. Snap beans are the second most-productive crop after tomatoes, so two rows are worthwhile. One row can be planted with green snap beans, the other with yellow wax beans or bush romano beans. Lettuce is an extremely useful and early crop. One row in the sample garden is devoted to looseleaf lettuce such as 'Oak Leaf'. It matures within 50 days. The other row is planted with a head lettuce such as 'Buttercrunch', which requires an additional 20 days to mature.

Small Garden—15x26'

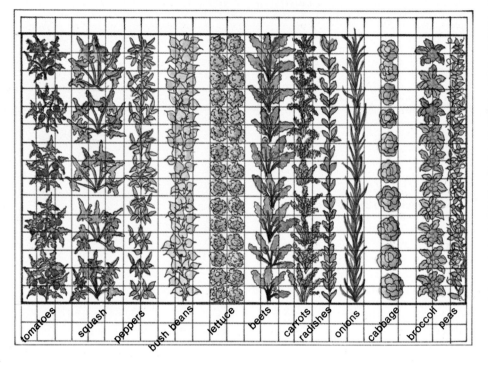

tomatoes, squash, peppers, bush beans, lettuce, beets, carrots, radishes, onions, cabbage, broccoli, peas

One square equals one foot.

Medium Garden—20x35'

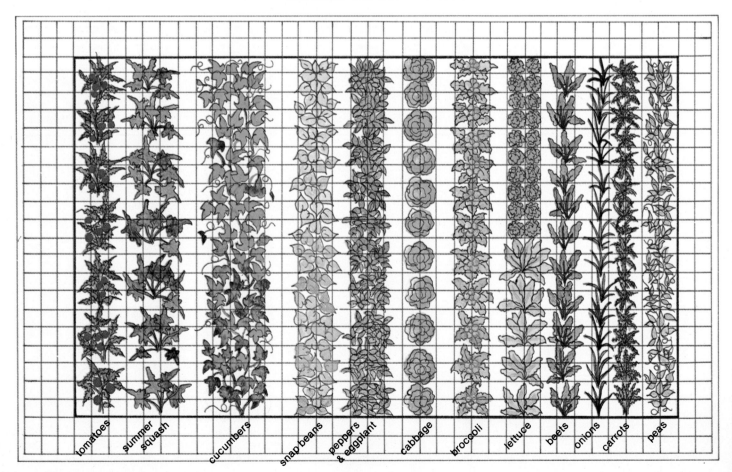

tomatoes, summer squash, cucumbers, snap beans, peppers & eggplant, cabbage, broccoli, lettuce, beets, onions, carrots, peas

Medium garden. Even if you have a garden that is 20x35', you also need to be selective in the kinds of vegetables grown. Corn and melons have been left out of the sample plan deliberately. These crops occupy too much space for the amount of yield.

Cabbage, broccoli, cauliflower and garden peas are included. Garden peas can be trained up chicken wire for support. Broccoli and cauliflower can share a 20-foot row. Broccoli can be planted in spring to mature in early summer, with cauliflower planted in its place after harvesting to mature in fall. Similarly, when the garden peas are finished bearing in midsummer, vines can be pulled up and the row planted with a fall-maturing vegetable such as brussels sprouts.

Large garden. The beauty of a large garden is the space available to grow favorites such as melons, winter squash and sweet corn. These vegetables demand a lot of room for worthwhile quantities, but they reward us with special tastes!

This garden features *perennial vegetables* such as asparagus, rhubarb and perennial herbs. These are crops that overwinter and remain productive for more than one year.

Large gardens are best sectioned into planting squares. This makes it easy to tend the rows of vegetables. Walkways are wide enough to allow you to take a wheelbarrow or cart into the garden for harvest or clean-up. You may wish to allow additional spacing between rows of vegetables if you plan to use a power tiller to cultivate the soil during the growing season.

Use each planting square to group plants that require similar care and growing conditions. Also practice *rotation planting,* which is moving the groups—except perennials—to a new bed each year. This may reduce the possibility of diseases.

Maximum productivity in any garden, no matter what size, can be accomplished by *double cropping* snap beans, radishes, beets, carrots and lettuce. This means making one planting in spring to mature by early summer, and a second planting in midsummer—after the first planting has been harvested—to mature in fall.

Succession planting, planting crops a few weeks apart instead of all at once, extends the harvest. Instead of picking all crops at one time, the harvest is staggered over several weeks.

Large Garden—30x34'

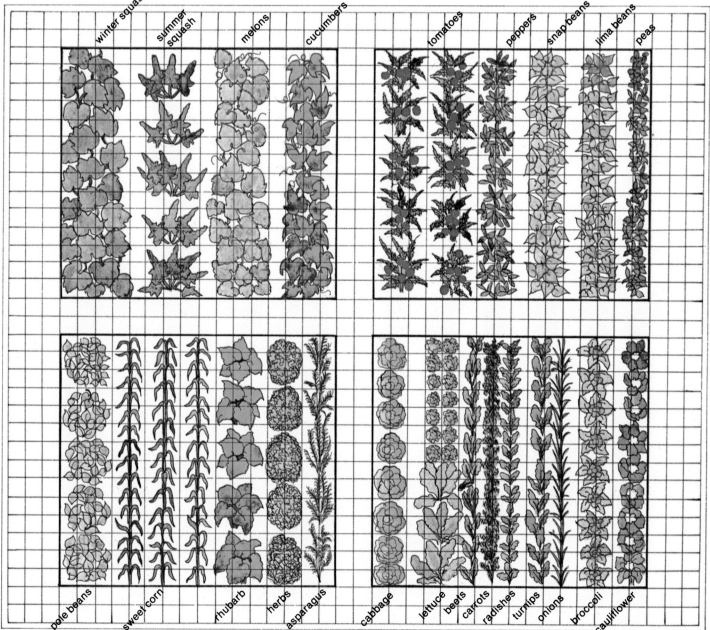

Automatic Vegetable Garden

How would you like to have a vegetable garden without weeds and pests, where the tedious chores of digging and watering are eliminated? Not only is the garden easy to care for, but it is extremely productive, yielding early harvests of your favorite vegetables. Sound too good to be true? It's not. With careful planning and proper techniques, you can grow such a garden. With some justification, I call this my *automatic vegetable garden.*

I have tested this gardening system for several years. Weeds are eliminated by mulching, including the use of black plastic as a mulch. After the ground is prepared the first year, you may not have to dig again. Instead, you garden in wide, raised rows and condition the soil each year with applications of compost or similar organic matter. An inexpensive drip irrigation system waters the garden automatically and efficiently. A reliable organic pest control program keeps pests to a minimum.

Here's how it is done:

The garden plot shown is approximately 15x40'. The size accommodates the use of two 150-foot lengths of drip irrigation hose. Coupled together, the hose is 300 feet long and waters 14 rows of vegetables, each row 15 feet in length. If you want a smaller or larger garden, plan it on the basis of the drip irrigation hose lengths. They are usually available in increments of 50 and 100 feet.

Prepare the planting rows. Dig the planting site in fall or spring. Divide the area into wide, raised planting rows 2 feet wide and 4 to 5 inches high. Place a 1-foot walkway between the rows. Rake soil from the walkways up over the wide rows to raise their height. Or add compost or soil amendment to build up the raised rows. The rows must be level across the top.

Lay irrigation hose. Start at a midway point along the edge of the garden, and lay a 150-foot length of drip irrigation hose along the middle of the rows. The hose should run from one garden row to the next, up and down the rows to the end. Lay a second 150-foot length the same way to cover the other half of the plot. Connect the two hoses to a water spigot by a Y-valve. When the garden needs moisture, turn on one water spigot and each row is watered slowly. When the soil is thoroughly moistened, turn the spigot off. Timers are available to make the drip system automatic.

Lay plastic. Take rolls of 3-foot-wide black plastic film and cover the raised rows. Smooth the plastic across the top of the level rows and down the sides. Leave a 1- to 2-inch border of plastic along the walkway. Cover it with soil to hold it in place. Put down several layers of newspapers in the walkways, and cover them with a thick layer of pine needles or similar organic mulch. The two layers form a weed-proof mulch that looks attractive

and wears well through a season.

Plastic has benefits most other mulches cannot provide. It is a solid barrier against weeds, warms the soil in spring to promote early yields, prevents moisture loss by reducing evaporation, protects the drip irrigation hose from damage and forms a barrier against soil insects in the fall. If you leave the plastic in place all winter, it warms the soil early in spring. However, you should remove the plastic to add compost or other soil amendment to the soil before planting. Replace old plastic with new any time you remove it.

Plant seeds and transplants. Make holes in the plastic for seeds and plants. Make two rows of holes in each raised planting bed for compact plants such as bush beans. Space them 12 inches apart, one row on each side of the drip irrigation hose. Make one row of holes for large, bush-type plants such as squash and tomatoes, spaced 3 feet apart. For peas, beans and corn, plant seeds in the holes. Plant transplants of tomatoes, peppers and cabbage.

For early harvests, start seeds of fruiting vegetables indoors in empty, quart-capacity milk cartons. The cartons have sufficient space to allow for vigorous root growth. At transplant time, the cartons are torn away and such plants as tomatoes, peppers and zucchini squash are transplanted without shock. In my area of Pennsylvania,

1. Make raised planting beds 2 feet wide and 4 to 5 inches high. This width accommodates 3-foot-wide roll of black plastic film.

2. Lay drip irrigation hose down the middle of each bed, snaking it up and down each row to the next. See diagram, page 56.

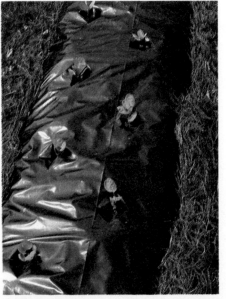

3. Roll plastic over the planting bed and secure edges with soil. To plant, cut an X in the plastic for each seed or transplant.

Automatic Vegetable Garden

Materials

Drip irrigation hose, 300 feet
Y-valve
Black plastic (1-1/2 mils thick) 3 feet wide, 300 feet
Granular fertilizer, 10 lb. bag—worked into soil before planting
Granulated limestone—to adjust pH according to soil test
Foliar fertilizer, 1 lb. bag—liquid fertilizer sprayed on leaves regularly
Seeds
Quart sprayer—to apply liquid fertilizer
Reinforced wire for tomato supports
Chicken wire fencing, 120 feet—to keep out rabbits

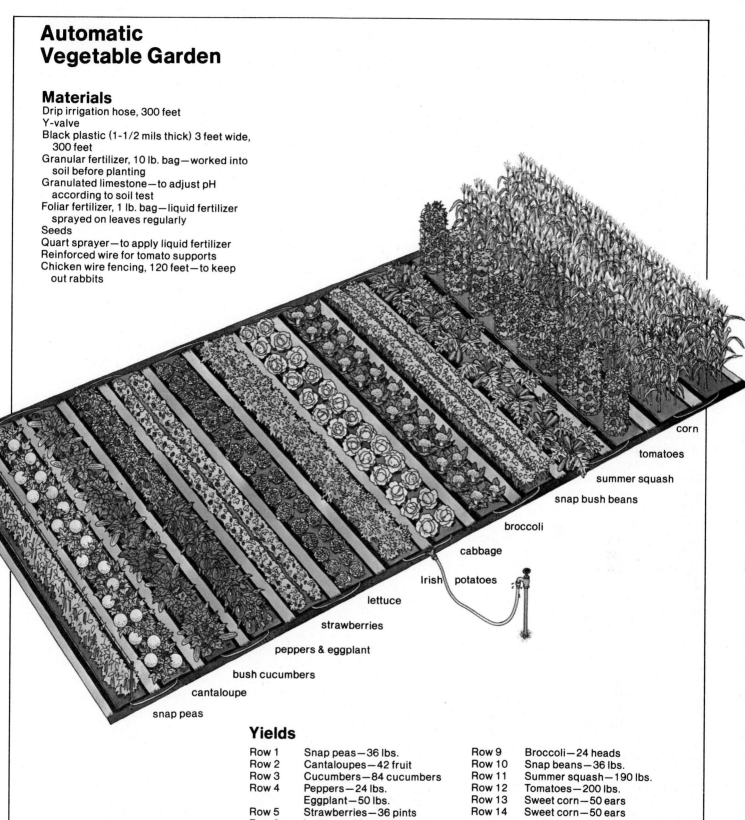

corn
tomatoes
summer squash
snap bush beans
broccoli
cabbage
Irish potatoes
lettuce
strawberries
peppers & eggplant
bush cucumbers
cantaloupe
snap peas

Yields

Row 1	Snap peas—36 lbs.
Row 2	Cantaloupes—42 fruit
Row 3	Cucumbers—84 cucumbers
Row 4	Peppers—24 lbs.
	Eggplant—50 lbs.
Row 5	Strawberries—36 pints
Row 6	Lettuce—38 heads
Row 7	Potatoes—86 lbs.
Row 8	Cabbage—24 heads
	Chinese cabbage—24 heads

Row 9	Broccoli—24 heads
Row 10	Snap beans—36 lbs.
Row 11	Summer squash—190 lbs.
Row 12	Tomatoes—200 lbs.
Row 13	Sweet corn—50 ears
Row 14	Sweet corn—50 ears

Spaghetti squash (not shown)—planted around edge of garden to climb up chicken wire fence—35 fruit weighing 5 lbs. each.

the average last frost date is May 15, yet I have picked zucchini squash May 31, cucumbers June 4, peppers, corn and tomatoes July 4, and melons July 18.

Control pests and diseases. I rely on organic insecticides that offer a broad control—either a rotenone-pyrethrum mixture or a diatomaceous earth-pyrethrum mixture. These two combination insecticides made from natural compounds leave no residues in the soil. They are effective against 90% of soil pests when combined with pest prevention methods. One of the most important prevention practices is a thorough winter clean-up of dead vegetation to prevent overwintering of pests.

The most important application of an insecticide is when you set out your cucumber, squash and melon transplants, or as soon as your beans are up. An early application prevents pests from becoming established.

Side dress with compost and fertilizer. Two other important aspects of this system are composting, and applications of liquid fertilizer to maintain plant nutrient levels. My compost is made in bins using kitchen and garden wastes. The compost, enriched with bone meal, is applied to the raised rows at the start of the season and raked into the upper soil surface. I grow lettuce without supplemental applications of compost.

Peas, tomatoes, peppers and cabbage need a *side dressing*—a booster application. A side dressing can be applied as a liquid fertilizer sprayed on the leaves of the plants or poured into the soil through the holes in the black plastic. The liquid spray is made by using fertilizer concentrate with a 1:2:1 ratio of nutrients, such as 5-10-5 or 15-30-15. See pages 26 to 29 for more on fertilizers.

Several side dressings during the growing season may be necessary to keep fruit-producing plants such as peppers and squash bearing prolifically.

Harvest. The combination of warm soil, fertile compost, side dressings of fertilizer, regular, deep watering and freedom from pests produces top-quality results. I have harvested tomatoes the size of grapefruit, 10-inch-wide heads of broccoli and huge, snow-white heads of cauliflower. Bush beans yielded 89 pods from a single plant. After the initial soil preparation and installation of the drip system, this was accomplished with little time and effort on my part.

BASIC GARDENING TOOLS

Few tools are required for vegetable gardening. A trowel for making seed furrows and planting holes, a spade for digging, a rake for leveling soil and a wheelbarrow for hauling are considered essentials. But a variety of tools are available that make certain tasks easier and less time consuming. Many of the following are easily obtained at auctions and garage sales for a fraction of their retail cost.

Garden fork. Valuable for lifting root crops from soil, turning compost piles, breaking up clay soil, digging heavy soil and loosening compacted soil. Also handy for lifting dense and fibrous materials such as piles of weeds, stable manure, compost and straw.

Garden hoe. For weeding between rows. The scuffle hoe, a variation of the garden hoe, cuts weeds off at the soil level. Other, more efficient systems of weed control are available, such as mulching. See page 58.

Garden hose. Essential for many low-rainfall regions to irrigate the garden plot. Hoses come in various lengths and diameters. A 5/8-inch-diameter hose is a common choice for an average-size garden. What the hose is made of will determine how easy it is to handle and its longevity. Avoid inexpensive vinyl hoses. Choose a quality garden hose reinforced with nylon cord.

Numerous hose-end adapters are available to perform a number of jobs. Misters, bubblers, extenders and adjustable nozzles allow you to direct a heavy jet of water or a fine spray to suit the task.

Garden rake. Essential for leveling soil prior to planting. The tines allow fine soil particles to pass through, but catch large stones and weed roots, helping to clear debris from a newly dug plot. A rake is also necessary to blend lime and fertilizer into the upper soil surface.

Garden spade. Apart from the obvious task of digging soil, use a spade to slice sod, loosen deeply rooted weeds, pry up large stones, shovel manure, spread compost and chop frozen ground to unearth root crops.

Garden trowel. Invaluable for transplanting seedlings, making seed furrows and prying up weeds.

Hand fork. Useful for working the top four inches of soil prior to transplanting and seeding. Also useful for weeding and lifting beets, radishes

Here's the Automatic Garden well into production. Summer squash are beginning to bear fruit—just 30 days from transplanting.

and other small root crops from the soil.

Pump-action sprayer. Essential for applying insect sprays, whether organic or chemical. Sprayer can also be used to apply liquid fertilizers as a foliar or soil feed. Pump-action and compressed-air sprayers are the least expensive and most efficient for home garden use.

Stakes and string. Helpful in marking out areas for digging and for creating straight rows at correct planting distances.

Plant labels. It helps to remember *what* you planted in *which* row. Don't trust your memory—it is too easy to forget. It is also helpful to remember what *variety* you planted and the planting date. You can then make comparisons between varieties for yield, flavor and earliness. Plastic plant labels are durable, but wooden tongue depressors, available from drugstores, are reasonably priced and long lasting.

Many experienced gardeners take record-keeping one step further and keep data on their garden's progress in a calendar or diary. Information that you have learned first-hand will prove to be invaluable as you garden year after year.

Power tiller. For large gardens, a power tiller saves time and effort. Many styles and price ranges are available. Study product brochures carefully before you buy. Owning one represents a substantial investment, so consider renting if all you need to do is turn the ground over or work in amendments each spring.

Wheelbarrow or garden cart. A wheelbarrow is more maneuverable than a cart, especially a wheelbarrow with a pneumatic tire. For large gardens, a cart is valuable because it is capable of hauling large loads of compost, fertilizer, weeds, produce and other materials.

Your tools will last many years if treated properly. Always store them out of the weather after use. Clean blades and other surfaces with a wire brush. Oil moving parts, such as wheelbarrow wheels and drive chains on power equipment.

Other garden supplies are covered on the following pages: *black plastic mulch* for weed control, page 58; *trellis netting* for climbing plants, page 75; *seed-starting aids,* page 36; *soil-test kits,* page 20; *irrigation systems,* page 53; *insect controls,* page 62; *fertilizers,* page 29 and *fungicides,* page 69.

Common Garden Tools

Garden spade is the most useful tool in the garden. Use it to dig soil and spread soil conditioners.

Hand fork breaks up crusted soil prior to planting. Use it to pull weeds growing close to vegetable plants.

Garden hoe allows you to uproot weeds without stooping. Keep hoe and other tools sharp by filing cutting edge regularly.

Garden fork helps in initial soil preparation by loosening soil. It can also be used to aerate your compost pile and dig root crops.

Hand trowel can be used to make seed furrows, dig holes for transplants, uproot weeds and spread fertilizer.

String and stakes make it easy to lay out your garden before digging, and mark planting rows prior to seeding or transplanting.

Soil, Compost and Fertilizer

Good soil is the foundation of a successful vegetable garden. If your garden produce is not up to par—midget-size corn, scrawny peppers, tomatoes with sparse, misshapen fruit and blemished root crops—your problem is probably caused by poor, infertile soil.

Soil anchors plants and supplies them with nutrients and moisture. Because nutrients are absorbed by plant roots in *soluble form,* dissolved by moisture, soil should have good moisture-holding capacity. This is created by air spaces between the soil particles. Air is also necessary for the plant roots to breathe. A good soil allows excess moisture to drain away. Without air in the soil, plant roots suffocate and die.

SOIL TYPES
There are many kinds of soil. Variables include the region where you live, the terrain, and whether the area was farmland or if the soil was graded or moved for a housing development. Soil differs in its *pH,* a measure of

acidity and alkalinity. Soil varies in texture and composition from light, sandy soil to heavy clay soil. There are also limestone soils, shale soils, humus soils, soils formed from volcanic ash, soils formed from decayed vegetation and stony soils. For the purpose of vegetable gardening, soils can be grouped into three broad categories:

Sandy soil. Sandy soil is composed of large mineral particles. If you squeeze a handful of moist, sandy soil, it crumbles when released. It holds plenty of oxygen and is a good growing medium for vegetables. Plant roots can penetrate it freely. The drawback of sandy soil is that water and nutrients drain away quickly. Also, sandy soil tends to be highly alkaline, which most vegetables dislike.

Clay soil. Clay is probably the most difficult soil to work with. It is composed of small mineral particles that tend to pack tightly together. If you squeeze a handful of moist, clay soil, it feels slimy and sticky, and compacts into a thick, heavy mass. Because of

this, it is heavy and cold in spring and can bake into a hard crust in summer. It does not drain well and acts as a barrier to plant roots.

Loam soil. This is the best kind of garden soil. It contains proportionate amounts of sand, clay and rock particles, and usually large quantities of organic matter. A loam soil retains water and nutrients in the root zone, yet drains well. If you squeeze a handful of moist, loam soil, it will form a loosely packed ball in your hand.

The only way to change a sandy soil or clay soil to a loam is by adding *organic matter.* Compost, decomposed manure, peat moss and ground bark products are commonly used. Instructions on how to improve the soil are given on page 23.

TESTING YOUR SOIL
A soil test won't tell you what type of soil you have or its organic content, but it will tell you about your soil's vital statistics—its pH and nutrient content. Technically, soil pH describes the soil's *hydrogen concentration,* in-

Left: Soil rich in organic matter is necessary to produce quality crops such as these freshly dug sweet potatoes. Above: Rich, dark compost has many benefits. It adds nutrients and organic matter to the soil and serves as an excellent mulch.

There are many kinds of soil, generally due to differences in mineral content and amount of organic matter. Here are examples of three basic types: Sandy soil at left is composed of large mineral particles. It drains well, but is not efficient at holding moisture and nutrients in the root zone. Clay soil at center is composed of small particles. It is dense, has poor drainage and is difficult to work. Loam soil at right has a good balance of mineral particles and is high in organic matter. It drains well and the spaces between its particles hold moisture and nutrients in the root zone.

dicating whether the soil is acid, alkaline or neutral. If the soil is too acid or too alkaline for the plants you want to grow, materials can be added to adjust the pH. Usually, lime is added to decrease soil acidity; sulfur or peat moss is added to decrease soil alkalinity.

The pH scale extends from 1 to 14, showing extremely high acidity at the low end of the scale and extremely high alkalinity at the high end. A reading of 7.0 is considered *neutral.* The difference between a reading of 6.0 and 7.0 might seem small, but because a pH scale is *logarithmic,* 6.0 is *ten times* more acidic than 7.0. For a further explanation, see the accompanying illustration.

It would be difficult to provide each row of vegetables with its preferred pH factor. The alternative is to establish a compromise soil condition in which the majority of vegetables succeed. Most vegetables prefer a soil pH that is *moderately* acid. Any garden soil that is too acid or too alkaline prevents plants from absorbing nutrients, even if nutrients are plentiful.

In addition to soil pH, you need to know the availability of nutrients in your soil. If you do not test your soil, you can add a general-purpose fertilizer with a ratio of 5-10-10, hoping that you are adding proper amounts of the important nutrients. Chances are, you will add too much of one nutrient and not enough of another. For example, a soil that has an overabundance of nitrogen and a poor supply of phosphorus generates leafy growth at the expense of producing fruit. Nutrients required by vegetables are discussed in detail on pages 26 to 29.

If you want to find out your soil's pH, you can use a do-it-yourself pH test kit. If you desire a wide range of information, from pH to nutrient availability, a laboratory soil test is in order.

Do-it-yourself pH test kit. This kind of kit is usually inexpensive and available from garden centers and mail order garden catalogs. It is not nearly as accurate as a laboratory test, but is simple to use. You mix small samples of soil from different parts of your vegetable plot into a test tube, pour in a solution, shake well and allow it to settle. You then compare the color of the solution with a chart provided with the kit to determine the pH range.

The color of the solution gives you an indication as to whether your soil is alkaline or acid. Directions with the kit tell you how much lime must be added to adjust the pH if the soil is acid, and what to do if the soil is too alkaline.

Laboratory soil test. A laboratory soil test is more precise than a test kit and a technician interprets the test results. It is therefore more expensive. With the exceptions of California and Illinois, all states perform laboratory soil tests for the gardening public. Look in your phone book under "U.S. Government," "Department of Agriculture," "County Agent" or "Cooperative Extension Service" to determine the agency in your state responsible for soil testing. Call and tell them you wish to have your soil tested. For a fee they mail you a package of instructions that contains a pouch for including a sample of your soil. Or you can contact the soil test laboratory direct for information.

Carry out the instructions and mail the package. Normally you will receive an analysis within a couple of weeks, but it sometimes takes longer. Your analysis will include detailed information on the make-up of your soil, its deficiencies and how to correct them. A sample soil test report from Pennsylvania is shown opposite.

If you live in California or Illinois, you must have your soil tested by a private lab. Look in the phone book under "Soil Laboratories" or "Soil Services."

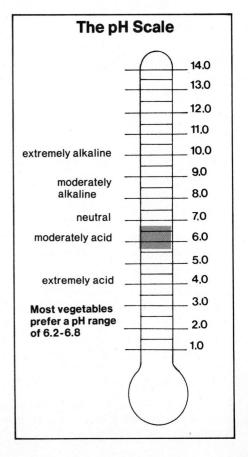

The pH Scale

	14.0
	13.0
	12.0
	11.0
extremely alkaline	10.0
	9.0
moderately alkaline	8.0
neutral	7.0
moderately acid	6.0
	5.0
extremely acid	4.0
	3.0
Most vegetables prefer a pH range of 6.2-6.8	2.0
	1.0

Sample Soil Test

Soil pH and pH buffer. Most flowers and vegetables do best with a pH range of 6.2 to 6.8—slightly acid. Analysis shows this soil sample to be 6.1, which normally indicates that the addition of lime is necessary to correct high acidity. Because of differences in composition, soils can have the same pH but require varying amounts of lime to adjust to proper levels. Therefore, the laboratory uses a more accurate rating known as the *pH buffer*. In this instance, the pH buffer is 6.8, allowing the lab to calculate how much limestone to add to bring the soil into proper balance.

Phosphorus needs are printed above the letter P. The number shows the pounds per acre of available phosphorus indicated by the soil sample. Phosphorus makes itself available to plants at a slow rate. For this reason, a *starter fertilizer*, a fertilizer high in phosphorus, should be mixed in the soil at the future root zone at time of transplanting, even though phosphorus is high.

Potassium and trace elements are shown separately by the letters K—potassium; Mg—magnesium, and Ca—calcium. These are expressed in milliequivalents per 100 grams of soil. The balance of these nutrients in combination with each other is also important. This is shown in the next column as cation exchange capacity (CEC).

Cation exchange capacity is a term measuring the soil's nutrient "storehouse." Clay soils high in organic matter usually have high CEC values. Sandy soils usually have low CEC values.

Percent saturation is the concentration of each nutrient expressed as the percent of CEC. It helps the lab determine how well the soil is balanced in available nutrients. A well-balanced soil will generally show 1 to 5% potassium, 10 to 15% magnesium and 80% calcium. In some soils, potassium is often higher than 5%. High levels are considered detrimental if the other elements are low. If potassium levels are excessive, plants tend to take up larger quantities of potassium at the expense of calcium and magnesium. A low amount of calcium is not considered bad, because it is needed by the plant in such small amounts. Excessive calcium saturation indicates less room for potassium and magnesium. Normally, a 10% magnesium saturation is desired. Calcium and magnesium ratio should be about 6 to 1. When greater than 10 to 1, the soil is out of balance.

These figures help the laboratory technician determine how to best adjust your soil. Because of their importance, the soil nutrient levels are shown graphically on the soil test form as "Low, Medium, High or Excessive."

Crops normally produce best when nutrients are balanced and present in the soil at high levels. If a nutrient is at a *low* level, applications of the nutrient should improve yields. An *excessive* level indicates that there is more than enough of a nutrient in the soil. Any further addition of the nutrient may reduce yields rather than improve them.

Nitrogen is not shown on the analysis. This is because available nitrogen in the soil constantly changes, even from day to day. A lot of rain, for example, tends to wash nitrogen from the soil. Addition of nitrogen is given among the recommendations for limestone and fertilizer.

Limestone and fertilizer recommendations. The report tells us how much to apply for each 100 square feet for three major crop groups. For *cole crops*, the *cabbage family* and *tomatoes*, this test says to add 4.5 pounds of 5-10-5 general-purpose fertilizer. In addition, 1 pound of 20% phosphorus or 1/2 pound of 46% phosphorus, should be added to increase the phosphorus level.

The recommendation for *vine crops* and *peppers* is 3.5 pounds of 5-10-5 general-purpose fertilizer, plus 1.5 pounds of 20% phosphorus or 3/4 pound of 46% phosphorus.

The recommendation for *beans, peas, lettuce* and others is 1.5 pounds of 5-10-5, and 2.5 pounds of 20% phosphorus or 1-1/4 pounds of 46% phosphorous.

The report also advises the application of 4.5 pounds of dolomitic ground limestone. Ground limestone contains magnesium. As it reduces high acidity, it corrects low magnesium content.

If only one fertilization recommendation can be followed, the report tells us to use the amounts given for *vine crops*.

- **LABORATORY RESULTS:**

6.1	6.8	73	0.4	0.4	9.2	12.0	3.3	3.3	76.5
pH SOIL	pH BUFFER	P (lbs/A)	K	Mg (meq per 100 gm.)	Ca	CEC	K	Mg % Saturation	Ca

- **SOIL NUTRIENT LEVELS:**

		LOW	MEDIUM	HIGH	EXCESSIVE
PHOSPHORUS	(P)				
POTASSIUM	(K)				
CALCIUM	(Ca)				
MAGNESIUM	(Mg)				

LIMESTONE AND FERTILIZER RECOMMENDATIONS FOR   HOME GARDEN

APPLY FOR EACH 100 SQ FT FOR THE FOLLOWING:
*** COLE CROPS, TOMATO, SWEET CORN, BEETS, CARROTS, ONION, CELERY, POTATO
   4.5 LB   5-10-5 ; PLUS 1.0 LB   0-20-0   OR   0.5   LB   0-46-0
***VINE CROPS, PEPPER, EGGPLANT, RASPBERRY, BLACKBERRY, ASPARAGUS
   3.5 LB   5-10-5 ; PLUS 1.5 LB   0-20-0   OR   0.75 LB   0-46-0
***BEANS, PEAS, LETTUCE, STRAWBERRY, RADISH, WATERMELON, TURNIPS, HERBS
   1.5 LB   5-10-5 ; PLUS 2.5 LB   0-20-0   OR   1.25 LB   0-46-0
APPLY FOR EACH 100 SQ FT FOR THE ABOVE CROPS:
   4.5 LB GROUND LIMESTONE. USE DOLOMITIC LIMESTONE TO SUPPLY THE
      MAGNESIUM NEEDS.
TO CONVERT ABOVE RATES TO LBS PER ACRE, MULTIPLY BY 435.
WHERE ONLY ONE FERTILIZER RATE IS DESIRED, USE VINE CROP RECOMMENDATION.

MODIFYING SOIL pH

Acid soils are common in forested areas of the country. Over the years, through composting of woody materials, soil increases in acidity. High acidity is not good because it chemically "locks up" nutrients in the soil, preventing them from becoming available to plants. The easiest way to adjust acidity to acceptable levels is through application of lime.

Lime is available in several forms. *Ground limestone,* also known as *dolomitic limestone,* is usually best because it is high in calcium, a trace element, and its effects are long lasting. Generally, lime is required every three years in acid-soil areas, applied at the rate of 5 pounds per 100 square feet. This amount lowers the pH one point.

Other materials that lower soil acidity are wood ashes and oyster shells. Oyster shells are high in lime and phosphorus. Wood ashes are also rich in potash. The harder the wood, the better its nutritional value to plants as wood ashes. For this reason, oak, walnut and cherry tree ashes are recommended. Wood ashes sprinkled over leaf surfaces discourage chewing insects. Sprinkled around the base of plants, ashes repel root maggots and slugs.

Alkaline soils are common in the Southwest. They are usually neutralized by adding sulfur, peat moss or other highly acid organic material such as leaf mold. Technically, the sulfur oxidizes and becomes sulfuric acid, which acidifies and neutralizes the alkaline compounds. Compost made from decomposed wood products is also used. All of these are normally available from nurseries and garden supply centers.

Use sulfur carefully to acidify an alkaline soil. Have the soil tested by a soil testing laboratory if you suspect your soil is alkaline, and receive an expert recommendation on amounts of sulfur to use.

Another product that is often recommended for acidifying soil is aluminum sulfate. It is generally applied at the rate of 1-1/4 pounds per 100 square feet in slightly alkaline soils. Be sure to read the package directions and follow them precisely to avoid an overdose.

PREPARING THE SOIL

As mentioned, a soil test is not the answer to all soil problems. Lack of organic matter can make it difficult for plants to make use of available nutrients. Organic matter also encourages beneficial soil microorganisms. If your soil is sandy, organic matter will improve its water- and nutrient-holding capacity. If your soil is clay, it will improve its structure and drainage. Compost, leaf mold, peat moss, decomposed manure and bark products are common sources of organic matter. Compost and leaf mold are the best. If you make your own, they are also the least expensive.

When you apply organic matter, the goal is to amend the structure of the soil. As a guide, the garden soil should be approximately one-third organic matter. Apply 3 to 6 inches of soil amendment over the existing soil. Till or spade all the materials thoroughly to a depth of 8 to 12 inches.

The actions of wind, sun and footsteps on a garden lead to soil compaction and dissipation of organic material. For these reasons, it is wise to add soil amendment to the garden every year.

Preparing a new garden. If possible, prepare the soil for a new vegetable plot in the fall. Fall preparation allows amendments to blend with the soil prior to spring planting. Soil preparation in the fall also uncovers eggs and larvae of harmful insects.

Fall is also the time to adjust the soil pH. Spread the recommended amount of lime, peat moss or other neutralizing material evenly over the soil. If you don't have the opportunity to prepare your soil in the fall, do it in spring as soon as the ground is dry and can be worked.

Digging a new plot is much different from preparing an established area, especially if the area you want to plant is covered with lawn or weeds. If your

Soil Structure and Plant Growth

These simplified illustrations point out the importance of good soil structure to plant growth. Soil at far right is composed of tightly compacted clay soil. In reality, clay soil particles are minute and cling together tightly, making it difficult for water, nutrients and air to reach the root zone. Soil at right has a balanced proportion of sand, silt, clay and organic matter. Spaces between these particles allow plant to receive necessary amounts of water, nutrients and air, yet soil drains well.

soil is manageable, small gardens can be dug by hand.

The easiest method is to stake out the site you wish to dig. If rains haven't done it for you, thoroughly moisten the soil the day before the area is to be dug. Don't dig or prepare soil when it is wet or dry—try for that moist, crumbly, in-between stage. Remove squares of sod with a spade and shake the valuable topsoil from the roots. If there is heavy grass, sod or weeds, remove them first—don't turn them under. Clumps of turf are difficult to break up and restrict planting. Also, some grasses such as bermudagrass can infest your garden if turned under the soil.

In preparing the soil for a new site, you may *single dig* or *double dig*. Single digging is simply turning over the soil to a depth of about 12 inches—the length of your spade blade. You then work that 12 inches of soil with a garden fork and rake to remove rocks, clods and other debris.

Double digging is more work, but plants with deep root systems respond to the additional depth of loose, fertile soil. First, dig a trench in the soil to the depth of your spade. Then dig down further with a garden fork to loosen the soil so you have a "double" depth of loose soil. Compost can be worked into the bottom level for a further improvement in the soil structure.

In most circumstances, double digging is worth the extra effort. But you can get almost the same effect by single digging, then raking the soil from the walkways to create 4- to 5-inch-high raised mounds. See Automatic Vegetable Garden, page 15.

As you turn over the soil, remove weed or grass roots and stones. Keep a sharp eye open for any insect pests such as wireworms and cutworms and remove them by hand. Use a rake to break up the clumps of soil. Level the site with a rake and clear away any debris collected in the prongs. Don't walk on the freshly dug soil. Instead, lay down wooden planks and walk over them.

Take care not to *over-prepare* the soil. If soil becomes too fine, it crusts and forms clods when wet.

Tilling. For large gardens or first-time gardens, it is probably best to rent a power tiller to mix soil, amendment and conditioners. If your soil is hard to work, you may want to use a tiller regardless of the garden's size. If you have a large garden, it may pay to buy a tiller, but rent the first time around. Check the classified section of your local newspaper and the Yellow Pages for tiller rentals.

Fertilizer should be added to the soil 7 to 10 days prior to planting, at rates recommended by a soil test. Or follow the fertilizer recommendations given on page 29.

EARTHWORMS IN THE SOIL

Earthworms improve soil by plowing tunnels in the soil, creating air and water passages. They also increase soil fertility. They ingest soil, pass it through their bodies, expelling it as *castings* that are richer in nutrients than the original soil. The Connecticut Experiment Station found that worm castings contain 5 times more nitrogen, 7 times more available phosphorus, 11 times more potash and 40% more humus than the surrounding topsoil. When an earthworm dies, its body adds nitrogen to the soil—up to 1,000 pounds of nitrogen per acre per year in a highly organic soil.

The total number of earthworms in an acre of ground can exceed 3 million—producing their own weight in castings every 24 hours. Earthworms are scarce in sandy soils and heavy clay soils. After the organic content of soil is increased, the earthworm population increases dramatically.

You usually do not have to buy earthworms—the microscopic egg clusters are present in most cultivated soils. To build up the populations in your soil, add plenty of organic matter and they begin to thrive on their own.

Materials normally added to the soil before planting include, from top: general-purpose fertilizer, lime or sulfur to adjust pH and compost.

Rear-end power tiller is used to prepare soil for planting. As a rule, rent a tiller before investing in one of your own.

Consider the earthworm as a friend of the garden, improving soil aeration.

Compost

Vegetable garden soils are constantly being depleted of plant nutrients, especially nitrogen. Plants use up nutrients, and rainfall and irrigation wash them from the soil. One of the best ways to combat loss of nutrients and maintain good soil texture in your garden is to add *compost*—the dark, fluffy material produced from well-decayed organic wastes.

The importance of composting cannot be overstated. I attribute much of the success of my garden to the generous amounts of compost I apply year-round. I use compost as a mulch around vegetables and in the rows to prevent weed growth. It conserves moisture and insulates the soil. As it decomposes, compost adds organic matter to the soil. This encourages earthworms, which further enrich the ground with their castings.

Compost can act as fertilizer, supplying plants with nitrogen, phosphorus and potassium, as well as other minerals. There is some disagreement as to whether compost can serve as a complete substitute for commercial fertilizer that contains essential plant nutrients. I believe that when compost is properly made and applied continuously over the growing season, it *can* replace commercial fertilizer. The problem with most gardeners, however, is the lack of space, time and materials to make enough compost to serve as a substitute.

MATERIALS FOR COMPOST

Garden refuse is excellent as material for compost. Remains of vegetable crops, lawn clippings and weeds are commonly used. Tough stems, leaves and hedge prunings are best shredded before adding to the compost heap. Household wastes such as potato peels, egg shells and coffee grounds can be easily composted. Meat scraps, fat and bones should *not* be used. They attract rodents and produce rancid odors.

In addition to your own garden and kitchen scraps, large quantities of waste material can be obtained from outside sources. One of the best sources is a local horse stable. Most stables are more than happy to have gardeners remove their piles of manure at no charge. Tons of stable manure—much of it already well decomposed—is often available. One or two trips a year can supply your compost pile with all the waste mate-

rial it needs. My own compost is made mostly from horse manure brought in from neighboring stables. It is heaped into my compost bin to decompose with garden and kitchen wastes.

Grass clippings and leaves are also available from neighbors, golf courses, cemeteries, and city and county cleanup crews. Before using grass clippings, inquire as to whether pesticides were used on the lawn. If so, do not add them to your compost.

One of the keys to making good compost is maintaining a balance between "green" material and "dead" material. Technically, this is a *carbon* (dead) to *nitrogen* (green) ratio. Under natural conditions, this ratio is approximately 12 to 1. There is a simple way to put this to work in your backyard compost pile. When you add a batch of grass clippings, fresh garden refuse or other green material, throw in a handful or two of sawdust, dead material. Some gardeners keep the sawdust in a can near the compost pile for ease of use.

The value of weeds as compost. When summer months turn hot and humid, we tend to slow down and spend more time in the shade, beside the pool or away on vacation. This is when the garden is most neglected and weeds begin to multiply.

But there is value in all those weeds. Removed from the garden and heaped into a compost pile, weeds are capable of decomposing into nutrient-rich compost.

Weed plants are efficient, penetrating deep into the soil or spreading across the soil surface to absorb water and nutrients. If allowed to decompose as compost, weeds release these nutrients. When this compost is used on a garden, it enriches the soil.

Some garden experts advise against using weeds in compost piles to keep weed seeds out of the garden. They also claim weed roots are slow to decompose. But properly made compost generates enough heat to kill weed seeds. To aid decomposition, tough weed roots like thistle, pokeweed and dandelion can be shredded by running a lawn mower over them or passing them through a shredder.

MAKING COMPOST

Anyone can make clean compost using common waste materials. Unfortunately, many people have an

image of compost as smelling bad and attracting flies and vermin. Properly made, it is clean, crumbly, odorless and completely free of diseases, pests and weed seeds.

Like good wine, good compost takes time and a lot of material to produce a small amount of quality finished product. Quality compost can be made in a short time by following these four fundamental steps:

1. Shred all waste material thoroughly before putting it on the compost pile. Smaller pieces decompose faster because there is more surface area for microorganisms to work on. Use a mechanical shredder, if possible, or run the lawn mower over the waste material. This is particularly important for tough weed roots, dry leaves and hedge prunings.

2. Turn the compost pile. Aeration is vital for speedy decomposition. Too little air will transform the pile into a putrid mess. Too much air will cause rapid heat and moisture loss. Use a garden fork to move the bottom of the pile to the top, and the inside of the pile to the outside. This helps improve air circulation and prevents compaction where microorganisms cannot work. Avoid thick layers of a single material—especially sawdust, grass clippings and leaves, which tend to cake. Mix these with other waste materials to improve air flow and drainage of moisture.

3. Use an activator. An *activator* is an additional source of nitrogen. It is a major ingredient in a successful compost pile. It serves as food for microorganisms and helps them work faster, raising the internal temperature up to 160F (54C). High temperatures destroy harmful pests, diseases and weed seeds.

In spring and summer, plenty of nitrogen is available in grass clippings, young leaves and weeds that you put on the pile. In fall, nitrogen is lacking. An activator will provide the nitrogen required. It can be animal manure, pure nitrogen fertilizer, fish emulsion, liquid seaweed, dried blood, bone meal—any material containing a rich supply of nitrogen. Activators made especially for composting are also available in package form from garden stores.

For acid-soil areas, a sprinkling of lime with the activator is helpful. Activators and lime can be applied between layers of waste materials, alternating the lime and nitrogen sources.

4. Keep pile moist but not wet. When adding dry waste material, wet it down before adding to the pile. Although moisture is essential in a compost pile, too much moisture will cause it to putrify and smell bad.

Mix each addition of moistened material into the pile. Level the top of the pile. For each 6-inch layer of garden and kitchen waste, add a layer of high-nitrogen material such as fresh animal manure, or sprinkle fish emulsion or chemical nitrogen fertilizer on top.

When the pile reaches about 4 feet high, cover with a layer of garden topsoil, an old blanket or sheet of plastic. This helps to keep the pile warm, which encourages bacteria to break down the materials. That is why composting slows in the cool winter months. Don't cover the pile so tightly that the oxygen necessary for decomposition is reduced. After covering, allow the compost to mature for 6 months. To maintain a continuous supply of compost, a second or third pile can be started. While one pile is being used, the others are in different stages of decomposition.

COMPOST BINS
You can make a simple, inexpensive, small-scale compost bin from wire fencing. Concrete wire mesh works well and can be purchased from a local builder's supply yard. Providing it rests on a level surface on bare soil, it makes a useful container for holding waste materials and compost in batches. Cost of materials is about $10.

A commercially manufactured compost bin with sliding panels is available in plastic or metal. The sliding panels provide access to the bottom of the pile while the upper layers are still decomposing. A ventilator grill under the bin and holes in the sliding panels provide aeration. A lid helps maintain warm temperatures.

Compost drums are designed for fast decomposition of materials. Waste material is heaped into the drum until full. The contents are turned daily by cranking a handle. Compost can be made in less time than with conventional methods.

More information on compost drums and sliding panel bins can be obtained by writing to The Kinsman Company, River Road, Point Pleasant, PA 18950.

Large-scale composting is best done in square or rectangular wooden bins. The first step is to construct a structure from wood, at least 4x4', but preferably 8x8', and 4 feet high. Wood preservative should be used on the lumber to resist rotting. Do not apply creosote or any other poisonous substance.

Build the bin so it sits solidly on bare soil. This way, worms and other beneficial soil organisms can freely enter the pile. Leave a 2-inch gap between the wooden slats that form the sides of the bin so air can penetrate the pile from all sides.

LEAF MOLD
Rich, black leaf mold is a kind of compost found naturally on forest floors. It has long been valued as a soil amendment. The moisture-holding capacity of leaf mold is up to 10 times better than ordinary garden topsoil. Leaf mold is also rich in trace elements and beneficial microorganisms.

It is easy to make leaf mold. Instead of burning leaves, create a storage bin from chicken wire curved to make a container on the ground. Leaves decompose much faster if they are shredded with a lawn mower before loading into the bin. You can also speed up decomposition by adding nitrogen. The nitrogen provides food for the microorganisms, so they multiply rapidly to do their job more efficiently. Nitrogen is available as animal manure and green plant parts such as green leaves and grass clippings. However, a packaged activator specifically made for composting works much faster, helping to reduce a mass of shredded leaves into leaf mold within weeks during warm weather.

The finished leaf mold is especially useful as a mulch. Be aware that it can make the soil more acid, so adjust with lime. Applied over the soil, it helps reduce soil temperatures. A bonus is its rich, earthy aroma.

Large-scale compost bin using the "layer" system. Every 6 inches of garden waste is layered with high-nitrogen material such as fish emulsion or fresh animal manure. Spaces between wooden side slats allow for air circulation.

Receptacle for a small-scale compost heap is made with wire fencing supported by stakes. Nothing fancy, but it works. This compost is ready to be used.

Fertilizer

Most vegetable plants cannot sustain themselves on nutrients found naturally in unimproved soil. It is necessary to provide plants with regular applications of fertilizer. Fertilizers are available in *natural* forms such as animal manure or compost, or *synthetic* forms made from chemicals. Both kinds contain varying amounts of the three major plant nutrients: *nitrogen, phosphorus* and *potassium (potash),* abbreviated to N-P-K. The numbers always appear in this order on fertilizer products.

Nitrogen is available in synthetic and natural forms. Synthetic nitrogen, nitrogen manufactured from chemicals, comes as either *fast release* (water soluble) or *slow release* (water insoluble). Fast release provides a quick effect, but soon drains from the soil. Regular applications during the growing season are normally necessary to maintain healthy green color. Fast-release nitrogen fertilizers can *burn* plants unless mixed into the soil a week to 10 days before planting.

Slow release is more efficient. Burning does not occur because the fertilizer is basically water insoluble, so it releases into the soil slowly. One application per season is usually sufficient to fertilize leaf-producing vegetables such as lettuce and cabbage. Read the product label to find out if your nitrogen is fast or slow release. Although nitrogen is the most important nutrient to have as slow release, because it can disappear so quickly, some brands of fertilizers also control the release of phosphorus and potassium. These are discussed on page 28.

Natural nitrogen is available as decayed living matter such as animal manure and compost. Liquid seaweed, fish emulsion and blood meal are other sources. Natural nitrogen is released slowly. If the material is thoroughly decomposed, there is no risk of burning.

Phosphorus is usually applied as bone meal, phosphoric acid and super-phosphate. If not used by plants, phosphorus stays in the soil for a long time. It is essential for early crops of fruiting vegetables such as melons and tomatoes. When fruiting crops fail to ripen, the problem may be a combination of too much nitrogen and too little phosphorus.

General-purpose vegetable fertilizers contain phosphorus, but a soil test will tell you how much extra your garden may need to bring it up to adequate levels.

Potassium acts like a vitamin tablet, and stays in the soil over a long period. The most common source of natural potassium is wood ashes. It is also an ingredient in general-purpose fertilizers.

Minor elements. Under normal soil conditions, minor elements such as calcium, iron, sulfur, copper, zinc, boron, magnesium and molybendum are available in sufficient amounts to promote healthy growth.

Occasionally, some soils suffer

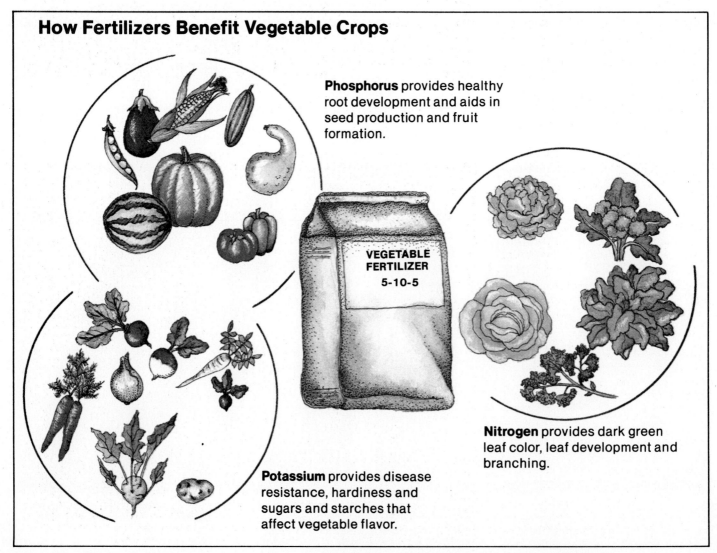

How Fertilizers Benefit Vegetable Crops

Phosphorus provides healthy root development and aids in seed production and fruit formation.

VEGETABLE FERTILIZER 5-10-5

Nitrogen provides dark green leaf color, leaf development and branching.

Potassium provides disease resistance, hardiness and sugars and starches that affect vegetable flavor.

minor nutrient deficiencies. Two of the most common are iron and calcium. Iron deficiency shows itself as *iron chlorosis*, a common problem in the Southwest. Leaves turn yellow but veins remain green. It can eventually be corrected by adding organic matter to the soil. The fastest way is to spray iron in a *chelated* form. Chelates are absorbed best by young leaves. Be sure to follow directions provided on the product label.

Calcium deficiency is most common in highly acid soils, causing blossom-end rot in tomatoes and peppers. Applications of lime or wood ashes will build up the calcium content. If in doubt about the availability of minor nutrients in your soil, a laboratory soil test can help.

READING A FERTILIZER LABEL

The amount of nutrients in a bag of fertilizer is shown as a percentage, such as 5-10-5. This means the fertilizer is approximately 5% nitrogen, 10% phosphorus and 5% potassium. The other 80% is filler, used as a distributing agent.

It pays to understand these numbers because they tell you how much of each nutrient you are getting for your money. For example, a nutrient analysis such as 20-10-10 delivers a total of 40% nutrients. The analysis also tells you which crops the fertilizer is best suited for. A high-nitrogen fertilizer such as **20**-10-10 is better for leaf crops. A high-phosphorus fertilizer such as 10-**15**-10 is better for fruit-producing crops such as tomatoes.

As a general guide, use a fertilizer with a 1-2-1 ratio such as 5-10-5 or 10-20-10. This will supply leafy vegetables with the nitrogen they require and fruit-producing vegetables with the necessary phosphorus.

NATURAL OR CHEMICAL FERTILIZER?

Natural fertilizers are composed of *organic* materials such as animal manure, bone meal and blood meal. Chemical fertilizers are made of *inorganic* or artificial materials. Each has advantages and disadvantages.

Chemical fertilizers are often termed *general-purpose fertilizers*. They are commonly available in garden centers. They increase soil fertility, but because they contain no organic matter, they do not improve soil structure.

Tomato plants show effects of nutrient deficiencies. Healthy plant at top left has been given proper amounts of nitrogen, phosphorous and potassium. Plant at top right did not receive nitrogen and died. Plant at bottom left shows lack of phosphorous. Plant at bottom right shows lack of potash.

Supplying plants with nutrients makes a dramatic difference in plant growth. After 20 days, fertilized lettuce plants, left, dwarf unfertilized plants, right.

Soil, Compost and Fertilizer **27**

If your garden soil is mostly sand or clay, compost or other organic matter should be added with the chemical fertilizers. It is difficult for chemical fertilizers alone to be effective without a good, loam-type soil to provide the conditions necessary to help plants absorb nutrients. See page 20.

Natural fertilizers. Natural fertilizers such as blood meal and seaweed tend to be high in nitrogen, but low in phosphorus and potassium. For example, blood meal has an analysis of 13-2-1. Other natural fertilizers are available in convenient packages from garden centers. These generally rely on a mixture of blood meal, cottonseed meal and bone meal for their high nutrient content.

Animal manures are natural fertilizers. They are composed of varying degrees of nutrients. For example, poultry manure is usually higher in nitrogen than cow or horse manure. What the animal has been fed, the age of the manure and moisture content are also factors. Animal manures are sometimes slow to supply nutrients, and large quantities are needed to supply plants with adequate nutrient levels.

Don't put fresh manure directly in the garden—allow it to decompose first. It can burn plants because of its high ammonia content. When you go to pick up a load of manure from a stable or farm, look for several piles in different stages of decomposition. If possible, choose manure from a year-old pile that already has the consistency of powdery soil.

Timed-release fertilizers. These are chemical fertilizers that release nutrients at a rate the plant can use efficiently. Many kinds are available. Some release only nitrogen at a slow rate and are identified as water-insoluble nitrogen. If you want a timed-release fertilizer that contains the three basic nutrients (N-P-K), read the label before you buy.

Presently, two leading brands of timed-release fertilizer are available that control the release of all three primary plant nutrients. They are sold under the trade names *Osmocote* and *Precise*. Osmocote is also sold under the brand name *Rain Bird*.

The fertilizer analysis of Precise is 9-12-6. Inside the capsule is a blend of nutrients in liquid form. When the capsule comes in contact with water, the liquid inside is released into the soil. After several months, the liquid

nutrients are depleted and the capsule wall decomposes into the soil.

Osmocote has a fertilizer analysis of 14-14-14. The capsule wall or shell is made from soybeans, so it breaks down in the soil. The nutrients inside are dry. They are released through the shell wall into the soil when penetrated by water vapor and when the temperature is 70F (21C) or more.

Which is best, natural or chemical? Plants cannot differentiate between nutrients in chemical fertilizers and nutrients in natural fertilizers. As a comparison, the human body cannot tell the difference between the vitamin C in a pill and vitamin C in an orange. But the orange provides other benefits besides vitamin C, such as the fiber found in the orange pulp. Similarly, many natural fertilizers supply benefits that chemical fertilizers don't. The composition of certain natural fertilizers such as manure helps improve soil structure.

A logical conclusion is to use chemical fertilizers in conjuction with natural fertilizers, unless indicated otherwise by the product label. Nutrients become available to plants immediately from chemical fertilizers, and natural fertilizers provide long-range benefits by improving the soil.

DRY OR LIQUID FERTILIZER?

Most vegetable fertilizers—chemical and organic—are sold in dry, granular form. They are sprinkled on the soil according to rates given on the package before planting and raked into the upper surface. But plants absorb nutrients in *soluble form*, dissolved by moisture, not as solids. Therefore, granular fertilizers begin to work only when sufficient soil moisture allows the plant to make use of them.

Too much moisture can produce negative results. During periods of excessive rains, a great deal of the fertilizer, especially nitrogen, can be *leached* or washed out of the soil before the plant has a chance to use it.

Dry fertilizer is mixed into the soil at the time of soil preparation. Application rates are supplied on the package. Fertilizer is spread over the soil area where seeds or plants are to be located, and mixed as deep as the future root zone. Once plants are up and growing, a small amount of fertilizer should be spread around plants, and raked and watered into the soil.

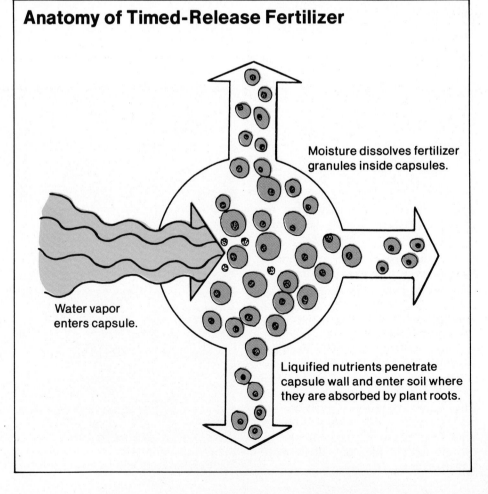

Anatomy of Timed-Release Fertilizer

Moisture dissolves fertilizer granules inside capsules.

Water vapor enters capsule.

Liquified nutrients penetrate capsule wall and enter soil where they are absorbed by plant roots.

This is called a *side dressing.* Side dressings should be kept about 8 inches away from plants. For larger plants such as tomatoes, apply fertilizer at the *dripline,* the outside perimeter of plants. This is where feeder roots are located.

Liquid-feed fertilizers, also called *soluble* fertilizers, avoid loss through leaching. The fertilizer is dissolved in water and applied to the soil directly around the plant's root zone. The plant is able to absorb the nutrients immediately. When applied according to label directions, liquid fertilizers are weak in strength so there is little risk of fertilizer burn.

Liquid-feed plant foods are easy to use. You mix a specified amount of dry crystal, powder or liquid per gallon of water. You then feed plants each time you water, or at weekly intervals, depending on the product.

Liquid fertilizer can be applied to the leaf surfaces as a *foliar feed.* However, leaves are not as efficient as roots in absorbing nutrients, so foliar feeding is not the best way to fertilize plants. Foliar feeding is mostly used as a *booster,* applied at the crucial period when fruit begin to form. If the timing is right, foliar feeding can increase yields. Be sure to apply according to label directions. An overdose of fertilizer can burn leaves.

GREEN MANURE
Certain plants such as soybeans, cereal rye and buckwheat leave the soil richer in nitrogen than before they were planted. The roots of these plants attract beneficial types of bacteria that have the ability to manufacture nitrogen from the atmosphere. These plants are called *green manure,* or *cover crops.* Nitrogen is an important nutrient for leaf vegetables such as lettuce, corn, cabbage and spinach. Many farmers and large-scale gardeners plant a green manure crop prior to planting these vegetables.

In small gardens, the practice of growing green manure crops is not common. Compost and fertilizer do a better job of enriching soil. For those home gardeners who want to try a green manure crop, the best is cereal rye. It is hardy and can be planted in fall after your garden has been cleared of crop residues. It is plowed under in spring prior to planting. The seedheads of cereal rye are sterile, so there is no problem with rye seeds coming up as weeds.

Although green manure crops add nitrogen to the soil, they can deplete the soil of phosphorus and potassium. A fertilizer that includes these two nutrients may still be needed to ensure yields of fruit-producing vegetables.

BACTERIAL FERTILIZERS
Certain kinds of soil organisms have the ability to manufacture plant nutrients when present in the soil, restoring exhausted soils to a naturally fertile condition. They feed plants, dissolve harmful salts, maintain an optimum soil pH and aerate soil. These bacterial fertilizers have a low nutrient analysis, 3-4-4, for example, but this is misleading. Once the microorganisms are added to the soil, they begin manufacturing nutrients much higher than the initial level stated on the label.

I have had good results with bacterial fertilizers. They improved yields of tomatoes, peppers and beans. I use them as a "booster," adding them to the soil at the start of the growing season. The most widely available bacterial fertilizer is *Restore,* available from Judd Ringer Research, 6860 Flying Cloud Drive, Eden Prairie, MN 55344.

A LOOK AT THE OPTIONS
After reading the preceding, it is obvious that there are many ways to

Nitrogen nodules on soybean plant are produced by soil bacteria. When garden plot is planted with a "green manure," it increases the soil's nitrogen content.

supply your vegetable plants with nutrients. Each form of fertilizer has advantages and disadvantages: *Timed-release* fertilizers are convenient and labor saving. Some products will see your plants through the growing season with just one application. But they are also more expensive than other methods, and require moisture before they begin to work. *Fast-release* liquid fertilizers provide nutrients to plants immediately, but they require the use of a sprayer and frequent applications—some as often as once a week. *Granular fertilizers* are convenient and generally inexpensive, but they, too, require moisture before nutrients become available to plants. *Animal manure* provides organic matter to the soil, but its nutritive content is difficult to determine. It also takes a large quantity to provide nutrients.

Use your own judgment as to the method best for you. Perhaps a combination of several methods is best, such as a timed-release fertilizer for sustained reliable feeding and a fast-acting liquid fertilizer at regular intervals as a booster. For your convenience, the following outlines a good fertilizer schedule. Adjust it to fit your own needs and situation.

SAMPLE FERTILIZER SCHEDULE
1. Add compost to your soil in fall or winter to improve soil structure and basic nutrient levels. Or, add compost to your soil early in spring, prior to planting. If compost is not available, add organic matter and animal manure. Both improve the soil structure; manure adds nutrients.
2. Apply a granular, packaged, vegetable fertilizer such as 5-10-5 to the soil 7 to 10 days before planting. Work into soil where plants or seeds are to be located. Most granular fertilizers are applied at the rate of 1-1/2 pounds per 100 square feet. Brands of fertilizer vary, so it is best to read the recommended rate on the package label and follow it carefully.
3. When plants begin to flower or fruit, apply a booster fertilizer in dilute liquid form to leaves and at base of plants at weekly intervals. Or, apply a side dressing of granular fertilizer along side of plants and rows. Keep the fertilizer away from plant stems to avoid "burn." Or, apply compost as a side dressing at time of flowering and just prior to harvesting.

Seed Starting and Planting

Seeds come in all different shapes and sizes, from tiny celery seeds that blow away if you breathe on them, to lima bean seeds that are large and easy to handle. Some seeds, like peas and corn, have seed coats that soften quickly on contact with moisture. Others, like okra, have extremely hard seeds. They should be soaked in lukewarm water 12 hours before planting. It adds up to a wide variety, with no one planting system suitable for all seeds.

Germination—the process of seeds sprouting roots and leaves—is one of the great miracles of nature. For most seeds, three conditions must be met before germination occurs: *adequate moisture, suitable temperature* and *air* (oxygen). Moisture is necessary to soften the seed coat and allow the *embryo,* the undeveloped plant, to expand and grow. Suitable temperature is needed to break dormancy. Some vegetable seeds like lettuce and spinach germinate at a temperature as low as 40F (5C). Tomatoes and peppers require at least 60F (16C) and

higher before they germinate. Air is required for seeds to live. If the soil is waterlogged for an extended period, seeds will die. For this reason, it is best to start seeds in a potting mix that drains well to allow air to enter the soil. See page 72.

Some vegetables have special germination requirements. *Light* is required for celery, lettuce and endive. When you sow seeds of these plants, press them lightly into the soil, and mist often to keep them moist. Onion and amaranth germinate best in *darkness.* If you start seeds indoors, place them in a cupboard or closet out of light.

SEED OR TRANSPLANT?
Some gardeners sow only easy-to-handle seeds directly in the garden, and buy inexpensive transplants of other vegetables from the nursery. But there are good reasons to start almost all of your vegetables from seed. Selection of ready-grown transplants is limited to a few popular varieties. For example, you'll be lucky to

choose from three kinds of tomatoes. 'Big Boy' hybrid, 'Rutgers' and 'Beefsteak' are commonly available at nurseries. Among peppers, the choice may be between two—'California Wonder' and 'Bell Boy' hybrid.

You may have trouble finding the vegetables you want, when you want to plant. Consider too, that it often takes years before transplants of new varieties become available to garden centers. Some excellent varieties never become available as transplants. A bonus of starting your own seeds is the satisfaction you experience knowing you are fully responsible for a crop from seed to harvest.

STANDARD OR HYBRID?
Vegetables are available in *standard* and *hybrid* forms. Sometimes standard varieties are called *open pollinated* because they are mass produced through pollination by bees and wind. Hybrids require *controlled pollination*—careful hand pollination between selected parent plants, usually different species that are sexually compatible.

Left: Block planting of lettuce eliminates need for walkways between rows of plants and uses garden space efficiently. Above: Indoor-started lettuce seedlings emerge from a flat.

The word hybrid comes from the Latin word, *hybrida,* meaning offspring of a wild boar and a domestic sow. A more familiar animal hybrid is the mule—a cross between a jackass (male donkey) and a mare (female horse). The mule is stronger and more useful than either parent. As with most hybrids, the mule is sterile and cannot reproduce itself. To create more mules, the original cross must be repeated. Seeds from plant hybrids are produced in a similar way. To make more seeds, you must make the original cross. A good example of a hybrid is seedless watermelon. See page 175.

The main advantage of a hybrid is its vigor, a quality called *heterosis.* This results in higher yields, increased size, improved disease resistance, earliness, heat or cold tolerance, improved nutritional value and other desirable characteristics.

Disease resistance has become such an important part of hybridizing that names of hybrid varieties often carry the initials of diseases or pests they are resistant to. An example is the tomato hybrid 'Supersteak VFN'. The "V" means it resists *verticillium* wilt, the "F" means it resists *fusarium* wilt, the "N" indicates resistance to *nematode* pests. Gardeners in hot, humid areas should look for such varieties.

SEED PACKETS, PELLETS AND TAPES
Almost every year there seems to be a new way to plant seeds. *Seed pellets, seed tapes* and other methods are said to make seed starting easier and more reliable. It can be difficult to sow tiny seeds such as carrots, but even these seeds can be planted properly by hand. You get better value with a seed packet because it contains many more seeds at less cost compared to seed tapes and other systems.

Seed packets have been significantly improved with the introduction of foil packaging. They are moisture-proof and keep seeds fresher longer. Some seeds deteriorate quickly and the traditional paper packet may allow seeds to lose viability. Under controlled conditions, seeds in moisture-proof packets maintain high germination until the seal is broken.

Pelleted seeds are probably the least gimmicky of the alternative seed-sowing systems. The pellet is a clay coating around small seeds that makes them larger and easier to handle. The coating dissolves on contact with moisture, and the seed germinates unhindered. Pelleted seeds tend to look like they have been manufactured, which might bother the gardening purist. But they do make it easier to sow small-seed vegetables such as carrots and lettuce.

Seed tapes are seeds bound into a transparent, biodegradable material, prespaced at regular distances. The material dissolves quickly after it comes in contact with moisture. Seed tapes save time with thinning, but they have some disadvantages. They are more expensive than conventional seeds from packets. And, if you don't get a high rate of germination, you will probably end up with wide gaps between plants. The tapes can also be a nuisance to plant. Because they are usually packed folded with sharp corners, they buckle out of the soil when you stretch the tape in the furrow.

SEED RACK OR MAIL ORDER?
Vegetable seeds are available in seed racks at retail outlets, or by mail order through seed catalogs. The advantage of rack displays in local stores is convenience. It is easy to go down to the nearest garden supply store and make your selections. The kind of vegetables and varieties offered depends on the type of store. Usually, garden centers carry more than one brand and offer the best selection.

Seed companies strongly represented in retail stores do not usually produce mail order catalogs. The largest of these are Northrup King of Minneapolis, Minnesota; Ferry Morse of Fulton, Kentucky; Asgrow of Kalamazoo, Michigan; Vaughans of Downers Grove, Illinois; and Fredonia of Fredonia, New York.

Rack displays offer a basic selection of traditional, established varieties. Occasionally, some hybrids are offered. If you plan to buy your seeds from these displays, it pays to shop early. Toward the end of the season, the rack is not refilled as often because the seed company must take back unsold seeds.

The big advantage of ordering your seeds through a mail order catalog is the huge selection available. Compared to 100 or 200 varieties normally offered in a large rack display, a major vegetable seed catalog will offer up to 2,000 varieties. There will also be a heavier concentration of hybrid varieties than in the rack displays.

Seed catalogs number in the hundreds. Some are filled with color pictures and mailed to millions of gardeners. Others are specialized, appealing to the interests of a few thousand gardeners. Large or small, printed in color or on mimeographed sheets, each year's catalogs offer far more than simple variety listings. Each catalog strives to establish an individual identity and personality. Along with variety listings, descriptions and pictures, you will often find valuable cultural hints.

The facing page lists some of the best vegetable seed catalogs.

Shopping from a rack at your garden supply store is the handiest and most economical way to buy seeds. Seeds from mail order catalogs take a little more time and effort to obtain, but the added selection can be worth it.

Seed Catalogs

AGWAY INC.
Box 4933
Syracuse, NY 13221
Color catalog with many exclusive vegetable varieties developed by the company's own breeders. Catalog free.

APPLEWOOD SEED COMPANY
Box 10761—Edgemont Station
Golden, CO 80401
Seeds for herbs, sprouts and wildflowers. Catalog free.

BURGESS SEED & PLANT CO.
905 Four Seasons Road
Bloomington, IL 61701
Fine selection of vegetable seeds. Many unusual seeds exclusive to this established company. Catalog free.

W. ATLEE BURPEE
300 Park Avenue
Warminster, PA 18974
Wide selection of vegetables, many developed by the company's own breeding program. Free catalog features flowers, bulbs, nursery stock and garden aids.

COMSTOCK, FERRE & CO.
263 Main Street
Wethersfield, CT 06109
Illustrated catalog lists old and new varieties of vegetables and flowers. Extensive list of herbs. Catalog free.

J.A. DEMONCHAUX CO.
827 N. Kansas Ave., PO Box 8330
Topeka, KS 66608
French gourmet vegetables. Catalog 50¢.

DOMINION SEED HOUSE
Georgetown
Ontario, Canada L7GYA2
An excellent selection of vegetable seeds for Canada. Will ship only in Canada. Catalog free.

EXOTICA SEED CO.
1742 Laurel Canyon Boulevard
Los Angeles, CA 90046
Rare and hard-to-get seeds from around the world. Catalog $2.

FARMER SEED & NURSERY CO.
818 N.W. Fourth Street
Faribault, MN 55021
Vegetable seeds, including midget varieties. Northern-grown nursery stock. Garden aids. Color catalog free.

HENRY FIELD SEED & NURSERY CO.
407 Sycamore Street
Shenandoah, IA 51602
Beautiful, full-color catalog offers a wide selection of vegetable and flower seeds, nursery stock and garden supplies. Catalog free.

GURNEY SEED & NURSERY CO.
Yankton, SD 57079
One of America's largest seed and nursery catalogs. Extensive selection of vegetable seeds, plus nursery stock and garden aids. Catalog free.

JOSEPH HARRIS CO.
Moreton Farm
Rochester, NY 14624
Exceptionally fine listing of vegetable seeds, many developed by the company's own breeders. Catalog free.

THE CHARLES C. HART SEED CO.
Main & Hart Streets
Wethersfield, CT 06109
Fine assortment of vegetable and herb seeds. Catalog free.

H.G. HASTINGS CO.
Box 4274
Atlanta, GA 30302
Assortment of vegetable seeds and nursery stock, especially suitable for Southern gardens. Catalog free.

HERBST BROTHERS SEEDSMEN, INC.
N. Main Street 1099
Brewster, NY 10509
An established seed company with an extensive vegetable department. Catalog offers more varieties than any other. Catalog free.

JOHNNY'S SELECTED SEEDS
Box 100
Albion, ME 04910
Vegetable, herb and farm seeds. Specializing in early, hardy varieties for the North. Catalog free.

J.W. JUNG SEED CO.
Randolph, WI 53956
Vegetable and flower seeds, nursery stock, fruit trees and gardening supplies. Catalog free.

OROL LEDDEN & SONS
Center Street
Sewell, NJ 08080
Large selection of vegetable seeds. Seedsmen since 1904. Catalog free.

MASON PLANT FARMS
Box 270
Reklow, TX 75784
Certified vegetable plants. Catalog free.

EARL MAY SEED & NURSERY CO.
Shenandoah, IA 51603
Vegetable seeds and nursery stock in a colorful catalog. Catalog free.

McLAUGHLINS SEEDS
Box 550 SP
Mead, WA 99021
Reliable vegetable seed supplier serving mostly West Coast gardeners. Catalog 50¢.

MELLINGERS, INC.
North Lima, OH 4452
Extensive listing of seeds, plants, organic plant foods and pest controls. Catalog free.

NICHOLS GARDEN NURSERY
1190 North Pacific Highway
Albany, OR 97321
Extensive listing of herb and vegetable seeds. Good source for many unusual and early maturing varieties. Catalog free.

L.L. OLDS SEED COMPANY
2901 Packers Avenue, PO Box 7790
Madison, WI 53707
Assortment of vegetable and flower seeds, nursery stock, lawn seeds and garden aids. Catalog free.

GEORGE W. PARK SEED, INC.
Greenwood, SC 29647
Recognized as flower seed specialists. Vegetable seed selection is also extensive. Color catalog free.

PIEDMONT PLANT FARMS
Box 424
Albany, GA 31703
Established supplier of field-grown vegetable plants. Free color catalog features many popular varieties.

SEEDWAY, INC.
Hall, NY 14463
Formerly Robson's Seeds. Vegetable varieties especially suited for Northeast conditions. Specialists in hybrid sweet corn. Catalog free.

R.H. SHUMWAY
628 Cedar Street
Rockford, IL 61101
Catalog is a blend of newly developed varieties and many established varieties. Source for plants, bulbs, shrubs and fruit trees. Catalog free.

STOKES SEEDS INC.
Box 548
Buffalo, NY 14240
Excellent selection of vegetables. Lots of growing tips. Catalog free.

THOMPSON & MORGAN
Box 100
Farmingdale, NJ 07727
Exclusive listings of vegetables, many rare and unusual. Useful nutrition and flavor charts. Catalog free.

OTIS S. TWILLEY SEED CO.
Box 65
Trevose, PA 19047
Vegetable seed specialists with extensive selection. Catalog free.

VERMONT BEAN SEED COMPANY
11 Garden Lane
Bomoseen, VT 05732
Complete line of all types of vegetable seeds, specializing in hard-to-find types. Source for sprouting seeds. Catalog 25¢.

VESEY'S SEEDS LTD.
York, Prince Edward's Island
Canada COA 1PO
Specialists in flowers and vegetables for Northern areas with short seasons. Catalog free.

WYATT-QUARLES SEED CO.
331 S. Wilmington Street, Box 2131
Raleigh, NC 27602
Wide selection of vegetable seeds for Southern gardens. Catalog free.

ALL-AMERICA SELECTIONS

Seed companies offer dozens of new vegetable varieties each year. Some are slightly different from existing varieties; others offer substantial improvements. Because of the number of new varieties, it is not always easy to decide which are worthwhile. For this reason, the American garden seed industry founded All-America Selections—the national seed trials. Each year, many new varieties are tested in trial gardens representing every area of the United States. Judges from the seed industry and academic areas grow and evaluate the varieties in their own test plots. They then make awards of recognition—a bronze medal, silver medal or gold medal, according to merit.

All-America Selections does not test every variety. Introducing a variety to the marketplace takes time, and some breeders are anxious to introduce their best varieties. They bypass the sometimes long periods required—up to three years—to gain an award.

For a current list of All-America Award-winning vegetables, write: All-America Selections, Box 344, Sycamore, IL 60178.

SAVING YOUR OWN SEEDS

Many gardeners like to save seeds from their garden plants for use the next season. This may seem like a good idea, but saving seeds is not as advantageous as it may sound. Plants grown from seeds from your own garden may give unpredictable results. Seeds saved from *F1 hybrids,* first generation hybrids, produce inferior re-

sults the second season. Saving seeds from standard varieties is also plagued with problems. Beets, chard, parsley, carrots, onions and celery are *biennials,* requiring two years before they flower and produce seeds.

Spinach, sweet corn, melons and cucumbers are pollinated by wind or insects. Cross-pollination can occur from a neighbor's garden or from other varieties in your own garden. Beet pollen, for example, can travel as far as two miles. This may cause your saved seeds to grow into something completely different than what you grew the previous year. Tomatoes, peppers and eggplant, which are considered self-pollinating, may give unpredictable results unless the varieties are isolated. Some vegetables such as lettuce and snap beans are also prone to carrying seed-borne diseases. This is especially true in the northeast United States and Canada.

Storing and testing leftover seeds. Most seed companies are generous with the quantities of seeds they provide in their packets. You may find that after planting you have a lot of leftover seeds in opened packets. To maintain viability, seeds must be kept *cool and dry.*

To store seeds, place packets in a wide-mouth jar that can be sealed with a tight-fitting lid. Put 2 heaping tablespoons of powdered milk in a paper envelope, and place this in the jar. The powdered milk absorbs moisture from the air inside the jar, keeping the seeds dry. Seal the jar and store in the vegetable bin of your refrigerator. How long seeds last depends to a great extent on storage conditions. High temperatures and high humidity deteriorate seeds

Viability of stored seeds can be checked by germinating them on a paper towel. See text for instructions.

quickly and reduce the rate of germination.

To see if seeds are viable, select about 10 seeds and lay them on a moist paper towel. Put the towel inside a plastic bag and place in a warm location. The plastic bag prevents the paper towel from drying out too quickly. After 10 days, count the number of seeds that have germinated. If 2 out of 10 germinate, this indicates a 20% germination rate—not good. If 5 out of 10 sprout, this shows 50% germination—acceptable.

Even if you have seeds left over from last year's seed order, it is probably better to start with fresh seeds. Some seeds are long-lived under ideal conditions, but high humidity and other factors can cause rapid deterioration. My advice is not to save seeds, unless you have a variety that is unobtainable from normal sources.

A Close Look At Seeds

Seed form, color and size are interesting to compare. From left: watermelon, sunflower, squash and beet.

Vegetables can be planted by sowing seeds directly into the garden or by transplanting seedlings. You can purchase transplants from a garden center or grow them yourself from seeds indoors or under glass, using the various techniques described in this section. If you choose to start seeds indoors, be sure to provide them with the following.

Regular moisture. One of the biggest problems with growing seeds indoors is maintaining moisture. Seeds grown in small peat pots and soil blocks tend to lose moisture rapidly. If a seedling is deprived of moisture for only a few hours, it will probably wilt and die.

When watering seeds in trays, apply water in a fine mist or add water to the tray. Pouring water directly on seeds disturbs the soil surface and hinders germination. To prevent rapid moisture loss, enclose trays or pots of newly planted seeds in a clear plastic bag. The bag helps prevent evaporation and keeps the soil moist.

Optimum temperature. Seeds require a certain temperature to germinate, which varies with the vegetable. Cabbage seedlings can be transplanted into the garden several weeks before the last frost date because they tolerate mild frosts. But cabbage seeds require a 70F (21C) temperature to germinate. Tender vegetables such as peppers and tomatoes germinate best at about 80F (27C).

Proper light. A major reason for poor-quality, home-grown transplants is inadequate light. Transplants become spindly and "stretch" when they do not receive enough light. Seedlings should be exposed to about 12 hours of sunlight each day. When growing transplants on windowsills, raise the pots to the level of the window pane. Also consider placing an aluminum foil reflector on the dark side of the seedlings so that light is bounced back to increase illumination. A simple reflector can be made by wrapping kitchen foil around a piece of cardboard.

Plant lights that simulate sunshine can be used to supplement natural light. Timers are available that automatically turn the lights on and off. Set seedlings a few inches away from lights to produce good growth. Give them at least 16 hours of artificial light per day.

Light units are available in a wide range of styles, sizes and prices. Standard fluorescent fixtures can be fitted with special plant "grow lights." Table-top models provide enough light for a tray of seedlings. Free-standing floor units accommodate up to eight planter trays.

Some seeds germinate better when exposed to light. Lettuce and celery should not be completely covered, but gently pressed into the soil surface. Read the packet information carefully to determine which seeds require light to germinate.

Prevent disease. The biggest killer of seedlings is *damping-off* disease, which causes seedlings to keel over at the soil surface. It is caused by a fungus present in unsterilized soil, dirty pots and unclean seeds. Overwatering, poor ventilation, poor light and high temperatures help to encourage the harmful fungus. It can attack seeds sown indoors or outdoors, but is most destructive to indoor sowings, often killing seedlings before they have a chance to emerge from the soil.

Prevent damping off by using new or clean seed-starting pots or trays. Also use sterile potting soil. Treating seeds with a fungicide such as benomyl before you plant helps avoid infestations.

Soil Temperature for Vegetable Seed Germination

Vegetable	30F	40F	50F	60F	70F	80F	90F	100F	110F
Asparagus			will	will	opt	will	will		
Bean, Lima				will	will	opt	will		
Bean, Snap				will	will	opt	will		
Beet		will	will	will	will	opt	will		
Broccoli		will	will	will	will	opt	will		
Brussels sprouts		will	will	will	will	opt	will		
Cabbage		will	will	will	will	opt	will	will	
Carrot		will	will	will	will	opt	will	will	
Cauliflower		will	will	will	will	opt	will	will	
Celery		will	will	will	opt	will			
Chard, Swiss		will	will	will	will	opt	will	will	
Corn			will	will	will	opt	will	will	
Cucumber				will	will	will	opt	will	will
Endive	will	will	will	will	opt	will			
Lettuce	will	will	will	will	opt	will			
Muskmelon (Cantaloupe)				will	will	will	opt	will	
Okra				will	will	will	opt	will	will
Onion	will	will	will	will	will	opt	will		
Parsley		will	will	will	will	opt	will		
Parsnip	will	will	opt	will	will	will			
Pea, English		will	will	will	opt	will			
Pepper				will	will	opt	will	will	
Pumpkin				will	will	will	opt	will	will
Radish		will	will	will	will	opt	will	will	
Spinach	will	will	will	will	opt	will			
Squash				will	will	will	opt	will	will
Tomato			will	will	will	opt	will	will	
Turnip		will	will	will	will	opt	will	will	
Watermelon				will	will	will	opt	will	will

will germinate ▒   optimum germination ▓

MATERIALS FOR STARTING SEEDS INDOORS

No ideal seed-starting system fits all situations. Generally, indoor methods can be classified as *one-step* and *two-step*. A one-step method is best for large seeds such as cucumbers and squash. You simply plant a few seeds in a pot filled with soil, or plant in a seed-starting device. Then you thin the seedlings to the most healthy specimen. At transplant time, you plant the seedling directly in the garden.

With the two-step method, seeds are first sown in a tray or flat filled with potting soil. They are then separated when large enough to handle, and transferred to individual containers. They remain there until they reach transplant size. Small seeds such as cabbage and parsley are best planted this way.

Following are descriptions of common materials and methods used to start seeds indoors. They include commercial products available from garden centers and mail order sources. Many household containers and packages that are normally thrown away can be recycled as seed starters.

Peat pots are small, round or square containers made of peat, an organic material. They are filled with potting soil, and seeds are planted in them. Plant roots are able to grow through the pot, which gradually decomposes in the soil. Transplanting is achieved without disturbing the roots. Be aware that uneven watering after planting can delay decomposition of the peat walls. To prevent the pot from restricting growth, it is best to remove the bottom of each pot gently, just before planting, unless roots are already protruding. This also gives the roots freedom to grow into the garden soil as soon as they are planted. When planting the pots be sure the top edge is *below* the soil surface, or it will act as a *wick* and draw moisture away from roots.

With small seeds, it's better to use peat pots in a two-step operation. Start seeds in a tray, then transplant to the peat pot after they have sprouted and are large enough to handle.

Peat pellets are made of compressed peat that expands to seven times its volume when moisture is added. Peat pellets are the most popular seed-starting product. Two kinds are available.

Jiffy-7 peat pellets expand to 1-3/4 inches in diameter and 2-1/8 inches high. Netting holds the peat together, and there is a depression in the top of each pellet for seeds. At transplant time, the entire pellet can be planted in the garden without shock to the seedling. It is a good idea to remove the netting before planting, because it may restrict plant growth.

Jiffy-9 does not have netting and is slightly smaller and less expensive. The peat is held together with an invisible binding agent. In my experience, it is superior to the Jiffy-7 because roots have complete freedom to grow once the pellet has been planted.

Both types are excellent for starting large-seeded vegetables in a one-step operation. They can also be used for small seeds. Tomatoes, peppers, cauliflower, broccoli and cabbage are good vegetables to start in peat pellets. About the only problem with peat pellets is their tendency to dry out quickly. Enclosing the pellets in a plastic bag helps prevent moisture loss.

Fiber blocks and cubes, like Jiffy pellets, have a depression in the top for seeds. They are light, clean and easy to use. Roots penetrate the block freely. When seedlings grow to proper size, the whole block can be planted without root disturbance.

Cell packs are small planting trays sectioned into four or six compartments. They are filled with a potting soil and used to start medium and large seeds. To remove plants from compartments, push up from the bottom of the pack with your fingers. Plants will come out, complete with soil and roots, allowing you to transplant without root disturbance. Cell packs are flimsy, but if handled carefully, they are reusable from one year to the next.

Peat, wood or plastic seed trays are good to start small, fine seeds such as parsley, celery and lettuce. The usual method is to fill the planters with a prepackaged soil mix. Make several furrows with a flat edge such as a ruler, then sow seeds thinly along the furrows. Keep the soil moist with a fine spray. When seedlings develop their first set of leaves, transfer to individual containers.

Recycled containers that are normally thrown away every day are excellent alternatives to manufactured products. The quart-size paper milk carton is, in my estimation, the best transplant container available. It allows plant roots plenty of room to grow. At transplant time, the rootball will be several times larger than the rootball started in a regular peat pot. Top growth will also be larger and capable of earlier, more productive yields. Be sure to punch drainage holes in the bottoms of containers so the soil mix does not become waterlogged.

Every year I start a number of vegetables in milk cartons to give them a jump over my peat-pot transplants. These generally include two plants each of cucumbers, tomatoes, peppers, eggplant and summer squash. The ample room provided by the milk carton allows summer squash and cucumbers to be transplanted with flower buds forming. Pepper, eggplant and tomato transplants have fruit already set. At planting time, it is simple to peel away the cardboard and set the rootball in the garden soil. Plants accept transplanting and continue growing without shock.

Use your imagination to seek out other seed-starting containers. Paper and styrofoam cups and the plastic bottoms of 1-liter soft drink containers are others. You can also use deep-dish plastic containers such as those used for holding dips, whipped butter and cheese spreads as seed-starting trays.

Preplanters are another type of seed-starting system. They are available at garden stores in the spring. These packs generally consist of a plastic container filled with planting soil and seeds preplanted and prespaced for reliable germination. All you do is strip away the clear film cover and add water. The packs are deep enough to allow plants to reach a good size before transplanting and fit easily on a windowsill.

Soil mixes are required to fill peat pots, cell packs and other containers for seed starting. Regular garden topsoil is a poor growing medium for indoor-started seedlings. *Soil substitutes* or *potting mixes*—combinations of materials such as peat moss, vermiculite and perlite—are much better. They are lightweight, free from disease and have better aeration and moisture retention than topsoil. Several ready-mixed brands are available from garden centers, including Jiffy Mix, Pro-Mix, RediEarth, Super Soil and Starting Formula. For more information on soil substitutes, see page 72.

Starting Seeds Indoors

One-Step Method

1. Moisten peat pellets to expand them. Large seeds such as cucumbers, squash and melons work best with this method.

2. When pellets are fully expanded, plant one seed in each pellet. Push the seed into the depression in the center of the pellet and pinch the sides to cover.

3. Two weeks after planting, squash seedling is ready to plant. You can plant the peat pot *with* the netting, but I prefer to remove it.

Two-Step Method

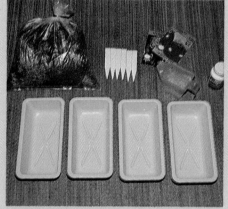

1. Materials needed for two-step seed starting: plastic seed trays, bag of potting soil, labels, seeds, water and benomyl fungicide to prevent damping-off disease.

2. Thoroughly moisten potting soil before planting. Squeeze bag so moisture is absorbed evenly.

3. Fill seed trays with soil. If you have more than one tray, plant one vegetable or variety in each tray.

4. Sow seeds thinly over the soil surface and cover with potting soil. Press firmly to ensure good seed-to-soil contact. Spray surface with benomyl to prevent damping-off.

5. Seedlings as they appear several days later. The time it takes for seedlings to emerge varies with the vegetable. Days to germination are given in the charts on pages 48 to 51.

6. Using a sharp pencil, lift seedlings from tray and transplant into larger container. Grow them in this container until they reach transplant size.

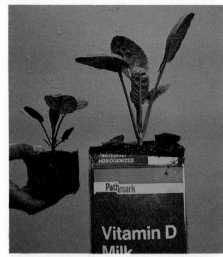

One of the best recycled containers for starting seeds is the paper milk carton. These cabbage seedlings were planted at the same time and grown under the same conditions.

Peat pots are filled with potting soil and planted the same as peat pellets. These are parsley seedlings.

Fluid seed sowing is a way to sow *pregerminated* seeds in the garden. It is especially effective for seeds that are slow to germinate.

FLUID SEED SOWING

Fluid seed sowing is a seed-sowing system that can help reduce poor seed germination. It also speeds up seedling emergence, and helps achieve earlier crops and higher yields.

Here's how the system works:

Seeds that are to be sown outdoors are germinated indoors between moist paper towels. Check the seeds daily. As soon as you see the seed coats split and the roots emerge, mix the germinated seeds in a toothpaste-like organic gel that comes with the kit. This free-flowing mix is then put into an applicator resembling a toothpaste tube. The pregerminated seeds are squeezed out of the tube, pre-spaced along the furrow. Subsequent thinning is either unnecessary or reduced.

Seeds in the furrow are then covered with soil. Within days they emerge from the soil with up to 10 days headstart over seeds sown the usual way. Even if cool temperatures follow sowing, the pregerminated seeds are not usually harmed, because seedlings will grow at cooler temperatures than required for germination.

The fluid seed sowing system is available as a kit from Thompson & Morgan. See page 33 for address. Kit contains different-size applicators to sow different-size seeds, a supply of gel and germinating trays. But you can probably take some shortcuts. With large-seeded vegetables, you can pregerminate the seeds on a moist paper napkin. Then pick up the individual seedlings with your fingers and place them in the garden furrow. Be careful not to bruise the delicate roots.

DIRECT SEEDING OUTDOORS

A common mistake many gardeners make is *planting seeds too deep.* If you are instructed to cover seeds with 1/4 inch of soil, don't roughly hoe a furrow and drop the seeds in, not realizing that you've planted them two inches deep. Seeds planted this way have little chance of survival. A rule of thumb is to plant seeds at a depth equal to four times their diameter.

Before you plant seeds outdoors, determine which tolerate frost in the seedling stage, and which are tender and susceptible to frost damage in the seedling stage. Don't plant seeds of tender vegetables until all danger of frost has passed.

Seeds need minimum temperatures in which to germinate. Certain seeds are susceptible to rot in early stages, caused by low temperatures and excess moisture. This is particularly true of beans and corn. Consider using *treated seed,* or treat your own seeds with an approved fungicide such as Captan.

Don't be impatient if some of your seeds take longer to germinate than the time indicated on seed packets. Some seeds germinate erratically under cool conditions, especially parsley, carrots and beets. Some seeds can be germinated indoors on paper towels and then planted. Pregerminated seeds have roots that are already growing through the seed coat so they get off to a fast start.

To plant small seeds, take a pinch in your fingers and trickle seeds into a furrow as evenly as possible. Or tear off a corner of the seed packet and gently tap seeds onto the seed bed. Cover with a layer of soil. Thin seedlings as soon as they emerge. One of the easiest ways to thin is to snip seedlings off with scissors at the soil level. Pulling seedlings, especially root crops, can disturb roots of adjacent plants. Carrots, celery and parsley may need thinning in several stages before they are properly spaced.

Larger seeds such as peas and beans can be planted exactly as you would like to have plants and rows in the gardens. Or you may find it better to plant closer together and thin seedlings in case you lose seeds or plants to pests. The same is true with onion sets. By planting the sets almost touching, you can harvest *scallions,* the young shoots, by picking every other one. This automatically thins the row. Similarly, lettuce and spinach thinnings can be used in salads or as sandwich fillings.

Watering. Drying out is a common cause of failure when seeds are sown directly in the garden, especially in low rainfall areas. Make it a standard practice to water the seed bed immediately after planting. Keep soil surface moist after seedlings emerge from soil. Water newly planted seed beds with a light spray. Disturbing the soil surface can interfere with seed germination.

To keep a seed bed from drying out and to prevent a crust from forming on the soil surface, add a thin layer of mulch. Compost or grass clippings work well. These mulches are light, water retentive and reduce the impact of the sun's heat. In warm, dry regions, some gardeners use burlap sacks or a couple of layers of newspapers as a moisture-retaining blanket to help encourage germination. However, the cover must be pulled back every morning to see if the seeds have made an appearance. If the covering is left in place, the seedlings "stretch" and lose vigor.

Pest protection. Birds can raid a newly planted vegetable garden and peck out the seeds and shoots. Pheasants, crows and pigeons seem to be the worst culprits. They usually leave treated seeds alone. Scarecrows and noise-makers can be effective. One of the most dependable deterrents is a tent of chicken wire placed over the furrow. This also keeps rabbits, woodchucks and other foraging animals out of the garden.

Some of the worst problem pests are soil-borne pests—not only insects such as cutworms and wireworms, but moles and shrews. Insect pests can be kept under control by sprinkling the soil with wood ashes, removing them by hand during soil preparation and by using seed treated with an organic fungicide. Effective chemical controls include diazinon and Sevin.

Shrews and moles are another problem altogether. They often tunnel just beneath a row of germinating seeds in their search for earthworms, and the germinating seedlings collapse into the burrow. Cats are effective in keeping down mole and shrew population. Several humane traps are also available.

When sowing fine seeds such as carrots and lettuce, a strainer is handy for applying a light, even covering of soil.

After planting seeds, discourage marauding birds with items such as this child's windmill.

DIRECT SEEDING TIPS

- Never walk on vegetable garden soil before or after planting. Heavy footprints compact soil and ruin a well-prepared seed bed. Use paths between rows or walk on planks.
- When fertilizing the seed bed, do not use fast-acting fertilizers at time of planting. They may "burn" tender seedlings. After applying fertilizer, wait 7 to 10 days before planting. Or, apply slow-release fertilizers at time of planting.
- A hand trowel is one of the best tools for creating seed furrows or planting holes. If you want a shallow, narrow furrow for small seeds, use the pointed tip of the trowel. To make a deep, wide furrow for larger seeds, press the trowel in deeper, or dig out a few scoops of soil to set transplants in place.
- Do not use the entire seed packet in one sowing. Save some seeds to fill in bare spots after the planting comes up, and to stagger the harvesting times. See Succession Planting, page 42.
- Firm soil over planted seeds with your foot or back of a spade. Don't compress the soil too much. Press just enough to eliminate air pockets.
- A strainer is handy for planting small seeds. To use, first spread seeds evenly on the soil surface. Fill the strainer with fine garden topsoil. Shake it over seeds until they are covered with about 1/4 inch of soil. Large stones, weed roots and other debris are left behind in the strainer. What a difference this simple method can make to your stand of carrots!

Seeds of plants that tolerate some crowding, such as spinach, carrots, radishes, looseleaf lettuce and many herbs, can be scattered over a wide row and lightly covered with soil.

TRANSPLANTING

Plants grown indoors and transplanted to the garden need to be handled with care. Treat them like eggs. Transplant shock can cause plants to grow slowly, and can sometimes result in death.

Hardening-off. Before a transplant is taken from a warm, comfortable indoor environment to the cool or sunny outdoors, it should be *hardened-off,* gradually acclimated to its new home. Even cold-hardy plants such as cabbage and broccoli should be given a gradual transition from an indoor environment to the outdoors. Hardening-off is most important with tender plants such as tomatoes, eggplant and peppers. A simple way to harden-off plants is to expose them to increasing amounts of cold or sunlight, depending on the weather situation. For example, place plants in the sun for an hour the first day, and gradually increase the exposure over a 10-day period until plants accept a full day of sun.

Placing transplants in a *cold frame* is a good way to get them adjusted to the outdoors. A cold frame is usually a wooden compartment that has a covering of glass or plastic. See photograph at right. It is often placed partially in the ground for insulation. The frame is left open during the day and closed at night. Normally, transplants are placed in a cold frame for about 10 days to ready them for transplanting.

Wood or aluminum cold frames can be purchased ready-made. The best of these are fitted with an automatic vent opener that is activated by the sun. For information on solar-powered vent openers write: Bramen Co., Inc., Box 70, Salem, MA 01970; or Dalen Products Inc., 201 Sherlake Drive, Knoxville, TN 37922.

If you don't have a cold frame, improvise with a wooden crate covered with a sheet of glass. Or place plants outdoors during the day and cover with plastic during the night. Anchor the plastic around the sides with bricks or stones, and keep the plastic from touching the plants.

Transplants should be planted when conditions are cool, such as on cloudy days or in late afternoon. After planting, do not let the soil dry out. You will probably have to water every day, maybe twice a day in warm weather. Place water directly in the root area. Protect seedlings with some sort of shade the first few days after planting if sunlight is intense.

Shop around for high-quality transplants. Choose plants that are sturdy, compact and healthy green.

Do not plant seedlings directly in the garden from a greenhouse or the warm, sheltered indoors. Placing them in a cold frame for several days helps seedlings acclimate before being planted in the garden.

Even after plants are *hardened-off,* some frost protection may be needed. A plastic milk jug with the bottom removed is perfect for individual plants. See page 45 for additional frost-protection methods.

TRANSPLANTING TIPS

• Buy sturdy, compact plants that have healthy green color. Avoid tall, lanky specimens that have yellow leaves and appear to be stretched. Their spindly growth may be caused by crowded roots. Or they may not have received enough light and tried in vain to grow toward the sun or light source.

• Ask nursery personnel if the plants have been *hardened-off*—gradually acclimated from greenhouse to the outdoors. If they have come straight from a greenhouse without being exposed to the outdoors for 10 days, they may sustain severe shock when transplanted to your garden.

• Examine the underside of leaves for signs of pests. If you find a cucumber beetle already on a cucumber transplant, chances are the plant will die from the wilt disease the beetles transmit. Eggplant with flea beetles and tomatoes with whiteflies should also be avoided.

• Do not buy transplants in flower or with fruit unless they are growing in a large container. The root system is simply inadequate to support the plant's advanced top growth. A tomato plant flowering in a 2-1/2-inch pot will probably die when transplanted.

• Water transplants in containers just before you plant them. It helps ease the rootball out of the container and lessens shock. If the transplant is in a plastic pot, take a knife and gently run it around the rim between the soil and the pot. The rootball can be pulled free without breaking roots and disturbing soil particles. The more original potting soil you can plant, the better transplants will grow.

• Cucumber and tomato plants form roots along their stems, so plant them deep to encourage extra roots to form. Plants that form edible parts at the soil surface such as leeks, celery and onions should be planted shallowly.

• Plants subject to cutworm damage should be protected with cutworm collars. See photo, page 63. If you have slug problems, take precautions to control them. It is not uncommon to set out a row of transplants in the afternoon and find them eaten by morning.

Planting

The most common method of planting vegetables is in a single row. For the sake of simplicity, it is the system described on seed packets to give spacing distances.

Block planting and *wide-row* planting are other common planting methods. These are new names to describe planting systems that have long been practiced in China and Europe. No single system of planting is ideal for all vegetables. Use the system that suits you, the available space and the growth requirements of the particular vegetable.

THREE EFFICIENT PLANTING METHODS

Single row. This is best for vegetables that require ample space, such as tomatoes, peppers, eggplant, squash, cucumbers and cabbage. Sometimes the single row is mounded into "hills" instead of continuous raised rows. The extra soil depth created by the hills benefits large plants with vigorous root systems, such as squash, melons, cucumbers and potatoes.

Wide row. Sometimes called *matted-row* planting and *French intensive.* Rows are generally 2 to 3 feet wide and raised 4 to 6 inches off the ground. It is efficient with vegetables that grow in a small space and tolerate crowding or close spacing. Looseleaf lettuce, parsley, dwarf peas, radishes, chives, thyme and mint can be planted this way.

Block planting. Sometimes called *square-foot* gardening. This system is efficient with vegetables that grow in a compact area but do not tolerate crowding—head lettuce, beets, carrots, turnips and onions. Block planting differs from a matted row in that plants are spaced uniformly, usually in a diamond pattern. The wide rows are usually 2 to 3 feet wide and mounded 4 to 6 inches high.

THINNING PLANTING BEDS

Some vegetables tolerate crowded conditions but require thinning to achieve adequate spacing of individual vegetables. Unfortunately, it is psychologically unpleasant to destroy healthy, useful seedlings. Keep in mind that it pays to be ruthless because crowded plants produce poor results.

Seed tapes and pelleted seeds also save thinning. Or mix fine seeds with

Single row is the traditional way to lay out a vegetable garden. Large vegetables such as tomatoes and potatoes are best grown this way. Other vegetables can often be grown more efficiently in a wide row or block planting.

Wide-row planting is best for vegetables that will tolerate some crowding. For more information, see pages 15 and 58. Shown here are two rows of dwarf peas at left and a row of radishes at right.

Block-row planting is similar to wide row, but only certain kinds of vegetables can be grown this way. *Heading* vegetables such as lettuce and cabbage are especially adapted to this method.

Many gardeners hate to thin seedlings, but consider it is a necessary evil. When plants compete for water, nutrients and space, they *all* suffer.

Succession planting, planting crops to mature at different times, extends the harvest period. Here, radish seeds are sown to replace a harvested crop.

This interplanting of low-growing parsley and upright-growing Swiss chard uses garden space efficiently.

sand or compost and broadcast in a wide row.

When thinning, take care not to disturb adjacent seedlings. Thin when the soil is moist, such as after a rain or watering, so roots pull up with least resistance. Or take a pair of sharp-pointed scissors and snip off the seedlings at the soil line.

Thinning may be necessary in several stages of plant growth. With carrots and beets, I like to make a superficial thinning as soon as the seedlings are up, then do a more thorough job after the plants are well established.

DOUBLE CROPPING AND SUCCESSION PLANTING

To get full value from a vegetable plot, practice *double cropping*. This means clearing a crop that has been harvested or has exhausted itself, and replanting with the same crop or a different crop.

For example, snap beans produce a flush of pods over 2 to 3 weeks, then deteriorate rapidly. By pulling out vines as soon as production dwindles, you can replant and obtain a second crop the same season. In most areas of the United States, you can obtain a third crop before fall frosts end the growing season. Similarly, two or three crops of lettuce can be harvested from the same garden space by double cropping.

Some vegetables cannot be replanted immediately because of the change in season. For example, English peas are grown in spring, and cannot be replanted because plants will not tolerate summer heat. Remove spent vines and plant a fast-growing summer vegetable in its place.

Succession planting is similar to double cropping. You sow vegetables at intervals during the season to provide a continuous harvest. One planting will come into harvest as another finishes bearing. Lettuce, snap beans, sweet corn and radish should be planted at two-week intervals to maintain a long harvesting period.

An additional way to extend harvests is to plant vegetables with *different maturity dates*. Certain vegetables are classified as "early," "mid-season" or "late." This is particularly true of tomatoes and sweet corn. By checking the "days to maturity" in this book, on a seed packet or catalog description, you can plan an extended harvest. For example, by planting 'Early Girl' hybrid (54 days), 'Better Boy VF' hybrid (72 days) and 'Super-steak VFN' hybrid (80 days), you can harvest tomatoes over several months. With sweet corn, by planting 'Earliglo EH' hybrid (65 days), 'Honey & Cream' hybrid (78 days) and 'Silver Queen' hybrid (92 days), you will enjoy sweet corn through the summer.

COMPANION PLANTING AND INTERCROPPING

Most vegetables seem to get along fine together. If rows are spaced properly, you should never have to worry about the carrots getting along with the cucumbers or the beans preferring to be near broccoli.

Many herbs possess exotic flavors and fragrances for repellent reasons—usually to repel certain insects and foraging animals. These repellent properties can sometimes be used to good advantage in the garden. Chives, parsley and garlic are often recommended for planting near vegetable crops for this reason. However, many horticulturists point out that there is too much speculation and not enough scientific evidence to support claims for repellent properties. Many herbs such as garlic and chives must be bruised before the repellent odor is released. They repel best when juice is extracted from them for spraying directly onto plants. See page 64.

In my opinion, the claims made for companion planting of herbs are exaggerated. Indeed, I have seen many vegetables ravaged by insects in spite of being close to "repellent" herbs.

Intercropping saves space in the vegetable garden. This is done by planting two vegetables close together, one to be harvested quickly before the other vegetable has matured and filled out. For example, lettuce and spinach can be grown between tomato plants. They can be harvested long before the tomato plants have grown to full-bearing size and begin to block out light. Similarly, tall, slender vegetables such as onions can be interplanted with compact vegetables such as beans and lettuce without being crowded.

Similar methods that save space, such as growing vegetables vertically and in raised-bed gardens, are discussed in the chapter Containers and Small Spaces, pages 71 to 75.

Planting a Garden

1. Lay out site according to plan, using stakes and string to mark the boundaries. Choose a site in a sunny, well-drained location.

2. Remove sod or weeds if they are present. Shake valuable topsoil from roots. After removing sod, take soil from several areas of the plot for a soil test. See page 19.

3. Most garden soil requires addition of organic matter to improve the soil structure. Spread 3 to 6 inches of amendment such as compost over the area to be planted.

4. Using a spade or power tiller, thoroughly mix topsoil and amendment. Dig down to the depth of the spade—approximately 12 inches.

5. Rake the soil surface to make it level. Remove stones and weed or grass roots. Keep a sharp eye out for larvae of harmful insects.

6. Scatter fertilizer over the soil. Lime or sulfur may also be needed to adjust soil pH. Rake into soil at root zone area. Wait 10 days before planting.

7. Using a trowel or similar tool, prepare furrow for seeds. Use string as a guide to keep planting rows and beds straight.

8. Sow large seeds in straight, evenly spaced rows. Cover and firm with soil. Many small-seed vegetables can be scattered over the soil surface. See photo, page 39.

9. Set out transplants according to their cold hardiness. Tomatoes, shown above, should be planted only after danger of frost has passed.

several distinct climates. The coastal area—from Santa Barbara south to the Mexican border—has 300 or more frost-free days of mild weather each year. This allows cool-season crops to be grown year-round. Summer fog is a factor where the warm interior air draws in cool Pacific air. The fog reduces the amount of sunshine, which slows development of many warm-season crops. Inland climates vary greatly, depending on elevation and proximity to the coast and desert.

Northern California also has micro-climates too complex to show on a map. Much of this area is influenced by the Pacific Ocean and summer fog. The immediate coastal area experiences moderate temperatures. Conditions are excellent for growing cool-season crops year-round.

In the interior valleys, summers are sunny and warm, creating exceptional growing conditions for warm-season crops, especially melons, sweet corn and tomatoes. Tropical vegetables such as jicama, chayote, winged bean and casaba melon do well in the valleys away from fog.

In many parts of these inland valleys, winters are mild enough to grow cool-season crops through winter. Otherwise, planting occurs mostly in February and March and again in August to September. April is the busiest month for planting warm-season crops. Because the season is long, a second planting can be made in June for a fall harvest.

Pacific Northwest. The climate of this area is unique. Western Washington and western Oregon have a long growing season—up to 250 days—with last spring frosts occurring in mid-March. But cool, cloudy summer weather reduces sunshine, and the soil warms slowly in spring. These cool conditions are excellent for cool-season vegetables, but warm-season vegetables require heat and sunshine to mature. Growing melons here is difficult. Tomatoes, peppers and sweet corn must be confined to early maturing varieties. Plant in raised beds to warm the soil early in spring, and take advantage of warm microclimates.

In eastern Washington there is enough summer sun to ripen long-maturing, warm-season varieties. In eastern Oregon the growing season is short. Cool-season crops are recommended. Grow early varieties and use season-stretching techniques.

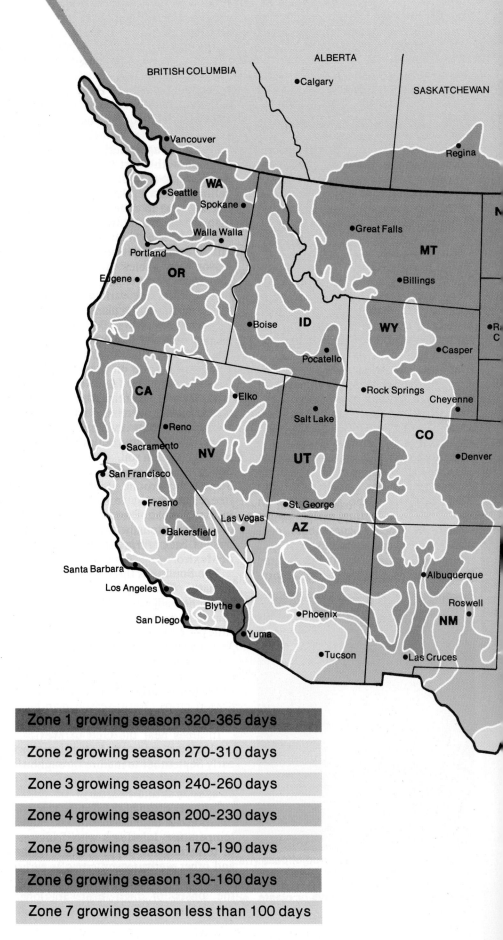

Zone 1 growing season 320-365 days

Zone 2 growing season 270-310 days

Zone 3 growing season 240-260 days

Zone 4 growing season 200-230 days

Zone 5 growing season 170-190 days

Zone 6 growing season 130-160 days

Zone 7 growing season less than 100 days

The climate of North America is complex. Microclimates and year-to-year weather patterns that affect zone divisions cannot be mapped. For these reasons, use the climate map as a guide and not an absolute. The same is true for the planting dates given in the following chart. They are based on mean spring and fall frost dates. Half the time, frosts will be sooner or later in a given year. For the most precise information on frost dates, check *locally* with nursery personnel, your county extension agent or state university extension service.

When to Plant

Vegetable	Zone 1	Zone 2	Zone 3	Zone 4	Zone 5	Zone 6	Zone 7
Amaranth	Feb 10-Apr 1	Mar 1-Apr 1	Mar 15-Apr 15	Apr 5-May 1	May 1-Jun 1	May 15-Jun 15	Jun 15-Jul 15
Artichoke, Globe	not recommended	Feb 5-Apr 1	Mar 20-Apr 1	Apr 5-May 1	Apr 20-May 15	May 10-Jun 10	May 15
Asparagus	not recommended	not recommended	Feb 1-Mar 10	Mar 1-Apr 10 Nov 15-Jan 1	Mar 15-Apr 15 Oct 20-Nov 20	Mar 10-May 15	May 1-Jun 1
Asparagus Pea	Feb 10-Apr 1 Oct 1-Dec 1	Mar 1-Apr 1 Sep 1	Mar 15-Apr 1 Sep 1	Apr 5-May 1 Aug 1-Sep 1	May 1-Jun 1	May 15-Jun 15	Jun 15-Jul 15
Bean, Broad	Jan 1-Feb 1 Oct 1-Dec 1	Jan 15-Mar 1 Sep 1	Feb 15-Mar 15 Sep 1	Mar 1-Apr 1 Aug 1-Sep 1	Mar 15-Jul 1 Aug 1-Sep 1	Apr 1-Jul 1	Apr 15-Jul 15
Bean, Cowpea	Feb 10-May 1 Jul 1-Aug 1	Mar 1-May 15 Sep 1	Mar 15-May 25 Sep 1	Apr 5-Jun 30 Jul 1	May 1-Jun 15	May 25-Jun 15	**
Bean, Garbanzo	Feb 10-May 1 Sep 1	Mar 1-Apr 1 Aug 15-Sep 30	Mar 15-Apr 1 Aug 15-Sep 30	Apr 10-May 1	May 1-Jun 1	May 15-Jun 15	**
Bean, Lima	Feb 20-May 1 Sep 1-Oct 1	Mar 1-Jun 1 Aug 15-Sep 30	Apr 1-Jun 15 Jul 15-Sep 1	May 1-May 10 Jul 1-Aug 15	May 15-Jun 30	Jun 1-Jun 15	not recommended
Bean, Scarlet Runner	Feb 1 Oct 1-Dec 1	Feb 5 Aug 1	Mar 15- Aug 1	Mar 15-Aug	May 1-Aug 1	May 15-Aug 1	Jun 1-Aug 15
Bean, Shelling	Feb 10-May 1 Sep 1	Mar 1-May 15 Jul 1-Aug 1	Mar 15-May 25 Aug 1	Apr 10-Jun 30	May 1-Jun 15	May 25-Jun 15	**
Bean, Snap	Feb 10-May 1 Sep 1	Mar 1-May 15 Jul 1-Aug 1	Mar 15-May 25 Jul 1-Sep 1	Apr 10-Jun 30 Jul 1-Aug 15	May 1-Jun 30	May 25-Jul 1	Jun 1-Jun 15
Bean, Soy	Feb 10-May 1 Sep 1	Mar 1-May 15 Jul 1-Aug 1	Apr 1-May 25 Jul 1-Sep 1	May 1-Jun 30	May 15-Jun 15	Jun 1-Jun 15	Jun 10-Jun 15
Bean, Winged	Feb 20-Jun 1 Jul 1-Aug 1	Mar 15-May 15	Apr 1-May 25 Jul 1-Sep 1	May 1-Jun 30	May 15-Jun 15	May 25	not recommended
Beet	Jan 10-Mar 15 Sep 1-Nov 1	Feb 5-Apr 15 Sep 1	Feb 15-May 15 Sep 1-Dec 1	Mar 15-Jun 1 Aug 1-Sep 15	Apr 1-Jun 15 Jul 15-Aug 1	Apr 15-Aug 1	May 1-Jun 15
Broccoli	Jan 1-Jan 30 Aug 1-Oct 1	Jan 15-Mar 1 Sep 1	Feb 15-Mar 15 Aug 1-Sep 15	Mar 1-Apr 15 Aug 1-Sep 15	Mar 25-May 1 Aug 1-Sep 15	Apr 15-Jun 1	May 10-Jun 10
Brussels Sprouts	Jan 1-Jan 30 Aug 1-Oct 1	Jan 15-Mar 1 Sep 1	Feb 15-Mar 15 Aug 1-Sep 15	Mar 1-Apr 15 Aug 1-Sep 1	Mar 25-May 1 Aug 1-Sep 15		May 10-Jun 10
Burdock	Jan 10 Sep 1-Dec 1	Feb 5-Mar 1 Sep 1	Feb 15-Mar 15 Aug 1-Sep 15	Mar 15-Apr 15 Aug 1-Sep 15	Mar 25-May 1 Aug 1-Sep 15	Apr 15-Jun 15	May 1-Jun 10
Cabbage	Jan 10-Feb 10 Sep 1-Dec 1	Jan 15-Feb 25 Sep 1	Feb 5-Mar 1 Sep 1-Dec 1	Mar 15-Apr 1 Aug 1-Sep 15	Mar 10-Apr 10 Aug 1-Sep 15	Apr 15-Jun 15	May 10-Jun 1
Cabbage, Chinese	Jan 1-Mar 1 Sep 1-Dec 1	Feb 1-Feb 25 Sep 1-Nov 1	Sep 1-Oct 15	Aug 1-Oct 1	Jun 15-Aug 15	Jun 1-Jul 15	May 15-Jun 15
Cantaloupe	Feb 20-Apr 1	Mar 15-May 15	Apr 1-May 30	May 1-Jun 1	May 15-Jun 15	Jun 1-Jul 1	**
Cardoon	Feb 10-May 1	Mar 1-Apr 1	Mar 15-Apr 1	Apr 10	May 1	May 15	Jun 1
Carrot	Jan 10-Mar 1 Sep 1-Dec 1	Feb 5-Mar 1 Sep 1-Oct 1	Feb 15-Mar 20 Sep 1-Nov 1	Mar 15-Apr 20 Jul 1-Sep 1	Apr 5-Jul 1	Apr 5-Jun 1	May 10-Jun 1
Cauliflower	Jan 10-Feb 1 Sep 1-Oct 1	Feb 5-Feb 20 Sep 1	Feb 15-Mar 10 Aug 1-Sep 15	Mar 1-Mar 20 Aug 1-Sep 15	Apr 1-May 10 Aug 1-Sep 15	Apr 15-Jun 15	May 20-Jun 15
Celeriac	Feb 10 Sep 1-Dec 1	Mar 1-Apr 1 Sep 1	Mar 20 Jul 15-Sep 1	Apr 10 Jul 1-Aug 15	May 1 Jun 1-Jul 15	May 15	Jun 1
Celery	Jan 10-Feb 10	Feb 5-Mar 1 Sep 1	Mar 1-Apr 1 Jul 15-Sep 1	Mar 15-Apr 20 Jul 1-Aug 15	Apr 10-May 1	Apr 10-Jun 1	May 20-Jun 15
Celtuce	Jan 10 Oct 1-Dec 1	Jan 15-Mar 1 Sep 1	Mar 1-Apr 1 Sep 1-Oct 1	Mar 15-Apr 15 Aug 1-Sep 15	Mar 25-Apr 30 Aug 1-Sep 15	Apr 15-May 1	Apr 15-May 15
Chard, Swiss	Jan 10-Apr 1 Jun 1-Nov 1	Feb 5-May 1	Mar 1-May 15 Jun 1-Oct 1	Mar 15-Jun 15 Jun 1-Sep 15	Apr 1-Jun 15 Aug 1-Sep 15	Apr 15-Jun 15	May 20-Jun 15
Chayote	Feb 10-Mar 1	Mar 5-Apr 15	Apr 1	Apr 15-May 1	May 1	not recommended	not recommended
Chicory, Leaf	Jan 10 Oct 1-Dec 1	Feb 5-Mar 1 Sep 1-Oct 1	Mar 1-Mar 15 Sep 1	Mar 15-Apr 1 Aug 1	Apr 5 Aug 1-Sep 15	Apr 20	May 15
Collards	Jan 1-Feb 1 Sep 1-Dec 1	Feb 5-Apr 1 Sep 1	Feb 15-Apr 1 Aug 1-Sep 15	Mar 1-May 1 Aug 1-Sep 1	Mar 15-Apr 15 Aug 1-Sep 15	Apr 1-Apr 15	May 1 Jul 1
Corn, Sweet	Feb 10-Apr 1	Mar 1-Apr 15	Mar 15-May 1	Apr 10-Jun 1	May 1-Jul 10	May 15-Jun 1	**
Cress, Pepper	Indoors all year	Indoors all year	Indoors all year	Indoors all year	Indoors all year	Indoors all year	Indoors all year
Cress, Upland	Jan 10-Feb 15	Jan 15-Mar 1 Sep 1	Feb 15-Mar 15 Oct 1-Dec 1	Mar 1-Apr 15 Sep 1	Mar 20-May 10 Aug 15-Oct 1	Apr 20-Jun 1	May 15-Jun 15
Cress, Water	Feb 10-Mar 1 Oct 1-Dec 1	Mar 15 Sep 1	Mar 15 Sep 15-Nov 15	Apr 10 Sep 1	May 1 Aug 1-Sep 1	May 15	May 30 Aug 1-Sep 1
Cucumber	Feb 20-Apr 1 Sep 1	Feb 15-Apr 15	Apr 1-May 1 Jun 1-Aug 15	May 1-Jun 1	May 15-Jul 1	Jun 1-Jun 15	**
Dandelion	Jan 10 Oct 1-Dec 1	Jan 15-Mar 1 Sep 1-Oct 1	Feb 15-Mar 15 Sep 1-Oct 1	Mar 1-Mar 15 Sep 1	Mar 15-Apr 1 Aug 1-Sep 15	Mar 15-Apr 1	Apr 1 Aug 1
Eggplant	Feb 20-Mar 15	Mar 1-Apr 15	Mar 15-May 1 Jun 1-Aug 1	May 1-Jun 1	May 15-Jun 10	Jun 1-Jun 15	**
Endive	Jan 10-Mar 1 Oct 1-Dec 1	Feb 5-Mar 1	Mar 1-Apr 1 Sep 1-Oct 1	Mar 15-Apr 15 Aug 1	Apr 1-May 1 Aug 1-Sep 15	Apr 15-May 15	May 1-Jun 1

**Difficult to grow in this zone. See Climate text.

How to Plant

Vegetable	Method of Growing	Cold Hardy or Tender	Depth to Plant Seed	Days to Germination	Weeks to Transplant	Spacing (in inches) Plants	Rows	Days to Harvest	Plants per Person	Comments
Amaranth	seeds	tender	1/4 inch	10-15 at 70F		16-20	20-24	60-70	15	Tolerates hot summers.
*Artichoke, Globe	seeds or roots	tender	1/2 inch	12 to 15 at 70F	8-10	36	36-48	180	5	Perennial in mild-winter areas.
*Asparagus	seeds or roots	hardy	1/2 inch	14-21 at 75F	10	12-18	36	2 years	10	See page 86 for root-planting method.
Asparagus Pea	seeds	tender	1/2 inch	7-14		4-6	12-24	70	30	Provide short trellis for support.
Bean, Broad	seeds	hardy	2 inches	7-14 at 55F		6-10	9-24	70	30	Plants must mature during cool weather.
Bean, Cowpea	seeds	tender	1-1/2 inches	6-10 at 70F		6-12	18-48	75	15	Young pods are edible as snaps.
Bean, Garbanzo	seeds	tender	1-1/2 inches	7-14 at 70F		12	24-30	105	15	Seeds susceptible to rot during cool, rainy conditions.
Bean, Lima	seeds	very tender	2 inches	7-10 at 70F		3-6	18-36	70-90	30	Seeds susceptible to rot.
Bean, Scarlet Runner	seeds	hardy	1-1/2 inches	5-10 at 70F		6	5 feet	70	6	Provide poles for support.
Bean, Shelling	seeds	tender	1-1/2 inches	6-10 at 70F		6	24-36	80	15	Bush and pole varieties available.
Bean, Snap	seeds	tender	1 inch	6-10 at 70F		2-6	18-36	50-60	30	Pick beans frequently.
Bean, Soy	seeds	tender	1 inch	10-14 at 70F		4-6	24-36	70	30	Pods shell easily if boiled.
Bean, Winged	seeds or plants	very tender	1-1/2 inches	7-14 at 70F	3	6-12	36	70-100	15	Provide poles for support.
Beet	seeds	hardy	1/4 inch	6-10 at 70F		3-4	12-18	50-60	45	Provide continuous moisture.
*Broccoli	seeds or plants	hardy	1/4 inch	5-10 at 70F	6	18	24-36	50-70	10	Heavy feeder, especially nitrogen.
Brussels Sprouts	seeds or plants	hardy	1/4 inch	8-10 at 70F	6	18-24	24-36	80-90	10	Usually best as a fall crop.
Burdock	seeds	hardy	1/4 inch	7-14 at 70F		24	36	100	30	Also known as *gobo*.
*Cabbage	seeds or plants	hardy	1/4 inch	5-10 at 70F	6	12-24	24-36	60-90	10	Protect transplants against cutworms.
*Cabbage, Chinese	seeds or plants	hardy	1/4 inch	3-5 at 70F	6-8	18-24	24-36	45	10	Pak choy, a nonheading cabbage, tolerates crowding.
Cantaloupe	seeds or plants	tender	1/2 inch	5-10 at 75F		12	4-6 feet	75-100	4	Protect from cucumber beetles.
Cardoon	seeds or plants	tender	1/4 inch	10-14 at 75F	6	24-36	36	120	3-6	Blanch stems before harvesting.
Carrot	seeds	hardy	1/8 inch	7-10 at 60-70F		1-1/2 to 2	12-18	55-80	90	Plant in short, wide rows.
*Cauliflower	seeds or plants	hardy	1/4 inch	4-10 at 70F	6-8	24	18-36	65-80	10	Bolts to seed with warm weather.
*Celeriac	seeds or plants	hardy	1/8 inch	10-20 at 65F	10	12	24	100	15	Grow for its edible roots.
*Celery	seeds or plants	hardy	1/8 inch	10-14 at 65F	10-12	12	24-36	95-150	15	Blanching stems improves flavor.
Celtuce	seeds	hardy	1/8 inch	7-14 at 55F		6-12	12-24	70	30	Harvest young leaves.
Chard, Swiss	seeds	hardy	1/2 inch	4-10 at 70F		12	18-36	45-55	15	Pay close attention to thinning.
Chayote	seeds	tender	bury fruit	7-10 at 75F		36	36	200	1	Plant whole fruit with top end exposed slightly.
Chicory, Leaf	seeds	hardy	1/4 inch	7-14 at 70F		6-12	18-24	90	15	Best grown as a fall crop.
Collards	seeds or plants	hardy	1/4 inch	4-10 at 70F	5-6	12-24	24-36	60-70	10	Slight frost improves flavor.
Corn, Sweet	seeds	tender	1 inch	6-10 at 70F		8-12	36	55-95	15	Plant rows in blocks for best pollination.
Cress, Pepper	seeds	hardy	surface-sow	1-2 at 70F		1/8	1/8	10	1 packet	Use as sprouting seeds.
Cress, Upland	seeds	hardy	1/4 inch	3-7 at 70F		6	12	60	30	Plants will survive cold winters.
Cress, Water	seeds or plants	hardy	1/4 inch	7-10 at 55F	6	4-6	12	70	30	Grows best in clear, running water.
Cucumber	seeds or plants	very tender	1 inch	6-10 at 70F	4-6	8-12	36-48	50-79	5	Protect from cucumber beetles.
Dandelion	seeds	hardy	1/4 inch	7-14 at 55F		6-9	12	95	30	Blanch leaves for best flavor.
*Eggplant	plants	very tender	1/4 inch	7-14 at 80F	6-8	18-24	36	70-90	6	Protect from flea beetles.
Endive	seeds	hardy	1/4 inch	7-14 at 70F		9-12	18	70-80	15	Bunch leaves over heart to sweeten.

*Transplants are preferred instead of seed.
Row spacings are based on single, straight rows.

Plants per Person indicates approximate amount of plants for fresh use.
Adjust according to personal preference or if you plan to store produce.

Vegetable	Zone 1	Zone 2	Zone 3	Zone 4	Zone 5	Zone 6	Zone 7
Garlic	Oct 1-Dec 1	not recommended	Feb 1-Mar 1 Aug 15-Oct 1	Feb 20-Mar 20 Sep 1	Mar 10-Apr 15	Apr 1-May 15	May 1-Jun 1
Ginseng	not recommended	not recommended	Feb 15-Apr 1	Mar 1-Apr 1	Mar 15-May 1	Apr 1-May 1	Apr 15-Jun 1
Gourd	Feb 20-Apr 1 Aug 1-Sep 1	Mar 15-Apr 1	Apr 1-May 1	May 1-May 15	May 15	Jun 1	**
Huckleberry, Garden	Feb 10-Apr 1 Sep 1	Mar 1-Apr 1	Apr 1-May 1	Apr 10-May 15	May 1	May 15	Jun 5
Husk Tomato	Feb 10-Apr 1 Sep 1	Mar 1-Apr 1	Apr 1-May 1	Apr 10-May 15	May 1	May 15	Jun 5
Jerusalem Artichoke	Feb 15 Jun 1-Dec 1	Mar 15-Apr 15	Apr 1-May 1	Apr 15-May 30	May 15	May 20	Jun 5
Jicama	Feb 20	Mar 15	Apr 1	**	not recommended	not recommended	not recommended
Kale	Jan 1-Feb 1 Sep 1-Dec 1	Jan 15-Feb 20 Sep 1-Oct 1	Feb 15-Mar 10 Aug 15-Oct 15	Mar 1-Apr 1 Aug 1-Sep 1	Mar 20-Apr 20 Aug 1-Sep 15	Apr 10-May 10	May 1-Jun 1
Kohlrabi	Jan 1-Feb 1 Sep 1-Dec 1	Jan 15-Feb 20 Sep 1-Oct 1	Feb 15-Mar 10 Sep 1-Oct 15	Mar 1-Apr 10 Aug 1-Sep 1	Mar 20-May 10 Aug 1-Sep 15	Apr 10-Jun 30	May 1-Jun 1
Leek	Jan 1-Feb 1 Oct 1-Dec 1	Jan 15-Feb 15 Sep 1	Feb 1-Mar 1 Sep 1-Nov 1	Feb 20-Apr 1	Mar 15-May 1	Apr 15-May 20	May 1-May 15
Lettuce	Jan 10-Feb 1 Sep 1-Dec 1	Feb 5-Feb 15 Sep 1	Feb 15-Mar 10 Sep 1-Nov 1	Mar 15-Apr 1 Aug 1-Oct 1	Apr 1-May 1 Aug 1-Sep 15	Apr 20-Jun 30	May 10-Jun 30
Mustard	Jan 1-Mar 1 Sep 1-Nov 1	Jan 20-Mar 1 Sep 1-Oct 1	Feb 15-Apr 1 Sep 1-Dec 1	Mar 1-Apr 20 Aug 15-Nov 1	Mar 20-May 10 Aug 1-Sep 15	Apr 15-Jun 30	May 10-Jun 30
Okra	Feb 20-Apr 15 Aug 1-Sep 1	Mar 15-Jun 1	Apr 1-Jun 15 Jun 1-Sep 10	May 1-Jun 15 Jun 1-Aug 10	May 15-Jun 1 Jun 1-Jul 15	Jun 1	**
Onion	Jan 1-Jan 15 Oct 1-Dec 1	Jan 1-Feb 15 Sep 1	Feb 5-Mar 10 Oct 1-Dec 31	Mar 1-Apr 1 Sep 1-Oct 1	Mar 15-Apr 15	Apr 10-May 15	May 1-Jun 10
Parsley	Jan 1-Jan 30 Sep 1-Dec 1	Feb 5-Mar 1 Sep 1	Feb 15-Mar 15 Sep 1-Jan 1	Mar 1-Apr 10 Aug 15-Nov 1	Mar 20-May 1 Aug 1-Sep 15	Apr 15-May 15	May 10-Jun 10
Parsnip	Jan 10 Sep 1-Dec 1	Feb 5-Mar 1 Aug 1-Sep 1	Feb 20-Mar 15 Aug 1-Sep 1	Mar 15-Apr 10 Jul 1-Aug 1	Apr 1-May 1 Aug 1-Sep 15	Apr 20-May 20	May 10-Jun 10
Pea	Jan 1-Feb 15 Sep 1-Dec 1	Jan 15-Mar 1 Sep 1	Feb 1-Mar 15 Sep 1-Nov 1	Feb 20-Mar 20 Aug 15-Oct 1	Mar 10-May 1 Aug 1-Sep 15	Apr 1-Jun 1	May 1-Jun 15
Peanut	Feb 10-Apr 1	Mar 15-Apr 15	Apr 1-May 1	Apr 10-May 15	May 1	May 15	not recommended
Pepper	Feb 20-Apr 15 Jun 1-Sep 1	Mar 15-May 1	Apr 1-Jun 1 Jun 1-Aug 1	May 1-Jun 1 Jun 1-Aug 1	May 15-Jun 10 Jun 1-Jul 1	Jun 1-Jun 15	Jun 15-Jun 30
Potato	Jan 10-Feb 15 Aug 1-Sep 1	Feb 5-Mar 1 Aug 1	Feb 15-Mar 15 Aug 10-Sep 15	Mar 15-Apr 1 Aug 1	Apr 1-May 10 May 15-Jun 15	May 1-Jun 15	May 1-Jun 1
Pumpkin	Feb 20-Apr 1 Aug 1	Mar 15-Apr 15	Apr 1-May 1	May 1-May 15	May 15-Jun 10	Jun 1	Jun 1-Jun 30
Radish	Jan 1-Apr 1 Aug 1-Sep 1	Jan 1-Apr 1 Sep 1-Nov 1	Jan 15-May 1 Sep 1-Oct 1	Mar 1-May 1 Sep 1-Oct 1	Mar 10-May 10 Aug 15-Sep 15	Apr 1-Jun 15	May 1-Jun 1
Rhubarb	not recommended	not recommended	Mar 1	Apr 1	Mar 25	May 1	Jun 1
Rutabaga	not recommended	Jan 15-Feb 1	Feb 1-Mar 1 Aug 1-Sep 1	Mar 1-Apr 1 Jul 15-Aug 15	May 1-Jun 1 Aug 1-Sep 15	May 1-May 20	May 10-Jun 1
Salsify	Jan 10-Feb 10 Sep 1-Nov 1	Feb 5-Mar 1	Mar 1-Apr 1 Jul 15-Aug 15	Mar 15-Apr 15 Jun 10-Jul 10	Apr 1-May 15 Jun 1-Jul 1	Apr 15-Jun 1	May 10-Jun 1
Scorzonera	Jan 10-Feb 1 Sep 1-Nov 1	Feb 5 Aug 1	Mar 1-Mar 15 Aug 1	Mar 15-Apr 1	Apr 1-Apr 15	Apr 15	May 10
Shallot	Jan 1-Feb 10 Oct 1-Dec 1	Jan 1-Mar 1	Feb 15-Mar 15 Aug 15-Oct 1	Feb 15-Apr 1	Mar 15-May 1	Apr 10-May 10	May 1-Jun 1
Spinach	Jan 1-Feb 15 Oct 1-Dec 1	Jan 1-Mar 1 Sep 1	Jan 20-Mar 15 Oct 1-Dec 1	Feb 15-Apr 1 Sep 1-Oct 15	Mar 15-Apr 20 Aug 1-Sep 15	Apr 1-Jun 15	Apr 20-Jun 15
Spinach, Malabar	Feb 20-Apr 1	Mar 15-Apr 15	Apr 20-May 1 Jun 1-Aug 15	Apr 20-May 1 Jun 1-Aug 1	May 1	Jun 1-Jul 1	Jun 10
Spinach, New Zealand	Feb 10-Apr 15	Mar 10-May 15	Apr 1-May 15 Jun 1-Aug 15	Apr 10-Jun 1	May 1-Jun 15 Jun 1-Jul 15	May 15-Jun 15	Jun 1-Jun 15
Squash, Summer	Feb 20-Apr 15 Jun 1-Sep 1	Mar 10-May 15	Apr 1-May 15 Jun 1-Aug 15	Apr 10-Jun 1 Jun 1-Aug 1	May 1-Jun 15 Jun 1-Jul 15	May 15-Jun 15	Jun 1-Jun 20
Squash, Winter	Feb 20-Apr 15 Aug 1	Mar 10-May 15	Apr 1-May 1 Jun 20-Aug 20	Apr 10-Jun 1 Jun 10-Jul 10	May 1-Jun 15 Jun 1-Jul 1	May 15-Jun 15	Jun 1-Jun 20
Strawberry, Alpine	Feb 1 Sep 1-Dec 1	Mar 1-Apr 1 Sep 1	Mar 15-Apr 15 Sep 1	Apr 10	May 1	May 15	May 15
Sunflower	Feb 10-Mar 1 Aug 1	Mar 1-Apr 1	Mar 15-Apr 15	Apr 10-May 15	May 1-Jun 15	May 15-Jun 20	Jun 1
Sweet Potato	Feb 20-Mar 1	Nov 15-Apr 1	Mar 15-Apr 15	Apr 10-May 15	May 15-Jun 15	**	**
Tomato	Feb 15-Apr 10 Aug 1-Sep 1	Mar 5-May 1	Mar 20-May 20 Jun 1-Jul 15	Apr 15-Jun 1	May 5-Jul 15 Jun 1-Jul 1	May 20-Jun 15	Jun 5-Jun 30
Turnip	Jan 1-Feb 15 Oct 1-Nov 1	Jan 15-Mar 1 Sep 1	Feb 1-Mar 15 Sep 1-Oct 15	Mar 1-May 1 Aug 1-Sep 15	Mar 10-May 1 Aug 1-Sep 15	Apr 1-Jun 15	May 1-Jun 15
Watermelon	Feb 20-Apr 1	Mar 15-Apr 15	Apr 1-May 1	May 1-Jun 1	May 15-Jun 15	Jun 1-Jul 1	**
Yam, Chinese	Feb 20-Apr 1	Mar 15-Apr 1	Apr 1-Apr 15	May 1-May 15	May 15-Jun 15	Jun 1-Jun 20	**

**Difficult to grow in this zone. See Climate text.

Vegetable	Method of Growing	Cold Hardy or Tender	Depth to Plant Seed	Days to Germination	Weeks to Transplant	Spacing (in inches) Plants	Rows	Days to Harvest	Plants per Person	Comments
Garlic	bulbs (cloves)	hardy	2 inches	10 at 55-70F		4	12	90	6 cloves	Each clove segment produces a new plant.
Ginseng	seeds or roots	hardy	surface-sow	7-14 at 70F	10	6	12	5 years	10	Roots develop slowly.
Gourd	seeds or plants	very tender	1 inch	6-14 at 70F	4	24-36	36	120	6	Provide vines with strong supports.
*Huckleberry, Garden	plants	tender	1/4 inch	7-14 at 70F	6-8	24-36	24-36	70-80	6	Boil berries briefly to remove bitterness.
*Husk Tomato	plants	tender	1/4 inch	7-14 at 70F	8	36	36	70	5	Also known as ground cherry and cape gooseberry.
Jerusalem Artichoke	roots	hardy	2-4 inches	14 days at 70F		15-24	36	110	15	Productive and hardy perennial.
Jicama	seeds or plants	very tender	1 inch	7-14 at 70F	8-10	24	6 feet	240	15	Tubers taste like water chestnuts.
Kale	seeds or plants	hardy	1/4 inch	3-10 at 70F	4	18	24-36	50-65	10	Hardy enough for winter greens.
Kohlrabi	seeds or plants	hardy	1/2 inch	3-10 at 70F	4-6	4-6	18	50-70	30	Turniplike bulbs form above the soil.
Leek	seeds or plants	hardy	1/2 inch	7-14 at 70F	4-6	2-4	12-24	140	45	Leave in garden until ground freezes.
Lettuce	seeds or plants	hardy	1/4 inch	4-10 at 55-65F	4	12	18	60-70	15	Space leaf types 6-8 inches apart.
Mustard	seeds or plants	hardy	1/2 inch	3-5 at 70F	4	12	18-24	35-60	20	Grow as a fall crop.
Okra	seeds	very tender	1/2 inch	7-14 at 70F		12-24	36	50-55	15	Harvest pods regularly.
*Onion	seeds, plants, sets	hardy	1/4 inch	7-12 at 70F	6	4	6-12	75	45	Space green bunching types 2 inches apart.
*Parsley	seeds or plants	hardy	1/8 inch	7-28 at 70F	6-8	6-12	12	50	2	Outdoor sowings are slow to germinate.
Parsnip	seeds	hardy	1/4 inch	15-20 at 70F		4-6	12-18	120	60	Leave in garden until ground freezes.
Pea	seeds	hardy	1-2 inches	6-15 at 60F		2-4	24-36	50-80	60	Bush types do not need staking.
Peanut	seeds	tender	1-1/2 inches	18-21 at 70F		18	36	110	15	Shell seeds before sowing.
*Pepper	plants	very tender	1/4 inch	10-15 at 70F	8	18-24	24	70-100	5	Harvest fruit regularly.
*Potato	tubers or seeds	hardy	1/4 inch	5-10 at 70F	8	12	30	90-105	15	Potato seed has recently become available.
Pumpkin	seeds or plants	very tender	1 inch	6-10 at 70F	4	4-6 feet	6-8 feet	85-120	1	Grow bush types to save space.
Radish	seeds	hardy	1/2 inch	4-6 at 60F		1	12	25-35	80	Provide with constant moisture.
Rhubarb	roots (crowns)	hardy	4 inches			36	36	2 years	2	Easy to grow from seed. See page 152.
Rutabaga	seeds	hardy	1/2 inch	3-10 at 70F		6-8	18-24	80-90	30	Turnips are easier to grow.
Salsify	seeds	hardy	1/2 inch	7-14 at 60F		4-6	12-18	110	60	Leave in garden until ground freezes.
Scorzonera	seeds	hardy	1/4 inch	7-14 at 70F		3-6	6-12	90-100	30	Provide with regular moisture.
Shallot	bulbs	hardy	surface-sow	7-10 at 55F		8	12	100	25	Bulbs form in clusters.
Spinach	seeds	hardy	1/2 inch	7-12 at 50-60F		4-6	12-18	40-50	30	Grow spinach substitutes during warm weather months.
Spinach, Malabar	seeds or plants	tender	1/4 inch	7-10 at 70F	6-8	6-8	36	70	15	Grow on trellis to save space.
Spinach, New Zealand	seeds	tender	1/2 inch	7-14 at 55F		12	24-36	70	15	Warm-weather substitute for spinach.
Squash, Summerer	seeds or plants	very tender	1 inch	6-12 at 70F	4	36	36	50-70	3	Protect from cucumber beetles.
Squash, Winter	seeds or plants	very tender	1 inch	6-12 at 70F	4	36-56	6-8 feet	85-120	3	Plant bush types to save space.
*Strawberry, Alpine	plants	hardy	surface-sow	14-21 at 70F	8-10	12	18-24	90	15	Seeds need light to germinate.
Sunflower	seeds	hardy	1 inch	7-12 at 70F		12	36	80-90	7	Roots emit a toxin that can affect nearby plants.
Sweet Potato	plants	very tender	3-4 inches	10 days at 70F	6	12	4 feet	120	15	One root produces many sprouts for planting.
*Tomato	plants	tender	1/4 inch	6-14 at 70F	6-8	24-36	36-48	55-90	3-5	Use wire cages for supports.
Turnip	seeds	hardy	1/2 inch	7-10 at 70F		3-4	12-18	40-60	30	Tops make delicious greens.
Watermelon	seeds or plants	very tender	1 inch	5-7 at 75F	4	5-6 feet	5-6 feet	75-100	3	Requires long, hot summer.
*Yam, Chinese	seeds or tubers	very tender	1/2 inch	10 at 70F	4-6	12	36	120	15	Grow on trellis for support.

*Transplants are preferred instead of seed.
Row spacings are based on single, straight rows.

Plants per Person indicates approximate amount of plants for fresh use.
Adjust according to personal preference or if you plan to store produce.

Water, Weed and Mulch

Water is the key to growth of all plants. In addition to supplying life-giving moisture, water dissolves nutrients so they can be absorbed by plant roots. Plants grow rapidly when moisture is plentiful, but become subject to both moisture and nutrient stress when water is scarce. Water is also the key to seed germination. It softens the seed coat and swells the seed embryo to stimulate growth. Because vegetables are composed mostly of moisture, their flavor is greatly affected by the water supply. Even the sugars responsible for sweetness move into the fruit from the leaves in soluble form.

The most common mistake when watering vegetables is failing to provide enough on a regular basis. Many gardeners wait until lack of moisture is noticed, then desperately try to water plants back to life. Vegetables need to be watered regularly to grow. Without continuous growth, many vegetables produce off-flavors or will not set fruit.

Too much moisture can have a nega-tive effect on vegetables. Waterlogged soil prevents air from reaching the root zone. Except for aquatic vegetables such as watercress, plants will die or suffer from root rot when deprived of air. Melons can crack open and rot. Vining crops such as cucumbers are more likely to get mildew diseases. Slugs and snails, which thrive in a moist environment, can cause complete destruction. Nutrients, especially nitrogen, can be leached from the plant root zone.

Good soil drainage is essential. If your proposed site for a vegetable plot has poor drainage, you have two alternatives: Put in a drainage system to take the water away or build a raised bed. A raised bed brings the garden soil up above the surrounding soil level so water drains freely. You may want to build up the sides with railroad ties, lumber or stones.

Supplying vegetables with proper amounts of water is an art, particularly with respect to timing. Vegetables have critical periods when they should be watered for greatest yields.

Some prefer watering in regular amounts at every stage of their growth cycle. Others need it more at certain critical stages such as flowering and fruiting.

All vegetables grow well with moderate, regular amounts of water throughout the season. But if you fine-tune your watering schedule to supply an abundance of water at the period of greatest need, you can expect better-than-normal yield and fruit size.

The period of "greatest need" varies with the different types of vegetables. For example, vegetables that produce fruit or set pods—beans, peas, corn, tomatoes, peppers and eggplant—need more water when they are flowering and setting fruit or pods. Leaf crops—cabbage, lettuce and spinach—need water on a steady, continuous basis to keep growing and produce largest weight gains. Root crops—turnips, potatoes, beets, carrots and parsnips—also need water on a steady, continuous basis to gain weight and size. If subjected to a dry spell, they simply stop growing.

Left: Droplets of water serve as a visual reminder that vegetables need *continuous* moisture.
Above: Straw mulch around zucchini plant helps simplify garden care. It reduces weed growth and cools the soil during the warm summer months.

Irrigation methods that supply water in steady, regular amounts, such as drip irrigation, are desirable. Failing that, you should time waterings so that each vegetable benefits from it the most.

WHEN TO WATER

Seeds and transplants. When small seeds such as carrots and lettuce are planted directly into the garden, water every day if it doesn't rain. These seeds are planted close to the soil surface and are more susceptible to drying out than seeds of peas, beans and corn, which are planted deeper. Moisture is also important immediately following germination, especially for root crops. When a good rain or watering follows germination, carrot roots grow straight down, helping to produce finely shaped carrots. If the root growth is slowed by lack of moisture, the carrot root can become distorted by harvest time.

When transplants are set into the garden, water immediately and keep soil moist until they are established. Transplanted seedlings often sustain root damage and need regular amounts of moisture for a couple of weeks to recover from transplant shock. If the temperature is warm when you set out your transplants, it is helpful to supply some kind of temporary shade until they become adapted.

Established plants. As soon as a plant begins to wilt, it needs water immediately or it will die. Lack of moisture shows itself in different ways, depending on the plant and its sensitivity to moisture stress. Beets stop growing and take on a fibrous quality. Radishes grow hollow and stringy. Melons will not set fruit. Sweet corn will not fill each ear to the tip. Leafy vegetables sometimes take on a bitter flavor. Snap beans grow distorted. Tomatoes suffer physical disorders such as blossom-end rot. Squash and cucumbers wilt.

Do not wait until plants show symptoms of water need. Check the garden soil regularly—every day if temperatures are warm—and supply plants with water in their root zone. An easy way to check moisture content of garden soil is to grab a handful of topsoil and squeeze it. If the particles cling together, the soil has adequate moisture. If the particles separate and feel dry, like sand, the soil needs moisture.

A frequent question asked about watering is, ''What time of day is best?'' Watering is best done in early morning. Watering at this time means less loss through evaporation and from wind.

MOISTURE-HOLDING CAPACITY OF SOIL

Different types of soil have varied capacities for holding moisture in the plant's root zone. Clay soils are prone to waterlogging, while sandy soils allow moisture to drain away too rapidly. The best kind of garden soil is a loam soil. Its composition is somewhere between sand and clay. A loam soil drains well, yet the spaces between soil particles retain enough water to supply plant roots.

WAYS TO WATER

The big problem with watering is getting it to your plants in sufficient quantities when Mother Nature proves uncooperative. If you live in an area that does not receive regular rainfall, irrigation will be necessary. The simplest source of water is from an outdoor faucet, whether it is attached to a city water supply or a well system.

Common methods of irrigation are furrow irrigation, hand-held garden hoses, lawn sprinklers set in the middle of the garden and drip irrigation systems that apply water to the root zone of plants.

Furrow irrigation is one of the most common methods of watering vegetables. Furrows or channels are created with a hoe or shovel and water is applied to the rows, which reaches the plant's root zone. Allow for dry pathways, or rows will be muddy after you water. This can be a mess when you walk between rows to harvest.

Any form of hand irrigation is generally the least-effective method. It seems as if you are applying more water than you actually are, and only the top few inches of soil are moistened. But if you have the time and the patience to wet the soil thoroughly to the root zone, it is still an acceptable way to water. Using an extension

Water Correctly

The illustration at right shows what happens when a plant is given frequent, shallow waterings. Roots grow where there is water—in the upper soil surface. During periods of warm, windy weather or if an irrigation is missed, the plant is unable to absorb the water it needs. The plant at far right is given deep, regular waterings. The roots penetrate deeply into the soil so they have a greater reservoir of water and nutrients to draw upon.

wand, which attaches to the end of the hose, makes hand watering easier and faster.

Lawn sprinklers are a big improvement over hand watering. They can be set in place to water as long as necessary to soak soil in the root zone. The biggest drawback with sprinklers is that they can waste water through evaporation on hot days.

DRIP IRRIGATION

When I first raised vegetables, I irrigated with a lawn sprinkler in the garden, or applied water with a garden hose. These watering methods usually did the job, but they were more *corrective* than *preventative*. During warm periods, plants can come under stress before you use the hose or sprinkler. Several years ago I started using *drip irrigation,* and I can honestly say that I will never again water any other way. The difference in plant performance is incredible, especially because the system *prevents* plant stress due to lack of water.

Drip irrigation is a system of hoses that lie across the soil close to plant roots, either on top of the soil or buried out of sight. Depending on design, drip hoses ooze moisture through pores along the hose wall, or drip moisture from *emitters,* tiny holes spaced at regular intervals along a hose. Drip irrigation is especially effective when installed under black plastic. This not only protects the hoses from damage, it reduces evaporation.

Spaghetti emitters have long, flexible tubes coming from a main hose. At the end of each flexible tube is a type of valve that does a fine job of dripping moisture. They are probably best suited for watering individual plants such as fruit trees or plants in containers.

The biggest benefit of drip irrigation is that you can water the whole garden regularly by a single turn of the faucet. Plants receive regular moisture, and are not subjected to water stress. The basics of watering correctly still apply—putting sufficient amounts of water in the root zone.

Economically, drip irrigation systems also make sense. They save water due to less waste—as much as 30%. Because plants make continuous, rapid growth, they produce early and bountiful yields.

Usually, the bigger your vegetable garden, the more complex the drip system. For a small area, it is sufficient to place drip hose up and down the rows with one end connected to a water spigot. With 1/2-inch diameter hose and emitters spaced 2 feet apart, and with average water pressure, water should be able to travel about 250 feet on level ground from your water spigot. This can be doubled to 500 feet if two hoses are connected to the spigot by a Y valve. For a drip system set-up such as this, see the Automatic Vegetable Garden, page 15.

To irrigate large gardens, you may have to consider a more sophisticated set-up. Such a system might involve lateral hoses connected to a larger line, called a *header* line, fitted with a water-pressure regulator. Some systems can incorporate a special fertilizer tank that injects soluble fertilizer into the water. Plants are fed automatically while they are being irrigated. Some drip-irrigation companies will help you design a system if you send them a plan of your garden with your order. Many have a specification sheet at the front of their supply catalog.

Drip systems vary in cost and quality. To decide which system is best for you, look for drip-irrigation advertisements in garden magazines. Send for their descriptive material and study it. Many retail garden-center outlets also carry drip-irrigation supplies that you can examine in the store.

One of the least-expensive systems is *Irrigro.* It consists of a white plastic hose with tiny pores. The pores allow water droplets to ooze through the sides of the hose, watering the soil all along its length. A source for Irrigro hose is International Irrigation Systems, 1555 Third Avenue, Niagara Falls, NY 14304.

Polyflex hose has emitters spaced at 18-inch or 24-inch intervals. Water drips from the emitters and saturates the soil in a wide circle until the soil is moistened along the length of the hose. If you are interested in more information on polyflex hose, write Submatic Irrigation Systems, Box 246, Lubbock, TX 79408.

Beads of water ooze slowly from tiny pores in drip irrigation hose. Water is supplied slowly and directly to the root zone of plants so there is less waste through evaporation. Other kinds of drip systems are available, including those with *emitters* or tiny valves set at regular spaces along the hose.

Drip irrigation hose is being laid to supply small garden with water needs. In this case, hose is placed up and down a series of narrow, raised planting beds.

Simple Drip System Layout

This drip system layout for a small garden is simple and effective. Y-valve connection—shown in circle—joins two sections of drip hose, each 100 feet long, to cover approximately 500 square feet of garden space. A design of this type works well with raised planting rows, designated by the color tint. See page 15 for additional information on drip irrigation systems.

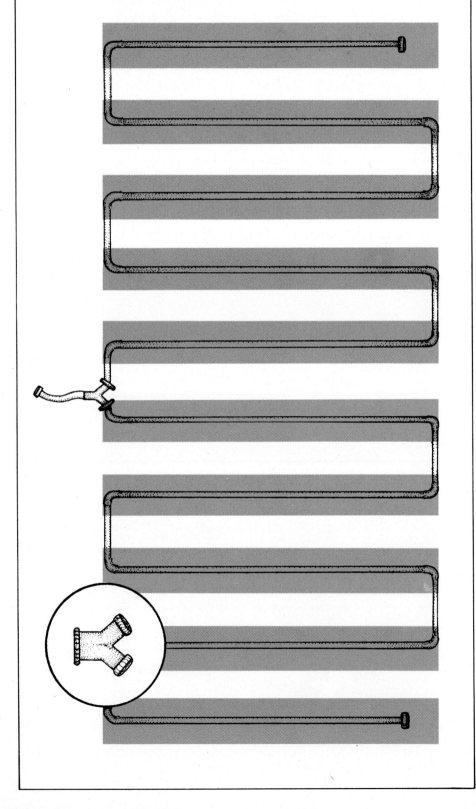

Weeding

The most frequent cause of vegetable garden failure is weeds. In a short time, unchecked weed growth can turn a neatly planted vegetable plot into a jungle. Weeds not only compete with vegetables for moisture and nutrients, they also block sunlight. It is easy to become discouraged when weeds claim your garden. The best way to combat them is to keep them from getting ahead.

A few minutes spent pulling young weeds at the end of each day is far more sensible than trying to catch up on a week of neglect. This is especially true in midsummer when weeds grow fast. I use every good rain as a signal. I go outside immediately after the rain has ceased. Weeds are easy to pull while the ground is wet and yielding.

When you do the initial soil preparation of your garden, remove all pieces of weed roots that you see. The smallest piece of plantain or dandelion root can grow into a full-size weed. Avoid walking on a newly cultivated garden. The surface compaction helps many weed seeds to germinate.

Use a mulch between rows to suffocate weeds. If installed correctly at the beginning of the gardening season, a mulch is actually the easiest way to control weeds. You may want to grow your vegetables through black plastic so weeds cannot grow up between plants. I eliminate weeds in my garden rows by laying down thick layers of newspapers, then covering them with a thick layer of dry pine needles. If you can't use a mulch, cultivate with a hoe or hand weeder.

When using straw or hay as a mulch, make sure it is clean and not full of dried weeds or grass seeds. These seeds will be in weed heaven in your garden, and can create havoc the next year or later the same season when the mulch decomposes.

HAND WEEDING

Even when you use a mulch, some weeds are persistent enough to break through. Two tools are excellent for hand weeding—a hoe for weeding between the rows, and a hand fork for scratching out weeds close to the row.

Wear gloves when removing weeds by hand. Some cause skin irriations. Try to remove weeds with roots intact. If the stem breaks above ground and the root remains in the soil, the weed will grow back.

When using a hoe or hand cultivator, take care not to disturb adjacent vegetable roots. For example, dandelion roots are long and tapering and come up without too much disturbance to the adjacent soil area. But plantain roots spread, and yanking them out can unseat nearby plants. This is especially true for root vegetables, which are bothered by any kind of soil disturbance.

HERBICIDAL WEED KILLERS
Use of chemical herbicides used to be confined to ornamental gardens, but now a few herbicidal weed killers are available for vegetables. You should read the label carefully and make absolutely certain the product *is* approved for vegetables.

Herbicidal weed killers are effective in keeping pathways clear of weeds. The most convenient kinds are available in dry granular form in a shaker box.

Usually, weed killers work by preventing the germination of weed seeds, so are best used as "weed preventers." If you have a weedy patch that you want to plant, it still must be cleared by hand. There is generally a waiting period before you can plant. Follow label directions carefully.

MECHANICAL CULTIVATORS
By planting rows of vegetables wide enough to accommodate a power tiller, you can use these groundbreaking machines as weeders to keep pathways clear. Mechanical cultivators that you push are effective if the rows are spaced wide enough. Be careful that the cultivator or tiller doesn't snag the roots of vegetables as you pass down the row. Proper spacing of plants and operating power cultivators in low gear helps prevent this kind of accident. You still need to weed by hand near the vegetable plants, but this is usually a minor chore compared to clearing long rows of weeds from pathways.

POSITIVE ATTITUDE
It helps to take a positive attitude toward weeding. Just think of all the exercise you are getting, and all the nutrient-rich compost you can make with each wheelbarrow-load! Most of all, consider how much water and nutrients those weeds are stealing from your vegetable plants. You are helping increase your harvests by eliminating the competition.

Keeping up with weed-pulling chores is the best offense against weeds taking over your garden. This wheelbarrow-full is destined for the compost pile. See page 24.

Mulching prevents many weeds from reaching the surface. Those that do grow through this pine-needle mulch are easy to pull.

The common garden hoe gets almost daily use during peak periods of weed growth. Hoe with caution around shallow-rooted vegetable plants.

Mulching

Mulching is a term used in gardening to describe a covering over the soil. A mulch performs three important functions:

1. It conserves moisture by reducing evaporation.

2. It prevents weed growth by cutting off light to germinating weed seeds, and prevents most weed seedlings from breaking through the soil surface.

3. It modifies soil temperatures by cooling or warming the soil, depending on the mulch and the time of year it is applied.

A mulch can be *organic,* such as straw, compost, leaf mold, bark chips, shredded leaves or lawn clippings. Or it can be *inorganic,* such as plastic, gravel, rock and strips of discarded carpeting. Each has advantages and disadvantages.

Before applying any mulch, organic or inorganic, the soil should be moist so the mulch will help keep it that way.

Organic mulches are *biodegradable,* meaning they eventually break down and add their matter to the soil. This improves the soil texture, which in turn increases the moisture- and nutrient-holding capacity of the soil. Organic mulches also tend to have a cooling effect on the soil. This is beneficial in summer when temperatures are high, but it is a deterrent in spring when warm temperatures are desired to germinate seeds and promote seedling growth. For this reason, organic mulches are usually applied after seeds and transplants are up and growing.

If you have access to a continuous supply, decomposed compost is an excellent mulch. Apply it up to 6 inches deep. Properly made, it is weed-free, disease-free and full of nutrients.

Black plastic is one of the best inorganic mulches. It has the advantage of being inexpensive and easy to install. It is best set in place before planting. It warms the soil early in spring, which helps crops grow faster.

In warm-summer areas, black plastic may overheat the soil when temperatures rise. If this is true for your location, it is best to cover the plastic with an organic mulch to decrease the soil temperature. The organic mulch also looks better and more natural than the black plastic.

It may be helpful to modify your planting habits somewhat when you use black plastic. Because plastic is

Black plastic is an effective mulch, shown here with block planting of onions.

Bark chips are decorative and functional between rows of radishes.

Grass clippings are normally available free. When they decompose, they add their nutrients to the soil.

Pine needles are attractive and easy to apply, but are not available in all areas.

Vegetable garden features a combination of black plastic film and wood chips. The plastic *warms* the soil in spring to help seedlings grow faster. When temperatures rise in the summer, bark can be placed over the plastic to *cool* the soil. This allows better root growth in the upper soil layer.

usually sold in rolls 3 feet wide, it is handy to create mounded planting beds 2 feet wide and 4 to 5 inches high. Leave 2 inches on each side for a covering of soil to anchor the plastic to the ground. In some cases, this bed is wide enough to grow one row of plants—tomatoes or peppers for example. With smaller vegetables such as lettuce and beans, there is room for two rows. After the plastic is installed, cut holes for seeds or transplants.

Some vegetables such as carrots and radishes cannot be planted through plastic—it is too tedious to make dozens of holes. Instead, mulch with a thin layer of grass clippings or compost that the plants can grow through.

Black plastic is available in degradable and nondegradable forms. In my experience, the nondegradable is best. It is actually easier to tear out than the degradable and is less expensive. It is simple to work the soil and put down new plastic to accommodate different crops the next season.

One disadvantage of mulches is that they can be hiding places for snails and slugs. These villains of the garden are prolific during wet weather and love to hide in moist, protected places. Some kind of control may be necessary, such as use of slug pellets, or liberal use of wood ashes to make the ground uncomfortable for them to crawl over.

The chart below describes a selection of common garden mulches. Some, such as cottonseed hulls, may be available only in certain areas.

Mulching Materials

Material	Thickness for Weed Control	Advantages	Disadvantages	Comments
Aluminum foil	1 layer.	Reflective surface increases light intensity in areas. Helps control aphids. They become disoriented by it.	Tears easily. Looks unnatural. Expensive for large areas. May reflect too much heat in warm-summer areas.	Cools soil. Allow soil to warm before using around warm-season crops. Best for short-season areas.
Bark chips and Ground bark	2 to 3 inches.	Attractive, natural appearance.	Harbors ants, ticks and termites. Expensive for large areas.	Cools soil. Allow soil to warm before using around warm-season crops. Bark products available in a variety of sizes.
Compost	3 to 4 inches.	Adds nutrients to soil. Usually attractive, natural appearance. One of the best organic mulch materials.	If compost is not made properly, it may harbor weed seeds.	Cools soil. Allow soil to warm before using around warm-season crops.
Corncobs, ground	3 to 4 inches.	Attractive, natural appearance.	Takes nitrogen from soil as it decomposes. Compensate with high nitrogen fertilizer.	Cools soil. Allow soil to warm before using around warm-season crops.
Cottonseed hulls	3 to 4 inches.	Attractive, natural appearance. Adds some nutrients to soil.	Lightweight—blows away when dry.	Cools soil. Allow soil to warm before using around warm-season crops. Available in South and parts of Southwest.
Grass clippings	2 to 3 inches.	Commonly available. Decomposes quickly to add organic matter and nutrients to soil.	Sometimes contains weed seeds. May need additional application midseason to be effective as a weed control. Thick layers will mat.	Cools soil. Allow soil to warm before using around warm-season crops. Best applied when dry. Don't use clippings treated with weed killers.
Hay and straw	6 to 8 inches.	Attractive, natural appearance. Adds nutrients to soil. Commonly available.	May contain seeds. May need additional applications midseason if used for weed control.	Cools soil. Allow soil to warm before using around warm-season crops.
Leaf mold	3 to 4 inches.	Attractive, natural appearance. Adds nutrients to soil. The best organic-mulching material.	Takes time to make. A lot of leaves are needed to make a small amount. Turns soil acid. Compensate with lime.	Cools soil. Allow soil to warm before using around warm-season crops. Good moisture-holding capacity.
Newspapers	1/4 inch.	Commonly available. Decomposes quickly.	Unnatural appearance, but can be covered with other, more attractive mulch.	Cools soil. Allow soil to warm before using around warm-season crops.
Peanut hulls	3 to 4 inches.	Adds nutrients to soil. Decomposes quickly to add organic matter to soil.	Lightweight. Blows away when dry. Not readily available outside Southern states.	Cools soil. Allow soil to warm before using around warm-season crops.
Peat moss	2 to 3 inches.	Attractive, natural appearance. Adds organic matter to soil.	Expensive for large areas. Better as soil amendment.	Cools soil. Allow soil to warm before using around warm-season crops. Good moisture-holding capacity.
Pine needles	3 to 4 inches.	Natural appearance. Readily available. Gradually adds organic matter to soil.	Slightly acidic, but no problem when lime is used prior to planting.	Cools soil. Allow soil to warm before using around warm-season crops.
Plastic, black	1 layer. Use 1-1/2 mil thickness.	Excellent for weed control. Maintains warm soil temperatures.	Unnatural appearance.	Warms soil. Use with warm-season crops to produce earlier, heavier yields. Best used in conjunction with drip irrigation system.
Plastic, clear	1 layer. Use 1-1/2 mil thickness.	Maintains higher soil temperature than black plastic, encouraging earlier yields with warm-weather crops.	Unnatural appearance. Weeds grow underneath.	Warms soil. Best used in conjunction with an irrigation system.

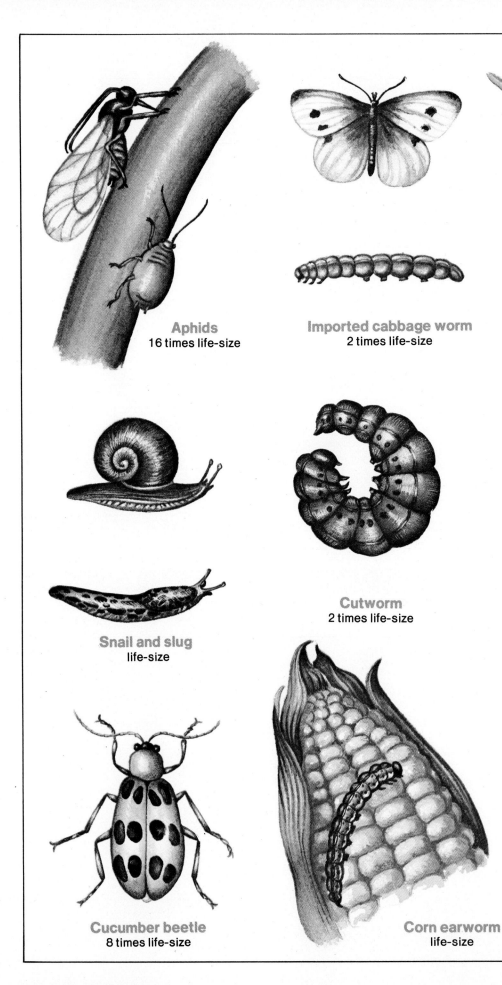

Aphids
16 times life-size

Imported cabbage worm
2 times life-size

Looper
life-size

Snail and slug
life-size

Cutworm
2 times life-size

Japanese beetle
4 times life-size

Cucumber beetle
8 times life-size

Corn earworm
life-size

Harlequin bug
3 times life-size

Pests and Diseases

In the world of gardening, the bigger the pest, the easier it is to control. Large animal pests such as rabbits, groundhogs, deer and raccoons can be kept out of a vegetable plot with fencing. Microscopic pests such as nematodes can be detected only after they have caused severe damage. Even after they are discovered, nematodes are extremely difficult to control.

Insects are the major pests in the garden. When they reach plague proportions, there is usually no way to stop them. To be effective, controls should be applied early and on a regular basis. Make a habit of inspecting your garden often. Small insect colonies are usually easy to eliminate. You can wash them off with a strong jet of water from a garden hose, or pick them off by hand, wearing gloves.

Realize that no matter what precautions you take, you cannot possibly protect your garden from *every* kind of pest. Ask local gardeners what pests have been troublesome in the past, and what controls have worked for them.

A GARDEN WITHOUT PEST CONTROL

One year I deliberately did not use pest controls so I could evaluate the effects of a "no-control" garden. I was amazed at the destruction. Cucumber beetles appeared first, immediately after transplanting. They ate flowers, stems, leaves and tendrils of my transplants. The young plants weakened rapidly, then contracted wilt disease. Soon, every squash, cucumber, melon and pumpkin vine I had planted withered and died.

Next came the slugs. It wasn't a particularly wet spring, but after a good downpour, they were out in force. They attacked the peppers first, stripping away every leaf down to the stem. They stripped the leaves from bean seedlings, and ate deep inside the lettuce and cabbage leaves.

After replanting the beans several times, a full row finally reached maturity. But just as they started bearing, I noticed that the yellow larvae of bean beetles had started to skeletonize the leaves, sapping the vines of

energy. Bean production slowed and then stopped and the vines shriveled from disease. On the underside of some leaves I found as many as 30 beetle larvae, packed in a tight colony on a single leaf segment. As a result, the bean crop was a disaster.

I was determined to grow healthy, pest-free vegetables in my next garden. I identified my worst enemies from the previous year—cucumber beetles, bean beetles and slugs. I formulated a pest-control program custom-designed to fight them. I selected a general-purpose, organic insecticide—a rotenone-pyrethrum blend—that was effective against a broad range of insects. Plants were sprayed as soon as they came up after being sown in the garden, or after they were transplanted, and sprayed repeatedly every week until the vines started to bear. The garden did not suffer damage from cucumber beetles or bean beetles all season, and encountered no damage from flea beetles, aphids or squash beetles.

The slugs needed a separate form of

Left: Gallery of common garden pests. Organic and chemical controls for these and others are listed on pages 65 to 67. Above: Natural pest control at work. Tomato hornworm is covered with cocoons of the braconid wasp. Larvae inside the cocoons will destroy the hornworm by sucking its body juices.

control. Slug bait was placed on shallow pans so the poison would not drain into the soil. All planting rows were dusted heavily with wood ashes and liberal amounts of compost were applied as a side dressing. The powdery texture of the compost and ashes had a repellent effect on slugs.

My entire garden was a picture of health. Visitors couldn't believe the earliness, productivity and insect-free condition of my plants. All that was required was *early, regular* controls designed to combat the most troublesome pests.

SIMPLE APPROACH TO PEST CONTROL

With most pests, you have a choice of chemical or organic controls. Many gardeners use a combination of the two, practicing organic controls as much as possible, resorting to chemicals as a last resort to save a crop from destruction.

There is also an in-between means of pest control that sometimes causes disagreement among organic experts. This method includes the use of *organic insecticides*—products such as rotenone and pyrethrum that are derived from plants. They don't leave harmful chemical residues in the soil, but they can destroy beneficial insects as well as harmful ones.

Most home gardeners don't like to handle a multitude of insecticides, either organic or inorganic. They would rather use one, all-purpose control that takes care of most insects most of the time. If this is the case, my recommendations are *rotenone* or *rotenone-pyrethrum* combination as an organic control or *Sevin* (carbaryl) as a chemical control.

Rotenone, also known as *derris dust,* is a substance refined from a tropical plant. It is best used as a dust, although it can be used as a spray if the sprayer is constantly agitated to mix the particles well.

Rotenone works on insects as both a *stomach* and *contact* poison. This means it kills insects when they eat it and when it lands on their bodies. It is especially effective against beetle pests. It is not seriously toxic to humans, dissipates from the soil quickly and leaves no harmful residues. Allow at least three days between an application and harvesting. Rotenone is highly toxic to fish, so do not allow spray runoff to find its way into a body of water. It is also lethal to honeybees and other beneficial insects such as ladybugs and praying mantis.

Rotenone is available combined with pyrethrum, another organic insecticide. The two used in combination are more effective than either used alone. Combination sprays and dusts are available from garden centers under various brand names. Check the labels to find a formula with the rotenone and pyrethrum combined.

Sevin is available both as a wettable powder and as a dust. It is an all-purpose insecticide and controls a greater variety of insects than rotenone. It is nontoxic to humans and can be applied to vegetables up to the day before harvest. Sevin is toxic to honeybees, so applications should be made during the late afternoon or early evening when bees are less active. Unlike many other chemical insecticides, Sevin leaves no harmful residues in the soil and is not absorbed by the plant.

Diazinon is an effective, general-purpose chemical insecticide, sold under the brand name *Spectracide*. Like Sevin, it is effective against a wide range of insect pests. It generally does a better job controlling soil pests, especially root maggots, when mixed into the soil at planting time.

ORGANIC CONTROLS

Organic pest controls are not always as effective as chemical controls, but do give you a certain peace of mind as to their impact on the environment. Many chemicals have a *residual effect.* This means they accumulate in the soil and have the long-range potential to damage the environment. Unfortunately, it takes a long time before a particular chemical is known to cause damage. Even chemicals regarded as "safe" today may be withdrawn from the market at a future date.

Organic insecticides quickly disappear from the environment, which is one of their principle drawbacks as pest controls—their effects can be rather short-lived. To compensate, a *regular and early program* of control should be followed.

Colony of Mexican bean-beetle larvae infests pole bean leaf. This photo shows why it is important to cover the *underside* of leaves when you spray.

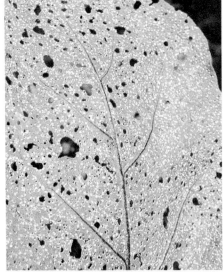
Eggplant leaf appears to have been riddled with a shotgun blast, a trademark of flea-beetle damage.

Colorado potato-beetle larvae feed on the tender stems of a tomato plant. Potato plants are more common fare.

Organic controls come in many forms. Some are plant derivatives, such as nicotine sulfate, pyrethrum and rotenone. These are mostly general-purpose controls effective against a large number of insects. They are acceptable to many organic gardeners because of their ability to break down and leave the environment clean.

Rotenone, as mentioned, is used mostly as a dust, but is also available as a wettable powder. A plant-derived insecticide, *ryania,* is less toxic to animals than rotenone. Similarly, *sabadilla* is used in place of rotenone because of its low toxicity.

Nicotine sulfate is obtained from tobacco leaves, and is sold as a concentrate. It is usually diluted with water at the rate of one teaspoon per gallon, and applied as a spray. It is particularly effective against soft-bodied pests such as aphids and mites. Care should be taken in applying it because it is poisonous to both animals and humans. As with chemical controls, apply all organic products carefully, according to the label.

Pyrethrum is a general-purpose contact poison derived from a South African daisy. It is short-lived, so regular applications are essential to control insects. Pyrethrum controls a wide range of insect pests, and is especially effective against bean beetles, leafhoppers, aphids and whiteflies. It is nontoxic to bees and animals but can be harmful to earthworms and adult ladybugs.

MINERAL-DERIVED CONTROLS

Diatomaceous earth, which is sometimes known as *fossil flour,* is a natural soil mineral. It is found in areas of the country that at one time were submerged under the ocean. It is the remains of tiny, marine crustaceans that have decomposed into a fine, white, dustlike material. The product is mined, refined and used in a variety of ways. Its most important benefit to home gardeners is its knock-down ability with insect pests. It can be purchased from garden centers and mail order catalogs. Pyre-kill and Perma Guard are common brands. For sources of these products, contact International Diatoms Industries, 904 23rd Street, Yankton, SD 57078.

Diatomaceous earth kills by puncturing the breathing system of insects and irritating their digestive organs to cause death in a short time. It is harmless to animals and humans, and to earthworms, which have the ability to digest it. It produces no harmful residues, and serves as a fertilizer on crops that benefit from its trace elements, which include calcium.

To broaden its effect, diatomaceous earth is usually combined with pyrethrum, which kills many insects on contact. The combination of the two has a 90% repellent effect on insects, as long as applications are made regularly. It is important to reapply diatomaceous earth after each rain for continuous control.

BIOLOGICAL CONTROLS

Another type of organic remedy is a specific biological control effective against a particular insect. Specific controls include the use of bacterial diseases, sex attractants and insect predators.

Bacillus thuringiensis is a bacterial disease sold under several brand names such as Dipel, Thuricide and Biotrol. It is effective against caterpillars. Spread over the vegetable garden and adjacent lawn areas, the disease attacks caterpillars and other leaf-eating worms. It has no harmful effects on humans, ladybugs, praying mantis, honeybees or earthworms. It can be applied anytime up to harvest.

It is mixed at the rate of 1 teaspoon to 1 gallon of water. *Bacillus thuringiensis* remains effective for 2 to 3 weeks after spraying, but should be reapplied within 2 days after every rain. Insects do not die from direct contact. They must eat a portion of leaf sprayed with the spores.

Bacillus popillae, also called *milky spore disease,* is sold as a powder. It is an effective control against Japanese beetles. Apply it over lawn areas. This is where the larvae stage of the Japanese beetle, a white grub, spends its life before emerging as a beetle. Treat the ground in spring, dropping one level teaspoon of powder on the lawn every two or three steps. *Bacillus popillae* can remain effective for up to 20 years.

Japanese beetle traps use sex to attract beetles. They contain a bait that

Snail and slug bait should be placed in a shallow tray to prevent the poison from leaching into the soil. Space trays about 2 feet apart to be effective.

Bottomless paper cup protects transplant against cutworm. Set cup in place at time of transplanting and bury lip in the soil.

Japanese-beetle trap uses a sex attractant to lure these pests into a disposable bag.

simulates the scent of a fertile female. This attracts male beetles in large numbers, and traps them in a disposable bag. See photo on page 63.

PLANTS WITH REPELLENT PROPERTIES

Two methods of pest protection are advocated with plants that have repellent properties. You can plant them close to pest-prone vegetables, or you can extract their juices to make a spray.

Generally, companion planting is much less effective than using the plants to make a spray. A plant normally must be bruised to release its repellent odor. Hot peppers, garlic, tansy, marigolds and parsley are commonly used to make repellent sprays.

The following recipes for *Tomato Spray* and *Garlic-Pepper Spray* utilize the natural repellent properties found in these common garden vegetables. Most of the ingredients for these sprays are easy to obtain, so you can make your own sprays at home.

The tomato spray and garlic-pepper spray are effective in repelling corn earworms and root maggots. Sprayed on corn silks, they repel or confuse the egg-laying moths. Sprayed around carrots, onions, cabbage and radish, they repel or confuse egg-laying flies.

Tomato Spray

2 cups of tomato stems and leaves, chopped
2 cups water
Combine and boil ingredients for 5 minutes. Cool and strain. Dilute liquid with 4 cups of water to use as a spray.

For a stronger spray, push tomato leaves through a blender or food processor until you have 1 cup of liquid. Add 1 tablespoon of cornstarch as a sticking agent and 8 cups of water.

Garlic-Pepper Spray

3 cloves of garlic, chopped
1 medium onion, chopped
3 tablespoons of hot red pepper
2 cups of water
Place garlic, onion and water in a blender. Blend at high speed for 1 minute. Add hot peppers and let stand for 24 hours. Strain through a fine sieve, cheesecloth or nylon stocking. Before use, dilute with 1 gallon of water to use as spray.

CONTROLLING ANIMAL PESTS

Rabbits and woodchucks. Fencing is necessary if these animals are abundant in your area. Enclose the entire garden with a low, inexpensive, but sturdy chicken-wire fence. Traps are available that capture the animals unharmed. Cats can also be effective in controlling populations.

Rodents and moles. Cats normally keep these pests under control. A variety of natural repellents and traps are available from hardware stores and mail order garden catalogs.

Deer. Hang strips of Venetian window blinds—they "crackle" in the wind. Metal pie tins that make clanging noises around the garden are also helpful. Fill cloth bags with human hair, available from barber shops, and hang on posts around the garden. An inexpensive, single strand of electrified wire at waist level may keep them out. Deer fencing is an expensive alternative but may be necessary for positive control.

Dogs and raccoons. Install a sturdy fence around the garden or string strands of electrified wire. Leave a portable radio playing in the garden at night and raccoons will usually stay away.

Crows, pheasants and pigeons. Most troublesome with newly planted corn and seedlings. Brightly colored objects that move in the wind help keep birds away. Cover new plantings with bird netting, or erect wood frames covered with chicken wire. Spray furrows with garlic juice. Planting seeds treated with a fungicide deters birds.

Beneficial Insects

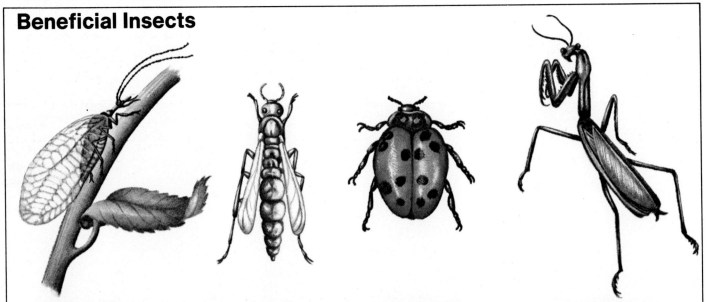

Lacewings. Available commercially, usually as eggs. The larvae are most beneficial, feeding on soft-bodied pests such as aphids and spider mites. A constant food supply is necessary for lacewings to remain in the vicinity of the garden.

Braconid wasp. These tiny, parasitic wasps lay their eggs, white cocoons, on pests. When the eggs hatch, the larvae sucks the body juices. Caterpillars such as the tomato hornworm are common hosts. See photo, top of page 61.

Ladybird beetle (ladybug). These are available commercially. Their main diet is aphids, but they also feed on other soft-bodied insects. Note that without a food supply, ladybird beetles will move out of your garden area.

Praying mantis. You can introduce this predatory insect into your garden by purchasing egg cases from commercial sources. Praying mantis feed mainly on large pests such as crickets and grasshoppers, but they also feed on bees and each other.

Pest Control for Common Insect Pests

APHIDS. Numerous species of aphids are common in vegetable gardens, including green, red, black and white kinds. They form large colonies around tender parts of plant stems and on leaf undersides. They suck sap from plants and produce a sticky substance called *honeydew,* formed from their excrement. Infested plants turn yellow, lose leaves and become stunted. Aphids are also carriers of disease.
Chemical control: Early in the season, begin a spray program of malathion or diazinon. Once they become numerous, aphids are difficult to control.
Organic control: Inspect plants frequently and blast colonies with a jet of water from a garden hose. Soap and water spray—1 teaspoon dishsoap to 1 gallon of water—can be effective. Add a layer of aluminum foil around base of plants. This reflects light onto the underside of leaves, making them an undesirable habitat. Ladybugs are natural enemies. Sprays of nicotine sulfate are also effective.

COLORADO POTATO BEETLE. Mature beetle resembles a ladybug, but is slightly larger—3/8 inch long. Body is yellow with black stripes. Eggs are yellow-orange, laid in clusters on eggplant, potato and tomato leaves. Larvae are hump-backed and red with black spots along the sides.
Chemical control: Spray infested plants with Sevin, malathion, methoxychlor or diazinon.
Organic control: Hand-pick egg clusters from plant leaves, checking undersides. Dust plants with rotenone and pyrethrum combination or diatomaceous earth.

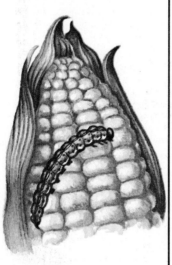

CORN EARWORM. Also known as *fruit worm.* The most common sweet corn pest. Corn earworm is the larva stage of a moth that lays its eggs on corn silks. Tiny larvae eat their way into the ear where they live on tender kernels. Worms are yellowish green, to 1-1/2 inches long. They cannot be detected unless the husk is peeled back. When corn is not available, these pests eat into tomato fruit, okra pods, pea pods and squash fruit.
Chemical control: When corn silks appear, apply 4 or 5 treatments of Sevin at 4-day intervals.
Organic control: Apply rotenone, pyrethrum or diatomaceous earth at 4-day intervals after silks appear and until they turn brown and brittle. Or fill an eye dropper with clear mineral oil and apply it to silks after the ear has started to fill out. Trim silks close with scissors once pollination has been achieved. Egg-laying moths prefer long, trailing silks.

CUCUMBER BEETLE. Striped and spotted cucumber beetles are yellow and 1/4 inch long. Spotted species is shown. They damage melons, cucumbers, squash, beans and potatoes by chewing stems, flowers, leaves and fruit. They usually cluster around the crowns of young plants and among blossoms. Look for brown scars along stems. Adult striped cucumber beetle spreads bacterial wilt to cucumbers, squash and melons, causing vine death.
Chemical control: Apply Sevin or diazinon when seedlings emerge and every 5 days until vines are established.
Organic control: Sprinkle leaves with wood ashes, pyrethrum, rotenone or garlic spray. Applying a thick mulch around plants also seems to help. For serious infestations, make an organic spray by mixing a handful of wood ashes and a handful of lime in 2 gallons of water. Helpful to apply sprays of rotenone-pyrethrum when you set out transplants, or when seedlings first appear.

CUTWORMS. Black, brown or gray, 1/2 to 1-1/2 inches long. Normally spend the day curled up in a C-shape, just below the soil surface. Often found in garden soil when digging or tilling. At night they chew on plant stems. Damaged plants keel over at soil level.
Chemical control: Drench soil with diazinon prior to planting. Or use Sevin by mixing 2 level teaspoons in 1 gallon of water. Spray plant bases and surrounding soil in late afternoon to early evening.

Organic control: Protect transplants with a paper or metal collar. Use bottomless paper cups slit along one side so they can be wrapped around the plant stem. Bury lip of cup in the soil.

FLEA BEETLES. Tiny black beetles, 1/16 inch long, cluster on leaf surfaces and jump when disturbed, like animal fleas. They are particularly fond of eggplant. Look for small holes in leaves, as though peppered with gunshot. Crops of secondary preference are radishes, turnips, beets, corn, potatoes and tomatoes.
Chemical control: Dust or spray with Sevin, diazinon or malathion.
Organic control: Dust with wood ashes, rotenone, pyrethrum or apply garlic spray. Remove all debris from garden in fall to discourage overwintering of pests. Till and rake garden soil after harvest to make it less sheltered for egg-laying females.

HORNWORM. The green hornworm is a large caterpillar 3 to 4 inches long. Eight diagonal stripes run along each side. A spike or horn emerges at the end of its tail. It is the larva of the hawk moth and feeds largely on leaves of tomatoes, peppers and eggplant. Look for bare branches and black droppings beneath plants.
Chemical control: Sevin, diazinon and malathion are effective.
Organic control: Hand-picking is the best control method. Inspect plants often and remove worms with a gloved hand. *Bacillus thuringiensis* is also effective.

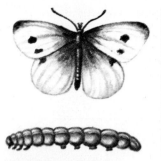

IMPORTED CABBAGE WORM.

Larvae of the cabbage white butterfly. Lays eggs on cabbage plants and other members of the cabbage family. Caterpillars are green, about 1 inch long, with a slender, orange stripe down the middle of the back. They eat ragged holes in leaves and chew channels into cabbage heads.

Chemical control: Sevin and methoxychlor are effective.

Organic control: Use *Bacillus thuringiensis*, a bacterial disease affecting caterpillars.

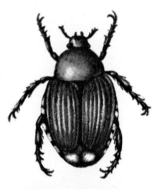

JAPANESE BEETLES.

Beetles are usually 1/2 inch long, shiny, coppery brown, with metallic green shoulders. They can be seen feeding on plants. When disturbed, they fly off suddenly, emitting a whirring sound. Larvae look like white cutworms. They overwinter in soil under sod, living on a favorite diet of grass roots. Adults devastate leaves and flowers of many plants, including corn, beans, okra and rhubarb.

Chemical control: Although malathion or Sevin controls them, a better control is a beetle trap.

Organic control: Hang a Japanese beetle trap on a pole near the vegetable garden. Sex hormone attracts male beetles to trap. Effective and capable of trapping thousands of beetles in one season. Wear gloves and hand-pick colonies.

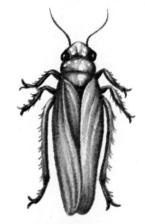

LEAFHOPPERS. These grasshopperlike insects are tiny, usually green and 1/8 inch long. They sit still on leaves, then hop abruptly into the air. Many different species attack different plants. They suck plant juices, causing leaf distortions. Leaf edges curl and appear burned. The biggest potential danger is introduction of virus diseases. Especially troublesome in fall.

Chemical control: Apply Sevin, diazinon, malathion or methoxychlor.

Organic control: Destroy garden debris to prevent pests from overwintering. Dust plants with rotenone, pyrethrum or diatomaceous earth.

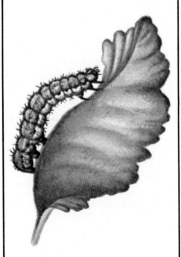

LOOPERS. These bright green caterpillars are the larvae of a moth. They measure 1-1/2 inches long and crawl by hunching the middle part of their back into a loop. They eat leaves, particularly members of the cabbage family. Inspect plants in spring for signs of looper droppings, which look like black pinheads. Holes and ragged leaf edges also indicate their presence.

Chemical control: Sevin and diazinon are highly effective.

Organic control: *Bacillus thuringiensis*, a bacterial disease affecting only caterpillars, is an effective control.

MEXICAN BEAN BEETLES AND BEAN LEAF BEETLES.

Larvae of Mexican bean beetle cause serious problems with beans. Adult beetles overwinter in dead vegetation. They are yellow, about 1/3 inch long, covered with spines resembling a pincushion. Examine undersides of leaves for egg clusters and for larvae. Adults feed on leaves. Larvae feed on roots. Damaged leaves often resemble fine lace because all but the leaf vein is eaten. Bean leaf beetles are most common in the southeastern United States, but are also found in midwestern and eastern states.

Chemical control: Spray with Sevin or malathion.

Organic control: Hand-pick colonies when small. Dust with rotenone, pyrethrum or diatomaceous earth. A spray using garlic concentrate or garlic-pepper may be effective. Destroy all bean stalks and garden debris in fall so beetles do not overwinter. Praying mantis is an insect predator.

MITES. Common spider mites are small, measuring only 1/50 of an inch. They are oval, and yellow, green or red. They suck plant juices, and are most prolific in dry weather, undergoing a complete life cycle in less than a week. Look for fine webbing over and under the foliage. Mottled, speckled, curling and wilting foliage is an indication of mite activity.

Chemical control: The miticide Kelthane is most effective. Treatment must be administered early in the season. Once these pests are established, they are difficult to bring under control. Diazinon and malathion sprays used at weekly intervals offer some measure of control.

Organic control: Destroy garden debris so mites cannot overwinter. Ladybugs are natural predators of mites.

NEMATODES. Microscopic worms live in soil and attack plant roots. Roots become shriveled, with swellings called *galls* ranging in size from a pinhead to 1 inch in diameter. Galls cut off flow of nutrients to the plant. Plants may become stunted, turn yellow and produce undersized, distorted fruit.

Chemical control: Soil drenches of insecticide are usually ineffective. Soil fumigation is effective, but requires the knowledge of a professional. Contact your county extension agent.

Organic control: Grow plants resistant to nematode attack. Certain varieties of tomatoes, for example, have the letter "N" after their name, such as 'Supersteak VFN'. These initials indicate resistance to *verticillium, fusarium wilt* and *nematodes.* You might try planting the garden one year with French marigolds instead of vegetables. Studies indicate that these marigolds repel nematodes.

ROOT MAGGOTS. These fly larvae resemble common house fly maggots. They are white, peg-shaped, 1/4 inch long. Several species exist. These include the cabbage maggot, which also attacks radishes; onion maggot; and carrot maggot, which also infests celery and parsnips. Fly lays its eggs at the plant base. Maggots crawl into the soil where they feed on the roots. Look for wilted leaves and stunted growth.

Chemical control: Use a soil drench of diazinon prior to planting. For onion maggots, dust or spray with malathion.

Organic control: Dusting with wood ashes, rotenone, pyrethrum and diatomaceous earth offers some measure of control. Spray with garlic concentrate or garlic-pepper spray. Covering soil with black plastic mulch and planting through the plastic helps prevent adult flies from laying eggs near crops.

SLUGS AND SNAILS. Slugs are basically snails without shells. Most active during wet weather and in early evening and early morning. Look for them under boards, stones or mulch during the day. They leave slimy, silvery trails that can be seen in early morning. Both pests do great damage by chewing leaves.

Chemical control: Use slug pellets marked "safe for fruits and vegetables." Scatter pellets on pans to prevent soil contamination. Using 4 tablespoons of Sevin 50% wettable powder to 1 gallon of water is also effective.

Organic control: Keep area around garden clean of trash, boards and other potential hiding places. Apply diatomaceous earth or wood ashes between rows and around plants. Beer in shallow pans lures some slugs and snails. They crawl into the pans and drown.

SQUASH BUGS, STINK BUGS AND RELATED SPECIES. Squash bugs and related pests such as the harlequin bug (shown above), stink bug and tarnished plant bug injure plants by sucking their juices. Each type of bug attacks a different vegetable. Harlequin bugs destroy cabbage, radishes and turnips. Stink bugs seek peas and beans. Tarnished plant bugs are partial to beets, celery and about 50 other vegetable crops. Squash bugs harm pumpkins, cucumbers and melon vines, as well as squash. Bugs vary in color, depending on species. Most are broad-shouldered and shaped like a shield. Injured plants show brown blotches or stunted, distorted growth.

Chemical control: Malathion, Sevin and diazinon sprays are effective.

Organic control: Place boards along rows for squash bugs to hide under. Hand-pick and destroy them each morning. Dust plants with rotenone, pyrethrum and diatomaceous earth. Remove debris from garden so bugs cannot overwinter. Check leaves frequently.

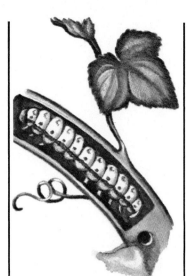

SQUASH VINE BORER. This is the caterpillar of a moth that lays its eggs at the base of plants. Larvae bore their way into stems. Borers are white, about 1 inch long. They are difficult to control because they work hidden inside stems. In addition to squash, they attack pumpkins, cucumbers and melons. Look for small, round holes along squash stems and a small pile of sawdustlike material. Plants wilt as larvae bore inside of vines.

Chemical control: Some control is possible by using sprays of malathion and methoxychlor. The most effective chemical control is Thiodan. As vines grow, treat them 3 times at 7-day intervals.

Organic control: Use rotenone, pyrethrum or diatomaceous earth to obtain partial control. Inspect vines for infestation. If you locate entry hole, insert a wire to determine location of the borer. Slit vine above the borer and destroy it. Bind slit shut again with twist-tie. Effective preventative control is to apply garlic spray to the base of each squash vine. Pungent odor helps repel the egg-laying moth.

WHITEFLIES. These small, sucking insects have white bodies covered with powder.

They resemble miniature moths. When disturbed, they fly up in a cloud like flakes of snow. They often hide underneath leaves, sucking plant juices. They are particularly fond of peppers and tomatoes. As many as four generations can be born during a warm, dry season. The young, called *crawlers,* are yellow and hatch from eggs laid under leaves. Plants are stunted and fruit yields are reduced.

Chemical control: Spray with malathion every 2 days for a 10-day period. Cover undersides of leaves. Diazinon is also effective.

Organic control: Whiteflies are attracted to the color yellow. Hang yellow boards covered with a sticky substance between plants. An aluminum mulch is also an effective control. It reflects light onto leaf undersides and disorients the insects. Ladybugs are a natural predator of whiteflies.

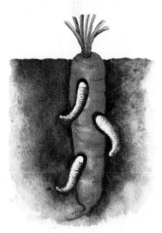

WIREWORMS. Yellowish brown insects measure up to 1-1/2 inches long. They feed below the ground on seeds and seedlings, and bore holes in root crops. You may see them when tilling garden soil. Harvest a few carrots or radishes and inspect for irregular holes where wireworms may be feeding.

Chemical control: Drench soil with diazinon. Do not use near pumpkins, eggplant or rutabaga. Read label for other precautions.

Organic control: Hand-pick wireworms from soil at time of cultivation. Flooding the soil occasionally helps to some degree. Good soil drainage reduces wireworm populations. Regular use of compost or wood ashes helps keep wireworms under control.

Disease Control

Plant diseases can be divided into two general groups: *parasitic* and *nonparasitic*. The parasitic group includes diseases caused by fungi, bacteria, viruses, mycoplasmas and nematodes. Parasitic organisms are microscopic and live off plant tissue, putting the plant under stress. In severe cases, they may cause the plant to die. The presence of these parasites is recognized as a disease.

The nonparasitic group includes diseases caused by physical disorders. These include injuries from sprays and unfavorable growing conditions—nutrient deficiencies or an improper balance of elements essential to plant growth.

THE IMPORTANCE OF PREVENTION

Prevention is more important with diseases than with insect pests. Insects can usually be eradicated when they become a problem, but most plant diseases cannot be destroyed after a plant is infected. Instead, the infected part has to be removed. Often, by the time a disease is noticed, it is too late. The plant must be sacrificed to prevent the disease from spreading. A preventative program aimed at controlling disease also helps control insect pests. Good gardening practices as outlined in this section will help keep diseases out of your garden.

Keep the garden clean. Many disease organisms overwinter in plant wastes. All plant debris including spent vines, roots, stems and leaves should be raked and burned or delegated to the compost pile. Avoid placing diseased plants on the pile, or the disease may be transferred to the compost.

Rotate crops. Diseases that cause slight damage one year could overwinter and devastate crops the next. By *rotating crops* each year—moving specific vegetables from one location of the garden to another—you help prevent diseases from gaining a foothold.

Buy virus-free plants. Do not purchase any vegetable plants for your garden unless they are certified "virus- and disease-free." This is particularly important with tubers such as potatoes, and roots such as asparagus. Before buying vegetable transplants, inspect leaves and stems carefully for any signs of disease or damage.

Plant disease-resistant varieties. Many vegetable varieties have been developed with resistance to a particular disease or group of diseases. Look for plants with the initials V, F, N or all three. This indicates that the plant is resistant to verticillium wilt, fusarium wilt and nematodes.

Destroy infected plants. Cut out infected plant parts. If serious, remove and destroy diseased plants so the disease is not spread to healthy plants. Certain parasites such as powdery mildew that live on the surface of plants can be eradicated by dusting or spraying with a fungicide.

Common Plant Diseases and Their Control

ANTHRACNOSE. Fungus disease that causes wilting of affected plant parts. White areas appear on leaves, causing them to wither. Infects members of the cucumber family, including melons, pumpkins and squash. Sometimes a problem on tomatoes. **Control.** Clear garden of all plant wastes in fall. Don't save seeds from pods infected by the disease. Plant disease-resistant varieties.

BACTERIAL WILT. When cucumber plants suddenly collapse from the top down, chances are they are infected by bacterial wilt disease. **Control.** Because this disease is spread by cucumber beetles, control of these pests is essential. See page 65. Plant disease-resistant varieties. Clean up garden in winter and burn or dispose of spent cucumber vines. Avoid growing cucumbers in same location the following year.

BLACK ROT. Cabbages are highly susceptible to rotting, especially during wet weather and when planted too close together. Heads become soft and yellow on one side then turn black and mushy. **Control.** Choose varieties described as being resistant to rot disease. Use sterile potting soil when growing transplants. Treat seeds with a fungicide such as benomyl.

BLOSSOM END ROT. A nonparasitic disease that usually occurs because of irregular or inadequate watering. Such watering causes the trace element calcium to be deficient. Tips of fruit such as tomatoes and peppers turn black. **Control.** Water transplants regularly until they are established. Use a mulch to conserve moisture. Mix lime or wood ashes into soil to provide plants with adequate amounts of calcium.

Protect plants with preventative controls. Certain diseases such as powdery mildew can be prevented by using fungicides *before* they occur. Complete coverage of plant parts is normally necessary, plus repeated applications. Fungicides are more effective when applied prior to rains because infection usually occurs during periods of high moisture.

Follow proper cultural practices. Healthy, vigorous growth allows plants to avoid many diseases. The plant nutrient potash helps plants fight diseases. Well-draining soil enriched with compost helps encourage healthy growth. Use of drip-irrigation systems that water plants only in the root zone reduces disease. Most diseases enter plants when they are wet.

Plant treated seeds. Seeds treated with mild organic fungicides can prevent seed decay and damping-off disease. Seed companies offering treated seed normally do so at no extra cost. In the case of bulbs and tubers such as onions and potatoes, plant *certified* virus-free stock.

Use disease controls. Fungicides are products that are toxic to *fungi,* which cause many diseases. They are applied as dusts or sprays. The most popular is a copper-based fungicide called a *Bordeaux* mixture. You can make your own Bordeaux mix. Mix 2 ounces of copper sulfate in 1 gallon of water. Add 2 ounces of hydrated lime to 2 gallons of water. Combine both to make 3 gallons of Bordeaux mixture.

FUNGICIDES

Although dozens of chemical and organic disease controls have been produced to combat specific diseases, a home gardener is not like a farmer who specializes in just one or two crops. A home gardener often has a dozen or more crops to care for, and would soon be overwhelmed trying to protect the garden from every disease. Gardeners generally want a broad-spectrum control that works against most of the diseases most of the time.

Here are brief descriptions of widely available, general-purpose disease controls.

Copper-containing fungicides. Bordeaux mixture is the best known, composed of copper sulfate, lime and water. See formula at left. The mixture is sprayed over foliage.

Sulfur-containing fungicides. Sulfur is one of the oldest, general-purpose fungicides. Wettable sulfurs, containing a wetting agent, allow the sulfur to be mixed easily with water to form an easy-to-apply spray.

Organic fungicides. Many organic fungicides are available. In many cases, they have replaced the older fungicides. Use them with caution, because some are toxic to fish, animals and people. *Captan, maneb* and *zineb* are examples. They are usually available as wettable powders for use as all-purpose fungicides. Captan is also used as a seed treatment to control damping-off disease.

FUSARIUM AND VERTICILLIUM WILTS. These are fungus diseases affecting tomatoes, peas, eggplant, peppers, potatoes, melons, pumpkins and squash. Vines turn brown, then wilt and die. Part of a plant may wilt then recover briefly, but soon the entire plant will perish. **Control.** Do not plant in the same spot where either disease has occurred in a previous year. Plant disease-resistant varieties such as 'Supersteak VFN' tomato or any other variety with the initials "VF" after its name.

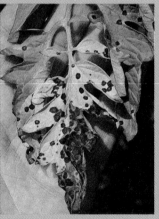

LEAF BLIGHT AND LEAF SPOTS. Several fungi cause leaf spots. Brown, circular spots with light-colored centers cover leaves, which eventually wither and die. Prevalent on beans, beets, cucumbers, eggplant, potatoes, melons and tomatoes. **Control.** Disease organism overwinters in soil and on seeds. Rotate crops so plants won't be grown in soil contaminated from previous year's growth. Do not save seeds from your own garden for replanting—they may harbor the disease.

POWDERY MILDEW. This fungus disease thrives in wet conditions. Powdery white patches appear on leaf and stem surfaces. They reduce the light that reaches the plants and cause leaves to shrivel. Susceptible plants include beans, melons, cucumbers, pumpkins, squash and watermelon. **Control.** Plant disease-resistant varieties such as 'Marketmore 76' cucumber. Irrigate carefully so leaves and stems do not get excessively wet, which encourages the disease. Spray with a preventative fungicide such as Karathane.

RUST. Red or dark brown, powdery pustules on leaves, stems and seed pods. Most abundant on lower leaves, causing severe injury and death. Prevalent on asparagus and beans. **Control.** The fungicide zineb prevents infections. Planting resistant varieties is best. Pruning infected plant parts helps bring disease under control. Disinfect pruning shears after each cut in a 50% bleach and water solution. Burn or dispose of infected branches.

Containers and Small Spaces

If you don't have space for a garden plot, many kinds of vegetables and herbs can be grown in containers. If you live in an apartment, condominium or mobile home, this may be the only way you can garden. Perhaps you simply want to grow a few vegetables like tomatoes and peppers, or maybe a salad garden. Containers offer a suitable alternative to growing them directly in the soil.

Mobility is an advantage with container gardening. You can get an early start on the season by placing vegetables outdoors during warm daylight hours. When cool evenings approach, you can move containers inside or under a sheltered area. If containers are heavy, you may have to install caster wheels to move them about.

Vegetables in containers can also be ornamental. Try planting vegetables in half whiskey barrels or terra-cotta pots. Make them part of your patio, porch or landscape.

CHOICES OF CONTAINERS

Containers are available in a wide range of sizes, shapes and materials. One of the best materials is wood. Containers made of redwood and cedar are best, because both types of wood resist rotting. Avoid growing vegetables in plastic pots. They have a tendency to heat up quickly in the sun. Too much heat damages plant roots and dries out the soil rapidly. Ceramic containers offer better insulation qualities but have a tendency to lose moisture through absorption and evaporation, especially clay pots.

When choosing containers for your vegetable plants, keep in mind the two conditions that often cause failure with container gardening—*rapid moisture loss* and *overheating*. A container with a double wall has better insulation than one with a single wall. If you make your own containers out of wood, it is a good idea to construct dual walls. The air space between the two walls supplies insulation. You can fill the space with moist, crumbled newspapers for additional cooling. Double-walled plastic containers are also available.

To make wooden containers rot-resistant, line the inside with plastic sheeting such as a garbage bag. Or apply a coat of asphalt emulsion for more permanent protection. If you use the plastic, be sure to punch holes in the bottom for drainage.

Some plastic containers have a liner that creates a humid air space between the potting soil and the plastic pot. This system also offers additional insulation.

Most fruiting plants such as cucumbers, tomatoes and peppers require pots that hold at least one gallon of soil. They may also require at least a quart of water every day. For specifics on container sizes, see Recommended Varieties for Containers, page 73.

All containers—wood, plastic, clay or ceramic—should have drainage holes in the bottom. Place stones, screens or broken clay pots over them to prevent the soil from washing away with each watering.

SOIL FOR CONTAINERS

The objective of any soil mix is to

Left: Homemade wooden planter holds 'Ruby' Swiss chard, grown for its ornamental and edible qualities. Above: Narrow side yard has enough space for a productive garden, featuring lettuce, carrots and beans.

create a growth medium that supports plants and holds moisture and nutrients in the root zone. Soil should also allow for sufficient drainage—air spaces between the soil particles are necessary for the roots to breathe. A soil that is made mostly of sand or peat drains too rapidly. Nutrients are washed from the root zone, and plants tend to dry out quickly. A soil composed mostly of clay is too dense in structure and does not have enough air space for plant roots. Topsoil from the garden is also too heavy and dense for most container plants.

The best choice of planting medium for containers is a "soil-less" potting mix. Such mixes are termed "soilless" because they do not contain soil or earth. Rather, all ingredients are sterile materials, such as peat moss, vermiculite, perlite, sand and ground bark, blended with a small amount of fertilizer.

Mixes are available under many different brand names, and can be purchased from garden-supply stores and home centers. As a rule, buy a bagged soil mix if you are going to fill containers that total up to 20 gallons capacity. Beyond that point, the economics begin to favor making your own.

Some prepared mixes are based on sand, which is heavy: Sand weighs about 100 pounds per cubic foot. Others are based on peat moss or fir bark and are so light that you can easily carry a 2-1/2 cubic-foot bale.

Two ingredients commonly included in potting soils are *vermiculite,* which is lightweight expanded mica, and *perlite,* porous volcanic rock. Both are granular materials capable of holding many times their own weight in moisture. Because of their structure, they also add air spaces to the mix.

MAKING YOUR OWN SOIL MIX

The most popular container mixes are available in two basic formulations. One has been developed for the East, where peat moss is available and relatively inexpensive. The other is more common in the South and West, where ground pine, fir bark or redwood sawdust is more available.

Cornell Mixes—for the East: After many years of research, Cornell University developed several lightweight soil mixes, primarily for professional growers. Many planter mixes available to gardeners today are based on the Cornell formula. A typical Cornell mix contains by volume:

- 1/2 sphagnum peat moss, coarse
- 1/2 vermiculite No. 2, 3, or 4 size
- Add *chelated* micronutrients to the water used for moistening the mix Micronutrients contain elements needed in trace amounts by plants. Lightly moisten ingredients and mix thoroughly. It helps if water is warm. Allow to stand in a pile for 24 to 48 hours so the dry peat will soak up moisture. To a cubic yard

of such a mix, add:

- 5 pounds ground limestone, preferably *dolomitic lime,* which contains both calcium and magnesium
- 2 pounds single superphosphate fertilizer
- 1 pound calcium nitrate or 1/2 pound ammonium-nitrate fertilizer

U.C. Mixes—for the South and West: The University of California developed this family of mixes for growers in the West, primarily for containers. A typical U.C. mix contains by volume:

- 1/4 small particles of fir or pine bark—diameter of 1/2 inch or less
- 1/2 aged or composted redwood sawdust, or "forest compost"—a sawmill mix of fine and coarse sawdust composted with a little nitrogen fertilizer. Or pulverized pine bark
- 1/8 coarse sphagnum peat moss
- 1/8 graded, 30-mesh, fine, sharp sand. Do not use sand from beaches. Omit sand or substitute perlite if weight of mix will be a problem
- To a cubic yard of the above, add chelated micronutrients and the same starter ingredients as for the Cornell mix

Mixing tips. For small lots, keep in mind that a *cubic yard* contains 27 cubic feet. A *cubic foot* fills about 7 to 10 1-gallon cans. Count on about a 15% to 20% loss of volume when you mix ingredients. The small particles

Redwood raised bed serves as a large container near a brick patio. Wide end piece is a handy seat when watering or weeding.

'Pixie' hybrid tomatoes are growing in pots inside a greenhouse. Compact growth habit of vine makes 'Pixie' ideal for containers.

Most herbs grow well in containers, such as lavender, left, and thyme, right. Containers are decorated coffee cans, with holes punched in the bottoms for drainage.

simply fill in between the larger ones.

To keep the soil mix sterile, blend materials on a plastic sheet or concrete pad that has been washed with a solution of 1 part bleach and 10 parts water. Use clean tools for mixing. To mix thoroughly, shovel the ingredients into cone-shaped piles. Drop material on top of pile so it cascades evenly down the sides of the cone. Build cone three times to ensure a complete mix. Store unused mix in plastic garbage cans or heavy-duty plastic bags to prevent contamination.

FERTILIZING CONTAINER PLANTS

Container plants require regular amounts of fertilizer. Nutrients, especially nitrogen, are continually being washed out of the soil. A slow-release fertilizer, see page 28, distributes plant nutrients over an extended period. But you will probably have better results by adding a diluted liquid fertilizer about once a week when you water. Plant foods designed to be mixed with water can be purchased in concentrated form as liquid or crystals.

For fruit-producing vegetables such as peppers and tomatoes, fertilizer should have a high phosphorus content, the middle number in a fertilizer analysis. Look for formulations such as 5-10-10.

Premium-quality soil mixes are fortified with starter fertilizer and micronutrients such as iron. If you use such mixes, do not feed plants for three to four weeks after seeding or transplanting. If you feed right away, the extra dose could injure your plants.

WATERING

Vegetables in containers generally require constant attention to water needs. Some may need watering every day, depending on the size of the container, the weather and the vegetable. Cucumbers, peppers and tomatoes require as much as a quart of water for every two quarts of soil. Hanging basket plants, because they are more exposed than container plants to heat and wind, are especially susceptible to drying out. They may need watering as often as three times a day to keep plants from wilting.

Viterra Hydrogel is a product that can be added to soil mixes to prevent rapid drying out and dehydration. In granular form, it is capable of absorbing up to 20 times its own weight in moisture. This product is useful when added to hanging basket soils and seed flats, which tend to dry out rapidly, especially in summer.

Drip irrigation is well-adapted to container gardening. Those with "spaghetti" hoses—numerous small tubes projecting from a main hose—are efficient in supplying individual containers and hanging baskets with water. Emitters at the end of each small tube slowly supply water to the soil. For more on drip systems, see page 55.

RECOMMENDED VARIETIES FOR CONTAINERS

Given sufficient soil depth, any vegetable can be grown in a container. Some varieties within plant groups are more successful than others. Here are some common vegetables that can be grown in containers. When a recommendation is given that a vegetable be grown in a "windowbox container," this means a container with at least 8 inches soil depth and 5 gallons soil capacity. For more information on the specific vegetables, see pages 82 to 175.

Artichokes. 'Grande Beurre' usually produces artichokes the first year. Grow in 15-gallon tubs.

Beans. 'Bush Roma' is a compact, heavy producer of fine-flavored romano beans. Grow in windowbox containers. Space each plant 6 inches apart.

Beets. 'Pacemaker II' is an early, uniform and sweet-flavored hybrid. Grow in windowbox containers. Space each plant 3 inches apart.

Broccoli. 'Green Comet' is early and compact. Grow in 5-gallon pots, or 15-gallon tubs, 3 plants per tub.

Brussels sprouts. 'Jade Cross' is early and heavy yielding. Grow in 5-gallon pots or 15-gallon tubs, 2 plants per tub.

'Salad Bowl' lettuce is a good choice as an edible ornamental, growing in this narrow space between path and garden.

The author uses half whiskey barrels to grow vegetables at the edge of his patio. Barrels are attractive as well as long lasting.

'Salad Bowl' lettuce grows in a hanging basket. Basket is made of wire and filled with sphagnum moss to create a mounded effect.

Cabbages. 'Stonehead' is early and compact. Forms a solid ball with few outer leaves. Can be spaced 15 inches apart, half as much space as other hybrids. Grow in 15-gallon tubs, 3 plants per tub.

Carrots. 'Short 'n Sweet' is early and sweet with small central core. Grows in windowbox containers. Space each plant 1 inch apart.

Cauliflower. 'Snow Crown' hybrid is early. Grow in 5-gallon pots or in 15-gallon tubs, 3 plants per tub.

Cucumbers. 'Pot Luck' hybrid and 'Spacemaster' hybrid are compact varieties that grow in hanging baskets as well as containers. 'Fembaby' hybrid is the best variety for containers, especially indoors. It is an all-female variety that sets fruit without cross-pollination. 'Fembaby' requires a short trellis for support and must not be allowed to cross-pollinate with other cucumbers. Grow in 1-gallon pots.

Eggplant. 'Oriental Egg' produces small, white fruit. 'Jersey King' hybrid produces black, medium-size fruit. 'Slim Jim' hybrid produces small, black fruit. All have a compact habit suitable for containers. Grow in 1-gallon pots.

Herbs. Containers are the best way to keep many invasive varieties within bounds. Parsley, chives, garlic, thyme, catnip, sage, lavender, sweet basil and chervil are adapted to containers. One plant is sufficient for most family's needs. Grow in quart-size pots or larger.

Lettuce. 'Tom Thumb' is a compact head lettuce that produces more heads per square foot than any other heading variety. Loose-leaf varieties tolerate crowding. 'Ruby' and 'Salad Bowl' are decorative with frilly leaves. Grow in windowbox containers.

Onions: Giant-size kinds such as 'Giant Walla Walla', and bunching kinds such as 'Evergreen Long White Bunching', are worthwhile to grow in windowbox containers.

Peppers. Sweet varieties such as 'Sweet Banana' and 'Early Prolific' hybrid are heavy yielding and early. Grow in 2-gallon pots or 15-gallon tubs, 5 plants per tub.

Potatoes. All varieties grow well in barrels. Sweet potatoes make excellent hanging baskets. Grow in 15-gallon tubs, 4 plants per tub.

Radishes. 'Cherry Belle' is earliest and has short tops, which allows for greater productivity. Grow in windowbox containers, each plant spaced 1 inch apart.

Rhubarb. 'Valentine' has brilliant red stalks. Grow in 5-gallon containers.

Spinach. 'Melody' hybrid is early and disease resistant. New Zealand spinach is a vining spinach substitute with heat resistance. Grow in windowbox containers. Space plants 4 inches apart.

Swiss chard. 'Ruby' has brilliant red stalks, making it highly ornamental. Grow in windowbox containers or 15-gallon tubs, 5 plants per tub.

Squash. Bush-type varieties of zucchini such as 'Gold Rush' hybrid and 'Early Golden' crookneck are excellent for growing in 2-gallon pots.

Turnips. 'Tokyo Cross' hybrid is a sweet-flavored, white variety. It is early and has good disease resistance. Grow in windowbox containers. Space each plant 3 inches apart.

Tomatoes. Many varieties are suitable for containers, but 'Pixie' hybrid is best of all. Vines are short and compact. Fruit are medium size. 'Tiny Tim' and 'Patio' are other common container tomatoes, but not as good as 'Pixie'. A hanging-basket variety is 'Tumblin' Tom'. Grow these compact vine types in 1-gallon pots or larger. For large-fruited, indeterminate types, use 15-gallon tubs.

Watermelons. 'Sugar Bush' has short vines requiring 6 square feet of space. It is the only variety suitable for containers, averaging 3, ice-box size, red-fleshed fruit. Grow in 15-gallon tubs, 1 plant per tub.

VEGETABLES IN HANGING BASKETS

Growing vegetables in hanging baskets is a very difficult method, but the ornamental effect can be dramatic. If gardening space is not available, hanging plants may be the only way you can garden. The problem with growing in hanging baskets is keeping plants watered. The soil in hanging baskets has a tendency to dry out much faster due to exposure to sun and wind. Using a drip irrigation system is one way to provide hanging basket plants with regular moisture.

You can make your own hanging containers from wire framework baskets and spagnum peat moss. The baskets are lined around the sides and bottom with the moss to form a "nest." This is filled with potting mix, and planted the same as any other container. The spagnum moss absorbs moisture and helps keep the soil cool. Plants can also be planted through the sides of the basket so that the entire basket becomes a "globe" of plants. See photo, page 73.

Watering is necessary at least once a day. Add a diluted liquid fertilizer to water once a week.

RAISED BEDS

Raised beds are planting areas raised above the normal soil level. Many are bordered by wood, brick or stone. They are in a sense large, bottomless containers. Because they are above ground level, the soil warms faster in the spring and drainage is improved. Raised beds help to create a neat, tidy

Raised beds are efficient, neat and attractive. Because soil is above ground level, it warms earlier in spring compared to conventional gardens.

appearance in the home landscape.

Rot-resistant redwood and cedar are good materials for building raised beds. Sturdy railroad ties are also popular. For extra-long raised beds, use telephone poles laid on their sides. These can be island beds or butted against a fence or wall.

The width of a raised bed should not be more than 6 feet, representing the total distance a person can comfortably stretch out with his hands from either side of the bed. If beds are butted against a wall, width should be reduced to 3 feet or less.

SPACE-SAVING TRAINING

Where space is limited, you may want to consider growing vegetables that can be trained up stakes, trellises and other forms of support.

Staking. There are several methods of staking tall-growing vegetables. Tomatoes, cucumbers and peppers can be trained to a single wood, metal or plastic stake, using string or twist-ties to secure stems to the supports.

Pole beans and tall varieties of peas can be trained up tripods and tepees. Use three or more poles set in a circle at the bottom, and tie poles together at the top.

Towers. The most efficient and easiest vertical-training method is growing plants inside cylinders of inexpensive wire *towers,* or cages. Tomato towers should be at least 5 feet high and 1-1/2 feet to 2 feet across. Concrete reinforcing wire with 6-inch mesh openings works exceptionally well. The wide mesh is necessary so you can harvest fruit by reaching through the wire, rather than trying to reach in from the top. Plant one tomato plant in the middle of each cylinder, and do not prune branches. As the plant grows, the branches push through the wire spaces so the plant becomes self-supporting.

Cucumber towers should be 3 feet in diameter and 3 feet high. Leave a gap about 1-1/2 feet wide along one side so you can reach inside to pick cucumbers from the middle of the tower. Plant several vines spaced 1 foot apart around inside and outside of the tower.

Squash towers can be made the same size as cucumber towers. Allow vines to climb up the middle and spill over the sides.

A-frames. These are short sections of trellis, usually 6 feet long. Frames are set over the soil like an ''A'' to support vining crops. They are usually constructed of wood and can be covered with chicken wire or plastic netting. They are useful for growing cucumbers, peas, vining squash, melons and similar vines. As melons gain weight, they should be supported with cloth or slings made of pantyhose or similar material. Without support, they may slip from the vine and burst when they hit the ground.

Netting and chicken wire. Use these attached between tall, wooden stakes to support many vining crops. Either can be draped against a wall to form a trellis.

Bamboo poles. Strong, long lasting and decorative, these can be used in countless ways to support beans, peas and other vining crops. For beans, it's best to erect them in a tripod or as an A-frame.

Recycled supports. Use your imagination to utilize throwaway materials for the garden. One of the most original trellising ideas I have seen was a collection of bicycle wheels randomly mounted against a wall. They supported cucumbers, balsam apples and spaghetti squash.

INTENSIVE GARDENING

Making every inch of space count is a good definition of intensive gardening. This can be done by growing vegetables in wide, raised rows—as matted rows with vegetables that tolerate crowded conditions, or in a block planting with vegetables that require more precise spacing.

An effective way of saving space in a vegetable garden is to plant vegetables with compact growth habits. When making vegetable selections among squash, avoid the *vining* varieties and try the newer *bush* varieties. Similarly, there are bush varieties of cucumbers, cantaloupes, watermelons, snap beans and other popular vegetables.

Intensive gardening also makes use of *interplanting.* For example, tall-stemmed chard can be interplanted among low-growing parsley. Quick-maturing lettuce can be planted among slow-growing brussels sprouts. The lettuce will be harvested and cleared from the bed by the time the brussels sprouts have spread to cut off the light. Pole beans can be grown with corn, using the corn stalks as supports.

Wire cage is set in place after tomato is planted. 'Pixie' grows to only 3 feet high. Large, indeterminate tomatoes require a cylinder 5 feet or more high.

Cucumber vine has been trained to a single pole to save space. An A-frame trellis, see photo, page 7, is more efficient for numerous vines.

Gardeners with little room are among the most imaginative. Discarded bicycle wheels support balsam apple vine.

Harvesting and Storage

The time has finally come to harvest your vegetables. After all of the effort, you will want to pick your crops when they are at peak flavor. Some vegetables can be harvested over a period of time without a noticeable loss in flavor. Others are at peak flavor for only a day, or at a certain time of day. For example, leafy vegetables, including herbs, have best flavor in early morning while they are still wet with dew.

The amount of time that passes from harvesting to eating or preparation has a bearing on flavor. Harvest the following vegetables as close as possible to preparation and meal time: asparagus, snap beans, broad beans, greenshell beans, lima beans, all root vegetables, broccoli, brussels sprouts, cabbage, cauliflower, cucumbers, eggplant, kohlrabi, leeks, okra, peas, peppers, summer squash, sweet corn, tomatoes, fresh vegetable soybeans and cowpeas. If these vegetables cannot be eaten soon after harvesting, store them in plastic bags or covered containers in the refrigerator.

If you are planning to freeze or can your garden produce, harvest just before preparing for preservation. How well vegetables taste after storage has a lot to do with their quality when fresh. Store only the freshest and the best.

HARVESTING VEGETABLES
Asparagus. Harvest when the spears are 6 to 8 inches long, before tops start to open. Cut or break off stems at soil line.

Beans—broad, greenshell, lima. Pick when pods feel plump. Eat seeds only—the pods are too tough.

Beans—snap. Pick when pods are plump but before seeds begin to bulge the pod wall.

Beets. Pick greens when leaves are 6 inches long. Pick beets when roots are 1-1/2 to 3 inches in diameter.

Broccoli. Harvest when heads are solid, before flower buds start to open and show yellow. Cut off 6 inches below head and save small, tender leaves. They are highly nutritious and delicious as greens.

Brussels sprouts. Do not harvest until after frost. A short period of cold temperatures improves their flavor. When sprouts (buds) at base of plant become solid, pinch out growing tip of plant to encourage development of sprouts higher on plant.

Cabbage. Harvest when heads become solid. To delay the splitting of mature heads, pull plants upward out of soil just enough to break a few roots. This reduces water intake and slows the maturation rate. Leave stems and roots of several plants intact. They will produce small, lateral heads later in the season.

Cantaloupe. Pick when blossom end feels soft under slight pressure. Also look for the "net" on fruit to become full and color of melon to turn light tan. Some cantaloupe, also called *muskmelons,* slip from the vine when ripe if you pull the stem where it is attached to the fruit. Not all varieties do this, so read seed packet or seed catalog description carefully.

Carrots. Dig roots when they are deep orange and have reached suffi-

Left: A summer harvest of mixed vegetables. Knowing the best time to pick can mean the difference between good and great flavor. Above: A freezer full of your own vegetables can make a measurable contribution toward reducing your food bill.

cient size. If they are to be stored, leave them in the garden until just prior to heavy frost.

Cauliflower. Harvest when curds are 4 to 6 inches in diameter, white and solid. Curds exposed to sunlight and rain become discolored and develop

Hety displays a basket filled with 'Sugar Snap' snap peas. Pick them when they are plump for eating fresh or for cooking.

For absolute maximum flavor, pick tomatoes when they are a rich, sun-ripened red.

an unpalatable texture. When curds are 1 to 2 inches across, cover heads by tying tips of the outer cauliflower leaves loosely above the curd. This is called *blanching*. Self-blanching varieties are available. See page 108.

Celery. Harvest when plants are 12 to 15 inches tall and stems have formed a thick cluster. Plants for storage should be lifted with roots attached. Place them upright and cover roots with moist sand.

Chard. Pick when plants reach 6 to 8 inches tall. Thinnings can be cooked. Thereafter, remove only outer leaves when they are young and tender. New leaves continue to grow from center of each plant. Leaves can be harvested well into winter—until the ground freezes.

Chicory, witloof. Pull roots after first fall frost. Cut tops to 1 inch and reset roots in soil or other moisture-holding material. Set in a dark, cool location, about 60F (16C). Cover tops of roots to a depth of 4 to 6 inches with loose soil or peat moss. Harvest compact, white leaf buds as they peek through the covering.

Chives. Cut leaves 2 inches above soil level to encourage new growth as it appears in early spring. Use young, tender leaves throughout the season.

Collards. Pick outer leaves when 8 to 10 inches long. New, leafy growth from center of plant will provide a continuous harvest.

Cowpea or black-eyed pea. Harvest pods as *snaps* like snap beans when seeds are near mature size but still bright green. Harvest seeds when pods turn brittle and seeds become dry, turning white with black eyes.

Cucumber. Different varieties are available for slicing and pickling. Read the descriptions on pages 119 to 123 to determine best use. For sweet pickles, pick when fruit are 1-1/2 to 2-1/2 inches long. For dill pickles, pick when fruit are 3 to 4 inches long. For slicing, pick when fruit are 6 to 9 inches long, but green and firm. Old fruit turn yellow and taste bitter.

Eggplant. Harvest black or purple kinds when firm and glossy. Older fruit become dull, soft and seedy.

Endive. Pick when plant is 10 to 12 inches across. Tie center leaves loosely to exclude light for 2 to 3 weeks. This blanching improves flavor.

Garden huckleberry. Pick when fruit are glossy black.

Garlic. Pull prior to first fall frost or

harvest after stalks have died down.

Jerusalem artichoke. Harvest any time of year. Best times to dig tubers are after early fall frosts and in early spring before new growth begins.

Kale. Pick outer leaves when 8 to 10 inches long. New leaves will grow from center of each plant for a continuous harvest.

Kohlrabi. Harvest when thickened stems reach 2 to 3 inches in diameter.

Leek. Pull when 1 to 1-1/2 inches in diameter, either before or after fall frost, and heap soil against stems to blanch and sweeten flavor.

Lettuce. Pick leaf types when outer leaves are 4 to 6 inches long. Harvest outer leaves first. New leaves will provide a continuous harvest of tender, tasty lettuce until hot weather brings on a bitter flavor, and plants go to seed. Harvest heading types when heads are moderately firm, before seed stalks appear.

Muskmelon. See Cantaloupe.

Mustard. Pick outer leaves when 6 to 8 inches long. New leaves provide continuous harvests until flavor becomes strong and leaves toughen from hot weather.

Okra. Pick when pods are 3 inches long and bright green, usually within two days of flowering.

Onion. Pull or dig after tops have died down. Mature onions from sets do not store well. Storage onions are best produced from seeds or plants. Pull with tops on, then cut tops 1 inch above bulb for drying.

Parsley. Pick when plants are established and branching freely. Pick sprigs from edges of plant through summer until ground freezes. Plants go to seed the second year if they survive the winter. Start a second batch of plants from seeds sown in pots about midsummer. Grow indoors over winter.

Parsnips. Dig in late fall, after early frosts. Cold temperatures improve their flavor.

Peas. Pick English peas when pods are plump and dark green. Harvest edible-pod kinds—snow and Chinese—before seeds start to bulge the pod wall. Harvest snap peas when pods are plump.

Peanut. Harvest just before first fall frost. To harvest, dig soil around plants with garden fork and lift plants with peanuts attached.

Peppers. Pick when green fruit are firm. Mature peppers should be harvested quickly before they turn soft, which usually occurs soon after the pepper turns red. Sweet bell peppers are usually blocky in shape. Hot varieties are long and slender.

Potatoes. Dig a sample to see if tubers are large enough. In cold-winter areas, harvest after plants have completely died down but prior to frost. Early potatoes can be harvested in midsummer before plants die down. Carefully dig into the upper soil surface and remove small tubers without disturbing rest of plant.

Radishes. Pull when 1 to 1-1/2 inches in diameter. Best eaten when young and tender, before flower stalks appear.

Rhubarb. Harvest when leaf stalks are 12 to 15 inches long. Flavor and tenderness is best in spring and early summer. Discard leaves—they are poisonous.

Salsify. Harvest in fall after frost. Cold temperatures improve flavor.

Spinach. Harvest whole plants when larger leaves are 6 to 8 inches long. Pull largest plants first. You cannot harvest outer leaves because this causes plant to wilt.

Squash. Pick winter squash before frost when fruit are hard. Harvest summer squash when fruit are young and tender. Do not allow fruit of either kind to reach maturity because it exhausts the plant's energy.

Sweet corn. Pull ears after silk turns brown and brittle. Kernels should be filled with milky juice.

Sweet potatoes. Dig in late fall but before the first early frost. Dig carefully to avoid cutting or bruising roots.

Tomatoes. For the best flavor and maximum sugar content, leave fruit on the vine an extra day after they have turned completely red.

Turnips. For greens, harvest leaves when they are 6 inches long. For roots, harvest standard varieties when turnips are 2 to 2-1/2 inches in diameter. In cold-winter areas, harvest before fall frosts. Japanese hybrids are best harvested the size of a golf ball.

Watercress. Pick tips of stems when 6 inches long. Harvest in early spring. Flavor deteriorates in summer.

Watermelon. Tap fruit with knuckles. *Dull sound* similar to tapping your forehead indicates fruit is not ripe. *Hollow sound* similar to tapping your chest indicates fruit is fully ripe. *Soft sound* similar to tapping your stomach indicates fruit is overripe.

Pick bell-type peppers when fruit are green and firm, before they turn red. This 'Big Bertha' hybrid pepper measured 10 inches long.

Although it is fun to grow huge summer squash, most are the best eating when about the size of your hand. This is 'Gold Rush' zucchini.

The easiest way to store certain vegetables is to let them *overwinter* in the garden. Spinach, especially 'Bloomsdale Long Standing', survives frosts if plants are established.

Storing vegetables is a suitable way to have a fresh supply of many vegetables on hand, especially during winter months. In some ways, dry storage is better then canning or freezing. Vegetables stored in their natural state retain more nutritive value and flavor.

One of the problems in storing vegetables at home is providing the different temperature and humidity conditions each vegetable group requires. Here are the main ways to store vegetables:

Cold-moist storage. Perishable vegetables such as asparagus and the vegetable "greens" should be stored at near-freezing temperatures. The vegetable bin of a refrigerator provides the best kind of cold-moist storage.

Cool-dry storage. Unheated storage areas such as attics and garages are usually suitable for storing dried peas, beans and onions.

Warm-dry storage. Most furnace rooms and indoor storage areas such as cupboards and closets are warm and dry. As long as it does not become too warm, this type of storage condition suits pumpkins and winter squash.

STORING VEGETABLES

Beans and peas—shelled. Allow pods to turn brittle. This includes snap beans, field beans, lima beans, English peas and soybeans. Spread pods to dry in a warm, ventilated location until completely dry. To eliminate potential weevil damage, freeze for 4 days before storing. Soybeans are not subject to weevil damage and don't require this treatment. Store dried seeds in closed containers in a cool, dry place as close to 32F (0C) as possible.

Beets, carrots and parsnips. Cut top off, trim taproot and brush soil from root. Store on a layer of damp sand or damp peat moss in wooden crates. Cover with more sand or peat moss. Continue to alternate layers of vegetables and sand or peat moss up to the top of the box. Store between 32F and 40F (0C to 5C) in a basement or root cellar.

Cabbage, cauliflower and kohlrabi. Cut cabbage and cauliflower heads from stems. Select only those that are solid and show no signs of splitting. Remove loose, outer leaves and leaves showing insect damage. Place each head in a plastic bag. Punch holes in bag to allow excess moisture

Beets and many other root crops can be stored in shallow boxes or crates. Cover with moist peat moss or sand and store between 32F to 40F (0C to 5C).

Winter squash should be stored with part of the dry stem attached. Fruit should not touch each other. Store as close to 50F (10C) as possible.

Pantyhose can be recycled to store onions. Onions are separated by knots and hung in a cool, dry place. Lop off onions from bottom when needed.

to escape. With kohlrabi, remove leaves and roots from the bulb and place a number of bulbs together in plastic bags. Store as close to 32F (0C) as possible, with high humidity.

Onions. Harvest onions when tops fall over and turn brown. Pull bulbs from soil with tops attached, then cut away tops to within 1 inch of bulb. Allow bulbs to cure for 10 days in a dry, well-ventilated area as close to 32F (0C) as possible. The variety 'Spartan Sleeper' is recommended for storage because it tolerates temperatures up to 70F (21C) without sprouting.

Onions that store poorly, notably sweet onions such as 'Giant Walla Walla', can still be stored for up to three months. Place onions in the legs of pantyhose and tie a knot between each onion. Suspend the onions from a nail in a cool, dark place. When you want to use an onion, clip off the bottom of the pantyhose.

Potatoes. Store in a dark place to prevent greening. The green color is

Storage Times
Beans, dry shelled—1 year or more, dried and stored in jars or bags.
Beets—up to 3 months stored in moist sand.
Carrots—up to 3 months stored in moist sand.
Cauliflower—up to 1 month stored in refrigerator vegetable bin.
Celeriac—up to 3 months stored in moist sand.
Celery—up to 2 months with roots sunk in moist sand.
Chinese cabbage—up to 1 month stored in refrigerator vegetable bin.
Kohlrabi—up to 1 month stored in refrigerator vegetable bin.
Onions—up to 12 months using long storage varieties. See page 138.
Parsnips—up to 3 months stored in moist sand.
Peas—1 year or more, dried and stored in jars or bags.
Potatoes—up to 3 months stored in boxes or burlap sacks. Store in dark place.
Pumpkins—up to 2 months stored in a cool, humid room.
Rutabagas—up to 3 months stored in moist sand.
Salsify—up to 3 months stored in moist sand.
Soybeans—1 year or more, dried and stored in jars or bags.
Squash, summer—up to 3 weeks in refrigerator vegetable bin.
Squash, winter—up to 3 months stored in a cool, humid room.
Tomatoes—up to 2 months, choosing long storage varieties stored in a cool, humid room.
Turnips—up to 3 months stored in moist sand.
Winter radish—up to 2 months stored in moist sand.

bitter and unfit for human consumption. Some potatoes may develop sweetness when stored below 40F (5C). To restore flavor, keep at room temperature for a few days. Potatoes held above 40F (5C) produce sprouts after two months.

Pumpkins and squash. Leave fruit on the vine as long as possible, but harvest before frost. Fruit should then be *cured* by keeping dry in a warm, well-ventilated area for 10 days before being placed in permanent storage. To prevent rot, leave part of the stem attached. Stem should be dry and hard. Best storage conditions are 50F to 55F (10C to 13C) with high humidity.

Rutabagas and turnips. These two vegetables are best waxed before they are stored to prevent shriveling. Before waxing, wash, dry and trim vegetables. Bring a large pail of water to a boil. Water should be deep enough so that the vegetable can be completely submerged. Float a layer of *paraffin,* a wax used in sealing jelly jars, on top of the water. Adding 10% to 20% clean beeswax to the paraffin toughens the layer and prevents wax from becoming brittle and cracking.

Roots should be dry and kept at room temperature for several hours prior to waxing. If vegetables are cold when waxed, they may accumulate too thick a layer of wax. Dip each root through the layer of wax and remove immediately. Do not leave in paraffin bath for more than three seconds. If layer of wax is too thick, add some salt to the water. This causes wax to cover in a thinner film. Store in boxes, alternating layers of vegetables with moist sand. Temperature of the storage room should be kept between 32F and 40F (0C to 5C) for best results.

PRESERVING THE HARVEST
In addition to dry storage, vegetables can be preserved for long periods in a variety of ways. Among these are canning, freezing, pickling and dehydrating. It is impossible in a book of this size to give specific directions on these subjects, but you should be aware of the alternatives. Where applicable, books are recommended to give you the necessary information.

Canning. High heat is required in canning to kill bacteria that spoil food and cause botulism. The safest system is using steam under pressure. The advantage of canning is the ease with which canned goods can be stored.

There are usually plenty of shelves around the home to store jars. The amount of frozen vegetables you are able to store is restricted by the size of your freezer. Canning is more time-consuming than freezing, and jars with special lids are required to ensure a safe seal.

These vegetables are recommended for canning:

Asparagus	Okra
Beans, lima	Peas
Beans, snap	Peppers
Beets	Potatoes, Irish
Carrots	Potatoes, sweet
Corn	Pumpkin
Eggplant	Squash, summer
Greens	Tomatoes

Each kind of vegetable requires different methods of preparation and boiling or steam-pressure times. For complete information, refer to the HPBook on canning, by Sue and Bill Deeming.

Freezing. Most vegetables freeze well. In fact, freezing is the easiest way to preserve vegetables.

The step-by-step photos at right show how to freeze snap peas. Follow these same steps for other vegetables, although blanching times vary.

Suitable containers for freezing include plastic freezer containers, plastic freezer bags or freezer jars. When closed, such containers should be moisture-proof. A large pot is needed for *blanching,* scalding vegetables with boiling water before they are stored.

Depending on the vegetable, most should be blanched for 1 to 4 minutes. Blanching kills harmful bacteria and maintains the bright, appetizing color.

These vegetables are recommended for freezing:

Asparagus	Greens
Beans, lima	Okra
Beans, snap	Onions
Beets	Peas
Broccoli	Peppers
Brussels sprouts	Potatoes, sweet
Cabbage	Pumpkin
Carrots	Squash
Cauliflower	Tomatoes
Corn	Turnip
Eggplant	

Pickling. Pickling is a form of canning. Vegetables are stored in *brine,* a mixture of vinegar and salt. The pickling process normally takes 4 to 8 weeks, depending on the vegetable. After pickling, vegetables have a crisp, clean, spicy flavor.

These vegetables make excellent pickles:

Beans, snap	Onions
Beets	Peppers, cherry
Cabbage	Shallots
Cauliflower	Tomatoes, green
Cucumbers	Watermelon rind
Okra	

Dehydration. Preserving vegetables by dehydration is one of the oldest forms of storage. In recent years, people have recognized the ease, economy and value of drying food.

Herbs are simple to dry. Stored in jars or other containers, they are handy in the kitchen. See page 177.

The principles of dehydration are very simple. Vegetables are chopped or sliced, then spread over screens to dry in the sun or in a special drying oven or dehydrator.

A dehydrator or oven dryer makes it easy to dry vegetables. Units are available by mail from garden catalogs and from appliance stores. Most important is to have thin, 1/4 inch or less, uniform slices for even drying. A food processor is helpful in this respect.

Pretreating vegetables is important to prevent spoilage. This consists of either *water-blanching* or *steam-blanching* to kill organisms responsible for spoilage, and to maintain the appetizing color of the vegetables. Steam-blanching is the preferred method for this.

To water-blanch, bring a pot of water to boil and submerge the sliced vegetables in the water using a wire basket. With steam-blanching, you suspend the vegetables over boiling water in a covered pot so the heat from the rising steam treats them.

Blanching times for vegetables differ. Variables include the vegetable, the amount to be processed at one time, thickness of the slices and altitude. Blanching normally requires only a few minutes.

These vegetables are recommended for dehydration:

Carrots	Parsnips
Corn	Peas
Garlic	Peppers, red &
Horseradish	green
Okra	Peppers, chili
Onions	Potatoes
Parsley	

For complete information on preserving, storing and using vegetables, read *How To Dry Foods* by Deanna DeLong, and *Cooking With Stored Foods,* by Carroll Latham and Carlene Tejada. Both titles are published by HPBooks.

1. To freeze snap peas, select firm, mature, unblemished pods. Pull strings and wash under cold water.

2. Blanch pods by submerging them in boiling water for 2 minutes.

3. After blanching, cool peas under running tap water.

4. Dry with towel and place in freezer bag. Squeeze out air and seal bag.

Gallery of Garden Vegetables

The following common and not-so-common vegetables are organized alphabetically for easy reference. Descriptions for most vegetables give background and cultural information, pest control and harvesting tips. Vegetable varieties are recommended, with reasons why they are superior.

Many vegetables have a section entitled "Inside Report." Most were compiled by interviewing the plant breeder responsible for creating a particularly outstanding vegetable variety.

Special emphasis has been placed on illustrating each vegetable as realistically and naturally as possible. The majority of vegetables pictured were grown in my own garden, using the growing techniques described in this book.

A special effort has been made to recommend varieties known to be widely adaptable. But some vegetables are better adapted to certain regions and these have also been noted. An additional source of variety recommendation is your local cooperative extension service. This agency is listed in the phone book under different names. Look under the "County" or "State University" headings for *Agricultural Extension Service, Cooperative Extension Service, County Extension Service,* or *County* or *Agricultural Agent.*

A way to obtain regional favorites is through catalogs of seed companies located in your area. For example, certain cold-tolerant varieties are better for cool-season areas of the Pacific Northwest and short-season areas of Canada. Seeds for such varieties are normally offered by seed companies located in Washington State, Maine and Canada. Similarly, there are varieties adapted to warm climates of the South and Southwest, offered by seed companies located in these areas. Page 33 lists various sources for seed by mail.

In addition to regional varieties, you need to consider regional planting dates. In the North, cool-season crops can be planted approximately three weeks before your last frost date in spring. In areas with mild frosts or *no* frosts, such as Florida, the Gulf States, southern California and southern Arizona, cool-season crops are best planted in fall—usually September and October. This way, crops can be harvested during winter and early spring before the onset of hot weather. For more on planting dates, refer to the climate information and planting chart on pages 44 to 51. Better yet, check locally among experienced gardeners or with your cooperative extension service.

Problems with pests and diseases also occur on a regional level. Common insect pests and diseases are noted in this chapter and in the chapter on pests and diseases, page 61. But it is impossible to describe every potential problem and every control. If you are a new gardener or new to an area, ask your neighbors which pests are known to bother certain crops in your area. You can then implement a specific control program to combat pests and diseases before they become established.

Left: A vine loaded with sun-ripened, 'Supersteak VFN' tomatoes. Above: Nothing else says freshness like just-picked vegetables from a back yard garden.

Seedhead of grain amaranth.

Artichoke 'Grande Beurre', grown from seed.

Amaranth

Two kinds of amaranth are commonly grown in home gardens. Leaf amaranth produces leafy greens that are excellent, hot-weather substitutes for spinach. Grain amaranth, popular in Aztec civilizations, produces large seedheads prized for their nutritive content.

Tampala (*Amaranthus* species) is the most widely grown leaf amaranth. It produces edible greens within 6 to 8 weeks after seeds are sown. Leaves can be used raw in salads or cooked like spinach. Young leaves are tender and require only a few minutes to cook. Stems can be braised like asparagus, imparting a flavor similar to artichokes.

Tampala freezes better than spinach or Swiss chard. It retains a more appetizing color, shrinks very little and has a better flavor.

Grain amaranths have edible leaves, but they are mostly grown for their huge, yellow, bronze and red flower plumes. They produce thousands of nutty seeds that contain high-quality protein.

How to grow: Sow seeds 1/4 inch deep directly in the garden after all danger of frost has passed. Thin seedlings so plants stand 16 to 20 inches apart in rows 20 inches apart.

Pest and disease control: Insect damage is normally minor, usually caused by chewing insects such as Japanese beetle. These can be easily controlled by rotenone organic dust or Sevin chemical spray.

Harvesting and use: Begin by picking young leaves, which are cooked like spinach. A large, decorative seedhead develops about midsummer. When seeds have turned brown, cut flowerhead and shake or thrash over a newspaper to collect seeds.

A favorite way to eat the seeds is to cook them like popcorn. Heat a metal skillet until hot, and pour in 1 tablespoon of amaranth seeds. Move the skillet constantly to keep seeds from burning while they pop. When popping subsides, seeds are ready to eat.

Recommended varieties: Tampala or 'Fordhook Spinach' (50 days) is an excellent spinach substitute. Available from Burpee.

Artichoke

Globe artichoke (*Cynara scolymus*) is an edible thistle, producing flower buds that are delicious to eat. Cardoon (*Cynara cardunculus*), described on page 105, is a close relative grown for its edible leaf stalks. Both of these vegetables originate in the Mediterranean.

The edible part of globe artichoke is the flower bud, which consists of a cluster of overlapping fleshy scales. Flower buds must be picked young, before the purple flower blossoms begin to show. A large, healthy plant will produce up to 50 edible buds.

When flowers are allowed to open they resemble a giant thistle head. They are greatly admired by floral designers who dry them for use in arrangements. Leaves of globe artichoke are large and deeply serrated—very striking in the landscape. Well-grown specimens can reach a height of 6 feet and are sometimes used in perennial flower borders as a dramatic highlight.

Artichokes have strict temperature and moisture requirements. Most commercial varieties produce poorly when the temperature falls below 65F (19C) during the May to September growing period. For this reason, over 90% of commercial artichoke production in the United States is confined to a small area of central, coastal California. Here winters are mild and coastal breezes keep summers cool.

Selecting the right variety for home use is important. Maturity dates range from 24 months for California artichokes grown from roots, to less than 8 months for certain European varieties grown from seed. Because of variety differences, traditional growing instructions for artichokes are misleading. The time-honored theory that artichokes can be grown only in the coastal valleys of California or in mild-winter areas of the South is now outdated.

The secret to growing artichokes in regions with snow cover and freezing temperatures is to start from seed. Choose a fast-maturing variety like 'Grande Beurre' (160 days) and grow it as an annual. Areas of the country with 100 frost-free days should be able to produce worthwhile crops of artichokes the first season.

How to grow: Start seeds indoors at the same time you start tomatoes. This is about 8 to 10 weeks before outdoor planting, which should not occur until all danger of frost has passed. Highest germination is assured if seeds are stored in the refrigerator for two weeks to help break dormancy. Plant seeds in individual pots and provide bottom heat to encourage faster germination. See page 37 for instructions on how to start from seed.

When seedlings are about 4 to 6 inches tall, set them 3 feet apart in rows spaced 3 feet apart in fertile soil. Artichokes are extremely heavy feeders and do best in soils enriched with garden compost, manure or leaf mold. If soil is lacking in fertility, rake into the soil an application of general-purpose fertilizer before planting. Read the package label for amounts. A booster application should be given to plants in midsummer.

Once planted, artichokes demand large amounts of water. Soil should always be kept moist. During hot, humid weather, plants may wilt but usually recover during the night.

If the ground freezes in winter in your area, it is best to dig up roots in fall. Brush soil from roots and store them in a cool, dark, sheltered place, preferably with an air temperature of 33F to 40F (1C to 5C)). If this is not possible, store roots in pots of soil in a cool, bright location such as in a cold frame. They will remain in a semidormant state until spring.

In areas free from snow cover and where winter temperatures stay above 20F (−7C), artichokes can be left in the ground. In spring, roots normally send up a mass of shoots called *suckers*. To make plants most productive the second season and thereafter, prune away all but four of the strongest shoots. These will use all of the plant's energy and produce heavy crops.

Pest and disease control: Aphids are the most serious pest. They congregate in groups along tips of new shoots and infest developing buds. Aphid colonies are usually green or black. The safest control is to blast them with jets of water from a garden hose. You can also rub aphids off stems with a gloved hand before colonies become numerous.

Slugs and snails can cause serious damage in the early stages of growth. Place slug bait in shallow pans so the poison does not contaminate soil. Be sure to use bait labeled "safe for vegetables."

Harvesting and use: Buds can be harvested when they are the size of a tennis ball or larger, before the purple part of the flower begins to show. Small buds are more tender to eat. Cut the bud from the plant using a sharp knife. See How To Cook And Eat An Artichoke for instructions on preparing the bud.

Recommended varieties: 'Grande Beurre' (160 days) produces a harvest the first year from seed. Available from Thompson & Morgan. 'Green Globe' (180 days), a widely available variety, will also produce edible buds the first year.

HOW TO COOK AND EAT AN ARTICHOKE

As much confusion surrounds how to eat artichokes as how to grow them. First, cut the artichoke from the flower stem immediately below the globe or *bud,* with about 1 inch of stem attached. Remove about 1 inch of the tip and hard, spiny leaves from around the base of the bud. Rinse the artichoke. Put salt, lemon juice and the artichoke in a pan of water and bring to a boil. Cook for 30 minutes or until the base is soft to the touch of a fork. After cooking, turn upside down to drain away water.

Prepare a dish of melted butter. To eat, pull away leaf sections of the artichoke, starting from the outside and working toward the center. Dip the base of each leaf section in butter and pull it between your teeth. The tender portion easily parts from the inedible, fibrous portion, which you discard. Each leaf toward the middle of the artichoke becomes more tender. Eventually you will reach the *choke,* or the immature flower head. Scoop this out with a spoon, leaving the *heart,* the tastiest part of all. Eat the heart and stem section with fingers or fork. Garnish with a squeeze of lemon juice if you desire.

Remove artichoke from plant with a knife. Leave 1 inch of stem attached.

Cut away sharp tips of bud scales. Peel away tough, lower leaf scales.

Cut off spiny top with sharp knife. Artichoke is ready to cook. See above.

Asparagus 'Mary Washington'.

Asparagus

Asparagus should be included in your garden for at least two reasons: One, it is an early crop. In most of the United States asparagus spears break through the soil in early spring, providing a succulent harvest that continues into early summer. Two, asparagus is a hardy perennial. It comes up year after year without having to replant. One mature asparagus plant is capable of producing 1-1/2 pounds of spears. A 25-foot row is normally sufficient to feed a family of three.

Asparagus does have some shortcomings—not least is the length of time required to produce a productive bed. Beds can be started from roots or seeds. Plants normally require 25 months to produce a harvest from newly planted roots. Add an extra 12 weeks if you prefer to grow from seeds.

An asparagus bed will remain productive indefinitely, as long as soil fertility is maintained. Do this by raking a general-purpose fertilizer into the soil surface in spring and fall.

Asparagus plants do not compete well with weeds. Keep beds weed-free through the growing season. The best form of weed control is to apply a layer of organic mulch such as peat moss or compost in spring when the spears begin to break through soil.

Plants are male or female. You can recognize a female plant in fall by the red berries that form among the foliage. Seeds inside these berries can be harvested in fall and used to start new plants.

Never cut an asparagus bed until the tops turn brown in the fall. The longer foliage stems are left on the plant, the more nourishment will reach the roots to ensure a bigger and better crop the following year. In cold regions plants go dormant and turn yellow naturally. In warmer areas water should be withheld to encourage dormancy. When tops are completely dead they can be removed.

How to grow: Rutgers University recommends the following seed-growing method. It allows you to harvest a seed-started crop the same time as a crop started from roots.

Start seeds indoors or in a greenhouse in late winter to early spring. Sow seeds in commercial potting mix of peat moss and vermiculite. The temperature of the seed-starting medium should be about 70F (21C). Plant seeds 1/2 inch deep in seed trays or flats. Place seeds 1 inch apart with 2 inches between rows. A weak solution of 10-10-10 soluble fertilizer mixed with water should be applied at 4-, 8- and 12-week intervals. Seedlings must receive plenty of sunlight. Supplemental fluorescent lighting can be used to help the seedlings along if natural light is poor. Allow 12 weeks from the time you sow seeds to the time you transplant to the garden. Transplant seedlings after all danger of frost has passed. At planting time you will have sturdy, 6-inch-tall, 12-week-old transplants capable of catching up with year-old, nursery-grown roots.

If you choose the slightly easier method of planting nursery-grown roots, start with 1-year-old roots rather than roots 2 or 3 years old. The larger the root, the more susceptible it will be to transplant shock and to root rot. Plant in spring using the furrow or mounded row method. See next paragraph. In desert or hot inland areas, plant in fall or early winter. Roots are long and fleshy. Position roots flat with the roots splayed out like the arms of an octopus. Space 12 inches apart in rows 3 feet apart.

There are two ways to plant asparagus—the *furrow* and *mounded row*. Soil for either method must be fertile and well drained. Slightly sandy soil is best with plenty of organic content, such as composted animal manure, garden compost or leaf mold.

To prepare soil, dig site 12 to 15 inches deep and add soil amendment if needed. See page 22. If you have poor soil, use the furrow system. Dig a trench 12 inches wide by 12 inches deep and cart in some good topsoil. Apply 1 pound of 5-10-10 fertilizer per 100 square feet of area and work into the soil. If soil is sandy and drains quickly, apply fertilizer according to package directions after plants are established. If the soil is too acid, add dolomitic limestone at the rate of 5 pounds per 100 square feet. Asparagus likes a slightly acid soil of 6.5 to 6.8 pH.

There is widespread disagreement over how deep the roots should be set in the furrow. The traditional way is to plant them 6 inches deep. The National Vegetable Research Station in England conducted an experiment, comparing the results of asparagus roots planted 4 inches deep to those planted 6 inches deep. Results were that heavier yields can be achieved by planting at the shallower depth and that roots are less susceptible to root rot.

The mounded-row method is easier to use if your soil is deep and rich in organic matter. Cultivate soil as you would for any other vegetable. Mix in fertilizer, peat moss and lime as necessary. Level soil and place roots in a row on the soil surface. Use a rake to mound soil from the sides of the row over the asparagus roots. Make the mounds 4 to 6 inches high. Each mounded row should be 1-1/2 to 2 feet wide at the base.

Pest and disease control: Rust disease can be a serious problem. It shows up as reddish orange, powdery blisters on plant stems. See photo, page 69. Most varieties offered commercially are rust resistant but not immune. Additional control can be obtained by spraying with maneb or zineb. Apply amounts as directed on the product label. Do not plant asparagus where strawberries have been grown—they are carriers of the disease.

Asparagus beetle is a troublesome insect pest. There are two kinds: common and 12-spotted. They cause damage by chewing holes in spears and laying eggs. Control by using an organic vegetable dust such as rotenone, or use a chemical spray such as Sevin.

Harvesting and use: To harvest asparagus, use a sharp knife and cut stem at an angle just below soil line. The most tender portion of an asparagus spear is toward the tip. When it's time to prepare spears for cooking, wash the stem, take the bottom portion of the stem between the finger and thumb of each hand, bend and let the asparagus stem snap where it wants to. Discard the tough, lower portion.

Asparagus tips are so tender they can be eaten raw in salads. Or they can be cooked for just a few minutes. It is best to harvest them just prior to cooking for best flavor. Serve with butter and breadcrumb dressing or cheese sauce. Asparagus not eaten fresh from the garden can be blanched and frozen. Frozen asparagus keeps well and retains its flavor.

Recommended varieties: 'Mary Washington' (2 years) is an old, reliable, rust-resistant variety available as seeds or roots from most seed catalogs. In the future look for varieties from Michigan State University with double the amount of edible stem per spear.

When planting asparagus roots, set 4 to 6 inches deep and splay them out like the legs of an octopus.

QUESTIONS ABOUT ASPARAGUS

Will sprinkling salt on an asparagus bed help ensure a good crop?

No. The theory is that asparagus can tolerate high levels of salt. The original home of asparagus is the salt marshes of Europe. Most garden weeds cannot tolerate salt, so it is considered an effective method of control. But too much salt in a garden is harmful to other neighboring plants. A mulch of bark chips or black plastic is better for controlling weeds.

I planted asparagus roots according to instructions provided by a catalog company, but only a few, weak stems came up. Some of the roots were moldy on arrival. Why?

Request a replacement or refund. All reputable mail order companies will honor their guarantees. It sounds as if the roots were in poor condition and rotted in the soil. Healthy asparagus roots should be dry and clean with no premature sprouting. Wait until fall before giving up on them entirely. Spring-planted roots can remain dormant well into summer.

How can I grow the white asparagus I've seen served in restaurants?

White asparagus is simply green asparagus that has been *blanched*. Blanching is done by heaping a covering such as shredded leaves or peat moss over the asparagus bed to exclude light when the spears break through the soil. Black plastic can also be used. At picking time it's simple to reach under the cover each morning to harvest the blanched spears.

Strands of wire support tall stems of asparagus to keep planting tidy and save valuable garden space.

Flower and pods of asparagus pea.

Hety checks progress of pole beans trained tepee-style.

Asparagus Pea

This vegetable deserves to be more widely grown in home gardens. Plants have the unusual characteristic of folding their leaves flat at night, like the prayer plant, a popular house plant. Asparagus pea is a fast-growing legume that grows like clover. Maturing in 70 days, it produces numerous, cinnamon-red, pealike flowers that are highly decorative and borne in pairs. Soon after bloom, flowers produce winged pods that are tender and delicious to eat. Cook them and serve with butter as you would edible-pod peas.

How to grow: Sow seeds directly in the garden after all danger of frost has passed. Plant seeds 1/2 inch deep in single rows. Space plants 4 to 6 inches apart, with 12 inches between rows. Plants can also be grown in wide, matted rows because they tolerate crowding. They have a tendency to sprawl, growing to 2 feet in height. It is best to grow them under a framework of chicken wire so the stems poke through the wire and become self-supporting. Plants do best in a fertile, compost-rich soil.

Pest and disease control: Foraging animals such as rabbits and woodchucks love the tender stems, so fence such pests out. Aphids may congregate along the plant tips. Control by rubbing them off with a gloved hand or blasting with water from a hose.

Harvesting and use: Pick pods when 1 inch long. Left to grow any larger they become tough and fibrous. Pods appear in pairs. Plants need cool conditions and will stop bearing at the onset of warm weather. Boil 5 minutes to cook pods, or stir-fry them.

Recommended varieties: Not sold by variety name, but the asparagus pea is sometimes sold under the name *winged pea.* Seed is available from Gurney or Thompson & Morgan.

Beans

Garden beans represent a large family of plants. This family includes common snap bean *(Phaseolus vulgaris)*, lima bean *(Phaseolus limensis)*, broad bean *(Vicia faba)*, edible soy bean *(Glycine max)*, cowpea *(Vigna unguiculata)*, mung bean *(Vigna radiata)*, shell bean *(Phaseolus vulgaris)* and garbanzo *(Cicer arietinum)*. Many other beans exist, but these are the ones most commonly cultivated in home gardens.

Beans come from all parts of the globe, including the Old World and New World. For example, cowpeas or black-eyed peas—favorites in the South—originated in central Africa. Yard-long beans *(Vigna unguiculata sesquipedalis),* a subspecies of cowpea, come from Asia. The largest genus of beans, *Phaseolus,* originated in South America. They were a food staple of the Indians when Europeans began settling America.

Cultural needs among beans vary greatly from species to species. Some prefer cool conditions, ideal for a short growing season. Others demand subtropical temperatures and a long growing season.

Snap Beans

After tomatoes, snap beans are the most popular home-garden vegetable. They are much easier to grow than tomatoes and produce earlier in the season. Green-pod varieties are the most popular and most nutritious. There are also snap beans with yellow pods, purple pods and speckled pods. The beans inside come in a variety of colors. They are usually white, brown or black but include speckled kinds that resemble a small bird's egg.

Many people insist on calling snap beans *string beans.* Old varieties had fibrous strings along the pod seam that were removed before eating. Plant breeders eliminated the strings more than 50 years ago. Today the majority of varieties offered in seed catalogs are stringless.

Snap beans are either *pole types,* which require supports to climb, or *bush types,* which grow in a clump form. Bush snap beans are more popular because they grow without training. Pole varieties do offer some advantages. They have a better flavor and are usually meatier. The cropping season for pole beans is longer, although they mature a little later than bush kinds. Pole beans have stamina to last through the growing season. Bush beans usually produce a flush of beans over a period of two weeks and then die. Pole types produce more beans. A single pole bean plant will out-yield six or more bush beans.

How to grow: Germination of snap beans occurs within about 15 days when soil temperature is 60F (16C). Plant seeds directly in the garden after danger of frost has passed. Sow seeds 1 inch deep, in rows spaced 2 feet apart. Or sow in wide, raised rows with 2 rows to each bed spaced 18 inches apart. Thin seedlings to 6 inches apart in the row after they are established. Bush beans will tolerate closer planting distances but crowding them together usually will not result in greater harvests.

To train pole types, erect a trellis 6 to 10 feet high. Sow seeds 1 inch deep and 4 inches apart on both sides of the trellis. Or use poles to form a tepee spread 4 feet in diameter. Plant several beans in a circle around each leg of the tepee. Thin to 4 best plants to grow up each leg, each plant spaced 6 inches apart.

Snap beans tolerate a wide range of soil conditions, but bear heaviest in sandy soils enriched with organic matter. A soil pH of 6.5 is considered best, which means they respond well to lime in acid soil areas.

Pest and disease control: Rot is a problem in cold, wet weather. It pays to purchase seed treated with a mild organic fungicide to resist rotting.

Bean beetles can cause extensive damage when the vines are established. Some control can be achieved by growing bush varieties only and removing vines from the garden as soon as they have finished producing. By removing spent vines, bean beetle adults and larvae are cleared from the garden. New populations of beetles take time to build up. In the meantime, make successive plantings for additional harvests. Most commercial growers use the chemical spray Sevin for protection against bean beetles. An effective organic control is pyrethrum, which should be applied soon after seedlings are up. Repeat every week or after rain. Pyrethrum is often combined with rotenone to make an effective, broad-spectrum organic insecticide. Rotenone alone is ineffective in controlling bean beetles.

Other pests include slugs and cutworms. Sow beans extra thick to compensate for losses. If fungus diseases cause destruction one year, plant next year's crop in a different area. If you cannot avoid planting in the same area, apply a general-purpose fungicide.

Harvesting and use: Pick beans on a regular basis. The more you pick, the more new beans will be formed by the plant. With round-pod varieties, pick as soon as beans have swelled to become plump.

Beans can be eaten fresh or shelled and left to dry. Fresh snap beans are excellent for freezing and for pickling. Dried beans can be stored indefinitely in a dry storage area.

Recommended varieties: Many fine varieties are available. 'Tenderpod' (50 days) grows tender, crisp, green pods. 'Goldcrop' (45 days), an All-America

Award winner, grows crisp, yellow pods with white seeds. 'Royal Burgundy (51 days) is a bush-type snap bean with tasty, purple pods. 'Kentucky Wonder' (58 days) is probably the most widely grown pole bean. 'Blue Lake' (55 days) has better flavor, with smooth, dark green, round, meaty pods unbeatable for canning and freezing.

Broad Beans or Fava Beans

Most beans prefer warm weather and tolerate hot summers, but broad beans demand cool conditions to grow their incredibly large pods. Pods measure up to 10 inches in length and have an inside lining that looks like white velvet. The pods themselves are not edible, but the shelled beans are delicious eaten fresh. Up to 10 beans are in each pod, each the size of a quarter.

How to grow: Broad beans are extremely hardy and tolerate frosts, but they must mature their large pods during cool weather. Sow seeds directly into the garden as soon as soil can be cultivated in spring. Plant seeds 2 inches deep with 6 inches between plants in

Bush snap bean 'Goldcrop'—an All-America Award winner—grows straight pods to 5 inches long.

'Royal Burgundy' is a purple-pod snap bean. Its bush growth habit saves space in the garden.

Snap bean 'Tenderpod' is also a bush-type variety. It's a prolific producer of tender, 5-inch-long pods.

'Kentucky Wonder' is probably the most popular pole bean. These were harvested from my garden.

HOW TO GROW BUSHELS OF EARLY BEANS IN A SMALL SPACE

No bean patch should be planted without pole beans. They have better flavor than their bush counterparts. They are also more productive over a longer period because most bush types exhaust themselves after two weeks of production.

Pole beans are more challenging to grow. They require training up poles for support. Bean beetles are much more difficult to control among the luxuriant vine growth of pole beans than they are on bush varieties.

Choice of varieties is really a question of personal preference. 'Kentucky Wonder' and 'Blue Lake' are my favorites, with the more flavorful 'Blue Lake' getting preferred space in my garden.

Beans are not normally transplanted because they do not accept root disturbance well. But it is possible, using seeds started in quart milk cartons so the bean has plenty of room for its vigorous root system. Root disturbance is minimal when the carton sides are torn away for planting. Start 4 to 6 plants 4 weeks before planting outdoors. Wait until the last frost date to do the transplanting. Beans are highly susceptible to shock from frost damage and take a long time to recover. *Hardening-off* is essential. Place plants in a cold frame or under glass for 10 days before planting outside.

Erect 4 bamboo or cedar poles like a tepee. Position poles over a mounded hill or a raised bed. As an alternative, make cages from builder's wire, as are often used to train tomatoes. See page 168. Fertilize the soil with a mixture of 5-5-5 organic fertilizer and garden compost. Cover the planting area with black plastic to ensure a warm soil and to check weed growth. You don't have to protect the transplants from cutworm damage—the stems normally "toughen-up" by the time they are put out. You do have to protect them from slugs. This is done by applying wood ashes over the surrounding soil and using slug bait.

Bean beetle control must begin at transplant time. Spray a rotenone-pyrethrum organic insecticide mixture, using a long adjustable spray nozzle that produces a fine mist. In addition to spraying the outer leaves, poke the nozzle inside the leaf canopy to cover the leaf undersides. The mixture is not long lasting and must be repeated after every rain, or once a week during dry weather.

Give the vines a feed of liquid fertilizer at 2-week intervals once they start bearing. Spray the solution on leaves as a foliar feeding and in the planting area around the base of the plants. Spray early in the morning to avoid problems with mildew. See page 29. By doing this, plants will continue to bear until frost. You'll be amazed what only 4 vines are capable of producing—enough to feed a family of 4 during summer and some left over to freeze! Make 'Blue Lake' one of the varieties you plant—it's the best for flavor and freezing quality.

double rows. Allow 9 inches between rows for dwarf varieties. To warm up soil so seeds won't rot, cover planting rows with glass *cloches* or plastic covers until seeds germinate. Broad beans can also be sown in quart milk cartons 6 weeks before outdoor planting. *Harden-off* plants by gradually adjusting seedlings to outdoor conditions. Transplant early to ensure large yields. Soil rich in nitrogen will produce best results.

Pest and disease control: The most common pests are black bean aphids that attack tender young shoots. Rub off colonies with a gloved hand or blast them with jets of water. Pinching off the lead shoot of each bean after it has flowered will also discourage aphids.

Harvesting and use: Pick beans as soon as pods are plump. Beans are delicious cooked and served with butter. Beans freeze well.

Recommended varieties: Seed catalogs do not usually offer much of a selection among broad beans. 'Long Pod' (85 days) grows to 3 feet tall. Occasionally a space-saving variety called 'The Sutton' (65 days) is available from Thompson & Morgan.

Cowpea Beans

Cowpeas are not peas but beans. The black-eyed pea, often listed by seed catalogs, is only one variety among a large selection popular in southern states. Even though plants have a bush growth habit, they require considerable space. They are not as easy to grow as bush snap beans. Plants require warm summers and at least 75 days of frost-free conditions to produce slender, 8-inch-long pods that contain 10 to 12 seeds.

How to grow: Seeds are extremely fragile and shatter easily. Handle with care. Plant extra thick to compensate for substandard germination. Plant seeds 1-1/2 inches deep directly into the garden after all danger of frost has passed. Space plants 12 inches apart. Allow at least 4 feet between rows. Plant's spreading habit can be made more compact by planting double rows 3 feet apart and setting a 2-foot-high, chicken-wire fence down the middle to train plants upon.

Pest and disease control: Control the destructive bean beetle with applications of Sevin or pyrethrum. These

Unlike most beans, broad beans require cool weather to grow their pods. Some reach up to 10 inches long. This is 'Long Pod' ready for picking.

same products will also help keep other chewing insects away. In the South, nematodes can be extremely troublesome. Fumigation may be needed for adequate control.

Harvesting and use: Young pods can be eaten as "snaps," but their most popular use is shelled and cooked as a vegetable side dish. Black-eyed peas have a strong, smooth, meaty flavor that most bean connoisseurs enjoy. Other varieties of cowpeas are sometimes preferred because they are less filling. 'Purple Hulls' (78 days) and 'Brown Crowders' (80 days) are popular in southern states.

Recommended varieties: 'Black-eyed Pea' (85 days) has white seeds with a black ring or *eye* where the bean joins the pod wall. It is resistant to wilt disease and nematodes. Hastings Seed Company and George W. Park Seed Company are sources of cowpeas.

Garbanzo Beans

Sometimes called *chick pea,* garbanzo bean is an important food staple in India. Although it resembles a brown bean, garbanzo is not really a bean or a pea, but a legume similar to clover.

How to grow: Sow seeds directly in the garden after all danger of frost has passed. Plant seeds 1-1/2 inches deep, 12 inches apart in rows spaced 2 feet apart. Plants have a spreading habit and do not need supports. They eventually reach 2 feet high. Garbanzos thrive in sandy, compost-rich soils. Although they respond to a high nitrogen content in the soil, they are sensitive to fertilizer burn from fast-acting nitrogen fertilizers.

Pest and disease control: Garbanzos are relatively pest-free and grow like weeds. New growth may attract aphids that can be rubbed off with a gloved hand or washed off by a blast of water from a garden hose.

Harvesting and use: Pods containing one or two large, round beans appear soon after the white, pealike flowers blossom in midsummer and late summer. Fresh beans are usually produced within 70 days. Beans are juicy and delicious, but shelling is tedious. Allow 100 days for harvesting as shelled and dried beans. Cook beans for a side dish or use in salads.

Recommended varieties: Because garbanzo beans have not attracted much attention from plant breeders, they are not sold by variety name.

Lima Beans

There are two kinds of lima beans: pole limas with vigorous vines that grow up to 30 feet high, and bush limas growing 2 feet high. Pole limas need training and support; bush limas require neither. Because bush limas save time and effort they are far more popular. Pods and beans are usually slightly smaller with three beans to the pod—one fewer than pole beans.

How to grow: Planting site should be in full sun with no shade during any time of day. Sow seeds 2 inches deep and about 3 inches apart. Germination occurs within about 10 days at 70F (21C) soil temperature. Thin to 6 inches apart in rows 2 feet apart. Plants need plenty of moisture during dry spells. A mulch will help conserve moisture; black plastic works well. It helps to warm the soil early so seedlings will grow quickly.

Pole limas need more room, and vines tend to be heavier than snap pole beans. The most reliable way to

Cowpea bean 'Black-eyed Pea'. Note how the beans are beginning to swell the pod. These are too old for "snaps," but soon can be harvested as shelled beans.

Garbanzo beans spread without supports. These plants are in flower prior to forming pods, which will contain one or two plump, round beans.

'Fordhook 242' is the best bush-type lima bean. Pick limas when the pod wall is bulging. You can feel the beans by squeezing the pod.

Romano bean 'Bush Roma' is a productive variety with long, flat, flavorful pods.

Runner beans require poles for support. Note the beautiful scarlet blossoms.

Bean seeds can be decorative. This colorful assortment includes 'Kentucky Wonder'—beige, 'Pinto'—speckled, 'Black-eyed'—white, and 'Kidney'—brown.

Soy bean 'Fiskby V' ready for harvesting at the "green mature" stage. Left on the vine to dry, beans can be gathered and shelled for dry storage.

grow them is on tripods, allowing 6 plants to climb up each pole.

High-nitrogen fertilizers or too much manure can encourage limas to produce excessive leaf growth. They will then have a tendency to delay pod formation. Phosphorus should be added to soil to encourage pod formation.

Pest and disease control: Limas are easy to grow but are subject to several hazards. If a cold, wet spell follows planting, seeds will often rot in the ground before germinating. To avoid problems with rot, wait until soil has warmed before sowing seeds. Cutworms relish the tender young sprouts, and bean beetles can strip the leaves, inhibiting growth. Generally, pest control is the same as for snap beans. See page 89.

Harvesting and use: Don't be tempted to pick lima bean pods too soon. It takes time for beans to swell up inside the pod after the pod has reached full size. It is difficult to tell by looking. If you can pinch the sides flat, the beans are not developed. If the pod bulges and you can feel the beans, they are ready to pick. Harvest pods as soon as they reach this stage for best flavor. Pods are not edible and are tedious to open. Squeezing the edges between thumb and forefinger usually springs them open if they are mature.

Limas are best cooked fresh. Beans of bush varieties have a meaty flavor. They can be stored frozen or dried and served as butter beans.

Recommended varieties: Best of the bush limas is 'Fordhook 242' (75 days), an improved, disease-resistant strain of the famous 'Fordhook' lima. It produces light green beans. Best of the pole limas is 'Prizemaker' (90 days). It grows the largest pods—up to five, giant, flavorful beans per pod, ivory-white in color.

Romano or Italian Beans

These pole beans have broad, flat, juicy pods. They are among the most flavorful of the pole varieties. Romano beans serve as a hot-weather substitute for runner beans.

How to grow: Sow seeds directly in the garden after all danger of frost has passed. Plant seeds 1 inch deep, 4 to 6 inches between plants and 2 feet between rows. Provide pole types with strong supports. A nitrogen-rich soil is recommended.

Pest and disease control: Same as snap beans. Bean beetle is the most serious pest. Control with Sevin chemical insecticide or pyrethrum organic substitute.

Harvesting and use: Same as snap beans. Romanos are excellent for freezing.

Recommended varieties: Pole types are not sold by variety name, but several dwarf bush varieties are available. Best of these is 'Bush Roma' (50 days).

Runner Beans

In cool climates, runner bean is often considered "king of the garden." In warm-summer areas, time plantings to mature in fall to produce worthwhile crops. Cool nights improve the flavor of the long, green, flat pods.

Vines are vigorous and highly ornamental, producing beautiful scarlet flowers that are used to decorate fences, trellises and other supports. Vines need 65 days to flower and another 10 days to yield mature beans.

Flowers are highly attractive to hummingbirds. The long pods—12 to 16 inches in length—are edible like snap beans, and contain black or red beans.

How to grow: Because plants grow to 10 feet high, they should be grown up poles or trellises for support. Sow seeds directly in the garden after all danger of frost has passed. Plant seeds 1-1/2 inches deep, 6 inches apart around each pole, or in straight rows along a trellis. If grown in straight rows, plant 6 inches apart in double rows, 1 foot apart between each row and 5 feet between each set of double rows. Thin seedlings to 12 inches apart.

Plants are hardier than snap-bean plants. It is worth trying an outdoor planting three weeks before your last frost date. Provide protection against a severe frost by using plastic covers or hot-caps.

Growth must be timed so pods mature in *cool* weather. For this reason most home gardeners prefer to plant them in midsummer to mature in fall.

A soil rich in organic matter produces best results. Plants also benefit from applications of a general-purpose fertilizer.

Pest and disease control: Discourage bean beetle with applications of Sevin chemical insecticide or pyrethrum organic spray. Mosaic disease can be avoided by planting resistant varieties.

Harvesting and use: Pick pods when 12 to 16 inches long while they are still flat. Some varieties are stringless. Others have strings that should be pulled before cooking. Use as you would snap beans. Plant more than you can use fresh as they retain their flavor superbly when frozen.

Recommended varieties: American seed catalogs generally do not offer runner beans by variety name, although many distinct varieties are available. English catalogs available to United States gardeners include Thompson & Morgan. For their United States address, see Seed Catalogs, page 33. You will find extensive selections from these catalogs, including dwarf types and white-flowered varieties.

Shelling or Dry Beans

These are grown mostly for baking and soups. Pods are normally too fibrous to be tasty, although some are edible as "snaps" when young. Probably the most popular of these is 'French Horticultural' (75 days), growing 8-inch-long, cream-colored pods streaked with red. Pods contain delicious green beans good to eat fresh or dried for storage.

Other popular shelling beans include 'Pinto' (85 days), which produces meaty, speckled beans popular in Mexican cooking. 'Red Kidney' (95 days), produces shiny, mahogany-colored beans used in soups and three-bean salads.

How to grow: Some shelling beans are bush types and can be grown like bush snap beans. Most are pole beans, requiring strong supports. Plant seeds 1-1/2 inches deep, 6 inches apart around poles. Or plant in straight rows to grow up a trellis. Sow directly in the garden after all danger of frost has passed. Organically

rich soil high in nitrogen will produce the most abundant yields.

Pest and disease control: Prevent the bean beetle from becoming established among the foliage. Use Sevin chemical spray or pyrethrum organic spray. Check plants frequently—especially leaf undersides—for any sign of bean-beetle larvae. Remove as many as possible by hand.

Harvesting and use: The pods of shelling beans are not edible. Let the pods turn dry and brittle before harvest. Shell and allow beans to dry by spreading on screens. Store in cans or cloth bags in a dry cupboard.

For a culinary guide to dry beans, refer to *Bean Cookery* by Sue and Bill Deeming, published by HPBooks.

Recommended varieties: In addition to the preceding varieties, consider 'Black Turtle' (85 days), the main ingredient of Black Bean Soup, a popular dish in the South. Vermont Bean Seed Company is a good source for this and other hard-to-find bean varieties.

Edible Soy Beans

Edible soy beans originated in Asia, where they were grown extensively as a protein source in areas where meat is scarce. They were largely ignored as a garden vegetable in the United States until the introduction of 'Fiskby V', developed in Sweden in the 1970s by Sven Holmberg.

In addition to a protein content of 40%, 'Fiskby V' is rich in vitamins A, B1, B12 and C, and contains high levels of calcium and iron.

'Fiskby V' produces a protein-rich crop within 80 days of sowing seeds. It thrives even in poor soil and takes nitrogen from the air in addition to the soil, producing rich green beans on bushy plants. Fresh-cooked 'Fiskby V' has a flavor as sweet as any other garden bean, and can be dried and stored for use during winter.

How to grow: Plant seeds 1 inch deep directly in the garden after all danger of frost has passed. Germination takes about 10 days at a soil temperature of 70F (21C). Sow in single rows with 4 inches between plants and 2 feet between rows.

Pest and disease control: Same as snap beans. See page 89. Use Sevin as a general-purpose chemical control or use a rotenone-pyrethrum combination.

Harvesting and use: To shell beans, cook them in boiling water for 15 minutes. Once cool, shells will slip away from the seeds with ease. Even easier is to add salt to the water and serve them the Japanese way—in bowls as hot snacks. Just pick up a pod, hold it between thumb and forefinger and squirt the beans into your mouth—delicious.

Recommended varieties: Since 'Fiskby V' (90 days) was introduced, other good home-garden varieties have been developed. Try the early-maturing 'Frostbeater' (75 days), available from Burpee, and the delicious 'Butterpea' (90 days), available from Johnny's Selected Seeds.

Winged Beans

Winged bean is found in its native Asian habitat from sea level to 7,000-feet elevation. It appears to need short days to flower and set pods. It is totally edible—

All parts of winged bean are edible—pods, leaves, stems, flowers and tubers. It thrives in long growing seasons of the South, but has not been tested fully in other areas.

Yard-long bean 'Orient Express' grows on a trellis for support. Beans may grow up to 3 feet long, but have best flavor when harvested at 12 inches long.

leaves, seeds, flowers, shoots and tubers. Its nutritional value is astonishing. The roots, which swell to the size of potatoes, are rich in protein, unlike potatoes.

Winged bean has been hailed as a new wonder food, but its adaptability to all parts of the United States and Canada is not yet known. It has been grown successfully for pods in Florida, Hawaii, Louisiana, Alabama and Texas. It has also been grown in northern states for its edible leaves and stems, which some years produce pods but rarely tubers.

How to grow: In areas with long growing seasons—200 days or more—the winged bean can be sown directly in the garden. Plant seeds 1-1/2 inches deep, 6 inches apart around poles so it will climb. Allow 3 feet between rows. To encourage germination, file a notch in its hard shell. This allows moisture to penetrate. In some areas with snow cover in winter and a shorter growing season, seeds are best started indoors. Start seeds 4 to 6 weeks before planting outdoors. Transplant to the garden after all danger of frost has passed. Plants need a fertile soil, especially one that is rich in nitrogen.

Pest and disease control: Generally free of pests and disease. Shows resistance to bean beetles.

Harvesting and use: Leaves are eaten as a cooked green like spinach. Stems taste like asparagus. Steamed or boiled, pods have a mushroom flavor. Flowers and tubers have their own distinctive tastes.

Recommended varieties: Presently, no named varieties are available. Reliable sources for seeds are Gurney and Twilley.

Yard-long Beans

Sometimes called *asparagus bean,* this bean is a food staple in tropical regions of the Orient. Some seed catalogs feature them. Worthwhile yields are possible in areas with a long growing season and hot summers.

How to grow: Sow seeds directly in the garden after all danger of frost has passed. Plant seeds 1-1/2 inches deep. Beans must have sturdy supports to climb. Plant 6 inches apart around poles or in straight rows to climb up netting. In short-season areas, a few beans can be started 4 weeks before outdoor planting. Plant in soil rich in organic matter. Water regularly and supply with regular doses of nitrogen fertilizer for best results.

Pest and disease control: Plants are resistant to bean beetles and other chewing insects. Concentrate on combating slugs. Use slug bait in shallow pans so the poison does not wash into the soil.

Harvesting and use: Although yard-long beans are capable of growing up to 3 feet in length, they are best picked when 12 inches long and used as "snaps." Simply chop beans into usable sections and cook like snap beans. Flavor is like asparagus.

Recommended varieties: Normally not offered by variety name. Thompson & Morgan does feature a Japanese variety, 'Orient Express' (110 days), that is 10 to 14 days earlier than the standard variety.

Beet 'Pacemaker II' hybrid, grown from seed in 50 days.

'Golden Beet' has a flavor like a standard red beet.

Beets

If you want maximum flavor and tenderness, give beets *regular, uniform moisture*. At the slightest hint of a dry spell, beets tend to stop growing. Many plants may fail to form beets if moisture is deficient in the early stages.

Crowding can produce an unusual number of mis-shapen plants. Many home gardeners do not understand that a beet seed is actually a dried fruit cluster of *three* or *four* seeds held together. Commercial growers pay extra to have them separated for precision planting, but home gardeners usually have to contend with a packet containing the regular seed cluster. No matter how careful you are at planting beet seeds, you will always have several seedlings growing closely together. As soon as possible after germination, thin out these groups to prevent overcrowding and a poor crop. Beets should be thinned to about 3 inches apart.

How to grow: Sow seeds directly in the garden in a fertile, sandy soil rich in organic matter. Ideal soil pH is 6.5. Seeds can be sown outside several weeks before the last expected frost in your area. Young seedlings will tolerate mild frosts. Plant seeds 1/4 inch deep in rows spaced 1 foot apart. Seeds germinate in 17 days at 50F (10C) soil temperature; 6 days at 68F (20C).

Pest and disease control: Rabbits and groundhogs love beet tops. Keep these pests out with an animal fence. Flea beetles and aphids can attack foliage. Control by blasting them with a water hose. Or use Sevin, a chemical spray, or dust with rotenone, an organic pesticide.

Harvesting and use: Beets will grow to the size of a baseball, but they are best harvested the size of a golf-ball. To store, cut off tops and cover beets with moist sand in a cool, humid basement at 32F (0C). They can be stored safely this way for up to 6 months. Beets are delicious canned and pickled. To prepare fresh beets, cut off top and taproot flush with the beet. Peel and cook whole in boiling water 30 to 40 minutes, or until tender. Slice into quarters for faster cooking.

Recommended varieties: Standard varieties such as 'Early Wonder' (55 days) and 'Ruby Queen' (54 days) are good performers, but you should try hybrid beets. You will be amazed how fast they germinate from seed and how soon they produce a crop. Flavor is superior—more moist and more sweet than standard beets due to their sugar-beet parentage. At present the only hybrid beets are red beets. The best is a variety called 'Pacemaker II' (50 days), developed by Dr. Warren Gabelman of the University of Wisconsin.

In addition to popular red beets, there is a golden yellow variety called 'Golden Beet' (55 days) and 'Burpee White' (60 days), a white variety. There is an unusual, elongated beet called 'Cylindra' (55 days). These beets have a flavor similar to standard beets, though not as good as a hybrid. You may also find the 'Golden Beet' weak in germinating. In other respects 'Golden Beet' is highly desirable. It does not "bleed" like a red beet, and the beautiful blue-green tops are delicious to eat like spinach. Among red beets, 'Lutz Green Leaf' (80 days) is best for edible tops.

'Pacemaker II' hybrid grows uniform, well-developed roots in spite of crowding.

Broccoli 'Premium Crop' hybrid.

Broccoli

This relative of cabbage originated in Europe. There are basically two types available to the home gardener—*heading broccoli* and *sprouting broccoli*. Heading types grow one, extra-large, terminal *head*, the edible part of the plant. The head is made up of hundreds of tiny flower buds tightly packed together to form a solid clump. After the head is cut it sends out smaller side heads. Sprouting broccoli differs in that it immediately sends up numerous small heads, which are replaced by more heads when the first are cut. Of the two, sprouting broccoli is hardier to cold.

How to grow: Broccoli is one of the easiest members of the cabbage family to grow. It needs cool conditions so plant it as an early spring crop. Or time plantings to mature in fall when cool nights favor proper development of heads. In desert and hot inland areas, it is grown as a fall crop. Summer plantings are not advised. Hot weather forces broccoli to quickly *bolt to seed*. This means the head doesn't form a tight bud cluster, but breaks apart and sends up a long flower stalk to produce seed.

It is usually better to start seeds indoors and transplant seedlings to the garden. Seeds require soil temperature of 70F (21C) or more to germinate. Plants tolerate mild frosts.

Broccoli prefers a firm soil. In sandy soils the heads will not form properly. Plant seeds 1/4 inch deep in single rows 2 feet apart with 1-1/2 feet between plants. Or start seeds in individual peat pellets or peat pots 5 to 7 weeks before young plants are to be set out. Plants should be about 6 inches high when they are transplanted. For fall harvests, plant 6 weeks before the onset of cool nights.

Broccoli is considered easier to grow than cauliflower. It seems to tolerate hot weather better, and the heads are not as susceptible to spoilage from adverse weather conditions.

Pest and disease control: If possible, do not plant broccoli in the same location twice or where cabbage, cauliflower or brussels sprouts grew the year before. By changing or rotating the planting site each season, you can usually avoid problems with soil-borne diseases.

Insect control is vital. Broccoli is a haven for all kinds of insect pests. Chief pests include slugs, cutworms, cabbage looper, cabbage root maggot, imported cabbage worm, aphids and flea beetles. Diseases include blackleg, black rot, club root and yellows.

It is impossible to safeguard your crop against every possible kind of insect and disease, but most damage can be prevented. Use paper or metal collars to prevent cutworm damage. Apply a safe vegetable dust such as a combination of rotenone and pyrethrum. Use Dipel or Thuricide organic products to keep caterpillars such as the cabbage worm under control.

Harvesting and use: Cut stems 5 to 6 inches below the base of the head. The tender stalks immediately below the head are edible, but once a head has formed, it must be picked quickly. Left even a few days past maturity, the buds will start to flower and show yellow. The texture changes from a tight, crisp formation to one that is loose and "ricey."

Wash stems well before eating. In spite of insect control, green worms sometimes hide among the stalks and are hard to see. Soaking heads in salt water for a few minutes usually dislodges them.

Broccoli is delicious raw in dips or freshly cooked as a vegetable side dish. Slice stems into small sections about 2 inches across for dips or to fit them into freezer bags. Broccoli freezes well.

Recommended varieties: Nothing is more important to the success of growing broccoli than choosing the right variety. For years 'Green Comet' has been the most popular among experienced gardeners. It produces the earliest heads—within 55 days of transplanting. All-America Award-winner 'Premium Crop' is only three days later in maturing and far superior in

Harvest broccoli as soon as it forms a head, or the bud clusters will open to produce flowers.

quality to 'Green Comet'. Individual heads of 'Premium Crop' grow up to 10 inches across and last longer than other varieties. Bud clusters are exceptionally tight, so heads have better flavor and texture than other kinds. Plants are uniform in habit and maturity. They produce handsome, blue-green heads that stand well above the foliage to make harvesting easy. Both 'Green Comet' and 'Premium Crop' are hybrids. Heads mature all at one time. For a high-quality, non-hybrid with variable maturity dates, grow 'Green Goliath' (55 days).

QUESTIONS ABOUT BROCCOLI

What is 'Romanesco' broccoli and can it be grown in the United States and Canada?

For generations, gardeners in northern Italy have been growing 'Romanesco' broccoli. It is unlike regular broccoli, forming highly decorative, light green clusters of heads that resemble sea coral. 'Romanesco' can be grown in many parts of the United States and Canada. It needs 85 days to reach maturity and must have cool weather when heads develop. For this reason it is best as a fall crop. Seed is available from Thompson & Morgan.

Japanese cooking features a broccoli that resembles an asparagus spear and tastes delicious. Is this a variety I could grow?

'Green Lance' broccoli (50 days) is an Oriental delicacy. It is very easy to grow and matures fast if allowed to develop during cool weather. It doesn't form a head like other broccoli, but has a main stem with a loose, tender tip that is delicious. The rest of the stalk, when peeled, can be eaten raw or cooked like asparagus. Seed is available from Stokes Seed under the generic name, Chinese broccoli.

Broccoli 'Green Lance' is an Oriental variety grown for its succulent, green tips and stems.

Brussels sprouts 'Jade Cross' hybrid.

Brussels Sprouts

Brussels sprouts are named for the capital of Belgium, where the plant first became popular after being developed from cabbage. Plants grow as a tall, slender stem, studded with miniature cabbage heads called *sprouts*.

Brussels sprouts require a longer growing season than other members of the cabbage family. In most of the United States they are successful only as fall vegetables. For a successful harvest you should transplant young seedlings to the garden in early summer. Plants make vegetative growth during the hot summer months then develop sprouts as cool conditions set in.

Plants like firm soil as opposed to sandy soil, and liberal quantities of compost or stable manure. If these are not available, apply a side dressing of high nitrogen fertilizer after plants are established. Pay close attention to water needs during dry periods. Moisture is responsible for firm development of the sprouts.

Brussels sprouts are perfect to plant in place of peas, lettuce or spinach after they have been harvested. These crops have usually ceased production by early summer, when they can be cleared from the garden.

How to grow: Start seeds 5 to 7 weeks before transplant time. Plant 1/4 inch deep in individual peat pots indoors. Germination takes 10 days at 70F (21C) soil temperature. Plants can be set in the garden 3 weeks before your last spring frost date or in midsummer. Set in the garden in rows spaced 2 feet apart with 2 feet between plants. Avoid planting where any member of the cabbage family was grown the previous year. Plants are subject to serious attacks from insects and diseases. Pests or diseases attracted to the first-year crop will usually destroy next year's crop. Control pests and diseases *early in the season*.

Pest and disease control: Rotenone is an organic insecticide used to combat a wide range of destructive chewing insects, but it is more effective when used in combination with pyrethrum. Sevin, a chemical spray, is also effective against the majority of insect pests.

Use Dipel or Thuricide organic products to keep caterpillars such as the cabbage worm under control.

Transplants can be protected from the cutworm and root maggot by using protective paper or metal collars fitted around the stems.

Harvesting and use: Pick sprouts when the lowest buds are the size of a golf ball or slightly smaller. Lowest sprouts on a plant develop first. If leaves between the lower sprouts are removed, sprouts will develop all along the stem. To speed up sprout development at top of the stem, pinch out growing tip. This stops further leaf growth and directs the plant's energy into enlarging the sprouts. Sprouts mature over a long period and are hardy enough that they can be left on the plant until the ground freezes. In fact, flavor is improved after a frost.

Brussels sprouts are excellent cooked fresh as a vegetable side dish, or used in soups or stews. They also freeze well.

Recommended varieties: Choice of variety is important. 'Jade Cross' (90 days) is the earliest and most productive. Sprouts will form at least 10 to 14 days ahead of standard varieties and are more tolerant of high temperatures. Yields can be three times more per plant than traditional varieties. A new variety called 'Cabbage Sprout' (100 days) is available through Thompson & Morgan. Although 10 days later than 'Jade Cross', it is equally productive and forms a small head of cabbage at the top. Other brussels sprouts form a loose crown of leaves.

Row of brussels sprouts 'Jade Cross' hybrid, showing proper spacing in fertile soil.

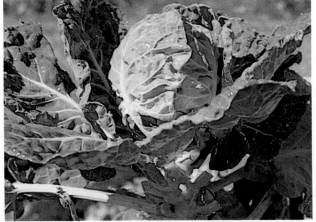
'Cabbage Sprout' produces brussels sprouts along the main stem *and* a small cabbage on top.

Edible burdock requires a lot of room.

Edible Burdock

Although burdock is regarded as a noxious weed in many areas, cultivated kinds have been grown in Japan for their large, slender roots, known as *gobo*. Roots have brown skins and grow up to 2 feet long.

How to grow: To grow the best-quality roots, plant in a deep, loose soil. Seeds can be sown directly in the garden in early spring, several weeks before frost. Plant seeds 1/4 inch deep, 2 feet between plants. Space rows 3 feet apart. In fertile soil, plants will grow as large as a healthy clump of rhubarb in one season.

Pest and disease control: Burdock survives like a persistent weed. Pest problems are few but sometimes wireworms and other soil pests tunnel into roots. Best control is to mix diazinon chemical insecticide into soil at time of planting.

Harvesting and use: Roots can be dug in the fall of the first year. Cut flowerheads before they have a chance to bloom. They self-sow readily and become invasive.

Roots for storage should be dug before the ground freezes. Cut stems flush with the root. Set the roots into boxes and cover with moist sand. Keep in a cool, dark place such as a root cellar or basement until needed. Tender, white flesh of roots is mild flavored when cooked.

Recommended varieties: 'Takinogawa Long' matures in 120 days from seed and achieves the best size among available Japanese varieties. It is offered by Johnny's Selected Seeds.

Roots of edible burdock can be harvested in the fall of the first year.

'Earliana' is the earliest of the spring cabbages.

Cabbage

Cabbage originated along coastal areas of western Europe. Wild varieties can still be found today in areas of England, France and other regions. They are cool-season vegetables and will split apart in hot weather. In recent years the Japanese have achieved considerable success in developing hybrids that will hold their heads a long time during summer heat.

As little as 50 years ago there was no such vegetable as a red cabbage. Other changes and improvements that are not so easy to recognize have been made. Disease resistance, especially to cabbage yellows, has been bred into some of the modern hybrids. Varieties have been developed that mature early, or are resistant to splitting during hot weather.

Cabbages are available in many colors and kinds. Brussels sprouts developed from cabbage. In fact, researchers have started to breed varieties of brussels sprouts that will produce cabbage heads in addition to sprouts along stems. See 'Cabbage Sprout', page 98.

Most popular among home gardeners is green cabbage, used mostly for boiled greens and sauerkraut. Red cabbage is best for pickling, although it also makes a delicious side dish. Savoy cabbage has decorative appeal. It is named for its wavy leaf edges and blistered leaf surfaces. It has a reputation for having the best flavor, with a tasty, buttery yellow interior.

How to grow: Even though cabbage is a cool-season crop, seeds will not germinate at low temperatures. It is best to start seeds indoors at a soil temperature of 70F (21C). Sow 1/4 inch deep in peat pots or peat pellets. Transplant seedlings to the garden several weeks before the last frost date. Seedlings will tolerate mild frosts if hardened off. Fluid seed sowing, page 38, is another way to start cabbage. It allows pregerminated seeds to be sown directly in the garden. Space plants 1 foot apart for small varieties, 2 feet apart for large varieties. Allow 2 to 3 feet between rows.

Cabbage prefers soil high in organic matter such as garden compost, decomposed animal manure and leaf mold. A general-purpose fertilizer worked into the soil ahead of planting is also beneficial.

Pest and disease control: Some control is vital for handsome heads of cabbage. Many gardeners dislike the idea of dust or spray getting into the cabbage head. If you choose to suffer with the insects—which usually chew the outer leaves first—hand pick them whenever possible.

The biggest problems right after planting are cutworms and slugs. To deter cutworms, fit cutworm collars around transplants. See page 63. To control slugs, lay slug pellets on dishes around cabbage, or spread out large amounts of wood ashes.

Another pest is the cabbage worm, a destructive caterpillar that chews on leaves and heads. They can be picked off by hand or blasted with a garden hose. Dipel and Thuricide are organic controls that transmit a disease lethal only to caterpillars.

Root maggots are the most difficult pests to control organically. The best remedy is to plant cabbage through black plastic mulch and fit a stiff, cardboard collar around the planting hole. This way the fly cannot enter the soil around plants to lay her eggs.

Broad-spectrum chemicals like Sevin and malathion are widely used by commercial growers and are effective against most cabbage pests. In extreme cases of root maggots, diazinon is used. Some of the milder organic sprays or dusts such as rotenone and pyrethrum offer good control, especially when used in combination. Cabbage diseases include black rot, black leg, club root and yellows. In areas where these diseases are prevalent, your best control is to plant disease-resistant varieties.

Harvesting and use: Begin picking when heads become solid. Plantings should be timed so that the

Cabbage 'Savoy King' hybrid grows enormous heads that are buttery yellow inside.

heads mature in cool weather. For example, early spring sowing will grow heads by early summer. Mid-summer planting will allow heads to form during cool fall weather. In some areas the midsummer planting is more successful than spring planting. Cabbage stores well for long periods in a refrigerator vegetable bin. It can also be stored frozen as coleslaw.

Recommended varieties: It doesn't pay to buy nonhybrid varieties—they split apart too quickly. Hybrids hold their solid form much longer. Of the hybrids, one of the best is 'Stonehead' (70 days) developed in Japan by T. Sakata. It won an All-America Award for its earliness, compact, solid heads and resistance to cabbage yellows disease. Heads measure 6 inches in diameter and require only 1 foot of space between plants. This means you can obtain more heads per row than with other standard cabbage varieties. The firm interior gives it longer storage capability.

Red variety 'Ruby Ball' hybrid (68 days) will stay in the garden at least a month without bursting, even during hot weather. It is also an All-America Award winner.

Savoy types include 'Savoy Ace' (75 days) or 'Savoy King' (85 days). Both are quality cabbages and both have won All-America Awards. Given a choice, 'Savoy Ace' is the better cabbage. Both are highly resistant to insect damage. For more information, see Inside Report at right.

Other good hybrids to consider are 'Emerald Cross' (63 days) and 'King Cole' (73 days). These varieties are widely available from major mail order seed catalogs.

Cabbage Crops

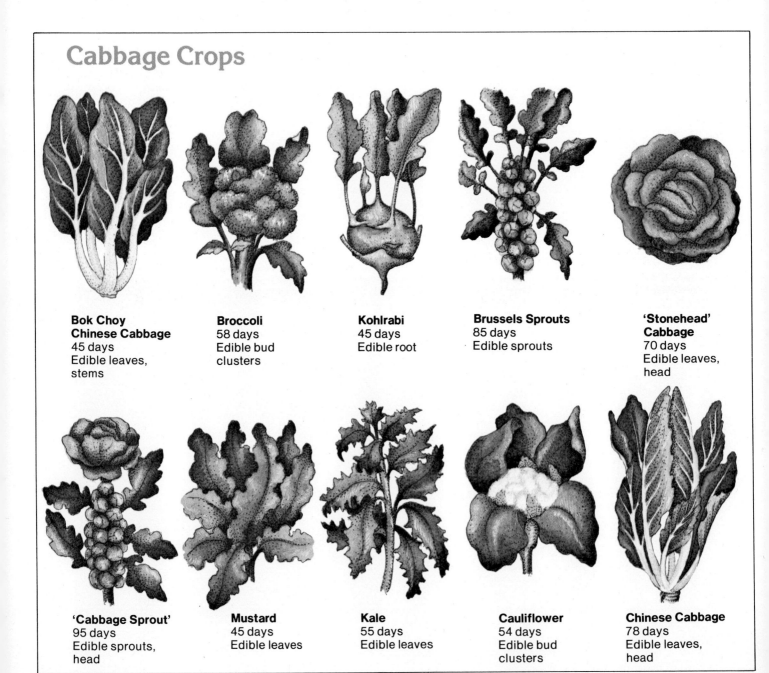

Bok Choy Chinese Cabbage
45 days
Edible leaves, stems

Broccoli
58 days
Edible bud clusters

Kohlrabi
45 days
Edible root

Brussels Sprouts
85 days
Edible sprouts

'Stonehead' Cabbage
70 days
Edible leaves, head

'Cabbage Sprout'
95 days
Edible sprouts, head

Mustard
45 days
Edible leaves

Kale
55 days
Edible leaves

Cauliflower
54 days
Edible bud clusters

Chinese Cabbage
78 days
Edible leaves, head

'Ruby Ball' hybrid, another All-America Award winner, can hold its shape for a month without bursting.

'Savoy Ace' hybrid won an All-America Award for its earliness and ability to stay firm a month or more before bursting.

Wide row planting is a good way to grow cabbages. Row is neat, easy to care for and accessible.

'Jade Pagoda' hybrid is the earliest heading variety of Chinese cabbage.

Pak Choy

This fast-maturing, nonheading variety of Chinese cabbage is grown in the Orient as fresh greens.

How to grow: Because plants tolerate crowding, they are generally grown in short, wide rows about 5 feet apart. Sow seeds 1/4 inch deep directly in the garden. Thin each plant to stand 2 inches apart. Space rows 12 inches apart. Make first sowings 3 weeks before your last frost date and continue until night temperatures exceed 70F (21C). Successive sowings should be made at 2-week intervals to ensure a continuous supply. Pak choy tolerates poor soil, but needs a continuous supply of moisture to ensure rapid growth during cool weather. Also grows well as a fall crop.

Pest and disease control: Flea beetles are the plant's worst enemy. Control with Sevin chemical spray or rotenone organic insecticide.

Harvesting and use: Harvesting can begin within 20 days of sowing seeds, and continue until the plant produces a flowerhead. Tip of the flowerstalk is tender and delicious until the buds open and display yellow flowers similar to broccoli. Cook by boiling or stir-fry.

Chinese Cabbage

Two kinds of Chinese cabbage are popular in home gardens—*heading* and *nonheading*. Heading kinds are oval shaped, with light green, crinkled leaves that are yellow inside. Heads mature within 70 days after sowing seeds under cool conditions. They usually do best as a fall crop, transplanted to the garden in midsummer.

Nonheading kinds are sometimes called *bok choy* or *pai tsai*. They are loose-leafed and much easier to grow than heading types. Leaves are dark green and have thick, succulent, white stems. Plants mature in only 45 days after sowing seeds. They can be grown as a spring or fall crop.

How to grow: Chinese cabbage will tolerate mild frosts and can be sown directly in the garden several weeks before the last frost date. It is better to sow seeds in peat pots or peat pellets for transplanting. Plant seeds 1/4 inch deep. Bok choy plants can be set into single rows or block planted in wide, raised beds, spaced at least 1 foot apart with 2 feet between rows. Space heading types 1-1/2 to 2 feet apart. Light soils enriched with garden compost or well-decomposed animal manure are best.

Pest and disease control: Similar to regular cabbage. See page 99.

Harvesting and use: Bok choy can be picked as soon as leaves and stems are large enough. Stems can be harvested from several plants, or an entire plant can be picked at one time. Heading Chinese cabbage is harvested as a whole plant. Use the same as regular spring cabbage.

Recommended varieties: Among heading varieties, try 'Jade Pagoda' hybrid (60 days). It is the earliest, largest, most heat-resistant variety. Handsomely savoyed leaves are highly ornamental. George W. Park is a source for seed. 'Crispy Choy' is the earliest of the nonheading varieties. It matures in 45 days, growing crisp, succulent, snow-white stalks edible raw or cooked. Burpee is a source for seed.

Chinese cabbage bok choy shows its crisp, succulent, white leaf stalks. These plants were ready to harvest in 45 days from sowing seeds.

Pak choy is a nonheading type of Chinese cabbage. If allowed to grow quickly during periods of cool weather, it produces tips that are delicous to eat as greens.

'Burpee Hybrid' cantaloupe is the most popular home garden melon.

Cantaloupe

Another name for cantaloupe is muskmelon, although purists will point out there is a botanical difference between the two. Cantaloupe belongs to the subspecies *cantalupensis*. It was named after the town of Cantalupo in Italy, where a particularly fine variety was cultivated. Fruit are mostly round, fragrant and have orange flesh. They stay connected to the vine when ripe. True muskmelons belong to the subspecies *reticulatus*. Their most distinctive feature is the prominent netting over the skin surface. Flesh is salmon or green with a musky fragrance. Fruit slips from the vine when ripe.

Honeydews, casabas and crenshaws are generally listed with cantaloupe because their cultural needs are similar. But they belong to the subspecies *inodorus*—meaning they lack fragrance. Plant breeders have created numerous hybrids between the three groups. This helps explain why seed catalog houses—for the sake of simplicity—group them all together. Most originate from Persia.

The most important requirement for quality cantaloupe is a warm, open, sunny location, free from any shade. Vines need to grow rapidly to ripen fruit to perfection. They will stop growing whenever the temperature falls below 70F (21C). Using black plastic as a mulch is highly beneficial. It helps to raise soil temperature early, maintains high temperatures at night and conserves moisture by reducing evaporation.

Melon vines produce male and female flowers. Fruit set occurs when female flowers are pollinated, mostly by bees. Most melon vines are *male dominant*, meaning they produce more males than females. Male flowers normally appear first, so patience is sometimes needed for fruit to set.

How to grow: Seeds are large and easy to handle. They can be sown directly in the garden after all danger of frost has passed. Or plants can be started indoors 4 to 6 weeks earlier, then hardened off and transplanted. Transplanting indoor-started seedlings rather than direct seeding is an advantage. Getting vines off to an early start helps them resist disease. Diseases generally appear at the onset of hot, humid weather. The stronger the vine by the time excessive heat and humidity occur, the better it is able to resist disease.

To plant, scoop a shallow saucer-shaped depression 1/2 inch deep in the soil and place several seeds around the edge. Mound with soil, creating a "hill." Space hills 4 feet apart with 6 feet between rows, thinning out the seedlings in each hill to leave 2 to 3 healthy vines. Seed germinates in 5 to 10 days at 70F to 80F (21C to 27C) soil temperature.

Soil should be fertile but not highly acid. Somewhat sandy soil is preferred, with plenty of organic matter included to retain moisture.

Melons need regular amounts of moisture because intake of moisture is what increases the size of fruit. An overabundance of moisture may cause cracking and rotting of fruit. When combined with cloudy conditions at time of ripening, overwatering can also cause poor flavor. Other factors that contribute to poor flavor are prolonged cold spells, foliage disease such as powdery mildew, and poor soil fertility.

Melons are sensitive to cold, suffering shock and setback below 50F (10C). Protect individual plants with *hot caps* until they are established. Hot caps are white plastic cones available at garden centers. You can make your own from plastic gallon milk cartons by simply cutting out the bottom with scissors.

To save space, cantaloupe may be grown up a trellis or fence. Support fruit with slings made from cloth or nylon pantyhose.

Pest and disease control: The most destructive insect is the cucumber beetle. It weakens the plant by eating stems and leaves. It also introduces wilt diseases, fatal to melons. The best method of control is to dust young seedlings with a safe vegetable dust as soon as they emerge from the soil, or when you transplant them to the garden. Rotenone, an organic insecticide, methyoxychlor and Sevin are three sprays used to combat cucumber beetle. These will also help control the vine borer, which eats its way up the middle of the

'Sweet 'n Early' hybrid cantaloupe is growing over black plastic mulch. Vines are just beginning to form fruit.

vine. If a vine suddenly wilts, look for a small hole with a pile of debris resembling sawdust near the base of the vine. This indicates where the borer has entered. Slit open the vine just above this hole and probe for the borer with a wire. After you have found the invader and disposed of it, close the wound on the stem. Hold it in place with twist-tie, if necessary. The wound will sometimes heal, and the plant may recover to produce fruit.

Three diseases are killers of melon plants: bacterial wilt, downy mildew and mosaic. Controlling cucumber beetle will help prevent bacterial wilt. Dusting with a garden fungicide will control downy mildew and other diseases. Certain varieties of melon have resistance to one or more diseases. Controlling aphids also helps reduce the risk of infection.

Harvesting and use: Melons should be picked at peak ripeness to ensure full-flavored, firm, sweet, juicy fruit. Different varieties show ripeness in different ways. A netted cantaloupe will have prominent ribs with heavy netting between the raised sections. A sign of perfect ripeness is when ribs remain green but netting turns a beige color. Another test for ripeness is to press lightly on the blossom end. If it gives a little, the melon should be ripe. Crenshaw melons show they are ripe by turning from dark green to bright yellow. Honeydew melons are ripe when they are silvery green with a flush of yellow. You can also lift the melon to your nose and smell the ripeness.

Recommended varieties: The most popular cantaloupe is 'Burpee Hybrid' (82 days). It produces large, handsome fruit weighing up to 6 pounds each, with prominent ribs and heavy netting. Flesh is deep orange, with small seed cavities. Flavor is absolutely delicious. 'Gold Star' (82 days), which closely resembles 'Burpee Hybrid', is also widely grown, and was developed by Joseph Harris Seed Company. Other fine varieties include 'Ambrosia' (86 days) 'Harper Hybrid' (74 days) and 'Sweet'n Early' (75 days).

Casaba

Casabas are large, pear-shaped fruit with ridges running along the length of the melon. They turn golden yellow at maturity. Flesh is white and delicately sweet. They need long, hot, dry climates in order to ripen to perfection. Arizona and southern California are the major production areas. An excellent variety is 'Golden Beauty' (120 days).

Crenshaw

Crenshaw is so highly regarded as a dessert melon that patrons of fancy restaurants pay over $2.50 a slice to savor its sweet, juicy flavor. Most varieties can be grown only in areas of the South and southern California. 'Early Hybrid Crenshaw' (90 days), is an exception. Generally, it will succeed wherever cantaloupe can be grown. Fruit are flavorful and weigh up to 20 pounds each. Skin is golden yellow when ripe and flesh is salmon-pink. Burpee is the originator and a source for this melon.

Honeydew

Most honeydew melons mature too late for northern states, but in recent years some early hybrids have become available. 'Earlidew' (75 days) is regarded as the earliest, green-fleshed honeydew type, offering high juice and sugar content.

Honeyloupe

The University of California at Davis has developed a cross between a cantaloupe and a honeydew melon, called a 'Honeyloupe' (86 days). It has the appearance of a honeydew but with white skin. Flesh is orange like a cantaloupe and has a delicious flavor. It requires about 90 days to reach maturity, and should succeed wherever cantaloupe can be grown.

Culture for casaba, crenshaw, honeydew and honeyloupe is identical to cantaloupe, except a longer growing season is generally needed to ripen the fruit.

Crenshaw melon 'Early Hybrid' generally succeeds wherever cantaloupe can be grown. Skin changes from green to yellow when ripe. Fruit weigh up to 9 pounds.

Honeydew melons are exceptionally sweet. Early maturing varieties such as 'Earlidew', above, can be grown in northern states.

HOW TO GROW MELONS IN CLAY SOIL

Sandy soil high in organic content is important to good melon crops. It's worth digging a special bed if your soil is mostly clay. Here's how:

1. Dig a hole about 1 foot deep and 3 feet in diameter. In center of hole dig a second hole 1 foot wide by 2 feet deep.

2. Fill smaller hole with soil amendment such as leaf mold or coarse garden compost. Tamp down firmly. This smaller hole will act as a water reservoir, and the coarse organic material will draw moisture up to plants.

3. Fill larger hole with two parts sand, one part decomposed manure or garden compost and one part garden topsoil. Create a mound so that the center is about 6 inches above soil level. Several days before planting, soak the hill thoroughly. Plant seeds or transplants when soil surface is dry enough to work. Allow three melon vines to grow from the hill.

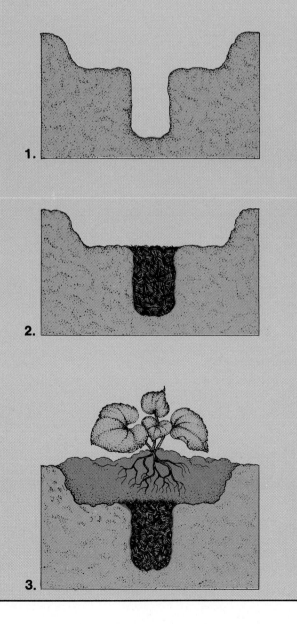

Cardoon is grown mostly for its edible leaf stalks.

Cardoon

Resembling a gigantic thistle, this tall-growing relative of artichoke requires so much room it is rarely grown in vegetable gardens. One plant can make a decorative highlight in a perennial border or against a building. Deeply serrated leaves are attractive, silvery gray. Large numbers of reddish, thistlelike flowers are also produced, often used in indoor arrangements.

As a vegetable, this Mediterranean native is grown mostly for its edible leaf stalks, which are used to flavor soups and stews. Cardoon is grown commercially in California, and can sometimes be found in Italian markets.

How to grow: Start seeds indoors 10 weeks before last frost in spring. Plant seeds 1/4 inch deep in peat pots or peat pellets. Space plants 3 to 4 feet apart. Long taproot requires a deep, fertile soil. Keep well irrigated during dry spells.

In areas free from winter freezing, cardoon can be grown as a perennial, coming up year after year. In northern states and high-altitude areas with severe winters, it is best grown as an annual for fall harvesting.

Pest and disease control: Aphids may congregate along young stems and infest developing flower buds. Dislodge them with strong jets of water from a hose. Slugs and snails are attracted to young plants. Control by putting slug bait in shallow pans so the poison does not wash into soil.

Harvesting and use: When plants are 3 feet high, arrange stalks so they are upright, and secure at top with a rubber band. Blanch stems by wrapping them in brown paper or burlap. This blanching takes about four weeks and improves the flavor, reducing fibrous quality of stalks. Plants are then cut at the soil line, and tops are trimmed off above the blanched area. This leaves a creamy white heart of stalks that resembles a large head of celery. Stalks can then be cut into sections and parboiled for 1-1/2 hours to reduce bitterness and render them tender.

'Short 'n Sweet' carrot grows well in clay or shallow soil.

Carrots

Wild species of carrots are widely distributed throughout Europe and have been cultivated for thousands of years in European gardens. But it wasn't until the French took an interest in carrot breeding that the vegetable lost many of its undesirable wild characteristics—thick, woody central core and pale color. The French seed house of Vilmorin made the most dramatic changes in carrot quality. This is why many good modern varieties such as 'Royal Chantenay', 'Danvers' and 'Nantes' have French names.

Today, American hybrids have begun to match and in some instances surpass the French varieties in quality and garden performance. 'Spartan Bonus' and 'Spartan Valor', developed by Michigan State University, are widely regarded as superior varieties. They color earlier, possess greater nutritional value and are more uniform in size and shape, with smaller central cores than the traditional French varieties.

Carrots have a particular nomenclature that is useful to understand.

Danvers carrots are long with a broad neck and a tapering root.

Nantes carrots are "stump rooted," meaning they are slender in shape and have rounded ends.

Chantenay carrots are medium size—broad at the top with a tapering shape, but ending in a stump-root.

There are other carrot varieties—particularly novelty carrots and extra-long varieties. Some look like beets, with round, ball-shaped roots. Others are shaped like long icicles, growing tapering roots up to 1 foot in length. This variation in size and shape allows you to pick a variety suited to your soil condition. For shallow, dense soils, short-rooted carrots are sensible choices. Deeper, sandy soils allow the long, tapering kinds to grow to perfection.

How to grow: Carrot seeds are tiny, and must be sown directly in the garden, with just enough soil covering to anchor the seeds. Care should also be taken not to cover with soil that will form a crust. Carrot seedlings are very weak, and the slightest crusting will impair their growth. Covering the seeds with silica sand to give them good soil contact is helpful. Germination takes 6 to 14 days at 60F (16C) soil temperature. Because carrots are hardy and tolerate mild frosts, seeds can be sown in the garden several weeks before the last frost date if the soil is sufficiently warm.

Having a well-prepared soil is important for quality crops. One way is to create a raised bed from sifted or improved topsoil. Carrots dislike dense, clay soils and prefer sandy soils. Organic matter is beneficial when added to soil but it must be well decomposed. Any coarse organic material such as fresh manure or rough garden compost can cause young carrot seedlings to fork and produce misshapen roots. Misshapen roots can also be caused by inadequate moisture at time of germination. Give carrots the best start by planting in well-prepared soil free of rocks and debris. Also supply with plenty of moisture so the taproot can grow long and straight as quickly as possible.

Thinning is best done in several stages. Sowing carrots thickly helps produce a healthy stand with no gaps. But as soon as the carrots are up begin to thin rigorously. Continue at weekly intervals until you have a solid line of carrots spaced 1-1/2 inches apart. It's also possible to sow carrots in matted rows, in raised planting blocks and interplanted among leaf crops such as parsley and lettuce.

Pest and disease control: In areas where they are a pest, carrot flies lay eggs around the roots of carrots. Maggots hatch from the eggs and burrow into the carrots. Diazinon applied to the soil in early spring will control carrot flies. Organic gardeners report a measure of control with wood ashes sprinkled over the soil, or garlic concentrate sprayed over seedlings. Nematodes can also be a problem, especially in sandy soils. Their control is best left to a professional. See page 65.

Harvesting and use: Carrots plucked fresh from the garden are much sweeter than those bought at the market, which lose flavor quickly once they have been harvested. Begin as soon as carrot roots have "sized-up" and "colored-up." Don't go by size of leaves. Carrots can create a lot of leafy growth without producing a sizeable root. Dig back soil around carrot top to see if it is big enough. Do not pull carrots out by their foliage stalks. They are brittle and will break away, leaving the carrot in the soil. Or, the carrot root itself may break. Instead, dig a garden fork or trowel into soil around carrots and gently ease them out.

To store carrots, brush off soil and trim leaves where they join the root. Place in moist sawdust or moist sand in boxes in a cool basement or root cellar. Carrots will remain in good condition for up to 6 months at temperatures of 32F to 40F (0C to 5C). Young carrots picked just before reaching maturity are also excellent for canning, and freeze well.

Carrots have long been popular in the health food movement for their high nutritional value and for the variety of ways they can be enjoyed. They are great to eat raw as carrot sticks and shredded as a garnish on salads. Or you can cook them whole, diced or sliced. Grated into small pieces, carrots are used as a flavoring for breads and cakes. Carrot juice and carrot jam are additional uses.

Recommended varieties: Carrots are most appealing

and have the best flavor when they exhibit deep orange coloring and small central cores. A good variety for clay soil is 'Short 'n Sweet' (68 days). It grows 3 to 4 inches long. A good early variety is 'Little Finger' (65 days). Roots are 3-1/2 inches long with smooth skins, small cores and extra sweet flavor when young. This is the variety to grow for gourmet flavor. Both varieties are offered by Burpee.

If your soil can accommodate a larger, long-rooted carrot, try 'Spartan Bonus' hybrid (75 days). In addition to being early for such a large carrot, it has deep orange color, an indication of high nutritional value. It also has a crisp, delicious texture.

For the longest roots of all, up to 9 inches, choose 'Trophy' hybrid from Joseph Harris. Maturing in 78 days, it is sweet and delicious with a brittle texture. The root itself is smooth, deep orange and elegantly tapered.

'Danvers' (75 days), 'Nantes' (70 days), 'Gold Pak' (76 days) and 'Royal Chantenay' (70 days) are old standards that produce quality crops.

'Royal Chantenay', a broad-shouldered, tapered carrot, will grow in average garden soil.

'Gold Pak', a long, narrow, tapering carrot, requires deep, sandy soil to grow to perfection.

'Purple Headed' does not require blanching like white cauliflower.

Cauliflower

Cauliflower is similar to broccoli in many respects. It is a cool-weather crop, grown for large, edible heads known as *curds*. These curds consist of tightly clustered, white, green or purple flower buds. They are more temperamental than broccoli in holding their tight shape. Poor soil and unfavorable weather quickly cause them to go to seed or discolor.

How to grow: Cauliflower seeds can be sown directly in the garden. Better results are obtained by starting seeds indoors 8 weeks before setting outside. Transplant seedlings when about 6 inches high, up to 4 weeks before the last frost date. Seedlings will tolerate mild frosts when adequately hardened off. Space plants 1-1/2 to 2 feet apart in single rows 2 feet apart. Seeds sown directly in the garden should be planted 1/4 inch deep. Seeds will germinate in 10 days at 70F (21C) soil temperature. Best planting times are early spring for a late spring to early summer harvest or in midsummer for a fall harvest. During fall, bunch together the broad leaves surrounding the head over the cauliflower. This will protect head from early frost damage. Cauliflower is often planted in fall to grow through winter in the desert and hot, inland areas.

Regular moisture and continuous growth are needed to form solid, quality heads. For this reason, heavy soils that retain moisture rather than fast-draining, sandy soils are preferred. The desired soil pH is 5.5 to 6.5.

Pest and disease control: Chief insect pests are cutworms, slugs, cabbage looper, cabbage root maggot, imported cabbage worm, aphids and flea beetles. Deter cutworms and root maggots by fitting paper or metal collars around stems of transplants. Control slugs with slug bait placed in shallow pans to prevent the poison washing into the soil.

To combat chewing insects such as flea beetles, apply the organic sprays rotenone or pyrethrum, which are best used in combination. To control caterpillars, use Dipel or Thuricide organic products. Sevin, a chemical spray, is also effective against most cauliflower pests.

Blackleg, black rot, club root and cabbage yellows are disease problems. These are difficult to control once they make an appearance. Plant resistant varieties as a defense. Winter clean-up and crop rotation will also help to keep these diseases at bay.

Harvesting and use: Harvest by cutting stem 5 to 6 inches below the head. Cauliflower can be served cooked or raw. It also freezes well and makes delicious pickles. Break head up into smaller sections for use or for fitting into freezer bags.

Recommended varieties: 'Purple-Headed' (80 days) has certain advantages over white kinds. It has higher nutritional value and does not discolor as easily from inclement weather. 'Chartreuse' (80 days) is an attractive, lime-green variety.

Michigan State University has done extensive work on producing special varieties with long, "jacket leaves." Called 'Stove Pipe' (50 days), leaves form a funnel around the head to give it self-protection from weather and insects. It is an improvement over the "self-wrap" kind, which has leaves that fully enclose the cauliflower head, preventing sufficient air circulation in warm climates.

The All-America Award-winner 'Snow Crown' (54 days), is a vigorous, early hybrid, growing curds that weigh 2 pounds apiece and measure up to 8 inches across. It matures a week earlier than other 'Snowball' varieties. A week often means the difference between a poor crop and a successful one. Joseph Harris, Gurney and Stokes Seed are sources for these varieties.

'Stove Pipe' cauliflower was developed by Michigan State University. Notice how the jacket leaves point straight up, offering protection to the head that grows deep down at the base of the leaves.

Side view of a harvested head of 'Stove Pipe'. Because of the upward growth habit of the leaves, the head does not need blanching. I have never had a plant that didn't grow a firm, round head.

Celeriac 'Alabaster'. Roots have a delicious, celery flavor.

Celeriac

Grown for its delicious swollen-root system, celeriac belongs to a family of herbs called *Umbelliferae,* widely grown throughout the world. Its closest relative is celery and its outward appearance and flavor resemble celery, but it is much easier to grow. Unlike celery, it does not produce edible leaf stalks.

It can be used any way you use turnips—diced or mashed as a side dish, or added to soups and stews as a flavor enhancer. It is one of the best vegetables for winter storage in the garden because it will tolerate frosts. Celeriac can be left in the garden for harvesting until the ground freezes. It will keep for months stored in damp sand or peat moss.

How to grow: Seeds can be sown 1/8 inch deep directly in the garden, but it is better to start seeds indoors. Start 10 weeks before outdoor planting. Sow in seed trays and transfer to peat pots when large enough to handle. Seeds germinate in 10 to 20 days at 65F (19C) soil temperature. Transplant to the garden after your last frost date. Too many cold nights can induce plants to bolt to seed. Space plants 12 inches apart in rows 2 feet apart. Apply a general-purpose fertilizer at the start of the season and at least two booster applications during growing season. Roots are ready for harvest about 110 days after planting, when they are 4 inches across. Inspect the root above ground to judge size.

Pest and disease control: Although not as susceptible to pests as celery, celeriac can become infested with vegetable weevils and wireworms. Both can be controlled with an organic vegetable dust such as rotenone or the more effective chemical Sevin.

Harvesting and use: Begin harvest in fall, when roots have reached full size. Celeriac is hardy and can be left in the ground after frost. Before freezing weather comes, pack roots in a box in moist sand or sawdust, and transfer to a cool place for storage.

Recommended varieties: 'Alabaster' produces extra-large roots, averaging 4 inches across. It reaches maturity in 120 days from seed. Offered by Burpee.

Celery 'Golden Self-Blanching' is an early, heavy producer.

Celery

Wild forms of celery are distributed throughout southern Europe. Prized for crisp, crunchy leaf stalks that are eaten raw or cooked, cultivated kinds derived from wild species have been grown in gardens for hundreds of years.

Edible leaf stalks grow as a clump from the soil line. Many gardeners prefer to *blanch*—whiten the stems—to improve the flavor. This is accomplished by wrapping stems with brown paper collars to exclude light. Heaping loose soil or shredded leaves against the stalks will also do the job. Be aware that blanching reduces nutritional value.

How to grow: Although seeds can be sown directly in the garden three weeks before the last frost date, it's best to start seeds indoors. Sow seeds in trays filled with a peat-based potting soil such as Jiffy-Mix. Plant 10 to 12 weeks before last spring frost date. Seeds are tiny and require light for best germination. Lightly press them into soil and spray with water. Cover tray with a plastic bag and place in indirect light. Fluid seed sowing, see page 38, is also a good way of sowing celery. It allows pregerminated seeds to be sown in the garden. Seeds germinate in 10 to 14 days at a soil temperature of 65F (19C). Space plants 6 inches apart in rows 2 feet apart, or plant in wide rows.

Celery's most vital need is regular moisture. Soil for celery should have good moisture-holding capacity, so an organically rich soil is important. Garden compost, leaf mold and decomposed stable manure are acceptable soil conditioners for a celery bed. Use drip irrigation or a lawn sprinkler set in the middle of the planting. Soak soil thoroughly when you water.

Celery is a heavy feeder and requires a fertile soil. Supply with booster applications of fertilizer during the growing season.

Pest and disease control: Watch for celery worms. They chew leaf stalks at the soil line, causing discoloring and rot. Remove by hand or dislodge with a jet of water from a garden hose. Sevin is the chemical spray to use. It will also control aphids. Organic gardeners use pyrethrum or rotenone to control insect pests.

Harvesting and use: Begin as soon as edible stalks are large enough to pull. Early pickings can be taken by pulling outer stalks of several plants and allowing plants to continue to grow more stalks from the center. Celery is hardy, and will tolerate mild frosts. It can be left in the garden well into fall. Heaping fallen leaves or similar insulating material against stems will help protect plants. For long periods of storage, celery can be moved to a root cellar or cold frame. Pull entire plant, roots and all, and stand upright in moist sand. Push roots in sand and leave tops uncovered. Celery is best when used with other vegetables in cooked dishes. For example, try them cooked with tomatoes or in vegetable soup.

Recommended varieties: Two kinds of celery are popular—green celery and golden or self-blanching celery. Most gardeners tend to prefer green varieties over golden kinds. 'Tendercrisp' (105 days) is considered best, combining earliness with heavy stalk production. 'Golden Self-Blanching' (115 days) is a popular pale-stalked variety.

Close-up view of 'Tendercrisp'. It is the best home garden celery, growing crisp, juicy stalks 10 to 14 days earlier than other varieties.

Left, leaves of celtuce. Right, mature stalks.

'Fordhook Giant' Swiss chard.

Celtuce

Celtuce is native to China and is closely related to lettuce. Because of its thick, central stalk it combines the uses of both celery and lettuce, hence the name *celtuce*. It is easy to grow and deserves to be more widely planted in home gardens.

How to grow: Plant and cultivate exactly as you would lettuce, either as a spring or fall crop. Sow seeds 1/8 inch deep. Space plants 9 to 12 inches apart in rows 1 to 2 feet apart, or block-plant in raised beds. Celtuce grows quickly. It produces greens within 60 days and stalks within 90 days of sowing seeds directly in the garden. Young leaves have four times the vitamin C content of regular lettuce.

Pest and disease control: The most troublesome pests are slugs and snails, which can devour young seedlings before they have a chance to become established. When the stalks start to mature, these pests also eat the skin, causing the stalk to split open and discolor. Control with slug bait placed in shallow pans so poison does not wash into soil. Rabbits and other foraging animals can be kept away by enclosing the garden with a fence.

Harvesting and use: When celtuce leaves are young they may be used as lettuce, either fresh in salads or boiled as greens. The most tasty part of celtuce is the heart of the stalk, which can be eaten raw or cooked once skin has been peeled away and discarded. The pale green hearts have a crisp and succulent texture. The flavor is hard to describe—something similar to the heart of an artichoke.

This is a good winter crop in areas with mild winters. It is excellent for growing in cold frames where winters are more severe.

Recommended varieties: Celtuce is not available in different varieties. Offered by Burpee, which first introduced it to the United States.

Swiss Chard

This extremely hardy, drought-tolerant leaf crop is grown primarily for its dark green, "blistered" leaves and crisp, crunchy leaf stalks. Because of its heat tolerance, Swiss chard, also known as spinach beet, makes an excellent substitute for spinach when cooked.

The more you harvest outside leaves, the more new leaves grow from the middle. The first picking of leaves can usually be made within 60 days of sowing seeds. Individual leaves can reach 3 feet in length.

How to grow: Sow seeds directly in garden 2 weeks before the last frost date in your area. Plant seeds 1/2 inch deep in rows spaced 18 inches apart. Thin seedlings so plants are spaced 12 inches apart, 2 feet between rows. Seeds germinate in 4 to 10 days at 50F to 70F (10C to 21C) soil temperature. Like beet seed, chard seed is a cluster of several individual seeds. Careful thinning will be necessary to space seedlings for good growth. Although plants will grow in poor, infertile soils, they do best in soil enriched with high nitrogen fertilizer.

Pest and disease control: Normally not bothered by pests. A few chewing insects may nibble holes in some of the leaves, but damage is rarely extensive enough to warrant control.

Harvesting and use: Begin as soon as the plants are established, pulling outer leaves from several plants so that more new leaves will grow from the center. Chard withstands frosts in fall, and usually remains productive until a hard freeze. Leaf stalks are highly nutritious, and can be cut away from the leaf and braised. Serve with buttered breadcrumbs as an excellent substitute for asparagus.

Recommended varieties: 'Fordhook Giant' (55 days) has large leaves and pearly white leaf stalks. 'Ruby' (55 days) is highly ornamental with red midribs and red leaf veins. 'Ruby' has such attractive, brilliant red stalks, it is often used in borders as an ornamental plant, or in containers for a dramatic highlight. Both are widely available from leading seed catalogs.

Chayote fruit hang from vines that require support.

'Sugarhat' chicory in the garden prior to harvesting.

Chayote

Chayote (pronounced *cha-yo-tay*) is a member of the gourd family, native to Mexico. Green, pear-shaped fruit are produced on vigorous vines that require a strong trellis or overhead structure for support. A single vine will cover 25 feet in a season, up to 50 feet in warm-climate areas. Fruit is solid. When mature, it drops from the vine like a bomb, burying its base in the soil so that it will sprout.

How to grow: Plant the entire fruit. Roots grow from the base and a shoot sprouts from the center. This sometimes occurs while fruit is on the vine. In mild areas that receive some frosts, plant in spring after danger of frost has passed, or start in 5-gallon container in a protected area.

Vines need 6 to 9 months of warm, frost-free weather to produce worthwhile crops. For this reason, chayote is grown mostly in Florida and southern California. In frost-free locations it grows as a perennial, yielding fruit for several years. In areas with mild frosts and where no freezing of the ground occurs, vines will die back to roots. At the onset of warmer weather, roots normally produce new shoots. Plants are highly productive. One vine will produce up to 100 fruit, weighing 1 pound or more each.

Pest and disease control: Protect young plants from cucumber beetles by using rotenone or Sevin.

Harvesting and use: Pick fruit when they have grown to the size of a large pear. Although fruit are best eaten fresh and boiled until tender, they will store for a month in the vegetable bin of a refrigerator.

To eat chayote, slice mature fruit into sections and boil for about 10 to 15 minutes. Chayote can also be sliced thin for eating raw. Flavor is similar to water chestnuts. Roots form swollen tubers and are also edible. They can be harvested the second season.

Recommended varieties: 'Perlita' (200 days), little pearl or chestnut chayote, comes from Guatamala. Fruit are about the size of a lemon. Its cooked texture is like a baked potato. It and a larger Mexican variety are available from Exotica Seed.

Chicory

Chicory has been a popular salad vegetable and medicinal plant since early Roman times. It is a common sight along the roadsides of America, producing beautiful blue flowers the size of cornflowers. Because it is so widespread, many people believe chicory is a native American wildflower. Actually, wild chicory is an escapee from cultivation, brought to the United States from the Mediterranean by immigrants.

Two forms of chicory are popular in home gardens. *Witloof chicory* is grown mostly for *forcing* during winter to produce golden yellow *chicons,* cone-shaped shoots popular in salads. See the following for forcing instructions. *Leaf chicory* produces a head of salad greens somewhat like lettuce.

How to grow: Witloof chicory is started from seed as an outdoor vegetable. The objective is to produce a healthy root system for storage during winter. Although seedlings will tolerate mild frosts, it is better to delay planting until season is well advanced. Three months of growing will produce the right size of root for top-quality chicons. Sow seeds 1/4 inch deep directly in the garden. Space plants 6 inches apart with 2 feet between rows. Plant in an open, sunny location in a well-drained soil rich in organic matter. Avoid adding coarse manure or coarse compost to the soil. They often contain obstructions that cause roots to split.

Dig roots before the ground freezes. Trim leaves back to within an inch of the root. Discard any roots that are less than 1/2 inch in diameter. Store roots in sawdust or moist sand at about 30F to 40F (−1C to 5C) for 6 to 8 weeks. To force, place roots in wooden crates deep enough to accommodate them. Roots can be trimmed from the bottom to form uniform lengths of 8 to 9 inches. Line crates with drainage material such as gravel. Add 3 inches of fine topsoil and push roots into soil so they stand straight up. Fill in around sides to top of roots with more fine soil until roots are covered. On top of this, add an 8-inch layer of sawdust or peat moss. Store in a cool, moist place.

For the forcing, crates must be stored at 50F to 60F

(10C to 16C). Soil must be kept moist. In four weeks chicons (shoots) should begin to appear. As the top of each chicon shows through the sawdust covering, dig down to the base and cut off chicon at the root. Chicons should measure about 5 inches long and 3 inches across. Once the main chicon has been harvested, several more smaller chicons will grow from root.

To grow leaf chicory, sow seeds directly in the garden as soon as the ground can be worked in spring. Seeds will germinate at low temperatures, like lettuce, and seedlings are frost hardy. Plant seeds 1/4 inch deep and thin to stand 12 inches apart, in rows 12 inches apart. Leaf chicory is also good to grow as a fall crop. Sow seeds in midsummer. Plants are hardy so they will normally survive in the garden until a hard freeze.

Pest and disease control: Slugs and snails may be a problem, even in greenhouses. Place slug bait in shallow pans near the plantings.

Harvesting and use: Leaf chicory is harvested like lettuce. Roots of chicory make an excellent substitute for coffee. Wash and peel, then cut into small diced pieces. Roast in an oven at 300F (114C) until crisp and brown. Grind and add one part chicory to one part coffee for a strong, dark brew.

Recommended varieties: With most varieties of witloof chicory, the sawdust covering over roots is essential to keep heads tight. Without a cover—just darkness—heads will be loose. Several new hybrid varieties are now available that can produce tight heads without the covering. Developed in Europe, the most popular varieties are 'Normato', early; 'Mitado', midseason; and 'Tardivo', late. Try growing them in a tub or pot. Cover with another upturned pot to provide the required darkness. Available from Thompson & Morgan.

A cross between chicory and endive results in 'Sugarhat' (90 days), usually listed in seed catalogs under chicory. It is a salad green like lettuce but hardier. Because of its hardiness, it is useful to grow as a fall vegetable. Available from Burpee and Twilley.

Witloof chicory produces *chicons*—young shoots from roots stored indoors in a dark area.

Collards are nonheading cabbages with tasty leaves.

Collards

These nonheading members of the cabbage family produce nutritious leaves popular in the South as a cooked vegetable green. They not only tolerate hot weather, but survive temperatures down to 15F (−9C).

Plants are taller than cabbage, standing 2 to 3 feet high at maturity. They tolerate poor soils, but respond well to high-nitrogen fertilizers and side dressings of stable manure.

How to grow: Seeds can be sown directly in the garden several weeks before your last frost date in spring. A midsummer planting is preferred because it allows plants to reach peak maturity by fall. Sow 1/4 inch deep in rows spaced 2 feet apart. Allow 1-1/2 feet of space between plants. Although seedlings tolerate mild frosts, seeds need high temperatures to germinate. To gain earliest crops, you can start seeds indoors in peat pots or peat pellets 5 to 6 weeks before outdoor planting. Seeds germinate in about 5 days at 70F (21C) soil temperature. Because young seedlings are susceptible to damage from damping-off disease, consider treating soil with captan.

Pest and disease control: Collards attract the same insect pests as cabbage. Rotenone organic vegetable dust or Sevin chemical spray will protect plants from most chewing insects. Dipel and Thuricide are good organic controls against caterpillars. Aphids are occasionally a problem. Blast them off plants with a water hose, or rub them off with a gloved hand while colonies are still small.

Harvesting and use: Pick leaves as soon as plants are established. If grown as a fall crop, pick leaves after frost—cold tends to improve their flavor.

Recommended varieties: 'Georgia' (80 days) produces juicy, blue-green leaves.

Sweet corn 'Jubilee' ready for harvest.

Corn

Corn was a staple of the Indians when Columbus discovered America. It originated as a cultivated crop during the Inca civilization, when wild varieties became extinct.

Probably no other vegetable in the world has undergone more drastic changes in the last 100 years than sweet corn. Some of the most startling changes have occurred within the last 10 years. Varieties that stir excitement one year can become out of date the next. An example is the sugar-sweet corn called 'Xtra-Sweets'. It was developed from a gene called the *shrunken kernel* by the University of Illinois in the 1960s. Shrunken kernel refers to the nature of the seed, which appears shriveled because of high sugar content. When dried it doesn't turn to starch and therefore shrinks. It caused a sensation at the time, because its sweetness was far superior to anything previously known in sweet corn. One of the first varieties, 'Early Xtra-Sweet' (71 days), promptly captured an All-America Award.

'Early Xtra-Sweet', 'Illini Xtra-Sweet' (both 85 days) and a host of others developed from the shrunken kernel gene have a serious drawback for home garden use. To obtain their sweetness they must be isolated from other corn so that cross-pollination does not take place. Cross-pollination with another type of corn can render the extra-sweet variety coarse and starchy, producing the worst corn taste you have ever encountered.

Strict isolation is difficult to achieve. A neighbor's corn or an adjacent field of cattle corn can be the source of pollen that will spoil the flavor.

Recently, plant breeders have developed super-sweet, hybrid varieties as sweet as the 'Xtra-Sweets', but with no need for isolation. The variety that has been the biggest hit is 'Kandy Corn' (89 days). It has a gene called *Everlasting Heritage,* or *EH.* These EH varieties retain their super-sweetness after cross-pollination and normally have higher germination than 'Xtra-Sweets'. Ears also retain their sweetness for up to 10 days after harvesting.

Some corn connoisseurs will quickly rally in support of a regular hybrid called 'Silver Queen' (92 days). It has no 'Xtra-Sweet' or EH genes in its parentage. By some quirk of nature, which even the original plant breeder cannot explain, 'Silver Queen' has superb, sweet flavor on a large cob.

'Silver Queen' does have some faults. It is a late variety, and tends to lose flavor soon after harvesting. But it has a tenderness and milkiness that cannot be improved for melt-in-the-mouth flavor.

With sweet corn varieties, there is another contradiction. The biggest-selling variety is 'Golden Bantam' (80 days). It is not a hybrid and has no super-sweet genes. 'Golden Bantam' is one of those vegetables that gained a tremendous reputation decades ago. Providing you eat the small cobs within hours of harvesting,

Two rows of sweet corn just before tassels appear. Rows are spaced 3 feet apart.

'Silver Queen' is the most popular white corn. These ears were grown in my garden.

the flavor is very sweet. But if you tried a direct taste-test between 'Golden Bantam' and one of the new EH hybrids like 'Kandy Corn', you would wonder how 'Golden Bantam' ever earned its reputation.

How to grow: It is best to sow sweet corn seeds directly in the garden. Many gardeners start a dozen or so plants indoors and transplant when 4 inches high to get extra-early yields. See How To Grow Early Sweet Corn, page 116. Seeds are easy to handle and should be planted at least 1 inch deep. Planting 2 inches deep is preferred because it helps hide seed away from birds. Seeds treated with a fungicide generally ensures higher germination. Such seeds resist rotting and are distasteful to foraging animals.

Don't plant seeds saved from your own corn crop. Most recommended varieties are hybrids. Seeds from hybrids are usually inferior the second generation.

Avoid planting corn in a single row. Corn is pollinated by the wind. Pollen from the *tassels,* male flowers, must fall onto the *silks,* female flowers, to ensure a well-filled ear of corn. It is far better to plant shorter double or triple rows. Both male and female flowers appear on the same plant. The female flower produces the kernels when fertilized. Under ideal conditions, two and sometimes three full-size cobs are produced on a single stalk.

Although sweet corn is killed by frost, it is amazingly frost tolerant in its juvenile stage. If a mild frost damages leaf tips, new growth usually surges from the center of the plant.

Sweet corn is a warm-season crop, growing best when daytime temperatures are 70F to 80F (21C to 27C). Soil should be well supplied with moisture. Adequate moisture at time of *tasseling*—flowering—is

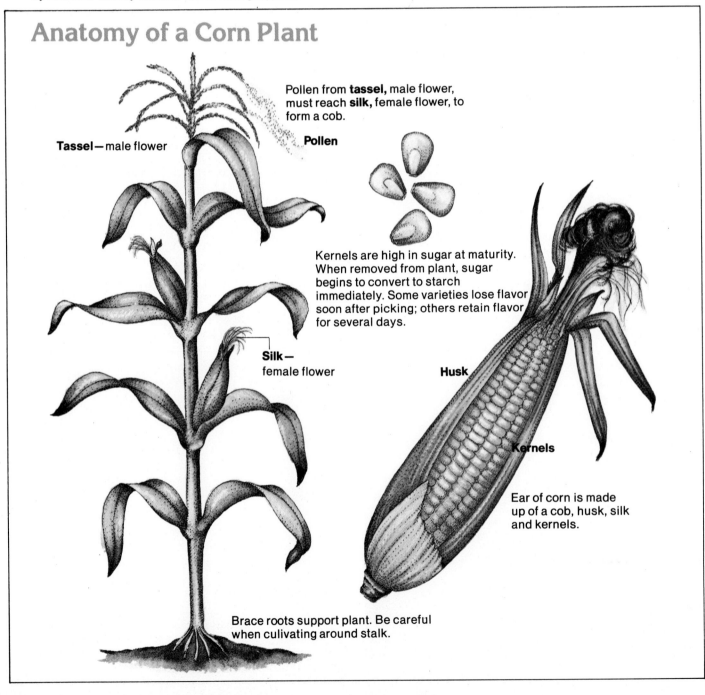

Anatomy of a Corn Plant

Pollen from **tassel,** male flower, must reach **silk,** female flower, to form a cob.

Tassel—male flower

Pollen

Kernels are high in sugar at maturity. When removed from plant, sugar begins to convert to starch immediately. Some varieties lose flavor soon after picking; others retain flavor for several days.

Silk— female flower

Husk

Kernels

Ear of corn is made up of a cob, husk, silk and kernels.

Brace roots support plant. Be careful when culivating around stalk.

probably the most important factor for abundant yields and well-filled ears.

Sweet corn is a heavy feeder and responds to high nitrogen fertilizer. For best results, mix fertilizer into the top 4 to 6 inches of soil prior to planting. Although sweet corn grows in a wide range of soils, deeply cultivated, well-drained soil with a pH between 5.8 and 6.5 is preferred. If soil is acid, liming may be necessary to meet this pH range.

Full sunlight is essential. If shade falls across the garden during peak sunlight hours, yields will be affected. Crowding also inhibits growth. Individual plants can be planted as close as 8 inches apart if at least 3 feet of space is allowed between rows. Corn responds well to mulch, especially black-plastic mulch. It helps increase soil temperatures in the early stages of growth.

Pest and disease control: Sweet corn is susceptible to a number of insect pests and diseases. Seed corn maggot, corn earworm, corn borer and sap beetle cause widespread damage. Bacterial wilt disease and smut disease are even more destructive. Seed corn maggots overwinter in soil and attack untreated seeds before they germinate, causing a poor stand. European corn borers overwinter in dead corn stalks and bore into new stalks the following year. This is why it is important to clean the garden in fall. Corn earworms hatch from eggs laid on corn silks, then eat into the husk where they feed on kernels. Damage generally occurs at the top of the cob, and is usually more of a nuisance than a menace.

The general-purpose pesticide Sevin is effective against the majority of corn insect pests. Organic gardeners report effective protection using organic controls such as pyrethrum and rotenone. Dust or

Varieties of Corn

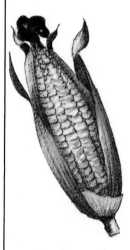

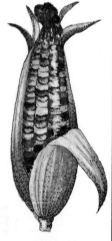

'Kandy Korn'
89 days
Sweet and tender

'Silver Queen'
92 days
Sweet and tender

'Honey & Cream'
78 days
Sweet and tender

Black Mexican
62 days
Ornamental

Rainbow Corn
100 days
Ornamental

Popcorn
83 days
Popping corn

Strawberry Popcorn
105 days
Popping corn

Calico Corn
100 days
Ornamental

Broom Corn
105 days
For making brooms

'Candystick II'
90 days
Sweet and tender

spray foliage to control corn borer. To control ear-worms, dust silks and repeat every three days until harvest.

In areas where bacterial wilt is prevalent, select disease-resistant varieties. Corn smut is difficult to control. Plant becomes infected in the early stages of growth. The disease becomes noticeable only when the cob becomes distorted and breaks out into black, powdery spores resembling soot. Treating seeds doesn't help—the spores generally overwinter in the soil. Removing and destroying smut spores before they burst is helpful. Burning diseased corn stalks in fall also helps control the disease. Larger, later-maturing varieties of sweet corn generally are more resistant than early, small varieties.

In Mexico, most gardeners don't worry if their corn patch becomes infected with corn smut disease. The spores are considered a delicacy and impart a delicious, mushroomlike flavor to meals. In fact, Mexican supermarkets sell corn smut in cans. Some Mexican gardeners encourage the smut by scratching the base of a plant, and pile soil against the scratch so that the fungus spores infect the plant's tissues.

Ornamental corn 'Rainbow' is grown for its decorative appeal. It is particularly striking in Thanksgiving centerpieces.

HOW TO GROW EARLY SWEET CORN

Four weeks before your last frost date in spring, start 6 to 12 plants in paper quart-size milk cartons. Let plants grow as much as they please. Then, 10 days before the last frost date, sow additional seeds directly in the garden. Space 1 foot apart in raised beds 2 feet wide and 1 foot between beds. Plants are therefore spaced 3 feet between rows. At the same time, plant most of the milk-carton seedlings through black plastic. They should be hardened off for 10 days before making the transition from an indoor environment to the outdoors. If you have a cold frame, it will work well for this.

If there is a mild frost, usually the outer leaves will get nipped, while the tender heart is protected inside the leaf whorl. Replace any corn plants that do get killed with spare plants that are kept growing in milk cartons. If you have more than enough milk-carton plants to fill in, pull up some of the weaker, outdoor-sown plants and replace them with the milk-carton transplants. Because the milk carton offers so much soil space and because the sides of the carton can be torn away, leaving the root area undisturbed, corn will transplant without so much as a wilted leaf.

When corn is about waist-high and just before it starts to tassel, spray the leaves and bases of the plants with a weak liquid fertilizer. This gives them a boost to form a healthy tassel and silk prior to cob formation. It also carries the cob through to full development.

Choice of varieties is important. If possible, plant more than one variety, preferably three. Plant two early varieties such as 'Quicksilver' (white) and 'Kandy Korn' EH (yellow) and a late variety such as 'Silver Queen' (white).

If you want to try corn smut, pick the cluster of pustules off plant, usually on the ear or tassel. Clean out any pieces of dried silk or tassel. Wash and serve spores in soups or on omelets, scrambled eggs, pizzas, tortillas—any food requiring a mushroom flavor. Broken or burst pustules can be powdered to use as a garnish.

Harvesting and use: Sweet corn is ready for harvesting when the silk has turned brown and brittle. An ear begins to convert its sugar into starch the moment it is picked. Super-sweet varieties such as the EH hybrids take up to 10 days to do so. In other varieties, starch conversion is complete within 12 hours. The old rule of picking corn only after the cooking water was boiling still applies unless you grow EH hybrids.

In areas where raccoons are prevalent, you might want to install a temporary electric wire fence to keep them out of the corn patch when harvest time approaches. They seem to have an instinct for knowing exactly when the corn is ripe and will strip stalks of every edible ear. Or place a radio, enclosed in a plastic bag, in the garden when harvest time approaches. Tune to an all-night talk show to keep raccoons away.

Sweet corn is most flavorful when eaten freshly steamed or boiled in water until kernels are tender. Cobs freeze well, which is the preferred method of storage.

Recommended varieties: The most popular sweet corn are yellow, white and *bicolor*—yellow kernels mixed with white kernels. Gardeners in short-season and northern areas should plant an early variety such as 'Polar Vee' (54 days), a yellow hybrid available from Stokes. Gardeners in warm climates, especially in the South, should plant varieties that have a heavy covering of jacket leaves around the kernels, such as 'Silver Queen' hybrid (92 days). This deters insect pests that are more numerous and abundant in these regions.

In addition, consider 'Jubilee' (84 days), a yellow

Popcorn requires a longer growing season than sweet corn. White popcorn is the most popular, but strawberry corn is ornamental. See illustration, page 115.

Broom corn produces fibrous tassels that can be made into brooms.

Corn nuts is a garden novelty. The large kernels of corn are tasty when roasted.

hybrid; 'Quicksilver' (75 days), similar to 'Silver Queen' but more than two weeks earlier; 'Stardust' (70 days), an early white hybrid; 'Earliglow EH' (70 days) and 'Kandy Korn' (89 days) both tender yellow hybrids; 'Honey & Cream' (78 days) a sweet bicolor; and 'Golden Cross Bantam' (85 days), the hybrid version of 'Golden-Bantam' (80 days).

Broom Corn

This is one of the tallest plants you can grow in your garden. Stalks tower 10 feet and more, topped with fibrous tassels that can be dried to make old-fashioned sweeping brooms. Cultural requirements for broom corn, ornamental corn and popcorn are the same as sweet corn.

Ornamental Corn

Several types of ornamental corn are offered by seed companies. The most popular is a mixture called 'Rainbow' (100 days). Cobs have multicolored kernels, sometimes showing as many as four different colors on a single ear—white, yellow, blue and red. 'Black Mexican' (62 days) produces black kernels.

Corn Nuts

A snack treat that is becoming popular is corn nuts—roasted kernels made from Peruvian corn. The white kernels are large, as are the ears, which vary in shape. Some ears are long and narrow; others are wide and fat. Kernels are unevenly distributed along the ear but are up to three times larger than regular corn. When stripped from the ear and roasted in the oven, they make a delicous, crunchy snack.

Popcorn

Popcorn is available in several different kinds. The most popular are white, hull-less types such as 'Japanese White Hull-less' (83 days). 'Strawberry Popcorn' (105 days) is edible but usually grown for ornamental effect. The golf-ball-size fruit are rich mahogany-red and grow on short stalks just 4 feet tall.

INSIDE REPORT: 'SILVER QUEEN'

'Silver Queen' is the most popular sweet corn among home gardeners. It is declared by many corn connoisseurs to be the most flavorful. To get the inside story on 'Silver Queen', I went to John V. Brewer, sales manager for Rodgers Brothers Seed Company, breeders of this highly regarded sweet corn. Here's what he had to say:

"'Silver Queen' was first introduced about 1958, but did not reach any volume until the 1960s. It was developed in a normal crossing pattern in our research plots at Caldwell, Idaho. It is not a "Super-Sweet" hybrid in the same sense as the Illinois types, which use the shrunken gene. 'Silver Queen' was derived from normal sweet corn breeding processes. We have no idea why it turned out so sweet and tender.

"I would feel confident in stating that 'Silver Queen' is the biggest-selling hybrid sweet corn today among home gardeners. But I doubt it is as widely grown as some of the more popular yellow types were at one time, such as 'Golden Bantam'.

"We sell substantially more seed of 'Jubilee' than we do 'Silver Queen', but a good deal of 'Jubilee' is used in the food processing industry. 'Jubilee' is gaining some favor with home gardeners, where its lack of disease resistance is not a limiting factor.

Many of us at Rodgers Brothers prefer 'Jubilee' to 'Silver Queen'. We do not like the high sugar content of 'Silver Queen'. We prefer 'Jubilee's' good, natural corn flavor and find it is nearly as tender as 'Silver Queen'."

Pepper cress grown indoors in a discarded produce tray.

Cress

Three popular kinds of cress are grown in home gardens: pepper cress *(Lepidium sativum)*, native to Western Asia; watercress *(Nasturtium officinale)*, native to Europe but naturalized in streams throughout the United States and Canada; and upland cress *(Barbarea verna)*, native to Europe and widely naturalized in meadows and waysides throughout the United States and Canada. All are easy to grow and pest-free.

Pepper Cress

The pungent, green leaves of this fast-growing annual can be harvested within 10 days of sowing seeds. Seeds sprout within 12 hours at room temperatures after watering.

Plants do not need soil to produce flavorful leaves. Sow seeds over moist paper napkins in a shallow dish and place in a cool window. Keep away from direct sunlight or the dish will dry out too quickly. Keep napkins moist and harvest sprouts with scissors.

Upland cress can be grown out of water. Its flavor is similar to watercress.

Watercress grows best in sandy soil. Provide with clear, running water.

Pepper cress can be used as a garnish for flavoring sandwiches, salads and egg dishes.

Watercress

A hardy perennial, watercress grows best in shallow streams with clear running water and sandy soil. Plants can be started from seeds indoors or outdoors. The best way is to buy fresh sprigs from the supermarket produce section and root them in water. Planting can be done at any time of year except during freezing weather. Started indoors, roots will take about a week to grow. Plants can then be transplanted to the stream bed. Space plants 6 inches apart. Place stones over the roots to anchor them, or plants may be washed away. Watercress can also be grown in garden soil. This method is tedious because the planting bed must be kept moist.

Watercress is a useful vegetable. It will survive frosts and freezing temperatures once established. Generous cuttings of flavorful greens can be harvested during winter months when other vegetables are finished. Winter and early spring harvests are best. Plants tend to grow tall and straggly during midsummer.

Watercress salad with a blue-cheese dressing is a gourmet's delight. The same is true for watercress soup and watercress butter. For watercress salad, pick the tender tips of watercress. Wash, dry and serve along with your favorite homemade or store-bought blue-cheese dressing.

To make watercress butter, finely chop watercress leaves. Wash in ice-cold water and dry. Cream with sweet butter, adding salt and pepper. For dark green butter, use equal parts chopped watercress and butter. For light green color, use one part watercress and two parts butter.

Upland Cress

This hardy biennial grows quickly into a healthy clump of watercress-shaped leaves within 8 weeks from early spring plantings. Seeds should be sown 1/4 inch deep directly in the garden as soon as soil can be cultivated. Thin plants to stand 6 inches apart in rows spaced 1 foot apart. If left in the ground over winter, plants will usually survive until spring—even in northern states—and then go to seed.

Pick young leaves as needed and add to salads. Upland cress is also useful as a substitute for watercress in salads, soups and butters.

How to grow: See the preceding individual descriptions.

Pest and disease control: Pepper cress grown indoors as ''sprouting seeds'' rarely encounters pests or diseases. If grown close with seeds touching or overlapping, molds may appear. Sprinkle seeds sparingly, leaving space between each seed.

Upland cress can attract flea beetles that chew the leaves. Sevin chemical insecticide or rotenone organic insecticide will control them.

Harvesting and use: Harvest peppercress in 10 days, watercress in 50 days and upland cress within 60 days. See descriptions for uses.

Cucumber 'Euro-American' produces fruit to 12 inches long.

Cucumbers

Two basic kinds of cucumbers are commonly grown in home gardens: slicing cucumbers *(Cucumis sativa)* and pickle cucumbers *(C. sativa, C. anguria)*.

Slicing Cucumbers

In recent years, plant breeders have made tremendous strides in improving slicing cucumbers. We now have a choice among many *monoecious* varieties—plants that produce both male and female flowers. These are termed *standard* varieties in the seed catalogs. In addition, so-called *all-female* varieties are available. On these varieties, *most* of the flowers are females, providing significantly greater yields. All-female cucumbers are referred to as *gynoecious.*

Sometimes an "all-female" cucumber produces a sufficient number of male flowers to ensure pollination of the females. Certain varieties produce almost 100% female flowers, requiring a standard variety to be grown nearby to provide pollination. I recommend avoiding these because it's more trouble to grow two varieties than one. You can tell the difference by reading the catalog or seed packet instructions. If the packet says "seed of a pollinator included," that means the plant is not capable of pollinating itself. The seedsman includes seed of a standard variety, either in a separate envelope inside the packet, or dyed a distinctive color.

To complicate the matter even more, some new kinds of cucumbers are all-female—set only female flowers—and are *self-fertile,* requiring no cross-pollination with males. This is known as *parthenocarpic.* A parthenocarpic cucumber comes in two types—indoor and outdoor. The first varieties introduced were for indoor culture only. They are seedless. If pollinated by bees or other insects, seed pods form inside the cucumber, making them gourdlike and inedible. Varieties of parthenocarpic cucumbers are available for outdoor culture. They cross with other cucumbers and still produce all-female, self-fertilizing flowers.

Vine types and bush types: In addition to sexual differences, cucumbers are available as *vine types,* requiring supports, and *bush types,* which sprawl on the ground. It is unwise to rely entirely on bush varieties for your cucumber crops in spite of their space-saving potential. Varieties such as 'Spacemaster' and 'Bush Champion' produce high-quality fruit earlier than vining kinds. However, plants are susceptible to mildew and other common cucumber diseases. You chance losing all your plants to disease before they have a chance to produce fruit.

If plants are allowed to grow naturally over the ground, they grow toward the sun. Cucumbers have tendrils that allow vines to climb naturally. Training plants on a trellis saves space and helps to produce fruit that are straight and uniform in shape.

How to grow: Seeds are large and easy to handle. Seeds can be planted directly in the garden after all danger of frost has passed. However, it is generally better to start seeds indoors. Sow 1 inch deep in individual peat pots, 6 weeks before outdoor planting date. Seeds germinate in 7 days at 70F (21C) soil temperature. Space each plant 1 foot apart in rows 3 feet apart.

To get a head start on the season, sow seeds in quart-size paper milk cartons filled with commercial potting soil. Poke holes in carton for drainage. Add a starter fertilizer to the soil mix before you plant. After the seeds germinate, water seedlings every day. When vines are about 6 inches high, tie them to a 1-foot-long stake for support. If left alone, the brittle stems may snap off at the soil line when transplanted.

Plants may have flowers formed at the time of transplanting, but the roomy milk carton allows flowering and growth without stressing plants. Because of their size and maturity, carton-started seedlings will be stronger when planted in the garden. Tear the carton away from the seedling to plant. Water immediately after planting.

Soil for cucumbers should be well drained and rich in organic matter. Optimum pH is 6.0 to 6.5—slightly acid. Cucumbers are sensitive to fertilizer overdoses.

These bush cucumbers are grown with a pine-needle mulch. Plants are spaced 1-1/2 feet apart to form dense, matted rows.

Apply fertilizer at half the recommended rate given on the fertilizer bag. Fertilizers high in phosphorus are preferred. A weak dose of fertilizer sprayed at base of plant or a side dressing of fertilizer or compost is also helpful when vines start to flower.

Weed control is essential for high yields. Weeds compete for moisture and nutrients. The best weed control is black-plastic mulch. It also conserves moisture, raises soil temperature earlier and maintains warm soil temperatures for fast growth of young plants.

Regular moisture is vital to cucumber production. Vines will wilt quickly when soil is dry. If moisture is lacking, flowers also fail to set fruit, or fruit will be distorted.

Pest and disease control: Insects are troublesome to cucumbers, particularly striped and spotted cucumber beetles. They chew leaves, flowers, fruit and stems—sapping vines of strength. They are also carriers of wilt disease, which can enter the vine as soon as a beetle bites it. To combat beetles, spray vines immediately after transplanting with a combination of rotenone and pyrethrum. Sevin also offers some protection. Commercial growers control cucumber beetle by garden dusts or sprays containing methoxychlor, which is applied to the transplants before they are set out into the garden. Guard transplants against cutworm damage by fitting stems with paper or metal collars.

Disease takes such a heavy toll among cucumbers you should plant only resistant hybrid varieties. Don't grow a cucumber because your grandfather grew it. Choose a hybrid variety like 'Marketmore 70' with resistance to several diseases. Some diseases that

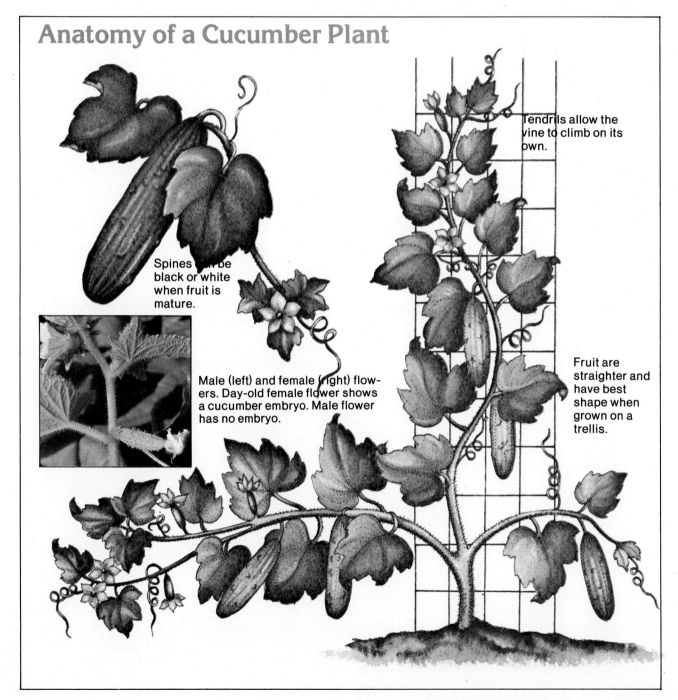

Anatomy of a Cucumber Plant

Spines can be black or white when fruit is mature.

Male (left) and female (right) flowers. Day-old female flower shows a cucumber embryo. Male flower has no embryo.

Tendrils allow the vine to climb on its own.

Fruit are straighter and have best shape when grown on a trellis.

infect cucumbers include downy mildew, powdery mildew, anthracnose, gummy stem blight and angular leaf spot. In addition to choosing disease-resistant varieties, plant your cucumber crop in a different spot in the garden each year. Also avoid planting where a crop of melons, pumpkins or squash grew previously. They all belong to the same family and harbor the same diseases.

If you had problems with these diseases and cannot avoid planting in the same spot, apply a garden fungicide with broad-spectrum control such as maneb.

Harvesting and use: Regular picking is essential for continous yields. Any cucumber left to turn yellow on the vine will quickly sap the vine's strength. Harvesting usually begins 45 to 55 days from planting and lasts for about 6 weeks.

The best way to store cucumbers is as pickles. If you want a supply of fresh cucumbers out of season, then grow some of the indoor, self-fertile cucumbers in a sunny window.

Recommended varieties: Seed catalogs often list slicing cucumbers as *white spine* or *black spine,* referring to the spines present on a mature cucumber. Spines are tiny and can be rubbed off with your fingers. They have no effect on taste or plant performance. 'Marketmore 70' (67 days) has a high degree of disease resistance. 'Spacemaster' (60 days) is recommended for gardens where space is limited. 'Burpee Hybrid' (60 days) and 'Victory' hybrid (60 days) have good disease resistance. 'Poinsett' (65 days) is a nonhybrid that does especially well in the South. Most major seed catalogs offer these varieties.

Cucumbers and Gourds

Slicing Cucumber
60 days
Edible raw

Burpless Cucumber
60 days
Edible raw

Pickle Cucumber
55 days
Raw and for pickles

Gherkin
60 days
Pickles

Armenian Cucumber
Raw and cooked

Lemon Cucumber
65 days
Edible raw

Bottle Gourd
80 days
Ornamental

Balsam Apple
65 days
Edible gourd

Luffa Gourd
80 days
Edible young, as scrub brush when mature

Snake Cucumber
90 days
Edible gourd

'Euro-American' hybrid is a cross between an American slicing cucumber—short, thick fruit—and a European cucumber—long, slender, mild-flavored fruit. The result is a vigorous-growing hybrid that incorporates the best qualities of both parents—mild, thick fruit that grow 12 inches long. I have had great success with this variety, and have harvested large cucumbers within 40 days of setting out transplants. See the head-start method described in the how-to-grow section under slicing cucumbers.

'White Wonder' (65 days) is an appealing variety, useful for pickles when small and for slicing when large. The skin is creamy white and so tender you do not have to peel it.

Pickle Cucumbers

As with slicing cukes, there is a choice of standard varieties, and hybrid kinds with *all-female* characteristics. Certain types of pickle cucumbers can be considered dual-purpose. When picked young, they can be used for pickling. If allowed to reach full size, they can be used as slicing cucumbers. 'Liberty' hybrid (54 days) is an example. It is an All-America Award winner and highly disease resistant, producing spectacular yields.

Lemon cucumber (65 days) is another dual-purpose cucumber. It is an appealing oddity, producing fruit the size of an orange. Fruit turn yellow when ripe. Vines are productive but generally die off early after setting a flush of decorative fruit. Young fruit make excellent pickles and mature fruit are suitable for slicing.

Gherkin cucumbers (60 days) are also popular. They are a type of pickle cucumber known for their spiny texture and sweet flavor. Gherkins should be picked when small—about 1 to 2 inches long.

'County Fair' hybrid (56 days) developed by the United States Department of Agriculture, and offered by Gurney, is the first "seedless" cucumber for outdoor growing. A pickling variety, it is self-fertile. Because it doesn't set seed, all energy from the plant goes into producing fruit. It's also resistant to several diseases. Other good disease-resistant pickle cucumbers include 'Saladin' hybrid (55 days) and 'Wisconsin SMR 18' (54 days).

Cultural requirements for pickle cucumbers are the same as for slicing cucumbers.

Burpless Cucumbers

Cucumber vines have a bitter taste as a means of protection from foraging animals. For an unknown reason, bitterness sometimes pervades the fruit. It is responsible for a condition known as *the burps.*

T. Sakata, a Japanese seedsman, developed the first mild-flavored cucumber. An American garden writer, Mrs. Kitty M. Simpson of Shreveport, Louisiana, suggested to him the name "Burpless" after growing a sample advance crop before its introduction. Mr. Sakata loved the name, and it has been successful in making these Oriental cucumbers popular. Fruit are long and slender with lots of spines. Despite the menacing appearance of the spines, skin is tender and fruit are crisp and delicious. They can be eaten fresh from the vine without peeling the skin.

If grown on the ground, fruit have a tendency to curl. For straight fruit, grow them on a trellis.

'Green Knight' hybrid (60 days) is an early, productive, burpless-type cucumber. It grows fruit up to 16 inches long. It is a distinct improvement over the original burpless variety, which most seed companies still offer under the name 'Burpless' hybrid (62 days). Burpee is a good source of seed.

Giant Cucumbers

Three types of giant cucumbers are available in seed catalogs: 'Snake Cucumber' (90 days); 'Armenian' (70 days); and 'Kyoto Long' (70 days). Only 'Kyoto Long' is a true cucumber, growing fruit up to 3 feet long for eating raw like regular cucumbers.

Burpless cucumbers grow long, slender, mild fruit. Train on supports so fruit will grow straight.

Cucumber 'Marketmore 70' is a disease-resistant slicing cucumber. It is ideal for growing on supports.

White cucumbers are more than a novelty. The skin is not bitter so the fruit can be eaten without peeling.

'Snake Cucumber' is actually a gourd. Edible fruit grow up to 3-1/2 feet long. Hollow inside, it can be sliced into rings and stir-fried.

The 'Armenian' or 'Yard-Long Cucumber' (60 days) is also an edible gourd, growing thick, ribbed, pale green fruit up to 3 feet long. It is best eaten young—about 1 foot long—sliced into round sections and boiled or fried like summer squash.

Gurney and Nichol's are sources.

Self-Fertile Cucumbers

You can grow cucumbers indoors during winter by using all-female varieties from Europe. They require no pollinator to set fruit, but do need special care. When grown properly, they will produce up to 15 fruit per plant.

Seed is expensive. For some varieties a packet of three seeds costs $4. Plant only one seed per peat pot—they are too precious to waste on thinning. If all you need is one plant the first season, store remaining seeds in the vegetable bin of your refrigerator. They will keep for several years.

Seeds normally sprout in 4 or 5 days at 70F (21C) soil temperature. Seedlings grow rapidly if given a southern exposure or if placed under fluorescent lights for 12 to 14 hours per day.

Once seedlings produce their first true leaves they can be transplanted into permanent containers. Two-gallon capacity or larger is preferred. These cucumbers need at least 2 pints of water per day to keep them productive.

When transplanting, set the stem of the seedling below the new soil line. This will encourage the plant to produce *brace* roots for extra strength when you begin training the vine to climb. This is important, because a juvenile cucumber stem is soft and will break easily if mishandled.

Regular applications of fertilizer are essential. Fertilizer is best applied as a soluble liquid feed at time of watering. Let vine grow up as a single stem and prune away any side shoots and flowers that develop until the leader reaches 3 feet high. Remove flowers along lower portion of stem or plant may be overburdened with fruit. Each flower will *abort*—fruit dies in the embryo stage. After 3 feet of vine growth you can allow fruit to form. After 4 feet of growth, pinch the lead shoot so vine will branch into two side shoots. Then train each side shoot in an arch.

Plants produce only female flowers, providing they are not cross-pollinated with another cucumber and demands for moisture are met. All flowers will set fruit—even during winter months.

If plants are grown in a greenhouse, all flowers that form along side shoots can be allowed to form fruit. If plants are grown in a window where lack of light and ventilation place stress on plants, it is best to remove every second flower.

Plants grow with incredible speed, produce abundantly and are delicious. They yield mild-flavored "burpless" fruit averaging 12 inches in length.

Recommended varieties: 'Toska 70' (70 days) will produce up to 50 cucumbers 15 inches long over a 6-month period under ideal conditions. Growers report a small percentage of male flowers, which must be removed. For windowsill culture and winter conditions, choose cold-tolerant 'Fembaby' (75 days). Fruit grow up to 8 inches long. Stokes, Burpee and Thompson & Morgan are sources for self-fertile cucumbers.

Self-fertile outdoor cucumbers: Outdoor cucumbers normally do not experience as much stress as indoor kinds. Make sure their need for adequate moisture is met. Train vines to climb, rather than sprawl on the ground. Sometimes after setting a first flush of fruit, flowers fail to set fruit until vine has gained enough new growth to support fruit production. With some plants, vine may automatically abort every other flower. A good, self-fertile pickle variety is 'County Fair' (56 days), developed by the USDA.

'West India' gherkin yields a large number of 2-inch-long fruit that are perfect for small pickles.

All-America Award-winner 'Liberty' hybrid is a productive, disease-resistant, pickle cucumber.

Fruit of *parthenocarpic* (self-fertile) slicing cucumber, beginning to grow fruit without cross-pollination.

Leaves and roots of dandelion are both edible.

Eggplant 'Dusky' hybrid.

Dandelion

Dandelions are a commercial vegetable crop used as salad greens. In Paris restaurants, a dandelion salad is often the most expensive salad on the menu.

How to grow: Sow seeds as soon as ground can be worked in spring. Plant seeds 1/4 inch deep in rows spaced 1 foot apart. Thin seedlings so plants are spaced 9 inches apart. Keep flower heads picked so all of the plant's energy is directed into producing leafy growth and thick roots. Plants prefer a soil rich in stable manure or garden compost. Plants sown in late summer will make strong growth by winter and produce early yields in spring, surviving severe freezes.

Pest and disease control: Dandelions are relatively pest-free, although rabbits are sometimes a problem.

Harvesting and use: The cultivated dandelion is very similar to the wild variety. It is grown for edible leaves and fleshy roots. A wine can be made from the blossoms. Blossoms for wine are usually gathered from wild dandelions because a large quantity is needed. Although leaves taste bitter when mature, they can be tied together in a bunch so light is excluded from the lower leaf sections. They then blanch white for a sweeter flavor. Leaves can also be cooked like spinach. Add a garnish of chives and a sprinkling of lemon juice for a gourmet touch. Dandelion coffee can be made from the roots and is caffeine-free. Dig roots in fall, dry and store in airtight jars. Roast roots and grind as needed to make coffee.

Recommended varieties: 'Thick-leaved' (95 days) is probably the most popular variety. It grows large, thick, dark green leaves, and is available from most leading catalogs.

Eggplant

Eggplant are tender perennials closely related to peppers and tomatoes. They are native to Africa and Asia. In most areas of the United States and Canada, eggplant are grown as annuals, planted outdoors after frost and harvested before fall frosts kill plants.

Shapes vary from round to oval, or egg to pear-shaped. Colors range from black, to purple, white, yellow and even a red variety that looks like a tomato. See illustrations on the facing page.

Pale pink flowers of eggplant are decorative. They are self-fertile so no cross-pollination is needed to set fruit. A slight movement of the flower is all that is required to mix pollen. This is usually achieved by the wind. Temperatures above 70F (21C) are required for good fruit set.

How to grow: Generally, the larger the fruit the more difficult it is to grow. Give eggplant an open, sunny location. Soil should be fertile and high in organic matter to provide for good moisture retention. Regular moisture is necessary for proper fruit development.

Start seeds indoors 6 to 8 weeks before your last frost date in spring. Sow seeds 1/4 inch deep in peat pots or peat pellets. Germination takes 7 to 10 days at 80F to 85F (27C to 30C) soil temperature. Harden-off transplants and set in the garden after danger of frost has passed. Space plants 1-1/2 feet apart, with 3 feet between rows. Black plastic is a beneficial mulch, helping to warm soil early in the season, conserving moisture and smothering weeds.

Use a general-purpose fertilizer at the start of the season. At 3-week intervals apply a side dressing of fertilizer, well-decomposed garden compost or mild liquid feed at least twice after fruiting begins.

Pest and disease control: Flea beetles can be troublesome. They are attracted to eggplant foliage like bees to honey. They pepper leaf surfaces with thousands of tiny holes, sapping the plant's energy. Most general-purpose vegetable dusts or sprays will discourage them, including pyrethrum and rotenone. Cutworm collars will protect young transplants from cutworm damage. See page 63. Colorado potato beetles have

Eggplant 'Easter Egg' grows edible, white fruit the size of a hen's egg. As the fruit ripen, they turn golden yellow.

also been known to take a liking to eggplant. Hand pick them from foliage or spray with rotenone or pyrethrum. Sevin is an effective chemical control.

Harvesting and use: Begin picking fruit as soon as they have reached a desirable size. Do not allow any fruit to overripen or turn brown or the plant will be weakened. The more you pick, the more productive a plant will be. Eggplant sliced into circles are popular fried and as an ingredient in casseroles. Try them chopped into sticks and deep fried.

Recommended varieties: The best variety is the hybrid 'Dusky' (60 days). It produces medium-large, pear-shaped, glossy black fruit up to 10 days earlier than similar-size varieties.

Eggplant are ideal for raising in containers. Those especially adapted are 'Scarlet Egg' (70 days), 'Easter Egg' (70 days) and 'Slim Jim' (65 days).

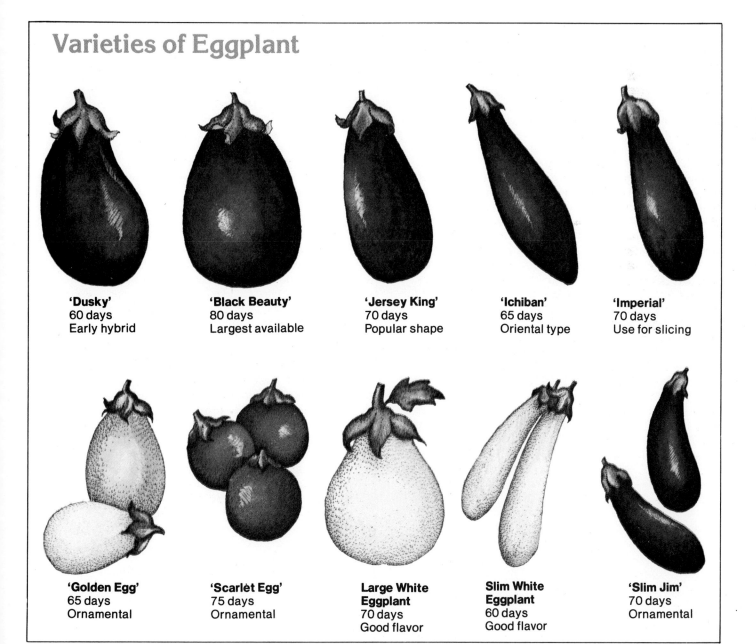

Varieties of Eggplant

'Dusky'
60 days
Early hybrid

'Black Beauty'
80 days
Largest available

'Jersey King'
70 days
Popular shape

'Ichiban'
65 days
Oriental type

'Imperial'
70 days
Use for slicing

'Golden Egg'
65 days
Ornamental

'Scarlet Egg'
75 days
Ornamental

Large White Eggplant
70 days
Good flavor

Slim White Eggplant
60 days
Good flavor

'Slim Jim'
70 days
Ornamental

Endive 'Green Curled' grows decorative, frilly leaves.

Garlic stores well when dried. Here it is braided into a garlic rope.

Endive and Escarole

Endive and escarole are closely related to chicory. They are used as a fresh green, imparting a bittersweet flavor to salads. Botanically, they are the same species, originating from Sicily, but they have been separated for garden use. Endive has *frilly leaves;* escarole has *smooth leaves.*

Both are cool-season crops, growing best in early spring and fall months. Cultural needs are similar to lettuce. They respond well to a fertile soil enriched with garden compost or well-decomposed manure.

How to grow: Sow seeds directly in the garden several weeks before the last frost date in your area. Seeds need some light for best germination. Plant 1/8 inch deep in rows spaced 1-1/2 feet apart. Or block-plant in raised beds, with 12 inches between plants. Water regularly to ensure rapid growth and tender leaves. Endive is hardy and can be left in the garden after fall frosts.

Pest and disease control: Concentrate on keeping young seedlings free from slug damage. This is easily done by setting out pans containing slug pellets or slug bait.

Harvesting and use: Begin after blanching the hearts to improve flavor and reduce bitterness. To blanch, tie tops of outermost leaves over the heart. Do this when plant is dry to avoid possibility of rot. Blanching is completed when the center of the heart turns a creamy yellow. This takes 2 to 3 weeks. Eat the heart only or the entire leaf, according to your preference.

Recommended varieties: 'Green Curled' (90 days) and 'Broad Leaved Batavian' (90 days).

A cross between endive and chicory done by the agricultural experiment station at Zurich, Switzerland, resulted in a variety called 'Sugarhat' (86 to 90 days). It is described under chicory, page 112, and is listed in most catalogs with chicory.

Garlic

This member of the onion family is valuable as a food flavoring, especially in French cooking. The juice of garlic cloves is also effective as an organic insect repellent.

The edible garlic bulb is made up of segments called *cloves* or *bulblets* wrapped in white, papery skin. Each clove is capable of producing a new plant.

How to grow: Plant bulblets directly in the garden in fall or early spring. Cover with 2 inches of soil. Space 4 inches apart in rows spaced 1 foot apart. Soil rich in organic matter will grow the biggest and best garlic bulbs. In areas with severe winters, a straw or leaf mulch will be necessary to help fall-planted bulbs survive cold temperatures.

Pest and disease control: Garlic is a natural insect repellent, so pest control is generally not necessary. Garlic cloves can be pressed to release a juice that many organic gardeners dilute with water to create an effective insect spray. See page 64.

Harvesting and use: Bulbs are hardy. Planting in fall will ensure the largest bulbs by the following summer. Harvest bulbs when plant tops die down. Bulbs can be dug and hung to dry in bunches. Leave a length of stem attached to bulbs so stems can be braided to form a decorative garlic rope. This is attractive and useful for hanging in the kitchen.

Recommended varieties: 'Elephant Garlic' grows extra-large bulbs that weigh up to 1 pound each. It has a milder flavor than regular garlic. To grow the biggest bulbs, leave some in the garden to overwinter for a second season's growth. Gurney is a reliable source.

Ginseng needs shade and cool soil to develop its fleshy root.

Luffa gourd can be grown on the ground, but it is better on supports.

Ginseng

When a reputable seed company listed ginseng in its catalog at the turn of the century, a stern warning was included. Many get-rich-quick claims told about fantastic prices being paid for the root of this wild, North American herb. This was supposedly due to its demand as a health tonic among Oriental families. "We are opposed to 'get-rich-quick' booms," the catalog stated, "and we would advise our friends to consider the special requirements of this plant before investing heavily in its cultivation. The plants require an equitable temperature, comparatively cool, and need to be constantly moist and shaded. They grow very slowly. Seedlings take from 5 to 7 years to reach marketable size. The crop requires considerable labor in keeping the beds stirred and free from weeds . . ."

The situation hasn't changed much today. Renewed interest in health foods has kept ginseng in demand. Get-rich-quick claims about growing it for sale still abound in the classified sectons of garden magazines.

How to grow: Ginseng grows in the wild from Maine to Georgia. It prefers natural, shaded areas such as woodland, and likes some shade when grown in the garden. Plants are hardy and seeds can be sown directly in the garden several weeks before your last frost date in spring. To grow larger roots the first season, it is best to start seeds indoors 10 weeks before setting in the garden. Soil should be loose with plenty of organic matter added.

Pest and disease control: Concentrate on repelling rodents—they love the root. Some rodent repellent flakes worked into the soil will keep them away.

Harvesting and use: Begin digging roots in fall. Left in the ground and covered with mulch, roots will survive the winter and will continue growing the following season. Roots are unusual in appearance, often suggesting a human form. Roots are grated into small pieces and dried, then steeped in boiling water to produce an herbal tea.

Gourds

This fascinating family of plants is closely related to pumpkin and squash. Most are native to Mexico. The majority of gourds are grown for utilitarian or ornamental value, but a few kinds are edible.

Gourds are vigorous, vining plants that do best when supported by a trellis. They have tendrils that allow them to climb untrained. Better-shaped fruit are assured when plants are kept clear of the ground.

How to grow: Plant seeds 1 inch deep in groups of 3 or 4. Space groups 3 feet apart and thin each group to one healthy vine. A light, fertile soil rich in organic matter—especially well-rotted animal manure—will help ensure good growth. Regular moisture is necessary for abundant yields, particularly for giant gourds.

Pest and disease control: Concentrate on thwarting cucumber beetles—they introduce wilt diseases. Spray with Sevin or rotenone as soon as seedlings appear. Continue protection according to label instructions until vines are well established. Squash vine borer can also be a problem. See page 67 for treatment.

Harvesting and use: When to pick depends on the variety grown. Generally, edible kinds need harvesting while young and tender. Ornamental kinds can be left until vines begin to wither and die, before fall frosts. See following descriptions for uses.

Recommended varieties: Many kinds of ornamental gourds are available. Here are some of the more popular *edible* kinds.

Balsam Apple

Balsam apple or bitter gourd (*Momordica balsamina*) (75 days), originated in the Orient. The Chinese have been eating it for centuries as a cooked vegetable. It is easy to grow, either on the ground or up a trellis as a climbing vine. It tolerates poor soil and drought. Plant quickly covers itself with brilliant yellow flowers, then produces dozens of cylindrical, pale green fruit covered with soft, decorative spines and warts. As fruit ripens to golden orange in color, it bursts at one end, opening outward, exposing more than a dozen, blood-red, shiny seeds that resemble enormous teeth. It is fas-

Chinese okra is a variety of edible gourd closely related to luffa gourd. These fruit are at the right stage for picking as a substitute for zucchini squash.

Hercules war club, called *upo* in China, is best when picked at an immature stage, as above. Like Chinese okra, the young fruit have a flavor similar to summer squash.

cinating for children to grow. Use it sliced in stir-fry vegetable meals. Park, Stokes and other seed companies offer seed. It is sometimes listed as Chinese bitter gourd, or bitter melon.

Chinese Luffa

Chinese luffa gourd is dried to produce a fibrous sponge, valued as a backscrubber. During a recent trip to China and Japan, I was surprised to discover that the luffa gourd is one of the most popular of all vegetables. It is grown along fence rails, up porch posts, trained along roof gutters and held by every other conceivable kind of support. Large, yellow flowers are highly ornamental and the lush, tropical-looking vines produce a dense screen and cooling shade.

Luffa is edible as well as functional. A healthy vine can produce dozens of dark green, ribbed fruit resembling giant cucumbers. Picked when small and immature, about 6 inches long, luffas can be used like summer squash. Eat them raw or slice for cooking.

Left to mature to full size, luffas will grow to 1-1/2 feet long, turning brown when fully ripe. This normally takes 80 days. At this stage the tender interior becomes fibrous and wiry. When the brown skin is peeled away the inside can be dried to make an instant backscrubber, dishrag or scouring pad.

Chinese Okra

This is not an okra, but a vegetable gourd *(Luffa acutangula)*. It produces dark green, ribbed fruit that grow 1-1/2 to 2 feet long. Chinese okra gets its name because its ridges or ribs resemble okra. It is also sold under its Chinese name, *cee gwa*.

Fruit are delicious to eat when young and tender. Pick when 6 to 8 inches long, and slice off the usually tough ribs. Prepare the same as zucchini squash.

If allowed to mature, fruit take on a fibrous quality similar to luffa gourds. They can be dried and skinned to make useful scrubbers and sponges.

Plants require 100 frost-free days to produce a worthwhile crop. Trellising the vines is important to produce straight fruit. Fruit will usually curl if grown on the ground.

Hercules War Club

Hercules war club *(Lagenaria longissima)* (80 days) is a popular Oriental vegetable, called *upo* in China. Vines are vigorous growers and require 10 feet of space to be fully productive. Although fruit will grow to 3 feet in length, they are edible only when small—about 6 inches long. At this stage they are tender and have a smooth, creamy, summer-squash flavor.

When ripe, fruit of balsam apple split open to reveal bright red seeds. Green fruit have an appealing, bittersweet flavor. Try them sliced thin and stir-fried with other vegetables.

Horseradish will grow in less-than-ideal locations.

When cooked, garden huckleberries are suitable substitutes for blueberries.

Horseradish

This deep-rooted perennial plant is a wild weed in parts of Europe and Asia. Cultivated garden varieties usually compete with the most persistent native American weeds, crowding them out. It is one of the easiest garden vegetables to grow. Because horseradish is so aggressive, it is best given its own corner of the garden. Try it where other vegetables have difficulty growing.

How to grow: Horseradish does not set viable seed and must be grown from root sections. These are usually small, pencil-thick side shoots taken from established plants. To plant, cover with 2 inches of soil in early spring. Place the small end of the root cutting facing down into the soil. Space plants 1-1/2 to 2 feet apart. For the largest, most flavorful roots, add plenty of organic matter to the soil. Supply with regular water.

Pest and disease control: Horseradish is one of the most tenacious plants in the vegetable kingdom, with few pest and disease problems.

Harvesting and use: Dig roots any time of year. They can remain in the soil year-round. Spring-planted root cuttings in a fertile soil will be sufficiently large enough to harvest by fall. Roots are usually dug from the soil in fall.

Roots are best used fresh. They will last up to three months in the refrigerator. Cut portions of horse radish stored in a jar of water in the refrigerator will keep for several weeks. Combine horseradish with sour cream to create a pungent relish for meats.

Recommended varieties: 'Maliner Kren' is a German variety. It has an extra-vigorous growth habit and is capable of producing the largest roots. Burpee is a reliable source.

Garden Huckleberry

Garden huckleberry is not a true huckleberry, but a fruiting member of the nightshade family. Plants produce thousands of glossy, black fruit the size of large blueberries within 70 days of transplanting. Although ripe fruit are edible raw, they have a slightly bitter flavor. After they are *parboiled*—cooked in boiling water—the bitterness is removed. Garden huckleberries make a good substitute for blueberries in jams, pie fillings or as a cooked dessert.

How to grow: Because plants are tender to cold, seeds are best started indoors in individual peat pots or peat pellets. Transplant to the garden after all danger of frost has passed. Space each plant 2 feet apart in rows 3 feet apart. Plants are so productive you won't need more than a single 15-foot row. Garden huckleberries grow well in poor soils and resist heat, but need watering during dry periods.

Pest and disease control: Troubled by few pests. Cucumber beetles and flea beetles can be controlled by Sevin chemical insecticide or rotenone, an organic alternative. Garden huckleberries will even tolerate competition from weeds.

Harvesting and use: Pick fruit when they turn glossy black. To cook, bring a pot of water to a boil. Add berries and 1 teaspoon of baking soda. Boil 1 minute and drain off water. This process will remove the bitterness and berries will be firm. Cool and pack in freezer bags for freezing. To make a delicious, blueberry-flavored dessert, mash berries and strain to remove skins. Add sugar to pulp and seed according to your personal taste. Serve alone or over ice cream.

Recommended varieties: No special varieties have been developed. Stokes, Gurney and Herbst are sources for seed.

Husk tomato 'Pineapple Cherry'.

Jerusalem artichoke flowers, left, and tubers, right.

Husk Tomato

A number of husk tomatoes are sold under different variety names. Some common names include strawberry tomato, cape gooseberry and ground cherry. All are native to South America. Fruit of husk tomatoes are encased in a husk resembling a Chinese lantern. Husk turns parchment-brown when ripe; fruit inside turns yellow. The problem with most husk tomatoes is that fruit are small and it takes quite a few of them to make a meal.

How to grow: Start seeds indoors 8 weeks before your last frost date in spring. Set outdoors after all danger of frost has passed. Space plants 3 feet apart in rows 3 feet apart. Provide stakes or cages so the bushy plants have support—plants grow to 6 feet in height. They prefer poor soils, generating too much leafy growth in fertile soils. They also produce best when nights are cool.

Pest and disease control: Apply Sevin chemical spray or rotenone organic insecticide to control cucumber beetles and Colorado potato beetles.

Harvesting and use: To harvest fruit, wait until the outside casing (husk) has turned brittle and brown. You will be able to see through the husk to the golden yellow fruit. Fruit may take a day or two longer to change color from green to deep yellow. Fruit can be eaten raw, used as a dessert topped with fresh cream or ice cream, or made into jams, jellies and pie fillings.

Recommended varieties: The best variety is 'Pineapple Cherry' (70 days), available from Gurney. It produces marble-size fruit with a delicious flavor. Fruit ripen to a golden yellow, and taste something like a ripe pineapple. Flavor improves after a mild frost.

Jerusalem Artichoke

This native American sunflower produces tall, weedy stems topped with masses of bright yellow, daisylike flowers. Its underground root system produces brown tubers that can be cooked and used like potatoes.

Jerusalem artichoke is low in calories, yet is a good source of many vitamins. It also stores well. Leave it in the ground and dig when needed if the ground is not frozen, or store in the vegetable bin of the refrigerator.

How to grow: Cover tubers with 2 inches of soil. Space 1-1/2 to 2 feet apart if you plant whole tubers. Space 6 inches apart if you cut tuber into smaller eye divisions. It is a hardy perennial but best grown as an annual. Tops will die down after frost. Tubers will live in soil through the winter, producing new growth in the spring.

Tubers have "eyes" on knobby protrusions similar to potatoes. Depending on size, each tuber can be cut into 6 to 12 eye-sections for individual planting. Plant in spring after the soil has warmed. Or plant in fall when cool nights and abundant rainfall help tubers establish a healthy, underground root system.

Given full sun, Jerusalem artichoke will thrive in poor soil. The only negative quality is the amount of space required for worthwhile production.

Pest and disease control: Relatively pest-free. Plants can become invasive pests themselves. It is best to locate plants in a special area of the garden, perhaps beside a fence or to act as a screen. Consider this when choosing a planting site.

Harvesting and use: Tubers from spring-planted roots can be dug in fall of the same year. Tubers from established plantings can be harvested any time of year. By storing tubers in boxes filled with moist sand in a cool basement, they can be used when the ground is frozen. Tubers can be prepared and eaten like potatoes.

Recommended varieties: 'Red Jerusalem Artichoke' has attractive, red skin. It is available from Gurney. Johnny's Selected Seeds offers a fast-growing variety called 'Stampede'.

Jicama tubers taste like water chestnuts.

Kale 'Dwarf Blue Curled Vates'.

Jicama

Also known as Mexican potato, jicama (pronounced *hik-ama)* is a vigorous, vining plant that produces edible tubers. They taste like water chestnuts without the starchiness. To grow full-size tubers as large as a grapefruit, plant needs 9 months of warm, frost-free weather. It will produce small, usable tubers with 4 months of warm weather. I have grown it with great success in my Pennsylvania garden.

Jicama is also grown as an ornamental to cover arbors and chain-link fences. The plants are spectacular, with large, shiny, heart-shaped leaves. Vines grow to 20 feet long in one season, bearing attractive, purple, pealike blossoms.

How to grow: In northern states and short-season areas, start seeds indoors at 70F to 80F (21C to 27C) soil temperature 8 to 10 weeks before outdoor planting. Because plants are damaged by frost, transplant only after all danger of frost has passed. In areas with a growing season of 250 days or more, seeds can be sown 1 inch deep directly in the garden. Plant in mounded rows spaced 2 feet apart and water during dry spells. Vines can be allowed to sprawl over the ground, but need at least 6 feet of space. To save space, they may be trained on a trellis. Large, heart-shaped leaves are highly ornamental.

Pest and disease control: Plant has its own built-in pesticide. Leaves, flowers and seeds are toxic to pests as well as to humans.

Harvesting and use: Dig tubers carefully from soil prior to frost. When the outside skin is peeled, the sweet, crisp inside flesh can be eaten raw or cooked.

Recommended varieties: Generally not sold by variety name. Gurney and Thompson & Morgan are sources for seed.

Kale

Kale is a cool-season plant originating from Europe and closely related to cabbage. It is valued for its nutritional content. It contains more Vitamin A, ascorbic acid and iron by weight than snap beans, corn or peppers. Kale is an extremely hardy plant, often surviving freezes and producing fresh greens during winter months. Several varieties are popular in home gardens, including plain-leaf and curly kinds. Colors range from light green to blue-green.

How to grow: Seeds can be sown directly in the garden in spring, or midsummer for a fall crop. Plant 1/4 inch deep in rows spaced 2 feet apart. Thin resulting seedlings so individual plants stand 1-1/2 feet apart. Do not allow the soil to form a crust because this will inhibit germination. Crusting can be avoided by frequent watering until seeds sprout, or cover soil with a thin layer of mulch.

Kale tolerates a wide pH range, from 5.5 to 6.5. Soil enriched with garden compost or well-decomposed animal manure is preferred.

Pest and disease control: Same as for cabbage. See page 99. Spraying with Sevin or dusting with rotenone organic pesticide helps to control flea beetles. Organic controls such as Dipel or Thuricide will reduce damage from cabbage worms. Planting through black plastic normally prevents entrance of root maggots into the soil. Kale shows some natural tolerance to attack from root maggots.

Harvesting and use: Plants that grow quickly have better flavor than those that grow slowly. Avoid eating older leaves because they are often bitter. Younger shoots and leaves have a sweet flavor. Frost also helps to improve flavor of leaves. Kale freezes well. Because it is so hardy, it may be better to maintain a few plants through the winter for greens out of season.

Recommended varieties: 'Dwarf Blue Curled Vates' (55 days), has low, compact growth habit and attractive, curly leaves.

Kohlrabi 'Grand Duke' hybrid stays tender even when large.

Leeks 'Broad London', with succulent white leaf stems.

Kohlrabi

The origin of kohlrabi is one of the mysteries of horticulture. Nothing even remotely resembles it in the wild. Because it is closely related to cabbage, horticulturists believe it may have developed by accident as a mutation from cultivated kinds of cabbage. Two kinds of kohlrabi are popular—white and purple.

The edible part of kohlrabi is a fat, turniplike bulb that forms along the stem just above the soil line. This bulb forms remarkably fast, especially during cool weather and periods of high rainfall.

How to grow: Sow seeds 1/2 inch deep directly in the garden. Space plants 6 inches apart in rows spaced 1-1/2 feet apart or in wide, raised rows. Because seedlings are hardy and tolerate mild frosts, plantings can be made 3 weeks before your last frost date in spring. Kohlrabi is a fine fall crop for northern states. Sow seeds at the end of summer. In desert and hot southern areas, sow in fall for a winter crop.

A fertile soil with a pH range of 6.0 to 7.0 is preferred. Add plenty of garden compost or decomposed animal manure.

Pest and disease control: Pests are usually not much of a problem. Applying an organic vegetable dust like rotenone or a chemical spray such as Sevin in the early stages will discourage flea beetles. If root maggots are prevalent in your area, add diazinon to the soil prior to planting. Or grow plants through black plastic. See Root Maggots, page 66, for more information.

Harvesting and use: Standard varieties become tough and fibrous when allowed to grow large. Pick when small—about 2 inches across. Newer hybrids stay sweet and flavorful even when left in the ground and allowed to grow up to 4 inches across. When the outside skin is peeled, the sweet, crisp, inside flesh can be eaten raw or cooked. The leafy, green tops are also edible and taste something like turnip greens.

Recommended varieties: 'Grand Duke' hybrid (45 days) is an All-America Award winner. The mild, sweet, crunchy flavor of the bulb is retained when it is allowed to grow large.

Leeks

These delicious, mild-flavored members of the onion family are easy to grow, forming thick, succulent stems from tightly folded leaves. Upper stalk of plant is green, fading to white toward the base. Plants are hardy to cold and can be left in the ground until freezing weather.

How to grow: Although seeds can be started indoors in trays for transplanting, they are best sown directly in the garden. Sow 3 weeks before the last frost date in spring. Sow seeds 1/4 inch deep. Thin to stand 1 to 2 inches apart in single rows 1 foot apart, or in matted rows or blocks. Like other members of the onion family, leeks prefer soils high in phosphorus and organic matter. Work a fertilizer high in phosphorus into the top 6 inches of the soil.

Pest and disease control: Wireworms and other soil pests can burrow into stalks at the base, causing brown discolorations and bitter flavor. Diazinon is a recommended chemical control. Or apply Sevin as a soil drench. Rotenone or wood ashes applied to the soil are organic controls that will provide some protection.

Harvesting and use: Begin in late summer when stems have thickened. Many gardeners like to pile soil against the stems to blanch them. Paper collars fitted around each stem exclude light, increase the amount of edible stem section and improve flavor. Leeks are delicious cooked as a side dish or added to soups and stews. This delectable vegetable deserves to be more widely grown in home gardens.

Recommended varieties: 'Titan' grows long, thick, succulent stalks. It matures up to 20 days earlier than the popular 'Broad London' (130 days), also known as 'Large American Flag'. Burpee is a reliable source for seed.

Lettuce 'Black-Seeded Simpson' growing in my garden.

Lettuce

Wild species of lettuce are widely distributed throughout the Northern Hemisphere. The earliest mention of cultivated varieties was in Persia around 500 B.C. Many of the ancient Greek and Roman writers mentioned it, and Pliny described nine distinct varieties. Today, more than 100 cultivated varieties are available to home gardeners. The wild progeny of modern cultivated kinds has never been positively identified, although it is generally believed to have originated somewhere near Turkey.

King of salad vegetables, lettuce is usually classified into four popular types: *leaf lettuce, crisp head lettuce, butterhead lettuce* and *cos or romaine lettuce.* All are cool-weather crops, so they grow best during spring or fall, going to seed during hot weather.

How to grow: Lettuce seeds germinate at relatively low soil temperatures, between 40F and 70F (5C and 21C). As soon as a warm spell begins in spring it is common to see volunteers come up where last year's crop went to seed.

Lettuce seeds are tiny and require a shallow soil covering—light is necessary for their germination. Cover with just enough soil to anchor the seeds—no more than 1/4 inch deep. Seeds can be sown directly in the garden as soon as soil can be worked in spring. Space rows 1-1/2 feet apart. Leaf lettuce and cos lettuce tolerate crowding and can be sown in matted rows with 4 inches between plants. They can also be grown in blocks with 12 inches between plants.

Head lettuce can be sown directly in the garden. Some gardeners prefer to start head lettuce indoors in peat pots and transplant 1 foot apart. Adequate spacing is the secret to proper head development. Evenly spaced blocks or rows are highly ornamental.

In addition to spring plantings, lettuce can be planted in late summer to mature during cool fall weather. If you live in a cold-winter area, you can grow plants under cover in a cold frame. Only in areas of the country that experience freezing weather during January and February is it difficult to grow lettuce during winter. During late summer, lettuce seeds are sometimes difficult to germinate. Temperatures above 70F (21C) hinder germination. Under such conditions consider germinating the seeds indoors in a cool location.

Regular irrigation and good soil fertility are necessary for best results. Lettuce responds well to high-nitrogen fertilizers and garden compost and animal manure. Some success can be expected even in poor soils using the looseleaf types.

Pest and disease control: The two most troublesome lettuce pests are aphids, which infest undersides of leaves, and slugs, which chew leaf ribs, causing them to turn brown. When plants are young, some growers use an organic dust such as rotenone to control aphids. Aphids can be controlled by blasting them regularly with a garden hose. To control slug populations, use slug bait. Place bait in shallow dishes so the poison does not contaminate soil. Be sure to use slug bait marked *safe for vegetables.*

Harvesting and use: Because lettuce is such a fast-maturing crop, it is usually cleared from the garden by early summer. Lettuce will go to seed when temperatures exceed 90F (32C). The space can then be replanted with warm-weather vegetables such as snap beans, or fall crops such as brussels sprouts, cabbage, broccoli, cauliflower or beets. Mature plants are best harvested before they produce seed stalks, which is when leaves turn bitter.

Recommended varieties: Variety recommendations are given in the following descriptions. Most varieties listed are available from leading seed companies. Exceptions are 'Chesibb' and 'Crisp Mint' (65 days). Seed of 'Chesibb' is offered by Michigan State University. 'Crisp Mint' is available from Thompson & Morgan.

Looseleaf lettuce such as 'Salad Bowl' tolerates crowding, so it can be grown in a wide, matted row. See photo, page 134, for a space-saving way to plant head lettuce.

Block planting is an excellent way to grow head lettuce such as butterhead, because it makes the best use of garden space. This method could also be called *growing shoulder to shoulder.*

Leaf Lettuce

Leaf lettuce types are the easiest to grow and mature the earliest, requiring 45 days from seed sown directly in the garden. Thinnings are available even sooner. Sow seeds 3 weeks before the last expected frost date for your area. Germination occurs at relatively cool temperatures, and seedlings are tolerant of light frosts. Because looseleaf varieties withstand crowding, they can be planted in wide, matted rows.

One of the great benefits of leaf lettuce is its ability to regenerate fresh, new leaves from the center whenever the surrounding outside leaves are picked. Instead of picking a whole head for salad fixings, pick outer leaves from several plants. This way your crop will last longer with less waste.

Choice of varieties among leaf lettuce is a matter of personal preference. 'Black-Seeded Simpson' (45 days) has light green, slightly crinkled leaves. 'Oak Leaf' (50 days) is early, tender and has a crisp rib that gives body to salads. 'Salad Bowl' (45 days) is highly decorative, with frilly leaves that are tender, sweet and delicious.

Butterhead Lettuce

Butterhead lettuce is the next easiest to grow. It does not form a solid head, but folds its leaves tightly in the middle, forming a soft head like a pillow. Although loose-head lettuce such as butterhead tolerates some crowding, it is best grown *shoulder to shoulder,* the heads just touching without crowding, in single rows or blocks. Seeds can be sown directly in the garden. Better results are assured if seeds are started indoors in flats and transplanted 6 to 12 inches apart.

The most flavorful of all lettuce varieties is a butterhead lettuce named 'Buttercrunch' (75 days). It was developed at Cornell University and is the winner of an All-America Award. Leaves are beautiful dark green, soft to the touch but with a crisp, delicious rib. Leaves at center of head are buttery yellow, crisp and full of sweet flavor. You can eat heads fresh from the garden, biting into the crisp, brittle interior like a juicy apple.

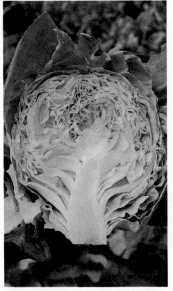

The inside of 'Buttercrunch' reveals the reason for its name. The heart is so crisp you can eat it like an apple.

'Oak Leaf' is a popular loose-leaf lettuce. Harvest outer leaves and new leaves will grow from center of plant.

Crisp head, or iceburg, lettuce will not accept crowding, and is the most difficult lettuce to grow. Space plants about 12 inches apart. One of the best varieties is 'Ithaca', which requires 72 days to reach maturity.

'Fordhook Fancy' mustard greens.

Crisp Head Lettuce

Sometimes called iceberg lettuce, these are the most challenging lettuce varieties to grow. They cannot be hurried like leaf lettuce, and they must not be crowded. The surest way of growing crisp head varieties is to start seeds indoors in seed trays or individual peat pots. Transplant to the garden about 3 weeks before the last frost date in your area. Allow 12 inches of space between plants. They can be grown through the winter in the southern part of the United States. Good soil fertility, plenty of moisture and organically rich soil will produce crisp, optimum-quality heads. One of the best overall varieties is 'Ithaca', developed by Cornell University. It requires 72 days to maturity, which is about 10 days earlier than 'Great Lakes', the traditional favorite.

Cos or Romaine Lettuce

This lettuce is highly regarded for its crispness, sweet flavor and upright growth habit, which keeps leaves clean of mud and dirt. If you have a liking for caesar salad, this is the lettuce used as the basic ingredient. One of the best varieties is 'Crisp Mint' (65 days), developed by the USDA. A more widely available cos variety is 'Parris Island' (76 days).

Lettuce for Greenhouses and Cold Frames

Lettuce cannot be stored successfully by freezing, canning or drying. But it can be grown easily during winter months in a cool greenhouse or a cold frame. Like most vegetables, lettuce has a high sunlight requirement. In northern states during the low-sunlight months of December and January, there is simply insufficient light intensity for most varieties to grow properly. 'Salad Bowl', a leaf variety, is fast growing and will produce through cloudy periods when most other lettuce varieties fail. 'Chesibb', developed by Michigan State University, is also tolerant of low light intensity. It is a cross between 'Cheshunt' (70 days), a European lettuce, and 'Bibb' (75 days), an American favorite. The result is a beautiful 'Bibb'-type lettuce in the butterhead category, with a flavor that is close to 'Buttercrunch'.

Cos lettuce grows upright, elongated leaves that stay clear of soil and mud splashes. Leaves have a crisp, succulent, central rib—one reason why it is the preferred lettuce in caesar salad.

Mustard Greens

This relative of cabbage is a fast-growing, cool-season vegetable. Mustard greens are high in vitamins A and C, plus B vitamins, calcium and iron. They are especially popular in southern gardens where they grow mostly as an early spring or fall crop. Some varieties are ready to harvest within 35 days after sowing seeds. *Frilly-leaf* and *broad-leaf* kinds are available.

How to grow: Seeds can be sown directly in the garden. Plant 1/2 inch deep. Space 12 inches between plants in rows 2 feet apart. Seedlings are hardy and tolerate mild frosts, so plantings can be made 3 weeks before your last frost date in spring. Soil should be fertile, with plenty of garden compost or decomposed animal manure worked into soil to aid moisture retention.

Pest and disease control: Concentrate on repelling cabbage maggots, cabbage worms and flea beetles. Use an organic spray or dust such as pyrethrum or rotenone. Sevin, a chemical spray, is also effective. Cabbage maggot damage is usually sporadic, and rarely affects all plants. If they are a problem, cabbage maggots can be controlled by planting through black plastic or by using a chemical control such as diazinon. To control cabbage worms, use organic products such as Dipel or Thuricide.

Harvesting and use: Pick leaves when they reach sufficient size. Choose young, tender leaves. Discard leaves showing signs of age such as browning or yellowing. Harvest before hot weather. Summer heat causes leaves to turn tough and gives them an unpleasant flavor. Mild frosts improve flavor. Many gardeners delay harvesting fall crops until after frost. Wash greens several times and steam in small amount of water. Mustard greens are also tasty fresh in salads.

Recommended varieties: 'Tendergreen' (35 days) is a heat-resistant variety. Leaves are broad, thick, dark green and have a spinach flavor. 'Foodhook Fancy' (40 days) is a frilly-leaf type. It is available from Burpee.

Okra 'Clemson Spineless' is an All-America Award winner.

'Yellow Spanish' grows round, mild-flavored bulbs.

Okra

Okra, also known as *lady's fingers* and *gumbo,* is related to hibiscus. It is a native of tropical Africa and Asia. Because of its heat resistance, it is a popular Southern vegetable.

Okra is grown for its long, green, slender pods, which form soon after its beautiful, hibiscus flowers fade. The tender, succulent pods must be harvested when young.

How to grow: Mature okra seed is hard. Because of this, germination can be erratic in dry or cool soils. One way to encourage germination is to soak seeds in warm water overnight before planting. Sow seeds directly in the garden after all danger of frost has passed. Plant 1/2 inch deep. Long periods of hot weather produce larger plants. In southern and western states, thin seedlings so that plants are spaced 2 to 3 feet apart. Space 12 inches apart in cooler areas. Allow 3 feet between rows.

Pest and disease control: Normally pest-free. Black aphids sometimes form colonies along the stems. Damage is rarely extensive. Aphids can usually be blasted off plants with a strong stream of water from a garden hose. Corn earworm can be a problem. Use Sevin chemical insecticide or rotenone organic alternative.

Harvesting and use: Begin harvest within about 55 days of sowing seeds. Once production begins, pods are best picked daily or they will soon become fibrous. If left on the plant, they eventually become dry and brittle. It is this stage that flower arrangers like to use them in dried arrangements. Care should be taken not to get pricked by the spines on pods. Even the so-called *spineless* varieties have some spines. Okra are delicious cooked as a side dish or added to soups and stews. Try them sliced and fried.

Recommended varieties: 'Clemson Spineless' (56 days) won an All-America Award. It produces quality, uniform, dark green, medium-long pods on 5-foot-high plants.

Onions

Onions are native to Western Asia. Large, edible bulbs grow the first year and flower the second when grown from seed. Onions will flower the first year when grown from *sets* or young bulbs.

In addition to yellow, white and red slicing varieties, there are bunching onions, valued for salads. Other kinds include Egyptian onion *(Allium cepa aggregatum)* and Welsh onion *(Allium fistulosum).*

Onions are hardy and can be planted in the garden in early spring as soon as the ground can be worked. Soil fertility, especially phosphorus, adequate moisture and cool temperatures in the juvenile stage, are necessary for best results.

Plants grow according to day length. As spring progresses into summer and days become longer, bulbs begin to enlarge. Different varieties have different day-length requirements. Onions recommended for northern states (long-day onions) may be unsuitable for the South (short-day onions), and vice versa. Read catalog and seed packet descriptions carefully to determine if a variety is suitable for a particular area.

Soil high in organic content, especially decomposed stable manure, produces the largest onion bulbs.

Because onions have shallow roots, it is important to maintain high moisture levels. Soil must be well drained or you may have problems with rot. Competition from weeds will hinder growth. Keep planting areas weed-free by shallow cultivation or mulch with straw. This allows air circulation and helps prevent rotting.

Although onions can be grown in single rows, a more practical way of growing them is in wide, raised beds. Plant 4 rows to a bed, 6 inches between rows. Leave 4 to 5 inches between plants.

In northern areas, the earlier you plant onions in spring, the heavier your yield. Tests have shown that onions planted in March can be 10% heavier by weight than those planted in April. In southern and western areas, onions are often planted in fall. Onions grown from transplants will mature about 6 to 8 weeks earlier than those planted from seed. Onions from sets will mature about 2 to 3 weeks earlier than those planted from seed.

Onions grown in hot, dry climates often develop a strong, fiery flavor. Mulching with straw will keep soil cool and conserve moisture to produce a milder flavor.

How to grow: Onions can be grown three ways: from *sets,* which are small bulbs, from *transplants* and from *seed.* Raising a crop from seeds or transplants will normally produce larger onions. Sets tend to put a lot of immediate energy into producing flowering stems at the expense of the bulbs.

Planting from sets is the most popular method. Plant 2 inches apart. As you harvest *scallions,* young onions, you eventually have onions properly spaced to produce large bulbs. Do not plant sets too deep. Scratch a shallow furrow and place root end of set in furrow. Fill furrow with just enough soil to anchor set.

Onions grow better with the bulb portion planted mostly out of the ground.

To obtain transplants, start seeds in seed trays 6 to 8 weeks ahead of outdoor planting. Scatter seeds over the surface of the tray. Cover with 1/4 inch of soil and maintain soil moisture. Let plants come up thick and fast—seedlings are easily separated for transplanting.

Transplants are also available by mail and from garden centers. As with sets, do not plant transplants too deep. Cover the base of the bulb with just enough soil to anchor it.

To sow directly in the garden, scratch a furrow and plant seeds 1/4 inch deep. Thin seedlings in stages so you can harvest scallions. Leave the strongest plants to mature into full-size bulbs. Space them 4 to 5 inches apart.

Pest and disease control: Concentrate on repelling onion maggot and thrips. Malathion is effective against

Onions

'Yellow Bermuda'
95 days
Mild flavor, cooking

'Spartan Sleeper'
100 days
Strong, sweet flavor, stores well

White Spanish
100 days
Mild flavor, slicing

Red Globe
100 days
Mild flavor, cooking

Leeks
130 days
Mild flavor, cooking

Bunching Onion
120 days
Mild flavor, salads

Egyptian Onion
100 days
Strong flavor, cooking

Garlic
100 days
Very strong flavor, cooking

Shallots
100 days
Strong flavor, cooking and pickles

Bottle Onion
100 days
Mild flavor, slicing

both. Rotenone controls onion maggot. Pyrethrum controls thrips. Sevin and diazinon chemical insecticides are good general-purpose controls.

Harvesting and use: Wait until tops of plants have died down before digging bulbs. Pull them up with their roots, brush off all soil and dry them for a day. Place them under shelter on screens or benches, or hang them in bunches. Good air circulation is needed for at least two weeks to fully cure and prepare them for permanent storage. To store, cut tops to 2 inches long and hang by their stems.

Recommended varieties: Most onions listed in seed catalogs are long-day types. 'Yellow Bermuda' (95 days) and 'Crystal White Wax' (95 days) are popular short-day types for planting south of Washington, D.C. 'Giant Walla Walla' (115 days) is a long-day type that has large bulbs. It is mild and can be eaten raw like an apple.

For long periods of storage, choose 'Spartan Sleeper' (110 days), a variety that will keep at room temperature without spoiling. Otherwise, choose among hybrids. 'Yellow Spanish' hybrid (110 days) has large, globe-shaped bulbs with a mild, sweet flavor. 'Bermuda White' hybrid (100 days) has large bulbs with white skin and a mild flavor. 'Giant Red Hamburger' hybrid (110 days) produces large bulbs with red skin and white, mild-flavored flesh.

Bunching Onions

Another way of growing scallions, in addition to harvesting regular onions before they form a bulb, is to grow bunching onions. Instead of each seed forming a large bulb like regular onions, a cluster of slender onions is formed. Some varieties mature quickly, such as 'Stokes Early Mild Bunching' (60 days). These can be grown in spring and early summer. Others, such as 'Evergreen Long White Bunching' (120 days), should be sown in spring or early summer for fall harvesting. Some bunching onions such as 'Evergreen Long White Bunching' are hardy and will overwinter. They will then produce early crops in spring as soon as a warm spell arrives.

Sweet Vidalia Onion

Only in Toombs and Tattnall Counties, Georgia, do you find the Sweet Vidalia onion (100 days). It is a peculiar combination of soil, sun, rainfall and farmers' know-how that produces the Vidalia. Nobody knows for sure why the same seeds and plants that bear regular hot onions produce succulent, sweet onions in southern Georgia.

Locals speculate that unique rainfall patterns and low soil sulfur content may do the trick. However it happens, the onion is esteemed for its unusually high sugar content, juiciness and digestibility. Onion connoisseurs will even eat it raw like an apple, with nary a hiccup.

Unfortunately, you must be careful where you buy the seeds and the onions. Disreputable dealers may sell regular Texas hot onions as Vidalias. To be certain you are getting the genuine article, contact the H.G. Hastings Company. See address on page 33. They mail thousands of boxes of Vidalia onions every spring. They also carry seeds and plants if you want to try growing your own.

A problem with Vidalia onions is storing them for future use. One way to prolong storage is to hang them in a cool, dark, dry place inside the legs of pantyhose. Tie a knot between each onion so they don't touch. When you want to use an onion, simply lop it off from the bottom of the stocking. One gardener I know buys 100 pounds of Vidalias for delivery in May. He eats his last Sweet Vidalia during Christmas week, using this method of storage.

'Evergreen Long White Bunching' produces clusters of long, slender onions that can be separated into scallions.

Onions in wide row appear close together, but harvesting young plants regularly thins the row.

Sweet Vidalias grow sweet in Toombs and Tattnall Counties, Georgia. Flavor is not as predictable elsewhere.

Parsley 'Extra Curled Dwarf'.

Parsley

Parsley is a hardy biennial. It may have originally come from the Mediterranean region, but its exact origin is unknown. It produces a healthy clump of aromatic leaves the first season and overwinters, even in severe climates. Plants go to seed in spring of the second season. If a loose mulch of shredded leaves or straw is heaped against plants at onset of freezing weather, plants will be protected. You will then have green sprigs during winter months. Parsley is an attractive landscape plant. Try it as a border or in containers.

How to grow: Outdoor plantings can take several weeks to germinate. Indoor sowings usually come up in several days, depending on soil temperature. Soaking seeds for 12 hours prior to outdoor sowing will hasten germination. Although young parsley seedlings are hardy and tolerate mild frosts, seeds need a warm, temperature, 70F to 75F (21C to 24C), in which to germinate. Darkness also aids germination. Because only a few plants are needed, even for large families, it makes sense to start seeds indoors in peat pots or peat pellets. Plant 8 weeks before outdoor planting time. Seed is small and should be sown thinly, covered with 1/8 inch of fine soil. Fluid seed sowing, page 38, is highly successful. It allows you to germinate seeds indoors on moist paper napkins. You can then sow pregerminated seeds directly in the garden.

Plants tolerate crowding. Thin seedlings to 6 inches apart. Spacing 3 to 4 inches apart will produce a more dense and attractive row. Parsley is also adapted to wide-row plantings—16 to 24 inches across.

Parsley is not particular as to soil quality and will grow in poor soil. Applications of high-nitrogen fertilizers and garden compost produce the bushiest plants.

Pest and disease control: Minimal control required. The parsley worm feeds on stems and leaves. It normally does not cause serious damage and can be removed by hand. Sevin chemical pesticide or organic controls Dipel or Thuricide effectively control this pest. Woodchucks are partial to parsley, but they can be fenced out.

'Spartan Sleeper' is the best variety to grow for storage. It will keep at room temperature without sprouting for several months—longer than any other variety.

Harvesting and use: Begin picking sprigs within 60 days from sowing seeds—as soon as plants have established themselves and started branching freely. The more you pick, the more new sprigs will grow in the middle of the plant. Parsley is used mostly as a garnish. It also improves the flavor of fresh salads and cooked dishes such as scrambled eggs, fish, chowders, mashed potatoes and stews. In addition to fresh use, parsley can be stored frozen.

Recommended varieties: There are basically three popular kinds of parsley: *plain or Italian parsley, curly leaved* and *parsnip rooted*. Parsnip rooted is also known as Hamburg or turnip rooted. It is grown for its parsnip-shaped roots. The most popular are the curly-leaved kinds. 'Extra Curled Dwarf' (85 days) is considered one of the best.

Parsnip 'Hollow Crown' grows tapered roots.

Wide-row planting of parsley. As plants mature, they will fill out to create a solid cover of decorative green leaves.

Roots of parsnip-rooted parsley, also known as Hamburg parsley, are used mostly in soups and stews.

Parsnips

Until the potato was discovered by Sir Walter Raleigh in South America, the parsnip was the single most important root vegetable in European cooking. Its native habitat ranges across southern and central Europe. Modern cultivated varieties are not far removed from their wild ancestors. Parsnip is tangy and sweeter than a carrot and more nourishing. The edible root is produced within 100 days of sowing seeds.

How to grow: Seeds are large and easy to handle. Sow them 1/4 inch deep directly in the garden. Space plants evenly to prevent tedious thinning. Plant seeds 4 weeks before your last expected frost date in spring. Thin seedlings to stand 4 to 6 inches apart, either in rows spaced 1-1/2 feet apart, or as a block planting in wide, raised beds. Seeds may be slow to germinate.

The secret of producing large, sweet parsnips is a rich, deeply cultivated soil. Work in plenty of decomposed organic material. A soil with stones or debris may cause malformed roots.

In the first few weeks following germination, water well. Regular soil moisture at this time helps to encourage young taproots to grow long and straight.

Pest and disease control: Controls are not usually necessary. Roots are not subject to attack from insects like many other root crops. Malformed roots are normally caused when roots grow into an obstacle in the soil rather than from pests or disease.

Harvesting and use: Begin in fall after cool weather has helped to improve flavor of roots. In southern areas with mild winters, plantings can be timed so roots mature in spring before hot weather. Roots can be stored for long periods indoors. Remove tops of plants, place in a box and cover with moist sand or peat moss. Store in a cool, dark area.

In Europe, parsnip wine is highly rated. A pie filling can be made by mixing raisins with pureed parsnips. French-fried parsnips are also a delicious side dish.

Recommended varieties: 'Hollow Crown' and All-America (both 105 days) are common, high-quality varieties.

Peanuts form large, mound-shaped, spreading plants.

Peanuts

Also called *goobers, groundnuts* and *monkey nuts,* peanuts are not nuts, but a South American legume related to peas and beans. They are fascinating to grow, educational for children and make excellent house plants in a sunny location.

The unique characteristic of a peanut plant is the way it forms nuts. First, the plant grows bushy and cloverlike. In about five weeks after planting from seeds, it produces many small, yellow, pealike flowers. Almost immediately they send out a long shoot called a *peg* from the center of the spent flower. The peg carries an embryo on the end. As it grows longer, it resembles a tendril. It arches downward and digs into the soil around the roots, then turns horizontal under the soil. There it forms a single shell containing from two to four nuts.

When you buy peanuts for planting, they are usually encased in their shells. Seed companies leave them in the shells to protect the peanut seeds. They are fragile and will split if mishandled. It is possible to plant the shell with seeds (nuts) inside. The preferred method is to break open the shell and plant the seeds separately. This way your package of seeds will go further. Also, you won't have as much thinning if the two seeds from one shell germinate side by side.

At least 100 days of frost-free weather are needed to grow peanuts. This means they can generally be grown wherever melons can be grown successfully.

How to grow: Plant seeds directly in the garden 1-1/2 inches deep. Plant after all danger of frost has passed. In short-season areas, start seeds indoors 6 weeks before outdoor planting. Space rows 3 feet apart and thin seedlings in each row to stand 16 inches apart. Although peanuts do best in a sandy soil, they will grow in a wide range of soils as long as the soil is not dense or compacted. Loose soil is necessary so the probes can enter it easily. In acid-soil areas, liming is important. If your soil is a heavy, clay type, consider planting in a raised bed. Mound soil to a height of 6 inches in a row 2 feet wide.

For maximum yields, plant varieties adapted to your area. Choose among four main types. The 'Runner' type, requiring 150 to 160 days to produce nuts, is grown principally in Alabama, Florida, Georgia and Mississippi. It has a sprawling habit. 'Virginia' peanuts need 120 days to mature and are grown mostly in Virginia and the Carolinas. Both vine types and bush types are available. 'Spanish' peanuts are bush types and are grown extensively in Oklahoma and Texas. 'Valencias', also a bush type, is grown in New Mexico. Both 'Spanish' and 'Valencias' are fast-maturing, requiring 100 to 120 days to produce nuts. If in doubt about a variety to grow in your particular area, consult your local county extension agent.

Pest and disease control: Peanuts are relatively pest-free, although they are subject to some of the same pests that bother snap beans. Nematodes can be a problem in some areas.

Harvesting and use: Harvesting is done in the fall, after frost has killed the vines. Use a garden fork and carefully lift out roots, picking peanuts from among the roots. Hang the peanuts to dry in a frost-free place for several days. Shake off soil and remove nuts by hand. Store them in air-tight containers to prevent dehydration. Roast nuts as desired. To roast, leave hulls on nuts and place in a pan or on a cookie sheet. Bake them in a preheated 300F (114C) oven for 20 minutes. Or, if you want to make your own peanut butter, you can do it with a food processor.

Using peanuts fresh is best. It is their garden-fresh quality that encourages many Southerners to eat peanuts when they are "green." Green peanuts are boiled in their shells in strong, salty water for 1-1/2 hours, and served warm as snacks. They are delicious and full of meaty flavor. Peanuts can also be hung in bunches to dry and then roasted.

Recommended varieties: The most popular peanut variety offered by seed catalogs is 'Jumbo Virginia' (120 days). It produces many large nuts. 'Early Spanish' (110 days) can be grown as far north as Canada.

INSIDE REPORT: 'PARK'S WHOPPER'

Geo. W. Park Seed Company offers a special variety with an interesting history. Called 'Park's Whopper' (120 days), pods are claimed to be the largest in the world, with some measuring over three inches in length. Here's the story as told by Bill Park, the company's president.

"An American soldier stationed in Brazil during World War II found two peanut plants growing in the wild that bore the largest peanuts he had even seen. He saved the seeds from these plants and after the war planted them around his home in Georgia, where they became a local curiosity.

"Some years later a gardener got seeds from a Mennonite farmer in the area, and the seeds were sent to Park Seed Company for evaluation. After testing at our research farm, we were able to confirm the spectacular claims. We made arrangements for stock seed increases, and released it to the home gardener in 1980."

Close-up of the popular 'Sugar Snap' pea.

Peas

Peas have been cultivated for thousands of years, and have been discovered buried in the tombs of Egyptian pharoahs. The original wild species has never been found, although evidence points to eastern Africa and western Asia as possible origins.

Three kinds of peas are grown in home gardens: *English peas,* which require shelling; *edible-pod peas,* which have tiny peas but edible pods; and *snap peas,* which produce plump, sweet peas and thick, edible pods. Snap peas are the newest of the three, developed from a breeding program in Idaho.

All three kinds prefer cool growing conditions. They are hardy and tolerate mild frosts. In the South and southern California they are grown as a winter crop.

Seed catalogs often classify peas as *smooth seeded* or *wrinkle seeded.* This describes the appearance of the peas when dried. It is an important flavor consideration. Wrinkle-seeded peas are considered much sweet-

er than smooth-seeded kinds, but smooth-seeded peas produce an extra-early crop.

Peas stop bearing at the onset of hot weather. In some instances, they can be cut to the ground and encouraged to sprout a second crop in fall. It is possible to plant a crop in summer for fall harvests.

How to grow: Because seeds are easy to handle and will germinate at 45F (7C) soil temperature, they are best sown directly in the garden early in spring. Plant 1 to 2 inches deep in double rows spaced 3 to 6 inches apart, 2 feet between the next double row. They tolerate crowding and can be spaced 2 inches apart in the row. Most pea varieties are climbers, requiring a trellis for support. Dwarf types are available and they help to support each other without a trellis if planted in double rows. Even dwarf varieties are more productive and resist rot if planted along a short trellis.

Pea flowers are self-pollinating. They set pods automatically once they start flowering. They prefer sandy soil with plenty of organic matter. Add a general-purpose fertilizer to the soil a few weeks before planting because seedlings are sensitive to fertilizer burn.

Pest and disease control: Usually not a serious problem. Deer love the young vines and may need to be fenced out. Occasionally, pea aphids are a nuisance. They can be controlled by a dousing from the garden hose, or by using a vegetable dust such as rotenone. Slugs and cutworms sometimes cause damage. See page 63 for controls. The pea weevil is a pest that enters the developing pods. It bores a hole and lays eggs inside the pea without leaving a noticeable mark. The larvae hatches while the pea is in storage and eats its way out. Sevin and rotenone control the adults. Peas are more susceptible to diseases than any other natural hazard. Seeds can be lost to rotting, which is why many seed houses offer seeds treated with a mild organic fungicide. Choose disease-resistant varieties, especially kinds that resist fusarium wilt, downy mildew and leaf curl virus.

Harvesting and use: Peas should be picked on a regular basis. Once vines start to flower, pods grow quickly,

English pea 'Burpeeana Early' can be grown without supports. Pick at this stage.

English pea 'Novella' is a dwarf. Because it has extra tendrils, it is self-supporting when grown in double rows.

'Oregon Sugar Pod' grows to only 28 inches tall, but is best grown on a trellis of chicken wire.

especially after rainfall. The more you pick, the more peas the vine will be able to produce. In addition to eating fresh from the vine, peas are excellent for freezing. English peas are favored for storing dry and for canning.

Edible-Pod Peas

The Chinese prize these peas and use them extensively. Sometimes called *snow peas* or *sugar peas,* they must be picked young before peas start to swell the pod. If allowed to mature, the pod takes on a fibrous quality. The current favorite variety is 'Oregon Sugar Pod' (68 days).

'Dwarf Gray Sugar' (65 days) is earlier than 'Oregon Sugar Pod' and can be grown without supports. A short trellis of chicken wire will encourage greater production and keep vines clean.

English Peas

These peas have two drawbacks. They must be shelled, which is tedious, and they require a lot of space to produce a sizeable crop. Some new varieties with extra-long pods have come onto the market. The best of these seems to be the disease-resistant variety 'Maestro' (61 days), developed by Cornell University. 'Maestro' yields up to 11 peas in each pod.

'Novella' (70 days) is a reliable, self-supporting pea. The unique quality of 'Novella' is its unusual number of tendrils, which intermingle with other pea plants to make a self-supporting row. The peas are small and sweet. Vines are high yielding. The tendrils can be eaten cooked, imparting a flavor similar to broccoli.

Other favorites include 'Burpeeana Early' (63 days), and 'Wando' (68 days). 'Wando' is one of the best for hot-summer areas.

Snap Peas

This variety makes pea growing worthwhile for space-conscious gardeners. Plump, sweet peas with thick, edible-pods ensure twice the amount of produce by weight compared to other pea types. 'Sugar Snap' (70 days) won an All-America Award for its many virtues.

This 15-foot row of 'Sugar Snap' peas produced over 1,000 pods at one picking. Vines were so heavy with peas they bent over the chicken wire fence used for support.

INSIDE REPORT: 'SUGAR SNAP' PEA

When I was director of All-America Selections, the national seed trials, I discussed the possibility of entering a new type of pea called a *snap pea* with Calvin Lamborn, a plant breeder from Idaho. The more he described its unique qualities—fat edible pods, plump sweet peas—the more I urged him to enter it.

The pea was duly entered, tested throughout the United States, and promptly carried off a Gold Medal—the highest award for any vegetable. It took three years for the breeder to grow sufficient seed to supply the anticipated demand. 'Sugar Snap' pea gained instant acceptance among home gardeners in a blaze of publicity never before accorded a new vegetable.

Let Calvin Lamborn tell you about it in his own words:

"In 1969, during my first year with Gallatin Valley Seed Co., Dr. M.C. Parker, then research director, explained to me his many research projects. Among these projects was a plant-breeding program to reduce parchment and strings in edible-pod peas. He had nearly abandoned the project because the pods with less parchment or strings were more distorted and therefore less desireable.

"Dr. Parker later showed me a mutant found in peas, called a *tight pod*. I examined this mutant form to learn why the pods were tight. I was surprised to find its pod walls were twice as thick as other peas. If the pod walls of edible-pod peas were twice as thick, perhaps, they wouldn't become distorted when the parchment and strings were reduced.

"This tight-podded mutation also had good-quality shelled peas. It appeared feasible that a cross between this rogue and a standard edible-pod pea might produce a thick pod without distortion and having good-quality peas.

"The cross was made and the result proved different enough from the standard edible pods and shelled peas to be considered a new vegetable. It has thick, crisp pod walls without parchment. Pods are tight and free from distortion. When the pod is bent, it will snap like a fresh, snap-bean pod, hence we call them *snap peas*. These peas can be used as a multipurpose vegetable. Pods and peas together are exceptional. Peas can be shelled out and used alone. One pod wall is as thick or thicker than the whole standard edible pod. They also can be cooked like standard edible pods.

"These snap peas are good either fresh or cooked. They are excellent for freezing, but not for canning. A good way to cook them is to stir-fry them in hot oil just a few minutes—long enough for the pods to change to a dark green color."

Dwarf varieties of snap peas are also becoming available. 'Sugar Bon', 'Sugar Mel' and 'Sugar Rae' grow 18 to 30 inches high. 'Sugar Bon' is said to be earlier and more heat resistant than 'Sugar Snap' Available from Park and Henry Field's.

Bell pepper 'Big Bertha' hybrid.

Peppers

Peppers are native to the tropical regions of South America. Two kinds are popular: sweet peppers and hot peppers, both identified botanically as *Capsicum annuum*. The sweet bell pepper is the most popular with home gardeners.

Although closely related to tomatoes, peppers are more demanding, requiring warm temperatures, abundant moisture and humidity to produce worthwhile yields. Generally, the smaller the fruit of the pepper, the easier it is to grow.

Bell Peppers

Bell types will not tolerate night temperatures under 60F (16C). They begin to wilt when the mercury stays above 70F (21C) at night. Maximum fruit formation occurs between 60F to 70F (16C to 21C) nighttime temperatures, and daytime temperatures below 80F (27C). But they will produce fruit under hotter conditions.

How to grow: Peppers are warm-season vegetables and are killed by frost. Buy transplants from local garden centers or start seeds yourself indoors 8 weeks before the last frost for your area. Plant seeds 1/4 inch deep in individual peat pots or peat pellets. Germination will occur in about 10 days at 80F (27C) soil temperature. Transplants should be 6 to 8 inches tall when planted in the garden. Set out plants after all danger of frost has passed. Space plants at least 1-1/2 feet apart in rows 2 feet apart.

To get a head start on the season, start seeds in a flat 10 weeks before the last frost date in your area. When seedlings are large enough to handle, transfer them to quart-size paper milk cartons, one seedling per carton. Give seedlings full sun and keep them watered. If they seem to grow slowly, provide with a diluted liquid fertilizer once a week when you water. Harden-off transplants 10 days before setting plants out in the garden.

If frost is not forecast, transplant one week before your last spring frost date. If frost does threaten, cover plants with bushel baskets or plastic cover-ups. At time of setting outdoors, plants should be in flower,

and the root system should fill the carton. Peel away the carton carefully, disturbing the rootball as little as possible.

Soil rich in organic matter helps maintain moisture levels. Soil in root zone should also be enriched with a high phosphorus fertilizer or with a side dressing of bone meal. Peppers react adversely to overly acid soils, growing best when the pH is 6.0 to 6.5. Liming in acid-soil areas will be necessary.

Peppers need an open, sunny location. Black plastic mulch over the soil is beneficial. It helps heat up the soil early, conserves moisture and maintains high soil temperatures during cool nights.

Water plants regularly. Spray a weak solution of liquid fertilizer on leaves and at the base of plants when plants begin to set fruit. Repeat spray every two weeks.

Flowers are self-fertile, requiring only a slight movement to mix pollen and achieve fruit set.

Pest and disease control: It may be necessary to protect plants from cutworms by fitting paper or metal collars around stems at transplant time. Aphids can be washed from plants with a garden hose or repelled by using a dusting of Sevin or rotenone.

Slugs and snails are attracted to peppers. They have been known to strip a plant down to its main stem overnight during periods of wet weather. They can be controlled by putting down slug bait in shallow dishes near the plants.

Flea beetles chew tiny holes in leaves. If infestations occur early, pepper plants are weakened and die. Sevin and rotenone repel flea beetles. The Colorado potato beetle is another pest that is controlled in the same manner.

Tomato hornworms are occasionally attracted to pepper plants. They are easily controlled by hand picking, although the organic bacterial controls Dipel and Thuricide are also effective. Some years stem borers may enter plant stems and burrow up the middle, causing the pepper plant to suddenly wilt and die. Sevin and rotenone offer some protection.

Tobacco mosaic disease can take a heavy toll of plants—not necessarily killing them, but weakening them sufficiently to reduce yields. It is best controlled by planting hybrid pepper varieties specifically resistant to the disease, such as 'Bell Boy' hybrid (75 days), 'Keystone Resistant Giant' (80 days) and 'Midway' (70 days).

Like tomatoes, peppers are susceptible to a condition known as *blossom-end rot*. This can occur when the pepper plant comes under stress, particularly from lack of moisture. It can also be caused by leaving transplants indoors in small pots for too long, resulting in flower formation before plant has developed sufficient leaf growth.

Harvesting and use: Fruit should be removed from plant carefully. Plant stems are brittle and it is easy to break them if fruit are pulled from the plant. It is better to remove fruit with a knife, scissors or a hand pruner. Staking plants is recommmended, or make supporting cylinders of inexpensive builder's wire.

Bell peppers are best harvested in the mature-green stage, when they have reached full size, just before turning red. A yellow variety, 'Yellow Banana' (75 days), eventually turns red. Once a pepper turns red it softens and deteriorates rapidly.

Peppers have many culinary uses. They are crisp and crunchy and can be eaten raw like an apple, or sliced and added to salads. They are excellent chopped and mixed with onions as a topping for pizza, steak or hamburger. Peppers also make tasty pickle and relish dishes. A basic dish is baked peppers stuffed with hamburger meat and herbs.

Recommended varieties: There are many choices among standard varieties and hybrids. Generally, it pays to grow hybrids. 'Tasty' hybrid (70 days) produces long, blocky fruit that turn from green to red. 'California Wonder' (75 days) is the most widely grown bell pepper. 'Early Prolific' hybrid (70 days) sets fruit early. Yields are heavy and the blocky, medium-size fruit are tasty. Available from Park Seed. 'Big Bertha' hybrid (72 days) is claimed to be the largest sweet bell pepper. I have grown numerous fruit measuring 10 inches in length and 4 inches wide at the top. Gurney and several others offer this variety.

Bell pepper 'Early Prolific' hybrid is cold tolerant and sets a heavy yield of block-shaped, medium fruit under adverse conditions.

INSIDE REPORT: 'GYPSY' YELLOW PEPPER

Paul Ledig, a horticulturist, was touring a vegetable garden near Chicago, trudging along rows of peppers in sticky mud after weeks of cold and rain. He was hearing complaints about what a dismal season it had been for peppers. "I was lucky if I could find two fruit on a plant. But when I came to a planting of 'Gypsy' hybrid pepper, it was loaded with fruit—up to a dozen big, beautiful yellow peppers. It's the closest you can get to a 'foolproof' pepper."

'Gypsy' was developed by Chinese plant breeder Elbert T. T. Yu at Petoseed, a wholesale seed grower, on its research farm in Woodland, California. It is early (65 days) and more tolerant of cool weather conditions than other, large-fruited sweet peppers.

Ledig further describes 'Gypsy's' benefits: "It's the best-tasting, large-fruited pepper for eating raw, like an apple. It's even sweeter in the red stage. If fruit is not harvested when yellow and allowed to turn red, its ornamental effect is magnificent."

'Gypsy' produces 12 to 18 fruit per plant. Up to 70 fruit per plant have been harvested in a single growing season, according to Ledig.

Seed of 'Gypsy' is widely available from mail order seed companies.

Bell pepper 'Tasty' hybrid ripens from green to red. If fruit reaches the red stage, pick them immediately. Otherwise, they will quickly turn soft and deteriorate.

Sweet pepper 'Gypsy' hybrid is early and prolific. Fruit ripen from yellow to red. Flavor is so crisp and sweet, fruit can be eaten raw like an apple.

A selection of peppers, from top, clockwise: sweet banana—sweet; bell pepper—sweet; 'Anaheim'—mildly hot; and red cherry—hot.

Hot pepper 'Hungarian Wax' ripens from yellow through orange to a mature red. It is highly ornamental and one of the most popular home garden varieties.

Other Sweet Peppers

A number of sweet peppers with distinctive shapes or flavors are available. 'Yellow Banana' produces abundant amounts of long, pointed fruit 6 inches in length, which turn from yellow to red. It is not uncommon to see 30 to 40 fruit on a plant at one time. Plants are ornamental and excellent for growing in containers. 'Yellow Banana' won an All-America Award for its productivity. More recently, the All-America judges made an award to 'Gypsy' (65 days), a hybrid yellow pepper. See Inside Report, page 145.

A variety of pepperoncini called 'Golden Greek' produces many thin, sweet, pointed peppers that turn from green to yellow to red. It is sold in supermarkets as a spicy, sweet pickle. But you will never find this variety offered in retail seed catalogs. Growers of 'Golden Greek' fiercely protect their interests by allowing no wholesaler or retailers to offer it. Many seed houses do offer a substitute, listed as 'Pepperoncini' (70 days).

'Sweet Cherry' (78 days) is a popular variety for pickling whole. Small, round peppers can be picked green or red. A mixture of red and green 'Sweet Cherry' on a relish plate is especially appealing.

Cultural requirements for these sweet peppers are the same as those for bell peppers.

Hot Peppers

Hot peppers vary considerably in shape, from pointed to round. They also vary in the degree of hotness and subtleties of flavor. Some, like 'Anaheim' (77 days), can be eaten raw, but they are mostly used for flavoring other foods. Chili peppers are also popular for drying and making decorative garlands.

'Anaheim' is one of the mildest hot peppers you can grow. Fruit grow up to 8 inches long and 2 inches wide, suitable for stuffing with meat or cheese filling. Plants are prolific and the fruit is edible in the mature green or ripe red stage. They are delicious raw or cooked.

'Hungarian Wax' (60 days) is a medium-hot variety growing long, pointed, yellow fruit to 6 inches long. Fruit turn red as they mature. Some varieties have been developed that set fruit on the top of plant, making them highly ornamental and popular in flower beds.

Long red cayenne (75 days) is a popular, fiery-hot pepper, with long, tapering pods that grow 6 inches in length. They start off green and change to red.

Jalapeño (70 days) produces lots of cone-shaped fruit that can be picked green or red. Taste is medium-hot. Its most popular use is for flavoring sauces, bean dips and cheeses.

Hot red cherry (75 days) is similar in appearance to 'Sweet Cherry', but extremely hot. It is most often pickled whole and served on a relish tray with Italian foods such as pizza.

Cultural requirements for hot peppers are the same as for bell peppers.

Far left: Long red cayenne is fiery hot. Plants are highly productive, producing more than 100 fruit per plant.

Left: Jalapeño is also quite hot, and is popular in Mexican dishes. It ripens from green to red.

'Norland' is a popular red potato variety.

Remove flowers from potato plants so energy goes to producing tubers.

Irish Potatoes

Potatoes are native to Peru, and were widely cultivated throughout South America when the Europeans first arrived. They gradually became an important economic crop in Europe because they were easy to grow and stored well. In Ireland, potatoes became an important food staple. When a series of bad harvests caused by potato blight produced shortages in 1846 and 1847, thousands of families died of hunger in The Potato Famine. The result was an exodus of Irish to America and other parts of the world.

Only the *tuber*—a swollen part of the root—is edible. All green parts including leaves, stems, seeds and fruit are poisonous. If a potato tuber is exposed to light and allowed to sprout, the green sprout will contain poison.

Potatoes are often grown in mounded rows or ridges. This allows extra room for the potatoes to develop. They also grow well on flat, cultivated ground with a covering of mulch. Many gardeners prefer this method. The tubers form in the ground and under the mulch. It is easy to part the mulch for early pickings without disturbing the whole plant.

I prefer to grow potatoes in a raised row under black plastic. Lots of tubers form on the surface of the soil. This makes it simple to peel back an area of plastic to reach the surface tubers.

How to grow: There are two ways to plant potatoes: from tubers, also called *seed potatoes,* and from seed. Garden centers and mail order catalogs sell seed potatoes. These are usually small tubers that are sliced in half. They are planted to produce a potato plant. Seed potatoes bought by mail are generally precut into planting pieces containing one or more *eyes.* The eyes of a potato are those small indentations from which sprouts appear. Each potato section for planting should include at least one eye, more if possible.

Wait until all danger of frost has passed before planting because potato sprouts are damaged by frost. In hot regions, potatoes are planted and grown in the cool time of the year. Space seed pieces 12 inches apart, 3 to 4 inches deep, in rows spaced 2-1/2 feet apart.

Soil should be light, fertile and slightly acid. Mix a general-purpose fertilizer into soil before planting. Water regularly for good tuber formation.

Growing potatoes from seed is possible using special varieties developed for earliness and uniformity. Regular potatoes grow slowly from seed and produce highly variable tubers. One of the big benefits of growing potatoes from seed is cost, because seed is cheaper to produce and ship than tubers.

The technique for growing potatoes from seed is the same as for tomatoes. After selecting a variety suitable for cultivation, start seeds indoors 8 weeks before the last expected frost date in your area. Sow seeds in peat pots or peat pellets. Transplant in the garden after all danger of frost has passed. Once the plants are set in the garden, culture is identical to growing from tubers.

Pest and disease control: Potatoes fall victim to a number of pests and diseases. The most common are Colorado potato beetle, flea beetle, leafhopper and aphids, all of which attack the foliage. Insecticides such as rotenone or pyrethrum organic controls are effective. Sevin chemical spray can also be used as a control.

Wireworms, white grubs and other soil insects damage tubers. They can be controlled by mixing wood ashes into the soil, by composting or by using the chemical diazinon as a soil drench. Rodents—especially mice—can damage tubers by burrowing under soil or mulch and nibbling holes in tubers. If rodents are a nuisance, set traps in the rows.

Early blight and late blight are diseases that kill the foliage. Scabby, brown, corky tissue on the surface of tubers renders the potatoes unpalatable. These diseases are best controlled by planting resistant varieties such as 'Butte', developed by the University of Idaho. Scab is a disease common in highly alkaline soils. Maintaining the soil pH between 5.0 and 5.5 will help control it.

Harvesting and use: Dig up a few tubers to see if they are large enough to be eaten. Crop usually requires about 100 days to reach maturity. If harvesting potatoes for storage, carefully lift roots and rake soil away

'Kennebec' is a popular variety of white potato. These were grown in my garden under black plastic.

to expose tubers. Brush off soil and place potatoes in burlap bags, boxes or baskets. Store in darkness at 50F to 60F (10C to 16C) for about 2 weeks in a humid atmosphere to cure. Remove to a dark, dry area and store as close to 40F (5C) as possible. Potatoes stored above 50F (10C) will sprout. Stored below freezing, they will rot and turn sweet.

Recommended varieties: 'Kennebec' is America's most widely planted potato variety. 'Katahdin' produces large, light-skinned potatoes that store well. Most popular of the red varieties is 'Norland'. Although it is earlier than 'Katahdin' or 'Kennebec', it is not recommended for long storage. 'Butte' potato, a 'Russet' type developed by the University of Idaho, has good, overall disease resistance and high nutritional value. 'Explorer' (100 days) is recommended if you start from seed. A single plant in my garden produced 30 beautiful, white-skinned tubers.

Colorful red or blue varieties are available from some mail order catalogs. See illustration below.

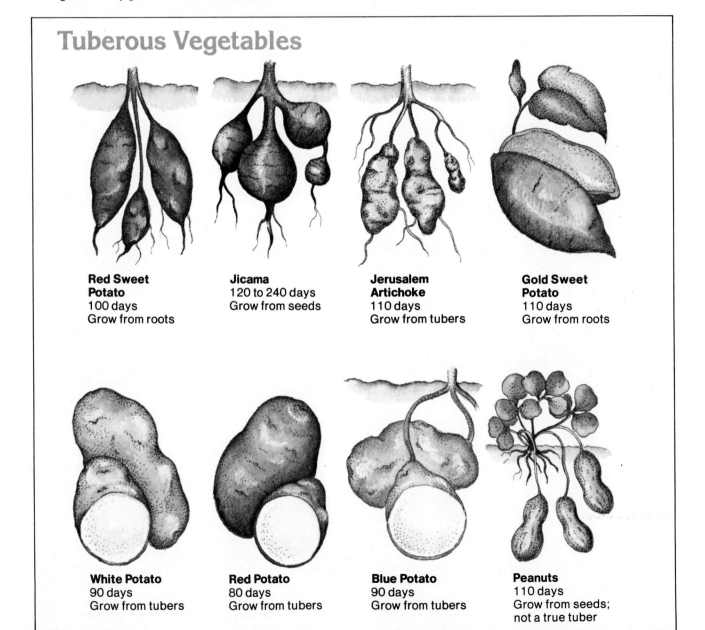

Tuberous Vegetables

Red Sweet Potato
100 days
Grow from roots

Jicama
120 to 240 days
Grow from seeds

Jerusalem Artichoke
110 days
Grow from tubers

Gold Sweet Potato
110 days
Grow from roots

White Potato
90 days
Grow from tubers

Red Potato
80 days
Grow from tubers

Blue Potato
90 days
Grow from tubers

Peanuts
110 days
Grow from seeds;
not a true tuber

'Jack O'Lantern' is the best pumpkin for Halloween carving.

Pumpkin

Pumpkins were a food staple of the Indians when the Pilgrims first arrived in America, and have been associated with Thanksgiving since those days.

Pumpkins are closely related to squash. Some large pumpkin varieties are not true pumpkins, but belong to families of winter squash. Although many wild varieties of gourds grow in Mexico, pumpkins have not yet been traced to a particular wild species.

Pumpkins are used mostly for pie filling and for decoration. Some varieties produce tasty seeds, particularly *naked-seeded* varieties. These are hull-less so require no tedious shelling. Pumpkins can vary in size from small, sugar pumpkins that are 6 inches in diameter to giant, contest-winning pumpkins that weigh over 400 pounds.

How to grow: Pumpkin seeds are large and easy to handle. Sow directly in the garden after all danger of frost has passed. Plant 1 inch deep in groups or *hills* 6 to 8 feet apart. Moisture helps make a pumpkin grow large, so work plenty of organic matter in the soil to improve water retention. Decomposed stable manure is an excellent soil conditioner. Soil fertility is also important. Lack of phosphorus will hamper development of fruit; lack of nitrogen will produce weak vines.

Both male and female flowers are produced on the same plant. Fruit formation occurs when a female flower, identifiable by an immature pumpkin underneath the flower, is pollinated by a male. This is usually done by insects. You can do it yourself using a camel's hair brush to transfer pollen from male flowers to female flowers.

Pest and disease control: Pumpkins are subject to the same pests and diseases as cucumbers and squash. A serious pest is the striped or spotted cucumber beetle, which weakens plants by chewing leaves, introducing diseases in the process. Later in the season the squash vine borer can cause portions of the vine to wilt and die. Eggs are laid along the vine by a moth. Upon hatching, the borer enters the vine, eating its way up the inside. Both can be controlled by applications of

HOW TO GROW A GIANT PUMPKIN

Growing a giant pumpkin—the kind capable of winning pumpkin-growing contests—is a special interest of many gardeners. The variety most often used is 'Big Max' hybrid, capable of reaching more than 100 pounds. It is not really a pumpkin, but a pumpkin-colored, pumpkin-shaped winter squash.

Seed from large 'Big Max' and other giant pumpkins are offered by private growers. You may find them in the classified section of garden magazines or at pumpkin fairs. If you want to compete in a giant-pumpkin contest, first attend a contest in your area, and wait to see which pumpkin wins the contest. At the end of the contest, the winner traditionally shares his seeds with other contestants. Everyone will then have an equal opportunity to grow an even bigger specimen the following year.

When the vine first starts flowering, let a lot of fruit form. Allow them to grow to the size of a grapefruit, then remove all except one. Choose the best fruit, taking into consideration color, shape and most of all, a thick growing stem. Pick off all other female flowers that form.

Pumpkins increase their weight by moisture absorption. To grow a big one requires the equivalent of 1 inch of rain each day for the pumpkin to grow 7 to 10 pounds per day. Fertilizer high in nitrogen is helpful. The more vigorous the vine, the greater its ability to grow large fruit.

Some pumpkin growers cheat a little and artificially feed their pumpkins with milk. They take a wool wick and enclose it in a plastic tube to prevent evaporation. They insert one end into the pumpkin stem and place the other end in a gallon jug of milk. The pumpkin takes up the milk through its stem, in addition to absorbing moisture from the soil through its roots. The result is a bigger and heavier pumpkin than normal.

'Big Max' is not a pumpkin, but a pumpkin-colored squash. Grow this one if you want to win contests.

Sevin or rotenone. Don't wait until you see the cucumber beetle before acting. Apply controls the same day you transplant, or as soon as seedlings emerge through the soil. Sometimes the squash borer can be detected before extensive damage is done. As soon as you see part of a vine wilt, check for a hole and look for a little pile of sawdustlike material. Poke inside the vine with a straightened paperclip to wiggle the borer out. Another method is to slit the vine to reach the borer and close the hole with masking tape to help it heal.

A number of fungus diseases can infect pumpkins, notably downy mildew, powdery mildew, anthracnose, stem blight and angular leaf spot. If you experience problems with these diseases, plant pumpkin crops in a different location the following year. If you cannot avoid planting in the same area, garden fungicides can provide control.

Harvesting and use: Begin as soon as pumpkins have turned ripe or when vines have died down after frost. Fruit should be deep orange in color before they are harvested. Cut pumpkins from vine with a knife, leaving 4 to 6 inches of stem attached. This stem should be hard and dry, or the pumpkin's keeping qualitites will be affected. Store in a dry place at about 50F to 60F (10C to 16C). Pumpkins will store up to three months.

Recommended varieties: 'Big Max' (120 days) is the variety to grow if you are interested in growing huge pumpkins. Best of the naked-seeded pumpkins is 'Triple Treat' (110 days), available from Burpee. It produces decorative orange fruit, edible flesh and hull-less seeds. It is a more sensible choice than 'Lady Godiva' (110 days), another naked-seed variety. For a space-saving pumpkin, try 'Spirit' hybrid (100 days). It won an All-America Award for its compact vine and medium-size, smooth, oval fruit. 'Jack O'Lantern' (110 days) is best for Halloween carving. 'Small Sugar' (100 days) is favored for making pies.

Sugar pumpkins are best for pies. Long, dry stems are preferred if pumpkins are stored.

Five radishes, clockwise from top: red 'Cherry Belle', 'Burpee White', 'Sparkle', 'Icicle' and 'French Breakfast'.

Radish

Cultivated varieties of garden radishes are unknown in the wild. They are thought to have developed from *Raphanus raphanistrum,* a weedy-looking species from the shores of the Mediterranean.

For such a simple vegetable, radish has many shapes and colors. Round, red radishes are the most popular. White, orange, black and two-toned varieties are also available, in round to oblong and icicle shapes.

The fastest-growing varieties mature in just 20 days from sowing seeds. These are best grown in spring. Days are cool and abundant moisture is available at this time to allow them to grow quickly. Deeper-rooted radishes, such as the Japanese long white and the long blacks, are known as *winter radishes.* They are better grown as fall crops.

How to grow: Sow spring radishes several weeks before the last frost date in your area. Also sow in fall in mild-winter areas. Plant in an area that has not been planted with any member of the cabbage family. This reduces risk of infestation by root maggot, a serious radish pest. Seeds should be sown directly in the garden, planted 1/2 inch deep and 1 inch apart. Germination takes just 4 days at a soil temperature of 68F (20C). Plant in straight rows or wide, block rows. A light, sandy soil enriched with compost and a general-purpose fertilizer will produce best results. If part of the radish root appears above soil surface, the sun can cause a hard, unpalatable crust to develop over the exposed area. Place some loose topsoil over them to prevent this.

The most important factor in growing tasty radishes is constant moisture. A single day without moisture can slow them down. The faster they grow, the better the flavor.

Pest and disease control: Concentrate on combating root maggots and wireworms, which is no easy matter. Commercial growers spray the soil with diazinon to kill them. Wood ashes raked into the soil and a spray of garlic oil are organic treatments that are said to be deterrents. Tiny flea beetles can also pepper leaf surfaces with holes. A vegetable dust such as rotenone will keep them away.

Harvesting and use: When to harvest depends on variety. Small-rooted radishes can be pulled as soon as they reach the size of cherries. Eat them raw or slice for salads. Left in the soil, radishes become pungent and take on a fibrous quality. At that stage they are good to eat sliced and steamed or stir-fried. Pungency disappears, and the texture is like water chestnuts.

Recommended varieties: 'Cherry Belle' (22 days) is an All-America Award winner developed in Holland. It is the best-selling radish variety. It is early and highly appealing, with bright red skin and crisp, white flesh. A radish variety that may eventually overtake 'Cherry Belle' in popularity is 'Inca' (25 days). It is a round, red type, resembling 'Cherry Belle' in outward appearance. But it possesses such good heat resistance

it can be grown as a summer crop in most areas. It grows large in hot weather as long as irrigation is adequate. The white interior stays crisp and firm when other radishes split or produce hollow centers. Another good red variety is 'Champion' (28 days), which reaches golf-ball size. Among so-called winter radishes, 'White Chinese' (60 days) has mild-flavored, pure white roots that grow to 8 inches long. Roots stay succulent for a long time until the ground freezes. Best of the all-white radishes is 'Burpee White' (25 days).

'Sakurajima Mammoth White Globe' (120 days) can reach up to 15 pounds. It is a late variety and difficult to grow, requiring a deep, loose soil. It can only be grown in frost-free areas of the country as a winter crop under short-day conditions. It is not suited for growing during spring or summer in short-season areas. Available from Gurney.

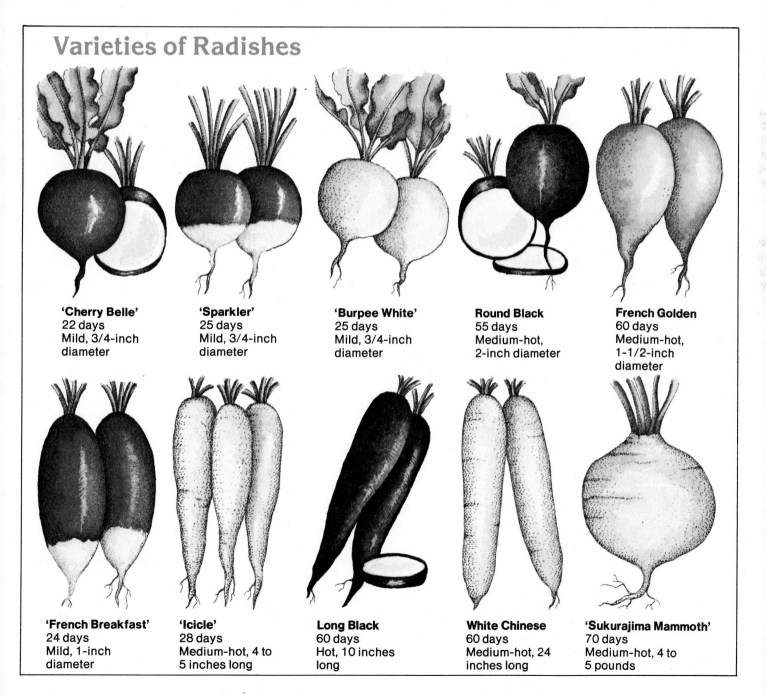

Varieties of Radishes

'Cherry Belle'
22 days
Mild, 3/4-inch
diameter

'Sparkler'
25 days
Mild, 3/4-inch
diameter

'Burpee White'
25 days
Mild, 3/4-inch
diameter

Round Black
55 days
Medium-hot,
2-inch diameter

French Golden
60 days
Medium-hot,
1-1/2-inch
diameter

'French Breakfast'
24 days
Mild, 1-inch
diameter

'Icicle'
28 days
Medium-hot, 4 to
5 inches long

Long Black
60 days
Hot, 10 inches
long

White Chinese
60 days
Medium-hot, 24
inches long

'Sukurajima Mammoth'
70 days
Medium-hot, 4 to
5 pounds

Rhubarb can be grown from roots or seeds.

Rhubarb

Wild varieties of rhubarb are widely dispersed throughout Asia, particularly in Turkey, India and China. But it wasn't until the 18th century that European gardeners began cultivating it in any quantity.

A hardy perennial, rhubarb is grown for its tart, succulent leaf stalks, which are usually boiled to produce a delicious sauce or pie filling. Stems are light green or red, depending on variety. The dark green leaf area itself is not edible. It contains poisonous amounts of oxalic acid.

Rhubarb is a cool-weather plant. It will not do well wherever temperatures are consistantly above 75F (24C) during summer, or above 40F (5C) during winter.

The coloring of rhubarb stalks is greatly affected by weather conditions. In cool climates such as the Pacific Northwest, the red coloring is intensified. Plants are larger in cool areas, with leaves reaching up to 10 feet high. The same variety in a warmer climate may grow no more than 3 feet high.

How to grow: Rhubarb is most often grown from roots or *crowns,* purchased through mail order catalogs or from local garden centers. These roots are usually planted in spring, allowing some pickings the second season. Rhubarb can also be grown from seed. If plants receive adequate moisture and nutrients, seed-grown rhubarb will also produce pickings the following season.

Planting from roots: When planting roots, the biggest danger is rot. Plant in full sun in well-drained soil. Do not bury the crown—place it level with the soil surface. Space roots 3 feet apart in rows 3 feet wide. If soil is poor quality, dig a trench or individual planting holes 2 feet wide. Fill with a mixture of equal parts garden topsoil, sand, and garden compost or decomposed stable manure. A fairly acid soil—pH 5.0 to 6.0—is best. Water regularly during dry spells. The importance of regular moisture cannot be overemphasized. In addition to soil quality, it is the most important requirement for rhubarb. Waterlogging should be avoided because it can cause rot. Planting in raised beds helps prevent rotting. In areas where winter temperatures fall to 10F to 20F (−12C to −7C), heap some protective mulch over the crowns after soil has frozen. Straw or shredded leaves will form a protective blanket that can be removed after the spring thaw.

Planting from seed: Seeds are large and easy to handle. Plant them directly in the garden 1 inch deep in groups spaced 3 feet apart. Thin seedlings in each group to the most healthy plant. If flower stems appear, cut them back. Seed production can drain the plant of energy. After plants have reached three years of age, roots can be divided to create more plants.

Pest and disease control: Concentrate on repelling the rhubarb curculio, also known as snout beetle. It bores into the stalks, crowns and roots, causing rot. It is usually found around wild dock, a common garden weed. Dusting plants with rotenone or spraying with Sevin will help keep this pest under control. Destroy plantings of wild dock around your garden, which can harbor the pest.

Harvesting and use: Do not harvest the first year after planting, and harvest only 2 or 3 weeks of the second year. Once plants are established the third year, begin as soon as leaf stalks are large enough. Once the ground thaws, growth is rapid. Rhubarb is one of the first vegetables to be harvested in spring. Harvest can continue until hot weather sets in, after which the stalks deteriorate in quality. To remove stalks from the plant, grasp a stalk firmly near its base and pull away from the plant. Stalk should come off cleanly, resulting in a "spoon" shape at its end. Do not cut stalks from the plant, as this can damage root and induce rot. Rhubarb freezes well for eating out of season.

FORCING RHUBARB

Roots can be *forced* into producing early yields. To force, follow these steps:

Outdoors. In areas of the country with severe winters, wait until daffodil bulbs start to poke through the soil. At this time, cover the dormant rhubarb roots with a garbage can, bucket or barrel. Heap straw or shredded leaves around the container for insulation. Check under the container in about five weeks. Stalks should be ready for harvesting.

Indoors. Before the ground freezes, dig up roots and plant in tubs. Leave them exposed to frosty weather for several weeks, then bring inside to a warm basement or greenhouse. Cover with a box or anything that will exclude light, and water to keep moist. Edible stalks should be ready for harvesting in 4 to 5 weeks.

Recommended varieties: Most gardeners prefer red-stemmed rhubarb to green-stemmed varieties. 'MacDonald' or 'Valentine' are most popular. 'Victoria' is a popular green-stemmed variety.

Salsify 'Sandwich Island Mammoth'.

Root of scorzonera is edible raw or cooked.

Salsify

Native to southern Europe, salsify has naturalized as a roadside plant throughout North America. It is grown mainly for its long, tapering roots that can be peeled, cooked and served like mashed potatoes. Prepared in this manner, the texture is smooth and creamy, with a delicate flavor that reminds many people of oysters.

How to grow: Salsify seeds should be sown directly in the garden. Plant seeds 1/2 inch deep, taking care that the soil does not crust, which can impair germination. Because salsify seedlings are hardy and tolerate mild frosts, seeds can be sown 3 weeks before the last frost date in your area.

A fine, loose soil is important to salsify, just as it is to other long-rooted vegetables such as carrots and parsnips. It dislikes clay soils, and prefers sandy soils enriched with garden compost or decomposed animal manure. Coarse organic material should be avoided because it can cause misshapen roots. Once seeds have germinated, water generously to help taproots grow long and straight as quickly as possible.

Thin seedlings so plants are spaced at least 4 inches apart. Space rows at least 1 foot apart. Salsify can also be block-planted in wide, raised beds spaced 6 inches between rows.

Pest and disease control: Generally not necessary. Salsify does not attract garden insects and is not bothered by diseases.

Harvesting and use: Delay digging roots until after frost in fall—cold weather improves their flavor. Plants are slow growing when young and normally require 100 days to produce useful roots. Because of their extreme hardiness, salsify roots can be left in the garden until the ground freezes. To store, cut tops to within 1/2 inch of the crown. Place in boxes of damp sand for the remainder of winter. See above for use.

Recommended varieties: Seed catalogs normally offer little choice of varieties. 'Sandwich Island Mammoth' (120 days) is the most widely offered selection. It grows roots up to 8 inches long and 1-1/2 inches across at the shoulder.

Scorzonera

This uncommon root crop is easy to cultivate, and deserves to be more widely grown in home gardens. Although roots have black skin, the interiors are white. After peeling, roots are edible raw and have a flavor similar to water chestnuts. They can also be cooked to eat like mashed potatoes.

How to grow: Plants are hardy. Seeds can be sown directly in the garden 3 weeks before your last frost date in spring. Cover with 1/2 inch of soil. Thin seedlings to 3 inches apart in rows spaced at least 12 inches apart. Plants need plenty of moisture, especially at time of germination. This helps the long, slender roots grow straight. Soil should be loose to a depth of 12 inches, so the roots do not become distorted. A fertile soil is essential, especially one rich in phosphorus.

Pest and disease control: Normally free of pests and disease. Root maggots and wireworms occasionally cause damage. To control these pests, use diazinon as a soil drench at time of planting, or mix wood ashes into the soil.

Harvesting and use: Harvest 90 to 100 days after planting. Lift roots carefully from the ground. Loosen soil around them first because they are as brittle as icicles and will break under pressure. Roots can be left in the ground until the ground freezes, or stored in a cool basement in boxes filled with moist sand. The thin, papery skin peels away easily, leaving a succulent, white root that resembles white icicle radish. It is mild in flavor and edible raw or cooked.

Recommended varieties: Not generally sold by variety name, although 'Russian Giant' (120 days), a large-rooted type, is sometimes offered. Johnny's Selected Seeds is a reliable source.

Use shallots as flavor enhancers and to make tasty pickles.

Spinach 'Melody' hybrid grown in my garden.

Shallots

Shallots, like garlic, chives and leeks, are related to onions. Their growth habit differs significantly from onions, forming a cluster of small, chestnut-brown bulbs at the base of the stalk.

How to grow: Planting can be done in early spring, as soon as ground can be worked. Buy sets and space 8 inches apart between plants, 1 foot between rows. Do not cover the bulbs completely. Push the base of each into the soil sufficiently to anchor it. Soil should be light and fertile, preferably enriched with organic matter such as decomposed animal manure or garden compost. A fertilizer high in phosphorus, which promotes root growth, should be added to the soil. The objective is to grow a large number of bulbs at the base of each plant, producing bulbs as large as possible. Give plants adequate moisture during dry spells.

Pest and disease control: Fly of the onion maggot lays its eggs on the shallots. When the eggs hatch, the maggots infest the bulbs. Diazinon used as a soil treatment at planting time is effective. Organic controls such as rotenone, pyrethrum and diatomaceous earth provide some control.

Harvesting and use: When tops have died down, shallots can be pulled from soil and separated. Spread on newspapers and allow to dry for about a week prior to storage. Use the largest bulbs for eating and save the smallest as sets for planting next year's crop.

Shallots have a strong flavor and are used mostly as a garnish and flavor enhancer. A popular way to enjoy them is whole as pickles, preserved in brine. The papery skin must be removed prior to pickling.

Recommended varieties: Shallots are not normally sold by variety name.

Spinach

Spinach is a hardy, cool-weather crop native to Persia. It has been cultivated since the 15th century in European gardens. It is one of the most nutritious leaf crops, with tasty, succulent leaves that are a source of iron, chlorophyll and Vitamin A.

Because spinach cannot tolerate hot weather, a number of spinach substitutes are offered in seed catalogs. All are flavorful when cooked, but they cannot quite match spinach as a fresh salad green. True spinach has a unique texture and succulent flavor. It is best to plant spinach substitutes for summer greens and grow the genuine article in spring and fall.

How to grow: Spinach likes a fertile soil, especially one enriched with garden compost or decomposed stable manure. Do not use fast-acting commercial fertilizers because spinach is sensitive to fertilizer burn. The medium-size seeds are easy to handle. Germination takes place within 23 days at 40F (5C) soil temperature. Sowings can be made directly in the garden as soon as ground can be worked in spring. In areas where the ground does not freeze, spinach can be grown as a winter crop. Sow seeds 1/2 inch deep in rows spaced 1 foot apart, or block-plant in raised beds. Seedlings should be thinned to stand 4 to 6 inches apart. Spinach will tolerate crowding and performs well in a matted, wide-row planting. Fluid seed sowing, page 38, is a good way to sow spinach. It allows you to sow pregerminated seeds for early crops. It also ensures a thicker stand in the row. Sown directly in the garden, spinach often germinates erratically.

Pest and disease control: Usually not many problems with pests and diseases. Even chewing insects seem to avoid spinach, and it grows when insects are not so active. In some areas, downy mildew and cucumber mosaic disease can infect a crop. The best method of control is to plant disease-resistant varieties.

Harvesting and use: Begin as soon as leaves are large enough to handle. Thinnings can be added to salads. When plants are mature, it is better to harvest whole plants rather than picking outer leaves. Loss of outer leaves tends to weaken plant too much for it to continue growth. Cook leaves or use as a tasty salad green.

Spinach leaves freeze well. If grown in a cold frame, harvests of fresh leaves are possible during winter. In areas with severe winters, you can sometimes maintain a crop of spinach in the garden. Make sowings about 40 days before the first fall frost date in your area. This allows plants to be half to three-quarters mature by the time frost slows their growth. When they are this close to maturity, plants are strong enough to resist freezing. At the first sign of a thaw in spring, they will quickly recover and produce early crops.

Recommended varieties: The All-America Award-winning 'Melody' hybrid (45 days) is early and heat resistant. Most of all, it is resistant to downy mildew and cucumber mosaic disease. Leaves tend to grow upward, clear of soil, so they stay clean and fresh for picking. As a winter crop, try 'Bloomsdale Long Standing' (48 days). Many varieties are available for local conditions. Consult your county extension agent.

New Zealand spinach is a spinach substitute that tolerates both drought and heat.

Malabar spinach grows as a vine. Use new leaves fresh in salads, or cook like spinach.

SPINACH SUBSTITUTES FOR HOT WEATHER

Three popular spinach substitutes normally grown during hot weather are New Zealand spinach *(Tetragonia tetragonioides)*, malabar spinach *(Basella alba)* and tampala spinach *(Amaranthus* species). All are easy to grow and delicious to eat, especially as cooked vegetable greens. In warm areas, a little afternoon shade will prolong the season.

New Zealand Spinach

Plants grow low to the ground, spreading in all directions like a ground cover. They usually reach 4 feet across by the end of the season. Tops of vines are the most tender. Seeds are joined together in clusters like beet seed, so thinning is essential in the early seedling stages. Seeds can be planted directly in the garden, but germination tends to be erratic in warm weather. Seeds need cool temperatures in which to germinate successfully, although plants enjoy warm weather to mature. For this reason, many gardeners prefer to start some seeds indoors. Transplant seedlings to the garden after all danger of frost has passed. Plant seeds 1/2 inch deep, with 1 foot between plants. Space rows 2 to 3 feet apart. Plants reach maturity in 70 days.

Malabar Spinach

This is a rapid-growing, vining plant, producing large, glossy, succulent leaves. It is best trained up a fence or trellis. Two or three plants are usually sufficient for home gardens. Seeds are best started indoors in peat pots 6 to 8 weeks before outdoor planting. Sow 1/4 inch deep and thin plants to 1 foot apart. They are highly sensitive to frost, so plant after all danger of frost has passed. Seeds can also be planted directly in the garden after frost. Plants require 70 days to reach maturity.

Tampala Spinach

A type of amaranth, tampala thrives in warm weather. Although it is rather coarse looking, the cluster of young leaves at the end of side shoots is tender and delicious. Sow seeds directly in the garden after all danger of frost has passed. Plant 1/4 inch deep. Thin seedlings to stand 1 foot apart in rows 2 feet apart. Normally two or three plants will supply the needs of an average family. Plants require 50 days to reach maturity. See page 84.

QUESTIONS ABOUT SPINACH

My spinach starts off fine, but develops yellow leaves and stays stunted. What's wrong?
This could be cucumber mosaic virus. Grow a resistant variety such as 'Melody' hybrid.

I never get good germination from spinach. Is something wrong with the seed I'm buying?
Spinach seedlings are highly susceptible to soil-borne diseases, especially damping-off disease. Treat seeds with damping-off fungus controls, such as captan or thiram, and you will probably see a noticeable difference.

Zucchini squash 'Gold Rush' hybrid.

Summer squash 'Cocozelle' or 'Italian Marrow'. These are often allowed to grow large so they can be stuffed and baked.

Summer Squash

Europeans never saw a squash until Columbus discovered America—all squash are native to South and Central America. This family of warm-weather vegetables becomes more diverse each year as plant breeders create new forms.

Summer squash are among the most valuable home garden crops. They are easy to grow, productive and have many culinary uses. Most of the popular kinds grow as bush-type plants, making them generally more compact than winter squash. Summer squash differs from winter squash in another important respect. Fruit have tender, edible skins when young and immature. Fruit should be harvested at this stage. If left on the vine to mature like winter squash, fruit become gourd-like with tough skins. Leaving fruit on the vine also quickly exhausts the plant's energy and reduces yields.

How to grow: Sow seeds 1 inch deep directly in the garden after all danger of frost has passed. Germination occurs in 7 days at 70F (21C) soil temperature. Plant 3 seeds in groups or *hills* spaced 2 to 3 feet apart. Thin to a single, healthy plant per hill. Space rows 3 feet apart.

If you want to get a head start on the season, sow seeds indoors 6 weeks before your last frost date. Plant in quart-size milk cartons. Fill cartons with commercial potting soil, and place 3 seeds in each carton. Planting an early-maturing variety such as 'Gold Rush' (50 days) is also helpful in producing early yields. After seedlings are up and growing, thin to one healthy plant. Keep the soil moist and be sure seedlings are exposed to full sun. Harden-off transplants for 10 days prior to setting them outdoors.

Set plants out in the garden one week *before* your last frost date. Listen for weather forecasts to see if there is a chance of frost. If frosts are predicted, cover plants with bushel baskets, hot caps or other devices.

Squash will produce earlier over a longer period if grown with a black-plastic mulch. Black plastic helps warm up the soil early, maintains even soil temperatures, conserves moisture and keeps fruit clean. In hot summer areas, an organic mulch should be placed over the plastic to keep roots cool.

Summer squash prefers soil high in organic matter, particularly decomposed stable manure. Failing this, high-nitrogen fertilizers are beneficial. To keep the vines productive and bearing summer to fall, they should be fed continually. Spray the leaves and base of plants with a weak, liquid fertilizer every 2 weeks. Plants also need lots of water on a regular basis for continuous fruit production.

Both male and female flowers are produced on the same plant, but most summer squash are *male dominant.* This means that vines produce more males than females, and the males generally appear first. Cross-pollination from a male flower to female results in formation of the fruit. This is usually performed by insects carrying pollen from one flower to another. When insect activity is insufficient, pollination can be achieved by hand. Rub pollen from the center of the male flower onto the center of the female flower.

Pest and disease control: Squash are susceptible to the same pests and diseases as cucumbers. Avoid planting squash where cucumbers grew the previous year. Cucumber beetles are probably the worst pest, sapping vines of energy in the juvenile stage and introducing wilt disease. Once established, cucumber beetles are difficult to eradicate. Control them with rotenone or Sevin. Make the first application as soon as the seedlings show through the soil or after transplanting.

Squash-vine borers are worms that hatch from eggs laid by a moth near the base of the vine. After hatching, the borer chews its way up the center of the vine, causing the end of the vine to wilt. Sometimes you can save the vine. Look for a hole with a little pile of sawdustlike material where the worm entered. Poke inside with a straightened paper clip to wiggle it out. Sometimes it may be too far inside. If so, slit the vine above the hole to get at the borer. Close and wrap the slit with masking tape and the vine will normally heal. Sprays of rotenone and Sevin help to control the squash-vine borer and cucumber beetle.

Diseases that affect squash include angular leaf spot, anthracnose, downy mildew and blight. Very few disease-resistant varieties exist. Apply a garden fungicide when these diseases show themselves. To prevent diseases, avoid planting squash in the same spot year after year.

Harvesting and use: Summer squash fruit vary in shape, but all are best picked when young. As they grow larger the skin hardens, seeds form and the edible flesh is not as flavorful. Even if you cannot use all the fruit produced on a vine, *keep fruit picked.* One fruit left to go to seed will quickly exhaust the plant of energy and productivity will diminish.

Most summer squash can be eaten raw, served as a substitute for cucumbers in salads. Try them steamed or pan-fried or stir-fried as a vegetable side dish, usually garnished with herbs for added flavor.

The large, yellow flowers of summer squash are edible. They are delicious dipped in batter and fried. Flowers usually open for just a few hours in the morning and close by noon. It is best to get into the garden early if you wish to pick blossoms for eating. Usually male squash blooms far outnumber females. Picking a few male blossoms for eating will not normally affect fruit yields.

VARIETIES OF SUMMER SQUASH

Gardeners have a wide range of choices when it comes to summer squash. It is impossible to cover every kind that can be grown in home gardens. The following varieties are the most useful and readily available.

Zucchini

Of all summer squash, zucchini is the most popular. It produces profuse numbers of slender, cylindrical fruit. A fast-growing plant, zucchini grows easily from seeds sown directly in the garden. It is such a versatile vegetable in the kitchen, that whole cookbooks have been written about ways to use it.

Basically, two kinds are available—those with green fruit and those with yellow fruit. Although green-fruited varieties are more widely known, yellow-fruited varieties are rapidly gaining in popularity.

Recommended varieties: 'Gold Rush' hybrid (50 days) is an All-America Award winner. It is favored for its earliness and excellent fruit quality. It produces a large number of female flowers, assuring heavier yields. 'Gold Rush' is so eager to bear fruit that seeds started indoors begin to produce female flowers before the first true leaves are fully developed. A small percentage of male flowers appear with the females—just enough to ensure pollination.

Another highly recommended variety, which some seed catalogs call a *zucchini squash* and others call an *apple squash,* is 'Gourmet Globe' (50 days). It grows round, green fruit that are best picked the size of an apple. You can eat the fruit raw, like an apple, skin and all, or you can slice it for cooking like regular zucchini. The interior flesh is ivory-white with a smooth, creamy texture. I grow this in preference to other kinds of summer squash. Park is a seed source. Thompson & Morgan offer it as apple squash.

How to Hand-Pollinate a Squash Blossom

'Gold Rush' with numerous, immature zucchini formed close to the stem. Flower buds are getting ready to open.

Female blossom, left, has a baby zucchini under flower. Male blossom, right, has no embryo—just a long stem.

Close-up of pollen-bearing male flower. Powdery yellow *anther* at center produces the pollen.

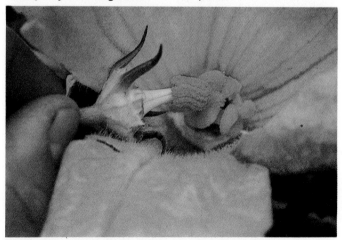
Pollen from the anther of the male flower is rubbed onto the *stigma* of the female flower to achieve fertilization. Pollination is normally performed by insects, but doing it by hand increases fruit set.

If your preference among zucchini squash is a standard green variety, then plant 'Aristocrat' (48 days), an All-America Award winner. It is early and holds its fruit pointing upward, like rockets. This keeps them clear of the ground and out of contact with soil and mud splashes. 'Cocozelle' (53 days), sometimes sold as 'Italian Marrow', is popular because it can be harvested small or large. It has delicious flavor at all stages, especially when the large fruit are stuffed and baked.

'Kuta' (50 days) is a hybrid between zucchini and winter squash. It grows pear-shape, light green fruit that are best harvested the size of a large pear. The interior white flesh is tender and smooth. Skin is soft, requiring no peeling. Park is a source for this interesting hybrid, which was developed in Germany.

Crookneck and Straightneck Squash

These productive, bush-type plants produce yellow fruit that usually have a narrow neck. Fruit are crooked, like a swan's neck, or straight. They are best eaten when young, about 4 to 5 inches in length. This is when they have a delicious, moist flavor and fine texture. Allowed to grow large, they often take on a warty, gourdlike appearance with a tough skin. Although they are not good eating at this stage, they can be used for decoration.

Recommended varieties: 'Early Prolific Straightneck' (50 days) is an All-America Award winner with heavy-yielding, bushlike plants. 'Golden Summer Crookneck' (53 days) is the most popular crookneck variety.

Scallop Squash

Scallop squash are shaped like discs. They come in a variety of colors, including yellow, white and green. These are best eaten when young, about 3 inches across. Left on the vine they will grow up to 8 inches across, looking something like a flying saucer. If allowed to get this big, they are useful mostly for ornamental purposes.

Recommended varieties: 'St. Pat Scallop' hybrid (54 days) is the best. It is a white variety that won an All-America Award for its productivity. Another valuable variety is 'Scallopini', a cross between scallop squash and zucchini. Plants are highly productive, yielding edible fruit within 50 days of sowing seeds. Young fruit are tender and can be eaten raw like an apple, skin and all.

Zucchini squash 'Gourmet Globe' is edible raw like an apple, and has a smooth, creamy flavor. Pick fruit when they are about the size of an apple.

'Kuta' hybrid is a cross between a zucchini squash and a pumpkin. For best flavor, pick fruit when the size of a large pear.

Fruit of 'St. Pat Scallop' is best eaten when 2 inches across. Fruit is tender and delicious and can be sliced to eat raw in salads.

'Golden Crookneck' shown at perfect size for picking—4 to 5 inches long. Fruit left on the vine become hard skinned and covered with ornamental warts.

Turk's turban is edible, but grown more for ornamental use.

Winter Squash

Four species of winter squash are most commonly grown in home gardens: *Cucurbita maxima*—banana, buttercups, hubbard and Turk's turban; *Cucurbita mixta*—striped cushaws and white cushaws; *Cucurbita moschata*—butternut, pumpkin squash and golden cushaw; and *Cucurbita pepo*—acorn, vegetable spaghetti and sugar pumpkins. All are native to Central and South America, where they are a food staple of the Indians. They differ from summer squash because the fruit produce a hard shell when mature. This makes them suitable for winter storage. They also require a much longer growing season than summer squash, and demand more space.

How to grow: Seeds are best sown directly in the garden after all danger of frost has passed. Sow seeds 1 inch deep. Plant vining kinds in rows 5 to 6 feet apart and bush varieties 3 feet apart.

Instead of allowing winter squash to spread over the ground, taking up valuable garden space, you can plant them in *squash towers*. These are wire cylinders similar to those used to train tomatoes. Vines climb up and over the towers, keeping plants more compact.

As with summer squash, winter squash thrive in soils that are organically rich, expecially with stable manure. Because moisture is responsible for heavy yields and optimum fruit size, they must be irrigated during dry periods.

Harvesting and use: Care should be taken to pick most winter squash varieties when they are fully mature. Picked too soon, fruit is watery and has insufficient sugar content. Certain varieties such as 'Hubbard' (110 days) and 'Golden Acorn' (85 days) can be harvested when young and eaten like summer squash. For tips on ripeness, see the following variety descriptions. Some varieties of winter squash will store up to four months. To accomplish this, storage conditions must be ideal. Store in a dry place with a 50F to 55F (10C to 13C) air temperature. Cut fruit from vine with at least 1 inch of neck attached. Necks of stored fruit must be hard and dry.

Winter squash may be cooked any way you serve potatoes, even as french fries. They make an excellent substitute for Irish potatoes, sweet potatoes or rice. Flowers are large and, like summer squash, can be dipped in batter for frying. Males and females appear together on the same plant, the males being more abundant.

Pest and disease control: Cucumber beetles and squash-vine borers can be destructive. Protect seedlings with a vegetable dust for early control of cucumber beetles. Discourage vine borers by clearing your garden plot of dead vines and stalks in fall. This prevents the insects from overwintering on the vines to infect new plants the following spring.

Angular leaf spot, anthracnose, downy mildew and blight are common diseases that affect squash. To prevent them, rotate crops each year. Use a general-purpose fungicide if diseases appear.

Hety shows off a plant of 'Jersey Golden Acorn' squash—an All-America Award-winning, bush-type winter squash.

Winter squash 'Blue Hubbard' grows vigorous, spreading vines. This vine spread is typical of winter squash, and underscores the importance of selecting bush-type varieties if garden space is at a premium.

Bush variety 'Table Ace' grows fruit comparable in size to vine varieties.

'Jersey Golden Acorn' can be picked golf-ball size to eat like summer squash.

'Blue Hubbard' grows up to 15 pounds. It's a good squash for long storage.

This is an immature 'Warted Hubbard'. Fruit grow to 12 pounds or more.

'Boston Marrow' has beautiful, deep reddish orange skin. It grows to 14 pounds, and is a good squash for long storage.

Acorn Squash

Two bush varieties, 'Table Ace' and 'Table King' (both 85 days), grow fruit that are similar to the vining kinds in size and quality. 'Table King' was developed by the University of Connecticut, and has the distinction of being awarded an All-America Award. It produces dark, ebony-green fruit with golden yellow flesh. Seed cavity is small. Matures earlier than vining varieties. Fruit are 6 inches long and 5 inches across. They have prominent ribs that create an attractive star shape when cut across the middle.

Both 'Table Ace' and 'Table King' are traditional types of acorn squash, having dark green skins. They are best harvested when fully mature. Test for ripeness by examining the underside of fruit. A patch of yellow forms where the skin touches the ground. An indication of ripeness is when this yellow patch changes to orange. Under storage conditions, the orange area may spread until the whole fruit becomes orange.

The best acorn squash is a golden yellow variety called 'Jersey Golden Acorn' (85 days). It was developed by Dr. Oved Shifriss at Rutgers University and was a winner of an All-America Award. Squash develop on bushy plants, and can be picked during two stages of their development. Pick two days after pollination when the fruit are the size of a golf ball, or when the squash reach their full size of 5 inches long. At the immature stage they can be eaten raw, and have a smooth, creamy flavor reminiscent of sweet corn. Fruit are tender and the pale, yellow skin requires no peeling. Left on the vine, skin hardens and the color changes to a deep golden yellow. At this stage the fruit can be cut in half and baked until tender. Extra fruit can be stored in a cool basement, garage or similar location.

A tasty dish can be prepared from acorn squash. Cut down the middle of a fruit and scoop out seeds. Fill the hollow with maple syrup. Bake in an oven for 30 minutes at 350F (177C), or until tender.

Blue Hubbard

Blue hubbard grow to be the largest of all edible squash—over 15 pounds. Skin is blue-gray and flesh is bright yellow. Because of their size, they are not always practical for the average family. Requires 120 frost-free days to produce ripe fruit. Fruit are ripe when the vines die down.

Flesh is sweet and the fruit store well. It can be used as a substitute for pumpkin in pumpkin pies.

Boston Marrow

This squash has a shape similar to blue hubbard. It possesses the most beautiful skin coloring of all squash. Its glowing, reddish orange color gives it value as an ornamental at Halloween or Thanksgiving. Unfortunately, the fruit size, 15 pounds or more, is too large for the average family to use efficiently. Fruit require about 120 days to reach maturity, and are ripe when the vines die down.

To cook, seeds must be removed and the flesh cut into manageable portions for baking, or for serving like mashed potatoes.

Buttercup Squash

It no longer pays to plant the vining types of buttercup squash. Varieties are available that produce top-quality fruit on bushy plants. The variety that does this best is 'Sweet Mama' hybrid (85 days), winner of an All-America Award. Tips of vines can be pinched off at 4 feet. A concentration of fruit will then mature near the base of plant. This variety shows tolerance to wilt disease and squash-vine borer. Fruit are ripe when they reach 5 to 6 inches across and cease growth.

Drum-shaped, dark green fruit have golden yellow flesh similar to acorn squash. Delicious steamed or baked, one fruit will feed two people.

Butternut Squash

Butternut is considered by many to have the finest flavor of all winter squash. It is not widely grown because of the room required to accommodate the sprawling vines. Home gardeners can now take a new look at butternut, due to two space-saving varieties. The first is a bush-type called 'Butterbush' (85 days). Fruit are not as large as 'Waltham Butternut' (85 days), the standard butternut variety, and the flavor is not quite as sweet. But crops mature ten days earlier on plants that grow 3 to 4 feet long. Yield is an average of 4 fruit per plant and fruit weigh 1-1/2 pounds each.

'Butter Boy' hybrid (80 days) produces fruit equal in quality to 'Waltham Butternut' in one-third the space. Fruit average 2-1/2 to 2-3/4 pounds each. They develop close to the base of the plant, rather than spread out along a rambling vine. Fruit are ripe when vine growth stops and skin changes from light tan to deep tan.

Cushaw

There are two species of cushaw squash. Golden cushaw (*Cucurbita moschata*) (110 days) has tan-colored skin. Green-striped cushaw (*Cucurbita mixta*) (110 days) has white skin with green stripes. Both have curved necks and grow on rambling vines. Fruit grow up to 10 pounds each.

Golden cushaw is ripe when vines start to die and skin turns from pale tan to deep tan. Striped cushaw is ripe when vines start to die and the pale green striping turns to bright green.

To cook either type, slice in half lengthwise and scoop out the seed cavity. Chop into manageable portions for baking in an oven. Or cut into sticks for deep frying.

'Gold Nugget'

This variety looks like a summer squash because of its bushy growth habit and the large number of fruit it produces. It stores and tastes like a winter squash. Each plant yields up to 8 fruit the size of a softball. They are deep orange with a contrasting white ring at the blossom end. Fruit mature in 95 days. You can tell fruit are ripe when they change from pale yellow to deep orange.

The thick orange flesh tastes superb steamed or baked. One fruit is sufficient to serve two people. Winner of an All-America Award.

'Sweet Mama' hybrid is a buttercup-type squash, growing large fruit with golden yellow flesh. Plants have a bush habit—good for small gardens.

Butternut squash 'Butter Boy' hybrid, harvested from my garden. Five fruit like this set within 3 feet of the crown.

'Gold Nugget' grows bushy plants and sets a lot of decorative orange fruit.

Tahiti squash produce enormous fruit with long necks. Plants are extremely vigorous—vines grow up to 10 feet long. Fruit can be eaten raw or cooked like potatoes.

'Banana' winter squash can grow large—the world's record is 135 pounds. This specimen weighs around 15 pounds—a good size for eating.

'Vegetable Spaghetti' winter squash grows well up any kind of support. At right, a squash after cooking shows the "spaghetti" interior scooped out with a fork.

Tahiti Squash, Melon Squash

Fruit is similar in appearance to golden cushaw. Flesh color is a slightly deeper, reddish orange. It also has a sweeter flavor than other winter squash. Fruit can be eaten raw. It has a carrotlike texture and flavor similar to sweet potatoes. Some think the flavor is slightly suggestive of cantaloupe, hence its second name, melon squash. It needs 100 days to produce ripe fruit. Any fruit that are green when frost hits usually turn a tan color during storage and ripening.

Turk's Turban

This is one squash grown for ornamental value rather than for eating, but it is certainly edible. Fruit are distinctively shaped like a Turk's turban and brilliantly colored, with bands of red, green and white. They have special appeal as Halloween or Thanksgiving decorations. Vines require at least 5 feet of space, in rows spaced 6 feet apart. Fruit ripen in about 100 days. Wait until the color contrast between the red, green and white stripes is bright before harvesting.

Vegetable Spaghetti

Mr. T. Sakata, a Japanese plant breeder responsible for introducing spaghetti squash, discovered the squash growing as a cultivated vegetable in Mainland China. He tried introducing it to American gardeners under the name Spaghetti Squash about 1930. But it did not sell so he took it out of his catalog. Thirty years later, he introduced it again under the name Vegetable Spaghetti, and sales took off. Today, it is one of the most popular of all squash. It sells at the supermarket produce counter—the ultimate acceptance of a vegetable. Fruit grow on rambling vines that can be trained to climb. In fact, training them up a trellis to save space is a good way to grow them. Initially fruit are ivory-white, and reach up to 4 pounds. At maturity they turn golden yellow—the best time to pick them.

Grown up a trellis or fencing, plants can be spaced 2 feet apart. If grown on the ground, allow 3 to 5 feet between plants in rows 4 to 6 feet apart.

To cook Vegetable Spaghetti (80 days), puncture fruit with a fork and bake in an oven at 350F (117C) for 45 minutes. Before cooking, the inside is solid. After cooking, slice fruit lengthwise and remove all seeds from the center. Scoop the spaghetti strands away from shell and fluff out the creamy white strands with a fork. See photo at left. Serve with a parsley-butter sauce or your favorite spaghetti sauce.

QUESTIONS ABOUT SQUASH

Will my squash cross with my melons and spoil their flavor?
Definitely not. It is genetically impossible for squash and melons to cross. Although squash, cucumbers and melons belong to the same family, *Cucurbitaceae,* they are totally different and incompatible species within that family. Certain squash can cross with each other, however. This is how plant breeders create new varieties.

Alpine strawberry 'Baron Solemacher'.

Sunflower 'Sunbird' hybrid grows large seedheads.

Alpine Strawberry

Alpine strawberry, *Fragaria vesca,* is similar to the common cultivated strawberry, *Fragaria x ananassa.* But many gardeners consider alpine strawberry a berry fruit rather than a vegetable fruit. Because it grows from seeds rather than roots, it is usually listed in the vegetable section of seed catalogs. The vegetable garden is only one place to grow the bushy, compact plants. They also make an attractive ground cover in the landscape. Berries are sweet and appear the first season if seeds are started early indoors.

How to grow: Start seeds indoors 8 to 10 weeks before planting outdoors. Seeds are tiny and need light to germinate, so do not cover them completely with soil. Press seeds into moist soil to anchor them. Germination can be erratic, but seedlings will make an appearance after 14 to 21 days. Plant outdoors after all danger of frost has passed, although alpine strawberry will tolerate mild frost. Space plants 8 to 12 inches apart in rows spaced 1-1/2 to 2 feet apart.

Never allow the soil surface to dry out after planting. Maintain moisture by misting soil surface with a spray bottle. Water flowing from a watering can or hose will disturb the seeds.

Pest and disease control: Generally pest and disease-free until plants begin bearing fruit. When fruit appear, cover rows with plastic netting to protect against birds and mice. If berries come in contact with soil they will rot. Prevent rot by applying a mulch of straw or other organic material over the soil.

Harvesting and use: Start picking fruit as soon as they are ripe—midsummer to fall—on a continuous basis. Eat fresh as a dessert fruit or serve with fresh cream. Berries can also be frozen and made into delicious jam.

Recommended varieties: 'Alexandria' (100 days), available from Park and Thompson & Morgan, produces the largest fruit. Plant breeders are in the process of creating varieties with even larger fruit. Seed of 'Alexandria' is sometimes in short supply. If unavailable, 'Baron Solemacher' (105 days) is a good substitute.

Sunflower

Giant sunflowers are native to the American continent. They are grown mainly for their highly nutritious seeds, which are edible when shelled. They grow quickly, producing beautiful flowers that mature into heavy seedheads measuring up to 24 inches across. In a single season, a sunflower can grow to 20 feet high. They are best confined to a special area of the vegetable garden, where they will not shade other vegetables. Sunflowers also emit a toxin from their roots that inhibits growth of nearby plants. This will affect vegetable plants if they are planted within 3 feet.

How to grow: Sow seeds directly in the garden in a sunny location after all danger of frost has passed. Seeds are large and easy to handle. Plant 1 inch deep, 1 foot apart in rows spaced 3 feet apart. Germination occurs in 10 days at 70F (21C) soil temperature. Soil should be fertile for largest heads and meatiest seeds. Plants respond to a general-purpose fertilizer worked into the soil at the start of the season. Follow with a booster application when flower heads appear.

Pest and disease control: The biggest pest problem is birds that strip seeds from the mature flowerheads. Many gardeners like to plant sunflowers around the home specifically to attract birds. If *you* want the seeds, tie cheesecloth or clear plastic bags with air holes around the heads when they are nearly ripe.

Harvesting and use: Begin when the seedhead becomes so heavy it appears ready to bend over and spill its seeds on the ground. Cut heads and hang in a warm, dry place. When heads have dried, rub the surface with your hand and seeds will fall out. Seeds are high in protein and can be roasted, shelled and eaten as snacks. Health food stores sell machines that will dehull seeds. Sunflowers are also rich in oil.

Recommended varieties: 'Sunbird' (68 days) is a dwarf variety, producing large heads on stems that grow half the height of regular giant sunflowers. Burpee is a source. The variety to grow for the largest seedheads is 'Mammoth Russian' (80 days), available from most mail order sources.

Sweet-potato vines showing width of plant spread.

Sweet Potatoes

Sweet potatoes are members of the morning glory family, native to South America. They produce dense, vigorous vines on top of the soil and large, sweetly flavored, tuberous roots underground. They are often called *yams,* a misnomer. True yams are species of the genus *Dioscorea,* an important food crop of the tropics. See Chinese Yam, page 175.

Although sweet potatoes are perennials in frost-free climates, they are treated as cold-tender annuals in cooler regions. The secret of success is to start with healthy transplants. They can quickly establish themselves in the garden after danger of frost has passed. Plants can then produce a worthwhile crop of large roots before fall frost kills vines.

How to grow: There are two ways to obtain transplants—from a mail order source, or grow your own. One large root is capable of producing 50 healthy transplants.

If plants are purchased by mail, open the package on arrival and plant as soon as possible. Expect mail order plants to look a little wilted or off-color on arrival. But don't be alarmed. Sweet potatoes are tough and will generally recover. Plant in late afternoon—exposure to direct sun and wind can shock plants. If planting must be delayed, place roots in moist sand or wet sawdust or inside a wet burlap bag.

To grow your own transplants, start a root indoors 8 to 10 weeks before planting outdoors. Select a firm, healthy root and sink it lengthways to half its depth into moist sand or potting soil. Keep at room temperature in a bright window, away from direct sun.

For the biggest crop, it is better to transplant young sprouts to a seed flat or box. The box should be filled with good growing medium such as a potting mix or decomposed compost. Give the sprouts warmth and light and feed with a weak, liquid fertilizer. When they are transplanted to the garden, they will usually grow rapidly.

Sweet potatoes are best planted in raised mounds. Mounds should be 10 inches high, 16 inches across at the base and 6 inches across at the top. Leave 4 feet of space between the mounded rows. A black-plastic mulch can be placed over this to help warm the soil, conserve moisture and eliminate weeds. Space transplants 12 inches apart. Because sweet potatoes sprout roots from their stems like tomatoes, transplants should be covered with soil along the stem. Leave the crown of leaves showing. Sweet potatoes prefer a pH of 6.5, which is slightly acid. They can tolerate even higher acidity—up to 5.0—without adversely affecting yields.

Four months of warm, frost-free weather are needed to produce worthwhile yields. Sweet potatoes are not fussy about soil, but respond best in soil that is sandy with high organic content.

Pest and disease control: Not a serious problem except in areas with nematodes. Prevent nematode infestations by rotating crops. To eliminate nematodes from the soil, fumigation may be necessary before the planting season begins. This is best left to professionals. See page 65.

Harvesting and use: Roots must be dug before frost kills the vines. The keeping qualities of the roots may also be adversely affected by cold. Use a garden fork to carefully lift roots and clean away soil. Separate potatoes into two piles—firm, unblemished roots for storage, and damaged roots for immediate consumption.

Unblemished roots should be cured at 70F to 80F (21C to 27C) air temperature. Curing is done by allowing roots to air-dry covered, out of direct sunlight, to toughen skins and heal minor blemishes. Properly cured and stored, they will keep up to 5 months.

Recommended varieties: 'Centennial' is America's leading sweet-potato variety. It has beautiful, deep orange flesh and deep orange skin, capable of growing extra-large roots. For gardeners interested in saving space, 'Porto Rico' is the best choice. It is a vineless, bush-type variety. Roots are medium size and have copper-colored skins and red flesh. Flavor is distinctive—like a chestnut—and excellent for baking whole.

Starting Sweet Potatoes Indoors
Half-submerge a sweet-potato root in a jar of water. Hold the top to the sides of the jar with toothpicks stuck in the root. Or sink a root lengthways to half its depth in moist sand or potting soil. Within a few weeks, the sides of the root will send up leafy shoots that sprout roots from the base. These can be removed and planted directly in the garden.

'Better Boy VFN' is disease resistant and produces large fruit.

Tomatoes

The tomato is native to Peru, although wild species are widely dispersed throughout Central and South America. The greatest concentration of wild species is in Mexico. Spanish priests found tomatoes growing in Mexico around 1550. They introduced the yellow-fruited kinds to Europe as an ornamental plant, where it was called *pomidoro,* meaning golden apple. Another popular term, *love apple,* comes from an early botanical name, *Poma amoris,* meaning amorous apple. "For the amorous aspect, or beauty of its fruit," according to an early English botanist.

No matter how you look at it, the tomato is America's most popular vegetable. Commercially, tomatoes are grown for fresh market use. They are used to make tomato soup, paste, catsup and sauce. More than 75% of America's home gardeners grow tomatoes in backyard plots. Snap beans are a close second in popularity, followed by sweet corn.

Despite this popularity, more misinformation seems to surround the tomato than any other popular vegetable. But it has always been that way. It took 400 years to accept the fact that tomatoes were not deadly poisonous.

From the moment of its discovery by Europeans, the tomato was treated with suspicion. The wild species closely resembles deadly nightshade, a related poisonous plant. Foraging animals would not touch it because of a toxin in the plant. When the leaves or stems were crushed or bruised, they gave off a repellent odor. Those people brave enough to venture a nibble of the wild fruit were not encouraged to venture a second bite. Fruit were seedy, rough skinned and sour tasting.

Until 1870, tomatoes earned little space in seed catalogs. Even then, they were usually placed in the ornamental section, among flowering annuals and perennials. What seems to have changed the fortunes of the tomato more than anything was an Ohio seedsman, Alexander W. Livingston. He set his sights on breeding varieties with smooth, round shapes and meaty flavor. After five years of work he introduced 'Para-gon', a mild-flavored, uniformly smooth-fruited variety. It became the world's first commercially successful tomato.

How to grow: Tomatoes are tender plants, susceptible to frost damage. Start seeds indoors 6 to 8 weeks before the last frost date in your area. Plant 1/4 inch deep in peat pots or other seed-starting devices. You can also buy transplants from garden centers. If seeds are started indoors on a windowsill, be sure they receive enough light. Elevate pots so they are level with the windowsill. Without sufficient light, seedlings stretch toward the sun, which weakens them. Set plants in the garden after all danger of frost has passed. Space plants 2 feet apart when staked, 3 feet apart unstaked. Allow 3 feet between rows for *determinate* types, 4 feet for *indeterminate* types. See bottom of page 168.

If you want to get a head start on the season, start seeds in quart-size milk cartons filled with a commercial potting mix. Plant 2 or 3 seeds in each container. When seedlings appear, thin to a single, healthy transplant. The size of the milk carton allows plants to develop large root systems. When the seedlings are transplanted, the paper cartons are easy to tear away, which lessens transplant shock.

Set plants in the garden when transplants reach about 6 to 10 inches tall. They should be *hardened-off*—gradually adjusted from the warm indoors to the cooler outdoors—before planting. See page 40. If you want to risk it, you can set plants out one week before the last average frost date. If frost or cold temperatures are forecast, be sure to protect transplants. Bottomless plastic milk containers placed over plants and held in place with a stone or a stake are ideal for this purpose.

Tomato plants should be set deep in the soil. A normal practice is to set plants in the ground up to their first true leaves. Roots are produced along the length of the buried stem, which makes a stronger, faster-growing plant.

Be careful not to damage the fine feeder roots when

Tomato flowers are *self-pollinating*—flowers have male and female organs. Shaking flower clusters distributes pollen to help increase fruit set.

seedlings are planted. If feeder roots are damaged, it may prevent plant from taking up sufficient amounts of moisture. Lack of moisture can result in a disorder called *blossom-end rot,* which shows itself as a blackened area on the underside of ripening fruit. This condition is actually caused by lack of calcium, a trace element. Damaged feeder roots and irregular watering prevent plants from absorbing sufficient calcium. Reduce the susceptibility of blossom-end rot by watering plants regularly. Mulching plants will also help the soil retain moisture.

A soil rich in compost or other organic matter is best for tomatoes. Also work a handful of general-purpose fertilizer and a handful of bonemeal—high in phosphorus—into the soil at each planting hole. Planting through black-plastic mulch, as shown on page 14, is also helpful. The plastic warms the soil to get plants growing faster. A slightly acid soil with a pH range of 6.0 to 6.7 is best. If soil is too acid, it will cause poor yields and late ripening. Liming may be necessary every other year in acid-soil regions. Liming also helps prevent blossom-end rot—lime is a source of calcium.

To keep plants productive, apply booster fertilizers. Spray leaves and base of plants with a dilute liquid fertilizer every two weeks when fruit begin to enlarge.

Tomatoes are *self-pollinating,* meaning flowers contain both male and female parts. To set fruit, all that is required is to mix up the pollen. This is done by breezes and movement of the flower trusses. Gardeners can help pollination by lightly shaking the blossoms. Best time to shake the blossoms is during the warm part of the day when humidity is low. Some gardeners use an electric toothbrush to vibrate the individual blossoms.

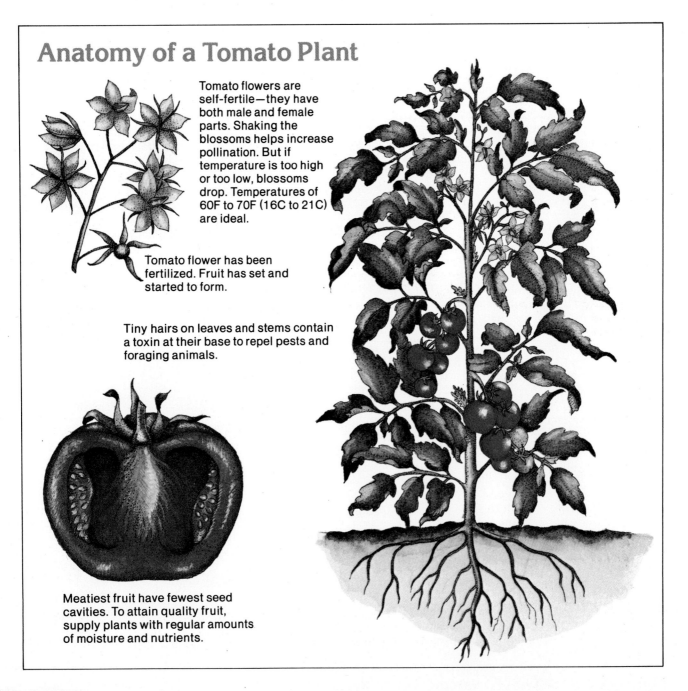

Anatomy of a Tomato Plant

Tomato flowers are self-fertile—they have both male and female parts. Shaking the blossoms helps increase pollination. But if temperature is too high or too low, blossoms drop. Temperatures of 60F to 70F (16C to 21C) are ideal.

Tomato flower has been fertilized. Fruit has set and started to form.

Tiny hairs on leaves and stems contain a toxin at their base to repel pests and foraging animals.

Meatiest fruit have fewest seed cavities. To attain quality fruit, supply plants with regular amounts of moisture and nutrients.

The tomato sets fruit within a fairly narrow temperature range of 60F to 70F (16C to 21C) night temperatures. Some gardeners encourage a more reliable fruit set by the use of a plant-growth regulator such as Blossom-Set. If temperatures are too hot or too cold, the plant has difficulty producing the necessary hormones on its own, so fruit fails to form. A commercial spray such as Blossom-Set supplies the tomato flower with hormones to help the plant set fruit.

Pest and disease control: When you visit your garden one morning and discover your tomato plants have wilted overnight, there is a good chance it is wilt disease. No cure is known. The only way to avoid wilt is to plant wilt-resistant varieties. These are indicated by the initials VF after the name—*verticillium/fusarium* resistant—such as 'Supersonic VF'. The name 'Better Boy VFN' indicates resistance to verticillium and fusa-

rium wilt and to nematodes. A condition similar to wilt disease can be caused by black-walnut trees. Roots of these trees give off a toxin destructive to tomatoes.

A number of other diseases can infect tomatoes, such as early and late blight, anthracnose and tobacco mosaic. Insect control, winter clean-up and not smoking in the garden—a source of tobacco mosaic—will help prevent these diseases. If a particular disease does establish itself, plant a resistant variety the next season. For example, the All-America Award winner 'Floramerica' hybrid (72 days) is resistant to 15 tomato diseases, including anthracnose and tobacco mosaic. 'Gurney Girl' hybrid (70 days) is resistant to tobacco mosaic, verticillium, fusarium and nematodes.

A number of tomato diseases, particularly anthracnose and early and late blight, can be controlled by using a broad-spectrum garden fungicide.

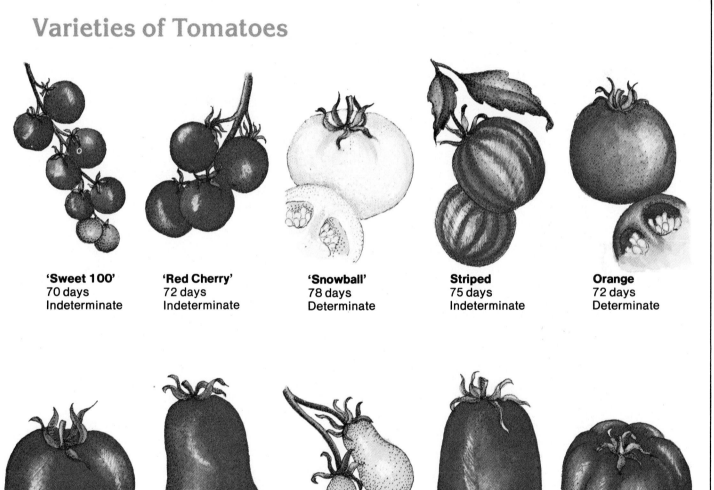

Varieties of Tomatoes

'Sweet 100'
70 days
Indeterminate

'Red Cherry'
72 days
Indeterminate

'Snowball'
78 days
Determinate

Striped
75 days
Indeterminate

Orange
72 days
Determinate

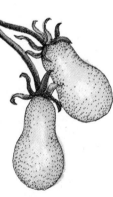

'Big Boy'
78 days
Indeterminate

'Roma VF'
67 days
Determinate

Yellow Pear
70 days
Indeterminate

Square Tomato
75 days
Determinate

Beefsteak
80 days
Indeterminate

Pine needles over black plastic serve as mulch between rows of tomatoes.

If you stake plants, drive stakes in ground before tomatoes are planted.

Wire cages are excellent as tomato trainers. You don't have to prune or tie plants. As they grow, branches push through the wire mesh so they become self-supporting.

'Beefmaster' hybrid allowed to sprawl on the ground. Fruit production is heavy, but vines take up a lot of space. Fruit and leaves are also more susceptible to pests and diseases.

Tomatoes are plagued by a few insects. Weekly sprays of pyrethrum-rotenone combination organic insecticide will control most pests. Cutworms are dealt with in another manner. They are fat, gray worms that live in the soil curled up in a semicircle. At night, they crawl to the surface and chew tomato seedlings off at soil level. Be alert for them while you are in the garden and remove them by hand. To prevent cutworm damage, you can make protective collars for each tomato plant. Take a paper or plastic drinking cup and cut a hole in the bottom. Slip the cup over each tomato plant. Bury the lip of cup in the soil and the cutworm will not be able to reach the tomato stem.

The tomato hornworm can cause considerable damage to the foliage. This pest appears later in the season. Worms can get up to 4 inches long or more, yet their markings allow them to blend with the leaves. To control, pluck them off by hand and dispose of them.

Colorado potato beetles also defoliate plants. They can be more destructive than the tomato hornworm. Fruitworms can spoil a lot of fruit. Sevin or rotenone will control these pests.

Tomatoes are a favorite target of nematodes, but there are several nematode-resistant varieties. Look for the "N" in the variety name.

TRAINING TOMATOES

There are three basic ways to grow tomatoes: sprawled on the ground; pruned and staked; and unpruned inside wire cages. The cage method is gaining popularity because it is easy and saves labor.

Generally, tomatoes grown on the ground produce more fruit, but they are susceptible to attack from pests and diseases. They also require a lot of room.

Tomatoes that are staked and have suckers and side shoots removed produce larger and better-looking tomatoes, but yields are less than with other methods. Tying and pruning can also be tedious.

Wire cages made of concrete reinforcing wire or similar material are simple to make. They are cylinders that encircle the tomato plant. As the plant grows, it pushes its branches through the wire, making it self-supporting. Plants produce well and the cages take up little space.

Harvesting and use: Tomatoes are killed by frost. When nights start getting cool, keep a close watch on the weather forecast. Just before frost hits, gather all tomatoes, green and red, and take them indoors. They will ripen gradually over a period of time. You can also pull up entire vines, tomatoes and all, and hang them in a frost-free garage or basement area. Tomatoes do not require light to ripen. In fact, bright sunlight shining directly on ripening fruit can cause *sunscald*—a pale, whitish patch that gives a bad taste.

Recommended varieties: Part of the fun of growing tomatoes is deciding the varieties to grow. During the gardening season you can compare them for earliness, yield and flavor with those of your neighbors, relatives and friends.

Tomatoes can be divided into several categories. There are hybrid and standard varieties. Hybrids are generally more productive. Tomatoes can also be classified by their growth habit. *Determinate* means vines are short and bushy and grow only to a certain height. These are ideal for growing on the ground or in containers. *Indeterminate* means that vines continue to grow indefinitely, until killed by frost or exhausted by age. They are long and rambling and do best with support.

Tomatoes are available in a variety of colors and shapes. There are red, orange, yellow and white varieties. There is also a yellow-and-red striped variety. There are giant-fruited tomatoes, sometimes called *beefsteaks,* large-fruited tomatoes, cherry tomatoes, pear or paste tomatoes, and a miscellaneous group known as *novelties.*

The following lists several popular varieties according to size. Unless stated otherwise, all are indeterminate plants.

Beefsteak or Giant-fruited

Although there is a 'Beefsteak' variety (80 days), beefsteak is more generally considered a category of tomatoes that grow extra-large, reaching up to 2 pounds in weight. 'Ponderosa' (80 days) is an old-fashioned beefsteak type, first introduced in 1892 by Peter Henderson. It has a pink coloring to the skin. Flesh is meaty and almost seedless, with rich, old-fashioned flavor, but it matures late. It is offered by Joseph Harris Company.

If you want to win contests, consider 'Delicious' (77 days). The world record is 6-1/2 pounds for one fruit. Also consider 'Supersteak VFN' hybrid (80 days). In my opinion, 'Supersteak VFN' is the best of the giant beefsteak types. Fruit ripen earlier than those of other tomatoes, and the average size is larger. I regularly grow 'Supersteak VFN' tomatoes that weigh over 2 pounds apiece. See cover photograph. The flavor is superb and the fruit is smooth and round.

Large-fruited Red Tomatoes

'Big Boy' hybrid (78 days) is the best-selling tomato ever developed. Plants are productive, producing flavorful fruit that weigh up to 1 pound. However, 'Big Boy' lacks disease resistance. You might want to consider 'Big Girl VF' (78 days), 'Better Boy VFN' (72 days), 'Supersonic VF' (79 days) or 'Floramerica VF' (75 days). All are midseason varieties and widely available from mail order seed catalogs.

Of all large-fruited hybrids, one of the best is 'Supersonic VF' hybrid, developed by Joseph Harris. It has good flavor and produces attractive, consistently round, deep red, blemish-free fruit.

Large-fruited varieties generally have less flavor, but the best of the early, large-fruited hybrids are still flavorful. Outstanding among these is 'Early Girl' hybrid (54 days). Fruit average 4 to 5 ounces. Taste tests have proven it to be among the best-flavored of the early varieties.

'Early Pick VF' hybrid (62 days) is a week later than 'Early Girl' hybrid but is disease resistant. It produces fruit that average 1/2 pound, some up to 1 pound. This is an impressive size for an early variety. Only Burpee sells 'Early Pick VF' hybrid. 'Early Girl' hybrid is widely available and can be purchased at local garden centers.

'Supersteak VFN' hybrid is my personal favorite of the large-fruited tomatoes. Plants are heavy producers of smooth, round, flavorful fruit.

'Supersonic VF' is heavy yielding, producing round, crack-resistant fruit that have great flavor. This handsome cluster was grown in my garden.

'Gardener's Delight' is a productive, medium-size tomato, perfect for cutting into segments for salads.

'Sweet 100' is a cherry type. Sometimes over 1,000 fruit can be picked from one vine over a growing season.

'Pixie' hybrid is the earliest ripening of all tomatoes, and grows to 3 feet high. 'Pixie' is also good to grow in pots indoors if given plenty of sunlight.

'Roma VF' is an Italian paste tomato, valued for canning. Fruit are medium size, flavorful and pear shape. It is the best paste tomato available.

'Golden Boy' is one of the most colorful yellow tomatoes. When combined with red tomatoes, it adds interest to salads and other dishes.

Small-fruited Red Tomatoes

This is the easiest class of tomato to grow. Disease problems such as blossom-end rot are rare. All varieties are early and plants stricken with disease are generally persistent enough to produce abundantly.

'Red Cherry' (72 days) is the standard variety by which all others are judged. A nonhybrid, it is still exceedingly productive. But other cherry-size tomato varieties bear earlier and have better flavor.

For outstanding productivity, plant 'Sweet 100' hybrid (70 days). It resembles 'Red Cherry' in size, and has the highest vitamin C content of tomatoes. It is so-named because each fruit cluster is capable of producing 100 ripe tomatoes. Because it is not uncommon to have 5 or more fruit clusters on a plant, a well-grown specimen can bear as many as 500 ripe tomatoes all at one time. Plants can produce over 1,000 fruit during the entire growing season. It was developed by Goldsmith Seeds, a commercial breeder, and is now offered by most mail order seed catalogs.

For extra-earliness try 'Pixie' hybrid (52 days). It is the earliest-ripening tomato of all. Plants of 'Pixie' are determinate, and the short, compact vines grow no more than 18 inches tall. This makes them ideal for growing in pots. Fruit are slightly larger than cherry size—1-3/4 inches in diameter.

'Pixie' hybrid is a good variety to grow out-of-season indoors. Start seeds in midsummer and grow in pots on a sunny windowsill or under fluorescent grow lights. If you use lights, be sure to keep plants close to lights or they will become "stretched." You will be able to harvest fruit until Christmas. Only during the shortest, cloudy days of January and February, in northern areas, will plants lose strength due to inadequate light.

Large-fruited Orange and Yellow Tomatoes

Yellow and other pale-fruited tomatoes are believed to be "low-acid." Actually, their acid content is similar to red tomatoes—they just taste less acid because of milder flavor. 'Jubilee' (72 days) is the most popular variety, but it lacks disease resistance. 'Sunray' (72 days) is now more widely grown. Developed by the United States Department of Agriculture, 'Sunray' is resistant to wilt disease. Available from Joseph Harris Company.

For a true, bright yellow, large-fruited tomato, try 'Golden Boy' (60 days). Fruit average 5 ounces each.

Paste Tomatoes

'Roma VF' hybrid (76 days), a determinate variety, is the most productive of all Italian paste tomatoes, also known as *pear tomatoes*. These are the best kinds for making tomato paste, juice and for canning whole. Developed by Joseph Harris Company and offered by all mail order seed catalogs.

Novelty Tomatoes

'Burgess Stuffing' (78 days) is a mutation discovered by a horticulturist at Burgess Seed Company. In outward appearance this tomato looks like a ripe bell pepper. The outside is lobed just like a pepper and the inside is hollow, with a few seeds clustered around the core. The walls of this tomato have the crisp texture of a pepper, but with a mild, unmistakably tomato taste. One scoop of the spoon and the fruit is ready to stuff.

Some people seem to enjoy tomatoes without the skin, but peeling can be a messy, tedious business. Fruit must be scalded with hot water before the peel can be removed. 'Easy Peel' (64 days) has the unique characteristic of an easy-to-peel skin without scalding. Round, red, medium-size fruit are also flavorful. Developed by Goldsmith Seeds, a California commerical breeder. Available from Park.

'Stakeless' (78 days) is a bush-type tomato for home gardeners. It grows upright without the aid of stakes. Main stem is so thick and leaf nodes are set so closely together that the plant supports its yield of fruit well above the ground. Growing to a height of 2 to 3 feet, it can be used effectively in flower borders as an ornamental. It has good resistance to fusarium wilt and sufficient resistance to early blight, so foliage usually stays green and attractive through summer into fall. Each plant requires 6 feet of growing space when planted singly. Plants can be set in rows about 4 feet apart to merge with each other. Developed by the University of Delaware. Available from Stokes Seeds.

Climbing tomatoes are special tall-growing varieties of tomatoes. They will not climb unaided, but can be trained up a trellis along the wall of a house, or up tall poles to attain heights of 10 to 15 feet. Most popular variety for this purpose is 'Trip-L-Crop' (90 days). Also offered as climbers are 'Early Cascade VF' hybrid (54 days) and 'Giant Tree' (90 days). All produce large fruit. In my experience, 'Early Cascade VF' is the best of the three. Available from Gurney.

'Square Tomato' (75 days) was developed by the University of California for mechanical harvesting. This variety is unusually flavorful when grown in a home garden and picked at the peak of freshness. The square shape is a practical development. Tomatoes will pack better and will not roll around and bruise as easily when shipped. Plants tend to ripen their fruit all at one time, which makes them highly decorative.

Over the years there have been numerous novelty tomatoes exhibiting strange colors. Perhaps the most interesting is 'Tigerella' (55 days), a red-and-yellow striped variety. 'Tigerella' was developed by the Glasshouse Crops Research Institute in England, and is available from Stokes.

'Tumblin Tom' (48 days) is an unusually early tomato developed for hanging baskets and container plants. The determinate vines cascade, bearing 1-1/2 inch fruit. Developed by Petoseed Co., a California tomato breeder. Available from most mail order seed houses.

'White Beauty' (84 days) produces ivory-white fruit with white skin and white flesh. Not as flavorful as red tomatoes. Available from Gurney.

'Yellow Pear' (70 days) has a mild, delicate flavor, making it good for preserves, cocktail snacks and for use in salads. Fruit measure 1-3/4 inches long and 1 inch in diameter. They hang in tight clusters and are highly decorative.

'Tigerella' is a medium-size, striped tomato sometimes sold as 'Mr. Stripey'. Stripes develop in the green stage. It's an interesting variety with good flavor.

'Burgess Stuffing' looks more like a ripe bell pepper. Use as you would sweet bell peppers, sliced raw in salads or stuffed and cooked.

'Yellow Plum' grows small, plum-shape fruit that are tasty in salads and snacks. A similar variety is the pear-shape, 'Yellow Pear'.

Turnip 'Purple Top' is best harvested when 2 to 3 inches across.

Turnip 'Tokyo Cross' takes just 35 days to grow from seed.

Turnips and Rutabagas

The turnip originated in Europe. Wild types can still be found there, from the shores of the Mediterranean to the steppes of Siberia. The rutabaga, also known as *Swedish turnip* or *swede,* is similar to a turnip.

Rutabagas are the result of a cross between cabbages and turnips, and generally produce larger edible roots than true turnips. Rutabagas generally do not do well south of the Mason-Dixon line, while true turnips are a successful southern crop.

Grown for both their delicious leaves and edible roots, turnip greens are even more popular in southern states than collard greens. Because of this dual benefit they are a worthwhile crop for home gardeners. They grow rapidly from seed and mature during cool spring or fall weather.

Some hybrid varieties from Japan such as 'Tokyo Cross' and 'Just Right' hybrid are quick to reach maturity. Roots can be harvested 35 days from sowing seeds directly in the garden, which is about 25 days ahead of standard varieties.

How to grow: For earliest crops, sow seeds 1/2 inch deep directly in the garden 3 weeks before your last frost date. For a fall harvest, sow seeds in midsummer. Plant in straight rows 1 foot apart or block plant in wide, raised beds. Thin seedlings to stand 3 to 4 inches apart.

Fertile soils enriched with garden compost or decomposed animal manure are best. Be sure to provide plants with continuous moisture. This is especially true for fast-growing hybrids.

Pest and disease control: Turnips and rutabagas experience problems common to cabbage. Aphids, flea beetles, root maggots and wireworms are insect pests that can infest a turnip crop. Dusting or spraying young plants with a safe vegetable control such as rotenone or pyrethrum will provide some measure of control over aphids and flea beetles. Sevin is also a good preventive spray. Diazinon can control soil-borne pests. Garlic oil spray is an effective organic repellent.

Harvesting and use: Pick leaves as soon as they are large enough. Cut a few leaves from several plants rather than from one plant. To cook, simmer in a small amount of water. Harvest time for roots depends on variety. Hybrid white kinds are most succulent when they are the size of a golf ball. Standard varieties do not have sufficient flavor until they are the size of a tennis ball. Turnips store well for long periods in a cool basement or root cellar. To store, cut tops to within 1/2 inch of the root and sink roots into boxes of sawdust or moist sand.

Recommended varieties: 'Tokyo Cross' turnip (35 days) is an All-America Award winner. Pure white roots grow rapidly to golf-ball size within 35 days. They can be left in the garden longer than standard varieties without losing quality. Flavor is sweet and succulent. Plants are disease resistant. Because 'Tokyo Cross' is a hybrid, seed is expensive to produce. Seed packets also tend to contain only small quantities of seeds. But this is such a superior variety the extra cost is worthwhile.

Among nonhybrid turnips, choose 'Purple Top White Globe' (55 days) or 'Early Purple Top Milan' (45 days), a flattened globe variety. Rutabagas require a much longer growing season than turnips, and are usually grown as a fall crop for winter storage. The leading variety is 'Purple Top Yellow' (90 days). It grows sweet, fine-grained yellow flesh that turns orange when cooked. Roots are smooth and round with purple shoulders.

QUESTIONS ABOUT TURNIPS

My seed supplier offers "sized seed" for both turnips and rutabagas. What does that mean?
Turnip seeds germinate at different times, depending on size. For this reason, some seed suppliers separate the seeds into different sizes to ensure an even rate of germination. Also, sized seed is helpful to commercial growers who use precision seed-planting machines.

Rutabaga 'Purple Top Yellow' is grown mostly for fall harvest. Rutabagas need twice the growing time of turnips, but roots are sweeter when allowed to grow large.

Turnip 'Red Ball' is an Oriental variety rarely seen in the United States. These were grown in a test garden at San Juan Bautista, California.

Root Crops

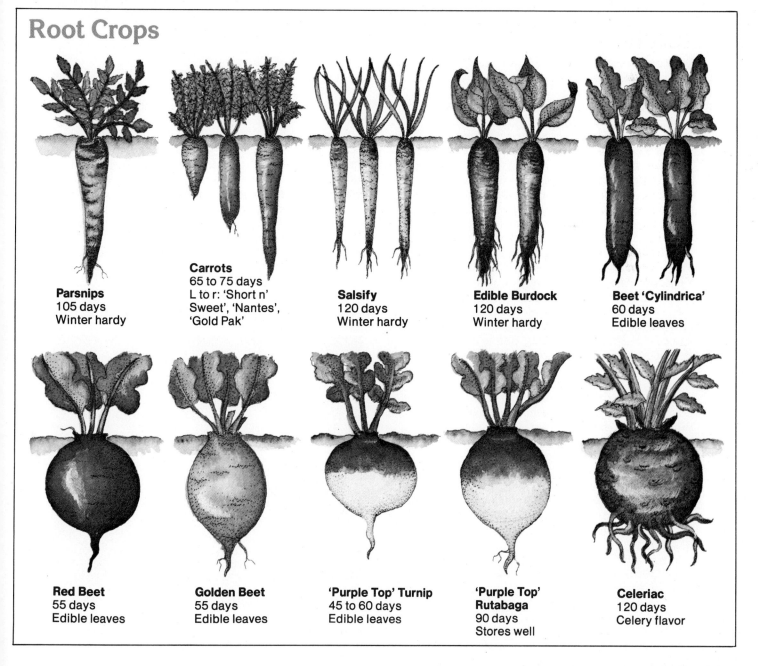

Parsnips
105 days
Winter hardy

Carrots
65 to 75 days
L to r: 'Short n'
Sweet', 'Nantes',
'Gold Pak'

Salsify
120 days
Winter hardy

Edible Burdock
120 days
Winter hardy

Beet 'Cylindrica'
60 days
Edible leaves

Red Beet
55 days
Edible leaves

Golden Beet
55 days
Edible leaves

'Purple Top' Turnip
45 to 60 days
Edible leaves

'Purple Top' Rutabaga
90 days
Stores well

Celeriac
120 days
Celery flavor

'Sweet Favorite' watermelons weigh up to 20 pounds.

Watermelon

Consider yourself an accomplished gardener when you can grow plump, juicy watermelons. It seems with watermelons you can do everything right and still fail to harvest a worthwhile crop. Generally, the larger the watermelon, the more difficult it is to grow.

Except for bush varieties with compact vines, watermelons need plenty of space. Give them 6 feet between rows in an open, sunny position. There seems to be a direct relationship between size of vine and flavor of fruit. If you try the new bush varieties, be prepared to sacrifice some taste quality.

Above all, watermelons love a hot summer, with adequate moisture at all stages to produce full-size fruit. The inside of a watermelon is mostly moisture. In short-season areas, stick with the ice-box varieties. These are about the size of large cantaloupe.

How to grow: Seeds are large and easy to handle. Sow them directly in the garden after all danger of frost has passed. Plant vining kinds 1/2 inch deep in groups spaced 6 to 8 feet apart. Later, thin to one vine in each group. In short-season areas, start seeds indoors in peat pots, peat pellets or empty milk cartons 4 to 6 weeks before outdoor planting.

A light, fertile soil is recommended. If you are serious about growing watermelons and have a heavy soil, mix builder's sand into the soil for added warmth and drainage. Also add plenty of organic matter to provide sufficient moisture-holding capacity.

At time of flowering and fruit set, side dress with garden compost or well-decomposed stable manure.

Pest and disease control: It is essential to protect young plants from attack by cucumber beetles. These beetles not only sap vines of energy, they introduce wilt disease, which is a killer. When seedlings emerge, apply rotenone, an organic dust, or Sevin, a chemical spray. Spray every 5 days until vines are established.

Watermelons are highly susceptible to diseases that infect cucumbers. Do not plant in an area where cucumbers were grown the previous year. If planting in the same spot cannot be avoided, then use a broad-spectrum garden fungicide to help control angular leaf spot, anthracnose, downy mildew and blight. There are disease-resistant watermelon varieties for some or all of these diseases.

Harvesting and use: A problem with growing watermelons is telling when they are ripe. During a visit to Taiwan to meet with one of the world's foremost watermelon breeders, Wun Yu Chen, I asked for an expert's advice. He offered this foolproof method:

Tap the watermelon with your knuckle and listen to the sound it makes. If it sounds like tapping your forehead, a dull sound, the watermelon is under-ripe. If it sounds like tapping your stomach, a soft sound, the watermelon is over-ripe. If it sounds like tapping your Adam's apple or your chest, a hollow sound, it is ripe and ready to be eaten.

Gardeners have other methods of determining ripeness: Look on the underside where fruit touches the ground. If it shows a patch of yellow, this is an indication of ripeness. Every watermelon fruit has a curly tendril immediately below the point where it is attached to the vine. When this tendril is green the watermelon is under-ripe. When it is brown and shriveled, the melon is ripe.

Recommended varieties: 'Yellow Baby' (70 days) is without question the best-flavored, most reliable, and earliest ice-box variety. Fruit are perfectly round and green with handsome, dark green stripes. They weigh up to 10 pounds each. The color is rich, glowing, pineapple-yellow. 'Yellow Baby' possesses 50% fewer seeds than other ice-box varieties. 'Yellow Baby' also has some tolerance to cold. Developed in the highlands of Taiwan where the seasons are short, it will be the first to ripen in your garden and the last to stop bearing.

'Sweet Favorite' produces fruit weighing up to 20 pounds within 80 days. It won an All-America Award because of its success in northern states where large watermelons previously could not be grown. Generally speaking, if you can grow cantaloupe in your area, you should be able to grow 'Sweet Favorite'.

'Sugar Bush' (80 days) is a compact-vine type, producing one or two ice-box-size fruit per vine. But

'Yellow Baby' is a popular "ice-box" variety. Because it reaches maturity in about 70 days, it is a good variety to grow in short-season areas.

plants are weak and not as early or as reliable as 'Yellow Baby'. To save space, watermelons can be grown up wire cylinders or a trellis.

For the South, favored varieties are oblong in shape, such as 'Congo' (95 days), 'Jubilee' (95 days), 'Charleston Grey' (95 days) and 'Dixie Queen' (96 days). All grow to 40 pounds in weight. 'Crimson Sweet' (96 days), a popular round variety in the South, grows to 25 pounds. 'Citron' (95 days), a small-seeded type used exclusively for pickles, grows to 12 pounds. It is available from Stokes.

INSIDE REPORT: SEEDLESS WATERMELONS

For the finest-flavored watermelons of all, grow "seedless" watermelons. A lot of people are putting off growing these because they don't understand how you can have seeds for a seedless watermelon. Admittedly, they are a challenge, but seedless watermelons are no gimmick.

The explanation is simple. It's rather like crossing a jackass with a mare to produce a mule—the mule is sterile. With seedless watermelons, the seeds in your packet are labeled *seedless* and *pollinator,* or dyed separate colors so you can tell them apart. Seeds of the seedless type are your female parent, and the pollinator is your male parent. By planting one male for every three females, watermelons on your female parent will be sterile, or seedless. The male will produce good-tasting watermelons, but these will have seeds. Label which seeds are which when you plant so you will be able to identify female and male watermelons.

Because energy is not wasted in producing seeds, seedless watermelons are more flavorful than regular kinds. Some varieties have three times the sugar content of a standard variety. One of the best is 'Triple Sweet Seedless' hybrid' (80 days). Fruit are oval, weigh up to 20 pounds, with bright, red supersweet flesh.

'Sugar Bush' grows 2 to 4 ice-box-size melons on each vine. Vines are compact, requiring one-third of the space of regular watermelon vines.

Chinese yam grows luxuriant vines above ground and delicious tubers below ground.

Chinese Yam

Chinese yam has been grown as far north as the Montreal Botanical Gardens in Canada. At Longwood Gardens, near Philadelphia, Pennsylvania, plantings started in 1969 have become so well established they have invaded other parts of the garden. Home garden plantings should therefore be confined to a special area where they are not likely to become invasive. In areas with frost, the foliage dies down in winter, but tubers and roots remain dormant and produce vigorous new growth when warm weather returns. There are no reliable mail order sources for seeds or tubers, but Chinese yams occasionally appear at Oriental food markets. Plants can be started from these. For planting methods see Sweet Potatoes, page 164.

How to grow: Chinese yams need deep, fertile soil and good drainage to produce tubers. They can be propagated from seeds, cut pieces of root and from stem cuttings rooted in water. The easiest and most reliable way to start plants is by sinking a tuber to half its depth in water or moist sand. Allow the tuber to sprout shoots. Separate these from the tuber and use as transplants. Plant after all danger of frost has passed. Although tolerant of drought, regular watering encourages larger tubers.

Pest and disease control: Because of their vigorous growth habit, Chinese yams are not normally bothered by pests or disease.

Harvesting and use: Small tubers can be harvested after 150 days of growth, and used any way you would sweet potatoes. In addition to their food value, yams make attractive, ornamental vines.

Recommended varieties: Not normally sold by variety name.

Edible Herbs

Herbs have played an important part in the history of civilization. Ancient cultures such as the Chinese, Abyssinians, Greeks, Romans, Egyptians and Aztecs took advantage of the culinary and medicinal properties associated with herbs. Many herbs became valued as cosmetics, fumigants, deodorants, insect repellents and dyes. Some were thought to possess supernatural properties and were used in religious ceremonies. Herbs were also associated with witchcraft and sorcery in ancient times—probably due to their potency. With most herbs, a little goes a long way.

Early settlers brought European herbs to America, mostly for use as kitchen flavorings and medicines. In colonial times, an herb garden by the kitchen door was regarded as a necessity. As cities became larger and stores made herbal products and substitutes more available, herb gardening declined.

Today, there is a renewed interest in growing herbs. People are discovering that herbs fresh from the garden are much more flavorful than dried, packaged products.

GROWING HERBS OUTDOORS

The most surprising fact about herbs is how easy most are to grow. In the wild, they exist in some of the most inhospitable places, sprouting and growing like weeds after every rainfall. The biggest problem with herbs in the home garden is keeping them tidy and within bounds. Sinking a container planted with herbs into the soil is a good way to keep some of the aggressive kinds from becoming invasive.

With most culinary herbs, a single, healthy planting is sufficient for a year's supply for an average family. Instead of planting herbs in rows as you would vegetables, tuck them into odd corners of the garden. Or create a special area where you can grow one or two plants, or many different kinds. If you are interested in an ornamental effect, herbs work well as borders, ground covers and low hedges. You may want to plant a traditional *knot garden.* See photo, opposite page.

Herbs generally require an open, sunny location and good soil drainage. Soil fertility is not always necessary, but the majority of popular herbs prefer a light, sandy soil amended with plenty of organic matter.

Planting and propagation. Many popular herbs can be grown easily from seeds, and are started the same way as vegetables. See page 37. Most herbs are *biennials,* plants that live for two years, or *perennials,* plants that live for more than two years. Perennials are easily propagated by dividing established clumps. This is done by digging into an established planting with a hand trowel or shovel. You can then separate a clump complete with roots and soil for transplanting.

In some cases, a stem cutting can be taken. Roots will sprout by immersing the cutting in water or moist potting soil. Mint can be propagated this way.

Left: Knot garden is created from low hedges of herbs at Filoli Estate, Woodland, California. Gentle curves produce a pleasing, informal atmosphere. Above: Chives in bloom create a beautiful border against picket fence.

Hardy annual herbs such as basil are usually grown from seeds. They die down after the first season but usually reseed freely. Hardy biennial herbs such as parsley generally survive the winter and go to seed the second season. Hardy perennial herbs such as chives, mint and lavender sometimes become permanently established, growing thicker and wider each year.

Although many perennial herbs are hardy to cold, a protective mulch of straw, pine needles or shredded leaves is advisable where freezing temperatures occur. Place over and around plants to a depth of 3 inches.

GROWING HERBS IN CONTAINERS

Many herbs grow well in containers indoors on a sunny windowsill. Some may not have as rich a flavor when grown indoors, but still provide zest to meals. Clay pots 6 inches in diameter are best if you have the room, but even 4-inch pots produce useful plants.

Container herbs should be grown in a soil mix composed of two parts sterile potting soil and one part course sand or perlite. See page 72. When plants get too tall and ''leggy,'' prune them back to a compact, dome shape. Position plants in a south- or east-facing window. Although most herbs tolerate warm, dry conditions, summer sun streaming through the window can burn plants. Mist plants in summer and keep soil moist but not waterlogged.

Although herbs generally do well in poor soil, give them a weak, liquid fertilizer once every two weeks at time of watering.

USING AND PRESERVING HERBS

With the exception of herbs grown for their aromatic seeds, pick *young* leaves and stems for culinary use. The top whorl of leaves of a basil plant, for example, is much more flavorful than older, lower leaves.

Drying is the most popular way to store herbs for extended periods. To dry herbs, harvest plant parts early in the day. This is when they are most flavorful. Rinse plants with cold water and hang them by their stems. Air-dry in a dry, dark, well-ventilated place, such as a garage or storage shed. Or spread herbs on cookie sheets lined with wax paper. Drying is complete when leaves feel crumbly, which takes about 7 to 10 days. Oven drying is the quickest method, but most volatile oils are lost and flavor is reduced. Low, gentle heat with good air circulation is preferred. If you choose to dry in an oven, spread on a baking sheet and set oven to 200F (76C). Drying times vary, but usually an hour or less is sufficient. Store dried herbs out of direct sun to preserve their oil content.

Certain herbs freeze well. Parsley, mint, basil and burnet are just a few. Harvest young leaves. Wash and blanch in boiling water for 50 seconds. Cool quickly in ice water, drain, then package and freeze. Basil, chives and dill can be frozen without blanching.

COOKING WITH HERBS

Some of the most basic foods take on gourmet flavors with the addition of a simple herb. Taste the difference in scrambled eggs with a sprinkling of chives. Add chopped parsley to mashed potatoes. Sprinkle finely chopped chervil leaves over a green salad. Crush a sprig of mint into a glass of iced tea. Sprinkle some flakes of chopped basil leaves over stewed tomatoes.

Use herbs sparingly until you learn how a given amount affects the flavor of a dish. Aromatic oils of herbs are often strong, and too much of any flavor can be objectionable.

Following is a selection of the most useful and easy-to-grow *edible herbs*. They have been chosen for their value as flavorings or herbal teas, rather than for medicinal or cosmetic uses. For further information on growing, drying and using herbs, refer to the HPBook, *Herbs: How to Select, Grow and Enjoy,* by Norma Jean Lathrop.

A fine example of a formal herb garden can be seen at the Royal Horticultural Society Garden, Wisley, England. Bronze urn serves as a focal point.

Herbs don't have to be planted in a formal garden or in a specific pattern. Casual grouping of assorted herbs combines well with stone walkway.

Mrs. Phyllis Shaudys, herb specialist, dries herbs on trays supported on frames used for drying laundry. Dehumidifier in room helps keep air dry.

Anise
Pimpinella anisum

An annual growing 1-1/2 to 2 feet high, anise has bright green, finely serrated leaves and small, whitish flowers in flat clusters. Leaves and seeds have a cool, sweet flavor suggestive of licorice.

How to grow: Plants grow rapidly from seeds sown directly into the garden. Sow seeds 1/4 inch deep after all danger of frost has passed. Plant in full sun and in light, well-drained soil. Water regularly. If planted in rows, thin 6 to 8 inches apart in rows 2 feet apart.

Pest and disease control: Generally free of pests and diseases.

Harvesting and use: Green leaves can be cut whenever plants are large enough. Use leaves to make an herbal tea, in salads or as a garnish. Gather seeds about 1 month after flowers bloom. Seeds are good to chew as a breath freshener. Use seeds to flavor confections such as cakes and cookies. Oil from anise seeds is used in medicines.

Recommended varieties: Not sold by variety name. A separate herb, *hyssop*, is sometimes sold as anise. See page 184.

Pure white flowers of anise appear at top of plants in midsummer. Seeds are usually ready to harvest in fall.

Whole anise seeds can be used as a licorice flavoring in cakes and cookies. Harvest when they are gray-green.

Basil
Ocimum basilicum

Sweet basil is an attractive annual that grows to about 18 inches tall. It produces light green, broad-pointed leaves and small, white, spikelike flowers.

How to grow: Plants grow easily from seeds sown directly in the garden. Sow seeds 1/4 inch deep after all danger of frost has passed. Thin plants to stand 12 inches apart. Basil likes full sun and moist, well-drained soil. Pinch stems to promote bushy, compact growth.

Pest and disease control: Basil is considered by some to be an insect repellent, but slugs and snails love it and will strip leaves from plants. Control with slug bait. Place bait in shallow dishes so the poison does not contaminate the soil. Japanese beetles are also attracted to basil. Use beetle traps or pyrethrum insecticide as organic controls. Use Sevin as a chemical control.

Harvesting and use: Green leaves can be picked about 6 weeks following planting. Harvest leaves for drying just before flowers open. Spicy-scented basil leaves, fresh or dried, are one of the most popular of all kitchen herbs. Cooks favor basil for all kinds of tomato dishes. Add it to soups, vegetables and Italian dishes.

Recommended varieties: 'Dark Opal' is highly ornamental with glossy purple leaves and purple flower spikes. Use it as a background planting in contrast to brightly colored flowers such as yellow marigolds. Other varieties include 'Lettuce Leaf', 'Lemon' and 'Well-Sweep Miniature'.

Rows of sweet basil are at peak maturity, just prior to flowering. Top whorl of new leaves is the most flavorful.

The bright blue, star-shaped flowers of borage are decorative as well as useful. Their cucumberlike flavor is refreshing in summer drinks.

Burnet has a cucumber flavor like borage. Add the fresh leaves to salads or cold drinks. Use dried leaves in salad dressings and soups.

Caraway is grown for its seeds, which appear soon after flowering. Add them to meat stews, fish casseroles, coleslaw and cheese spreads.

Borage
Borago officinalis

This decorative annual has beautiful, sky-blue, star-shaped flowers. Gray-green leaves grow to 5 inches long. Plants grow 2 to 3 feet tall with an equal spread.

How to grow: Borage is best grown from seeds sown directly in the garden. It is difficult to transplant. Sow seeds 1/4 inch deep after all danger of frost has passed. Thin plants to stand 2 feet apart. Borage does best in dry, sunny places.

Pest and disease control: Chewing insects such as Japanese beetles may attack the leaves. Pyrethrum or Sevin will control them. Also consider beetle traps.

Harvesting and use: Sprays of borage flowers and leaves are used to give a cool, cucumberlike flavor to summer drinks. Pick blossoms as they open. Use young, fresh leaves—they are not as flavorful when dried.

Burnet
Poterium sanguisorba

This vigorous perennial herb forms dense, mound-shaped clumps. Leaves are dark green and toothed, and unfold like an accordion. Plant grows 2 feet high and spreads 2 feet wide.

How to grow: Plant in full sun. Burnet is best sown directly in the garden. Its long taproot makes transplanting difficult. Sow seeds 1/4 inch deep and thin plants to stand 12 inches apart. Burnet tolerates poor soil but does best in sandy, well-drained soil. Propagate by dividing roots of a healthy, established clump.

Pest and disease control: Relatively pest- and disease-free.

Harvesting and use: Pick leaves as soon as they are large enough to handle. Burnet lends a cucumber flavor to cold drinks and wines. Leaves can also be chopped fine and sprinkled over salads. Drying destroys the flavor, so store leaves by freezing.

Caraway
Carum carvi

Caraway is a biennial plant that grows in a mound to about 30 inches high. Flowers appear in flat, white clusters. Finely cut, bright green leaves resemble carrots.

How to grow: Caraway is easily grown from seeds. Plants do not usually bear seeds the first year. If planted in fall, they produce seeds the following year. Caraway is not easily transplanted. Sow directly in the garden 3 weeks before last frost date. If planted in rows, thin 8 to 12 inches apart in rows 3 feet apart. Plant prefers loose, well-drained soil. Protect roots with a mulch in winter.

Pest and disease control: Relatively free of pests and diseases.

Harvesting and use: Seeds should be harvested when ripe. This is usually a month after flowering when seeds turn grayish brown. Seeds have a distinctive, aromatic odor and flavor. Oil of caraway seeds is an important ingredient in liqueurs. Use seeds in Hungarian-type dishes, coleslaw, cheese spreads, meat stews and fish casseroles.

Catnip

Nepeta cataria

Catnip is a hardy perennial plant that grows 3 to 4 feet high. Heart-shaped leaves are gray-green. Flowers are purple.

How to grow: Plant seeds or propagate by division. Sow seeds 1/4 inch deep. Thin plants to stand 2 feet apart. Catnip is best planted in spring or late fall. Prefers fertile, sandy soil. When young, plants are decorative and compact. As they grow older, they become straggly. Use catnip as an ornamental background plant.

Pest and disease control: Generally free of pests and disease, but *cats* can be pests. They can destroy new plantings. Protect plants with netting or a wooden frame covered with chicken wire until they become established, and are better able to withstand "attention" from cats.

Harvesting and use: Cut and dry mature leafy tops and leaves at any stage of development. Catnip leaves are used for tea and seasoning.

Chervil

Anthriscus cerefolium

This is a hardy annual that grows up to 2 feet high and spreads 1 foot wide. Lacy leaves resemble parsley but are a lighter shade of green. Small, delicate, white flowers appear in flat clusters.

How to grow: Sow seeds directly in the garden 3 weeks before last frost date. Seedlings are difficult to transplant. Thin plants 3 to 4 inches apart. Plant in fertile soil in a sunny site. Keep soil moist. For denser foliage, cut flower stems before they bloom.

Pest and disease control: Generally free of pests and disease.

Harvesting and use: Leaves are best used fresh. Pick them just before buds open for maximum flavor. Cut, dry and store the green, tender leaves. Use as a garnish on salads, soups and egg dishes. Add it to melted butter for a fish or chicken baste.

Chives

Allium schoenoprasum

Chives are small, dainty, onionlike plants. They grow in clumps that reach about 10 inches high. These hardy perennials with decorative, bright pink flowers make attractive border plants.

Garlic chives, *Allium tuberosum,* are similar in appearance to regular chives but leaves have a slight garlic flavor. Plants are a little larger and produce clusters of beautiful white flowers on tall stems. They are perennials, and are harvested and used like chives.

How to grow: Seeds can be sown directly in the garden 3 weeks before last frost date. However, it is better to start them indoors. Sow seeds 1/4 inch deep in a tray filled with potting soil. Transplant small clumps of seedlings 12 inches apart in rows spaced 2 feet apart. Chives thrive in poor soil, but perform best in an organically rich soil high in phosphorus. They require little care, other than dividing plants when overcrowded. Easily propagated by division.

Catnip is often grown in perennial borders as an ornamental. It is also valued for its aromatic leaves, which make a refreshing tea.

Chervil is best grown in a clump planting rather than a row. Harvest the leaves like parsley. Chervil gives a mild, anise flavor to soups, salads and egg dishes.

This 2-year-old clump of chives is growing in my own garden. Leaves add a zesty, onionlike flavor to foods. Flowers are edible and highly ornamental.

Comfrey plants grow in a neat mound. Chop the vitamin-rich leaves very fine and add to salads, or cook small amounts to eat like spinach.

Coriander in full bloom. The seeds that follow are valued for their perfume scent and flavor. Use them as a condiment in confections.

Pest and disease control: Remarkably pest- and disease-free. Chives are regarded as an effective insect repellent. They are often used around other vegetables for natural insect control. Chives do attract greenfly on rare occasions. They can be washed off plants with a soap and water solution.

Harvesting and use: Use chives to impart a delicious, subtle, onionlike flavor to foods. Grow them in containers on a sunny windowsill and cut fresh leaves whenever you need them.

Comfrey
Symphytum officinale

More curative powers are claimed for comfrey than any other herb. The name is a corruption of *con firma,* alluding to its reputation for healing broken bones and wounds.

A popular catalog describes comfrey as follows: "This is one of the key plants in herbal remedies. Up to 33% protein is contained in the leaves and it is high in vitamins and minerals. Probably the only plant known to man that contains vitamin B12, normally found only in raw liver and raw egg yolk. It also contains vitamins A, C, E and the B complex. It has a case history of benefits to the kidneys and urinary tract. Herbalists claim it is one of the only herbs that help prevent cataracts of the eyes in middle age."

Comfrey is a hardy perennial. It grows as a vigorous clump of large, pointed, dark green leaves to 3 feet high and 2-1/2 feet wide.

How to grow: Plants are easily grown from seeds, but are easier to cultivate from root cuttings. Roots are brittle. A small piece of root will sprout a new plant. If you start from seeds, sow 1/4 inch deep directly in the garden 3 weeks before last frost date. Thin seedlings to stand 2-1/2 to 3 feet apart. Comfrey is not particular as to soil quality, but grows best in soil rich in organic matter. Requires regular amounts of water.

Pest and disease control: Relatively pest- and disease-free. Snails may eat holes in leaves, but damage is rarely extensive enough to worry about.

Harvesting and use: Harvest leaves selectively, choosing some from each plant. Leaves can be chopped fine and sprinkled on salads or cooked like spinach. Use comfrey sparingly.

Recommended varieties: In addition to green varieties, there are pink, red and green-and-white variegated types.

Coriander
Coriandrum sativum

Coriander is a dainty annual that grows to 2 feet tall. Aromatic seeds are known as *coriander.* Leaves are known as *Chinese parsley* or *cilantro.* White or purplish-tinged flowers appear in small, flat heads.

How to grow: Easily grown from seeds. Sow directly in the garden after all danger of frost has passed. Long taproot makes transplanting difficult. Plant seeds 1/4 inch deep and thin plants 6 to 10 inches apart. Does best in well-prepared garden soil that has good drainage. Requires regular amounts of water.

Pest and disease control: Generally free of pests and diseases.

Harvesting and use: Gather seeds as they ripen in midsummer. They are round, about 1/8 inch in diameter, and have a delicious taste and perfume smell. Coriander seeds are used as a condiment in confections. Freshly chopped leaves can be added sparingly to soups, salads and stir-fried dishes.

Dill
Anethum graveolens

This popular annual herb has bluish green stems that contrast with finely divided, yellow-green, plumelike leaves and yellowish flowers. Plants grow about 2 to 3 feet high and 1 foot wide.

How to grow: Seedlings do not transplant well, so grow from seeds sown directly in the garden. Sow 1/4 inch deep 3 weeks before last frost date. Thin plants to stand 9 to 18 inches apart. Plants may need staking in rich, loose soils.

Pest and disease control: Generally free of pests and diseases. Rabbits sometimes eat young dill plants. Keep rabbits out with fencing. Aphids and greenfly are occasionally attracted to young stems. Wash them off with spray from a garden hose, or rub them away with a gloved hand. Sevin is an effective chemical spray. Dill becomes a pest itself unless confined to a special area of the garden. Seeds scatter and come up like weeds the following year.

Harvesting and use: For best results, pick leaves just as flowers open. Pick seeds when they are flat and brown. Leaves and seeds are popular for flavoring pickles, sauerkraut and beet dishes. Dill can be combined with garlic and pepper to produce a highly flavored, Mediterranean or East European pork roast.

Fennel
Foeniculum vulgare azoricum

Two kinds of fennel are frequently listed in seed catalogs. *Florence fennel,* the more popular type, is grown for its stems and succulent, bulbous base. *Wild fennel* is grown for its anise-flavored leaves.

Fennel is a tender perennial but is usually grown as an annual. It looks similar to dill and grows 2 to 3 feet high, spreading 2 to 3 feet wide. Leaves are feathery and light green. Small yellow flowers are formed in flat clusters in late summer and early fall. Where leaf stalks meet the soil a fleshy, white bulb is formed. Bulb is crisp, crunchy and has a flavor like licorice. Sometimes listed in catalogs as "Finocchio."

How to grow: Fennel grows easily from seeds. Sow seeds 1/4 inch deep directly in the garden 3 weeks before last frost date. Thin plants to stand 10 to 12 inches apart. Plants like full sun but produce larger bulbs under cool conditions. Supply with fertile soil high in organic matter for best results. Space rows 3 feet apart and thin plants 10 to 12 inches apart.

Pest and disease control: Concentrate on eliminating infestations of wireworms and other soil insects. They can chew bulbs, causing discoloration and poor flavor. Compost and wood ashes mixed into the soil may discourage them. Recommended chemical treatment for

Dill in full bloom. All parts—flowers, seeds, stems and leaves—are edible but should be used sparingly. Use to flavor meats, pickles and vegetable dishes.

Florence fennel forms a cluster of fleshy stems close to the soil. Cooked or raw, these crisp, succulent stalks have a delicious licorice flavor.

Horehound leaves are the source of a distinctive flavor used in confections and candies. When steeped in hot water they make a refreshing herbal tea.

soil pests is diazinon. Greenfly occasionally attacks young stems. Wash off with soap and water solution.

Harvesting and use: To use as a condiment, pick seeds when dry but before they fall from plant. Stems for eating should be picked before the flower stalks bloom, and before the onset of hot weather. Leaves have an aniselike, licorice flavor. Lower part of the stems can be eaten like celery. Seeds can be used to add flavor to cheese spreads and vegetable dishes.

Horehound
Marrubium vulgare

This tender perennial resembles mint, except plants are covered with a velvety down. Grayish green leaves are crinkled and tend to turn downward. Flowers are white and appear in clusters on stems of plants at least 2 years old. Plants form dense clumps up to 2 feet high with an equal spread. Because of its weedy growth habit, horehound is best placed in the background. Or plant in a sunken container to keep it from becoming invasive.

How to grow: Horehound can be propagated from seeds, cuttings or by division. Sow seeds 1/4 inch deep directly in the garden 3 weeks before last frost date. Thin seedlings to stand 1 to 2 feet apart. Plants grow well in light, sandy soil and withstand full sun and intense heat. Horehound survives mild winters but needs protection in cold-winter areas.

Pest and disease control: Generally free of pests and diseases. It can become a pest itself if allowed to reseed continually.

Harvesting and use: Leaves and small stems can be cut for use before plants bloom. Horehound is the source of the familiar, old-fashioned candy of the same name. It is also used to make an herbal tea.

Recommended varieties: 'Black', 'White', 'Silver' and 'Variegated' are available from herb catalogs.

Hyssop
Hyssopus officinalis

Hyssop is an evergreen perennial that grows to no more than 2 feet high, spreading to 3 feet wide. It has woody stems, small, pointed green leaves and spikes of small, blue, white or pink flowers. If pruned, it makes an attractive border or small hedge.

How to grow: Hyssop is easily grown from seeds. Sow directly in the garden after all danger of frost has passed. Sow 1/4 inch deep and thin seedlings to stand 2 to 3 feet apart. After hyssop is established, it is a hardy plant. Tolerant of poor soil.

Pest and disease control: Generally free of pests and diseases.

Harvesting and use: Pick leaves just prior to flowering. Pungent leaves are used to flavor liqueurs and as a garnish with meat and fish. Use sparingly to flavor soups and stews. Oil obtained from leaves is used in making perfume. Store by freezing or drying.

Recommended varieties: Common hyssop is the most widely available variety. Some herb specialists also offer 'Anise' hyssop and 'Camphor' hyssop. These names describe the fragrance of their aromatic leaves.

Hyssop is an attractive, compact-growing plant that does best in partial shade. Leaves have a strong, bitter flavor but can be used sparingly to flavor meat dishes.

Lemon Balm
Melissa officinalis

Closely resembling mint in appearance and growth habit, lemon balm spreads like a weed. Confine it to a small planting. Plants grow 2-1/2 feet high, spreading to 2 feet wide. Light green leaves are heavily veined. A variegated type is also available.

How to grow: Plants are easy to grow from seeds. Start them indoors for transplanting or sow directly in the garden. Sow seeds 1/4 inch deep 3 weeks before last spring frost date. Thin plants 2 to 3 feet apart. Tolerates poor soils. Plants die down in winter, but roots are perennial and new growth appears in spring.

Pest and disease control: Generally free of pests and diseases. Sometimes attracts greenfly, which can be washed off plant stems with soap and water solution.

Harvesting and use: As the name suggests, this plant imparts a wonderful lemon fragrance and flavor. Leaves make a delicious herbal tea and can be used as a flavor enhancer in place of lemon. Try it on fish, salads or fruit dishes. When added to iced tea or alcoholic beverages, a crushed sprig of leaves has the same flavoring effect as a slice of lemon.

Marjoram
Origanum majorana

Marjoram is one of the most fragrant and popular of all herbs, usually grown as an annual. Its growth habit is low, reaching about 1-1/2 feet high spreading up to 2 feet wide. It makes an attractive border plant. Small, oval, gray-green leaves are velvety to the touch. Sweet marjoram is preferred by most gardeners over the similar wild or pot marjoram.

How to grow: Marjoram is easily grown from seeds or cuttings. In cold climates, it is best treated as an annual, or grown in a container and brought inside during cold weather. Sow seeds 1/4 inch deep directly in the garden after all danger of frost has passed. Thin seedlings 1 to 2 feet apart. Plant in an open, sunny location in a well-drained soil.

Pest and disease control: Generally free of pests and diseases.

Harvesting and use: Use leaves fresh anytime or dried as a flavoring in cooking. To dry, cut leafy stems when plant is flowering. Oil derived from leaves is often an ingredient in perfume.

Oregano
Origanum vulgare

Also called *wild marjoram,* this plant is much coarser than sweet marjoram, *Origanum majorana,* and has a scent more like thyme. It is a hardy perennial with sprawling stems that can reach up to 3 feet high. Small flowers are pink or white.

How to grow: Plant seeds 1/4 inch deep 3 weeks before last frost date. Thin plants to stand 10 to 12 inches apart. Plants can also be propagated by division. Tolerates poor soil. Stimulate foliage growth by cutting back flowers. Replant in three or four years when plants become woody.

Pest and disease control: Generally free of pests and diseases.

Fresh leaves of lemon balm add appealing color and flavor to summer drinks. Use dried leaves to make tea, but don't steep too long or flavor will be overpowering.

Marjoram, also known as *sweet marjoram,* is a popular herb that can be used fresh or dried. Add it to omelets and vegetable and meat dishes.

Oregano is often used in Italian cooking. It is similar to marjoram except it is a cold-hardy perennial; marjoram is an annual.

Peppermint displays its dainty flower clusters and deep purple stems. Use leaves to make a fragrant tea, but don't steep too long or the flavor becomes too strong.

Harvesting and use: Use fresh leaves in salads or teas. Preserve leaves by drying or freezing. Oregano is used extensively as a flavoring on pizza. Sprinkle leaves over lamb or steak rubbed with lemon juice, or add to Italian-type sauces.

Parsley
Petroselinum crispum

See page 139.

Peppermint
Mentha piperita

Peppermint has an interesting history. It was introduced in England in 1676, a hybrid of watermint and spearmint. It was the first commercial crop grown in England, beginning in 1750. A botanist of the time coined the name "peppermint" to describe it. Today all peppermint crops are derived from those 17th century English hybrids.

Plants are hardy perennials. They produce many upright stems to 2 feet or more high, spreading 1 foot wide in a single season. Dark green leaves and reddish-tinged stems have a pleasant, minty fragrance. Tiny, purplish flowers appear in thick, terminal spikes 1 to 3 inches long.

How to grow: Peppermint grows best in a rich, moist soil, in sun or shade. Propagate by seeds, division or cuttings. Cutting sprigs frequently promotes fast growth.

Mint cuttings root easily in water. This is the preferred method of propagation. Plants can be divided by their roots. If you want to grow from seeds, sow 1/4 inch deep directly in the garden 3 weeks before last frost date. Thin plants to stand 6 inches apart, and allow them to form clumps or matted rows.

Pest and disease control: Mint leaves are susceptible to rust disease. Prune and destroy infected foliage. Winter clean-up of dead plants helps control the disease.

Harvesting and use: Use leaves anytime. To dry for storage, leaves are best harvested just as flowers begin to appear. Leaves are used to make an herbal tea and for other flavorings. Oil from the plant is used in products such as chewing gum, confections, toilet water, soap and liqueur.

Recommended varieties: There are two main varieties—black peppermint and white peppermint. Black peppermint is the variety grown commercially in the United States as a source of peppermint oil. It can be identified by its deep purple stems. White peppermint is less vigorous, less flavorful and has light green leaves and stems. For other forms of mint, see Spearmint, page 188.

Rosemary
Rosmarinus officinalis

Rosemary is an evergreen shrub in areas where winter temperatures stay above 5F (−15C). Plants have dark green, needlelike leaves, woody stems, and tiny, pale blue blossoms. Fragrance is suggestive of nutmeg and pine needles. In colder areas, this perennial should be brought indoors and kept as a pot plant during winter.

Rosemary is an attractive plant in the landscape, and a popular flavoring for stews and meat dishes such as pork and veal. Use leaves fresh or dried.

Varieties vary in form and size. Most are dense, spreading shrubs up to 3 feet wide. With time, plants can be trained and pruned into topiary figures and tree forms.

How to grow: Rosemary grows best in well-drained, sunny locations in soil containing lime. Lime should be added each year in acid-soil areas. Plants can be propagated by cuttings or grown from seeds. Sow seeds 1/4 inch deep directly in the garden 3 weeks before last frost date. They require up to 3 weeks or more to germinate. You may also start seeds indoors and transplant. Thin seedlings to stand 1 to 2 inches apart for a dense, hedgelike effect. Plants grow slowly, adding about 6 inches of height each season. Keep moist and mist often during hot weather. Otherwise, plants may drop their leaves. Pinch tops of plants to keep compact.

Pest and disease control: Plants sometimes become infested with red spider mites. They are difficult to control once established. Malathion and dicofol are common chemical sprays used to control mites. Frequent dousing of plants with a soap and water solution is an organic control.

Harvesting and use: Narrow leaves have a spicy fragrance. Use fresh leaves as needed any time of the year. Rosemary is a popular flavoring for meats and dressings, or as a garnish on roasts. Oil from leaves is used in medicines.

Recommended varieties: Over 20 varieties are sold by herb specialists. Different flower colors are available, from deep blue to pink. 'Prostrate' grows to 2 feet high and spreads to 5 feet wide. 'Tuscan Blue' grows upright to 5 feet high.

Sage
Salvia officinalis

This is a woody, hardy, perennial plant with oblong, woolly, gray-green leaves. Sage grows 2 to 3 feet or more high, sprawling 2 to 3 feet wide.

How to grow: Start from seeds or cuttings. Sage is slow to begin growth. Sow seeds indoors 8 weeks before outdoor planting date. Plant in garden in full sun 3 weeks before last frost date. Space plants 2 to 2-1/2 feet apart. If a hedge effect is desired, space plants 6 to 12 inches apart. Plants eventually become woody and should be renewed every 3 to 4 years. Pick leaves before or at blooming. Cut stems back after blooming to encourage new growth.

Pest and disease control: Nematodes can be highly destructive. French marigolds are said to help repel these soil pests. Soil may require fumigation for complete eradication. See page 65.

Harvesting and use: This aromatic and slightly bitter herb is often included in stuffings for poultry, rabbit, pork and baked fish. It is also used to flavor sausage and meat loaf.

Recommended varieties: Over 25 varieties are available. Mail order herb catalogs are the best sources. Pineapple sage, *Salvia elegans,* has a pineapple fragrance. Garden sage, *Salvia officinalis,* has an anise fragrance. It is the most common variety. It grows 2 to 2-1/2 feet high. Oval leaves are gray-green. Purple sage is a gray-leafed variety. Young leaves have a purple cast.

Sage can be grown as a border plant. Leaves are strongly flavored and can be added to poultry stuffing and meat, egg and vegetable dishes.

Sage is adapted to growing in containers, as shown by this healthy specimen. Purple basil and thyme are growing in containers in background.

Summer savory adds a peppery taste to salads, soups and stews. It has a milder flavor and is preferred over the similar winter savory.

Close-up view of winter savory shows its dainty white flowers. Culinary use is the same as for summer savory. Its flavor is more potent, so add to dishes sparingly.

Spearmint is one of the most popular garden herbs. Top whorl of leaves can be used to flavor cold drinks, make mint sauce and create a refreshing herb tea.

Summer Savory
Satureja hortensis

This is a tender annual that grows up to 18 inches high and spreads 12 inches wide. It has small, bronze-green leaves, and small, lavender or white flowers. Leaves are pungent and spicy.

How to grow: Summer savory grows best in a well-prepared, loam-type soil. Seeds can be sown directly in the garden after all danger of frost has passed. Sow 1/4 inch deep and thin plants to stand 10 inches apart.

Pest and disease control: Generally free of pests and diseases.

Harvesting and use: Harvest leafy tops when plants are in bud. Hang in an airy, shady place until crisp and dry. Use as a condiment with meats and vegetables. Summer savory is generally more sweetly flavored than winter savory.

Winter Savory
Satureja montana

This woody, perennial plant has dark green, shiny, pointed leaves. It grows to 2 feet high and spreads as wide. Flowers are small, in shades of white and lavender. It is a perennial plant, whereas summer savory is an annual. It has a stronger flavor and is normally used sparingly with other herbs.

How to grow: Propagate by cuttings or grow from seeds. Sow seeds 1/4 inch deep directly in the garden 3 weeks before last frost date. Thin seedlings to stand 12 inches apart. Prefers a light, sandy soil. Keep dead wood trimmed out of plant. Leaves are evergreen in mild-winter areas.

Pest and disease control: Generally free of pests and diseases.

Harvesting and use: Pick young shoots and leaves anytime. Leaves are best dried for winter use. Winter savory is a condiment, often used as a flavoring in liqueurs. It can also be used in small quantities with other herbs to flavor soups and stews.

Recommended varieties: Several named varieties are available. 'Nana' is a dwarf variety.

Spearmint
Mentha spicata

Spearmint is a hardy perennial. Pointed, slightly crinkled leaves are lighter green than peppermint. Plants grow 1-1/2 to 2 feet tall, spreading 12 inches the first season. They form thick clumps each season by sending out underground runners. Plant has a sweet, minty fragrance.

How to grow: Cuttings and root division are the most common forms of propagation. Plants can also be started from seeds. Sow seeds directly in the garden 3 weeks before last frost date. Plant 1/4 inch deep and thin seedlings to stand 6 inches apart. Spearmint grows best in moist, fertile soil. Growth is more vigorous with frequent harvesting.

Pest and disease control: Susceptible to rust disease. Prune away and destroy infected foliage. Cleaning garden in winter helps prevent rust. Mealybugs sometimes form colonies on spearmint. Dab them off with cotton swabs dipped in rubbing alcohol.

Harvesting and use: Pick fresh leaves and leafy stem tips for use anytime. To dry leaves for later use, harvest just as flowering begins. Leaves are used to flavor cold drinks and teas and to make mint sauce. Oil from leaves is used in confections.

Recommended varieties: Spearmint is the most popular home garden mint. In addition, there are dozens of other varieties available. 'Apple' mint, 'Ginger' mint, 'Orange' mint and 'Pineapple' mint are just a few. See Peppermint, page 186.

Sweet Cicely
Myrrhis odorata

Every part of this plant is edible and has a sweet, licorice flavor. Plants grow to 3 feet tall and spread to 2 feet wide. They produce lacy leaves and beautiful white flower clusters. A hardy perennial, sweet cicely is one of the first herbs to flower in spring.

How to grow: Jet-black seeds take up to a month to germinate. Sow directly in the garden 3 weeks before last frost date. Or sow in early fall so plants can grow during cool weather and go dormant after a hard frost. Mild-winter climates do not have enough cold for dormancy. Plants will grow vigorously the following spring. Plant seeds 1/4 inch deep in fertile soil enriched with plenty of organic matter. Space plants 2 feet apart. Soil should be kept moist. Plants can tolerate light shade.

Pest and disease control: Generally free of pests and diseases. Young stems occasionally attract aphids, which can be rubbed or washed off.

Harvesting and use: Finely chopped leaves are useful as a garnish for salads, egg dishes and seafood. Immature seeds taste like licorice, and are delicious to chew before they become hard.

Sweet Woodruff
Galium odoratum

A low, spreading, perennial plant, sweet woodruff grows in clumps about 8 inches high. Slender leaves are borne in star-shaped whorls. Tiny, white flowers are formed in loose clusters. When plant leaves are crushed, they have a sweet scent similar to vanilla and fresh-mown hay.

How to grow: Sweet woodruff is a hardy perennial and usually survives through winter if grown in sheltered areas. Plants thrive in semishade. They make an attractive ground cover under taller plants and around bases of trees. Sow seeds directly in the garden 3 weeks before last frost date. Thickly broadcast seeds over the soil surface and rake into soil. Plants tolerate crowding, and grow in dense, spreading, matlike clumps. Soil should be fertile, preferably mixed with plenty of organic matter such as peat moss, leaf mold or garden compost.

Pest and disease control: Generally free of pests and diseases.

Harvesting and use: To store, harvest and dry plants in spring when flavor is the strongest. Leaves can also be frozen. Sweet woodruff is used most often to lend its distinctive flavor to German May wine.

Flowers of sweet cicely appear in spring. Clusters of pods that follow contain black, aromatic seeds flavored like licorice. Leaves are sweet and make a tasty tea.

Sweet woodruff makes an excellent, ornamental ground cover in partial shade. Leaves, fresh or dried, can be added to drinks or used to make tea.

Edible Herbs **189**

French tarragon, not *Russian* tarragon, is best for culinary use. Plant is sterile so it cannot be grown from seed, but grows readily from cuttings.

Tarragon
Artemisia dracunculus

This woody perennial grows to 2 feet high with an equal spread. Tarragon has a branching habit with narrow, needlelike green leaves. The French consider tarragon the king of all culinary herbs. But it is French tarragon and not Russian tarragon they refer to. See recommended varieties.

How to grow: French tarragon does not set viable seeds. When seeds are offered in catalogs, it is Russian tarragon, which is not the quality of the French version. Tarragon grows in full sun but seems to do better with some shade. It prefers well-drained, organically rich soil. Propagate from root cuttings or by division. Although it is somewhat hardy, tarragon needs protection during winter in cold climates.

Pest and disease control: Susceptible to root rot. This can be avoided by planting in well-drained soil.

Harvesting and use: Use fresh, young leaves and stem tips. Flavor is lost when tarragon is dried. Chopped leaves have a distinctive flavor similar to anise. Add leaves to salads, marinades and sauces. Used sparingly, tarragon enhances the flavor of potatoes, omelettes and chicken. Helps reduce strong fishy flavors in seafood. Leaves add flavor to vinegar when steeped for two weeks.

Recommended varieties: 'Sativa' French tarragon is preferred over 'Inodora' Russian tarragon. Russian tarragon is vigorous, growing to a height of 6 feet. It has an unpleasant flavor. If you buy tarragon seeds, Russian tarragon is what you will get. True French tarragon is sterile and can only be grown from cuttings or from root divisions.

Thyme
Thymus vulgaris

Thyme is a low, wiry-stemmed perennial that grows to about 10 inches high. Plants spread about 8 inches wide the first year, and eventually create a thick, dense mat. It is an attractive edging plant and an effective ground cover in rock gardens and dry walls. Stems are stiff and woody. Gray-green leaves are small, oval and highly aromatic. Lilaclike flowers are borne in small clusters.

How to grow: Plants grow best in light, well-drained soil in full sun. Sow seeds 1/4 inch deep 3 weeks before last frost date. Thin plants to stand 8 to 12 inches apart. Also propagate by cuttings and by division. It is best to renew plants every few years.

Pest and disease control: Generally free of pests and diseases.

Harvesting and use: Harvest leafy tops and flower clusters when first blossoms open. Dry and store for later use according to instructions given on page 178. Leaves also freeze well.

Thyme is widely used as a seasoning. It goes well in gumbos, bouillabaisse, clam chowder, poultry stuffings and slow-cooking beef dishes.

Recommended varieties: More than 50 varieties of thyme are available. English thyme, *T. vulgaris,* is the most popular. Other varieties have exotic flavors, such as lemon, nutmeg, oregano and balsam thyme.

English thyme creates beautiful, spreading clumps of fragrant flowers, and is often grown as a ground cover. Use it to flavor soups, stuffings and stews.

INDEX

Bold face indicates most important reference.

A

A-frame, 7, 75
Acid soil, 20, 22, 24
Acorn squash, 159, 160
Activator, 24
Agricultural agent, 83
Agricultural extension service, 83
Alkaline soils, 20, 22
All-America Selections, 34
Allium schoenoprasum, 181
Alpine strawberry, 48-51, 163
Aluminum foil, 59
Aluminum sulfate, 22
Amaranth, 48-51, **84**
Anethum graveolens, 183
Animal pests, 64
Anise, 179
Anthracnose, 68
Anthriscus cerefolium, 181
Aphids, 60, 65
Armenian cucumber, 121
Artemisia dracunculus, 190
Artichoke, 73, 84
   how to eat, 85
Asparagus, 13, 35, 48-51, **86**
   harvesting, 77
Asparagus pea, 88
Automatic Vegetable Garden, 6, 14-16

B

Bacillus popillae, 63
Bacillus thuringiensis, 63
Bacterial fertilizer, 29
Bacterial wilt, 68
Balsam apple, 121, 127
Bamboo poles, 75
Bark chips, 58, 59
Basic gardening tools, 16-17
Basil, 179
Bean beetle contol, 90
Bean leaf beetle, 66
Beans, 48-51, 73, **88-94**
   broad, 89
   cowpea, 90
   garbanzo, 91
   harvesting, 77
   lima, 35, **91**
   romano, 92
   runner, 92
   shelling (dry), 93
   snap, 35, **88**
   soy, 93
   storage, 79
   winged, 93
   yard-long, 94
Beefsteak tomato, 169
Beets, 12, 13, 35, 48-51, 73, 80, **95,** 173
   harvesting, 77
   storage, 79
Bell peppers, 79, 144-145
Beneficial insects, 64
Benomyl, 37
Biological controls, 63
Black plastic, 14, 58, 59
Black rot, 68
Blanching, 81
Block planting, 31, 41, 134
Blossom-end rot, 68, 144, 166
Blue hubbard squash, 160
Bok choy cabbage, 100
Borage, 180
Borago officinalis, 180
Bordeaux mixture, 69
Boston marrow, 160
Bottle gourd, 121

Braconid wasp, 64
Broad beans, 48-51, **89,** 90
Broccoli, 12, 13, 15, 35, 48-51, 73, **96-97,** 100
   harvesting, 77
Broom corn, 115, 117
Brussels sprouts, 35, 48-51, 73, **97-98,** 100
   harvesting, 77
Bunching onions, 138
Burdock, 48-51, 98
Burnet, 180
Burpless cucumbers, 121, 122
Bush beans, 12, 15
Bush cucumbers, 15, 119
Bush snap beans, 89
Bush varieties, 75
Buttercup squash, 161
Butterhead lettuce, 133, 134
Butternut squash, 161

C

Cabbage, 7, 12, 13, 15, 35, 48-51, 74, **99-101**
   harvesting, 77
   illustration of crops, 100
   storage, 79
Cabbage sprout, 100
Calcium deficiency, 27
Canning, 80, 81
Cantaloupe, 15, 48-51, **103-105**
   harvesting, 77
Captan, 69
Caraway, 180
Cardoon, 48-51, 105
Carrots, 12, 13, 35, 48-51, 74, **106-107,** 173
   harvesting, 77
   storage, 79
Cart, 17
Carum carvi, 180
Casaba melon, 104
Catnip, 181
Cauliflower, 13, 35, 48-51, 74, 100, **107-108**
   harvesting, 78
   storage, 79
Celeriac, 48-51, 108, 173
Celery, 35, 48-51, **109**
   harvesting, 78
Cell packs, 36
Celtuce, 48-51, 110
Chantenay carrot, 106
Chard, Swiss, 35
   harvesting, 78
Chayote, 48-51, 111
Chemical fertilizer, 27
Chemical pest control, 62
Cherry tomatoes, 170
Chervil, 181
Chicken wire, 75
Chicons, 111
Chicory, 111
Chicory, witloof, harvesting, 78
Chinese cabbage, 48-51, 100, **102**
Chinese luffa, 128
Chinese okra, 128
Chinese yam, 48-51, 175
Chives, 177, 181
   harvesting, 78
Clay soil, 19, 20, 105
Clear plastic, 59
Climate and planting dates, 44
Climate map, 46-47
Cold frame, 40
Cold-hardy vegetables, 11, 44, 49, 51

Cold-moist storage, 79
Cold-tender vegetables, 11, 44, 49, 51
Collard, 48-51, 112
   harvesting, 78
Colorado potato beetle, 62, 65
Comfrey, 182
Companion planting, 42
Compost, 19, 23, **24-25,** 59
   bins, 25
Containers, 71
Cooking with herbs, 178
Cool-dry storage, 79
Cool-season vegetables, 44
Copper-containing fungicides, 69
Coriander, 182
Coriandrum sativum, 182
Corncobs, as mulch, 59
Corn earworm, 60, 65
Corn nuts, 117
Corn, sweet, 48-51, **113-117**
   harvesting, 79
   illustration of anatomy, 114
   illustration of varieties, 115
Cornell soil mix, 72
Cos lettuce, 133, 135
Cottonseed hulls, 59
County agent, 83
County extension service, 83
Cowpea bean, 48-51, **90-91**
   harvesting, 78
Crenshaw melon, 104
Cress, 118
Crisp head lettuce, 133, 134, 135
Crookneck squash, 158
Cucumber, 7, 12, 13, 35, 40, 48-51, 74, 75, **119-123**
   harvesting, 78
   illustration of anatomy, 120
   illustration of varieties, 121
Cucumber beetle, 60, 65
Cultivators, 57
Cushaw, 161
Cutworms, 40, 60, 63, 65

D

Damping-off disease, 37
Dandelion, 48-51, 124
Danvers carrot, 106
Deep watering, 54
Dehydration, 81
Determinate tomatoes, 168
Diatomaceous earth, 63
Dill, 183
Direct seeding, 38
Disease control, 68
Disease prevention, 35
Disease-resistant varieties, 32, 68
Dolomitic limestone, 22
Double cropping, 13, 42
Double digging, 23
Drip irrigation, 14, 55
   sample layout, 56
Dry beans, 93
Dry fertilizer, 28
Drying herbs, 178
Drying vegetables, 81

E

Earthworms, 23
Edible burdock, 98, 173
Edible-pod peas, 142, 143
Eggplant, 12, 15, 48-51, 74, **124-125**
   harvesting, 78
   illustration of varieties, 125
Egyptian onion, 136

Emitters, 55
Endive, 35, 48-51, 126
   harvesting, 78
English peas, 142, 143
English thyme, 190
Escarole, 126
Everlasting heritage, 113

F

Fava beans, 89
Fennel, 183
Fertilizer, 19, 21, 23, **26-29**
   container plants, 73
   how to read a label, 27
   sample schedule, 29
Fiber blocks and cubes, 36
Flea beetles, 62, 65
Fluid seed sowing, 38
Foeniculum vulgare azoricum, 183
Forcing rhubarb, 152
Fork, garden, 16
Formal herb garden, 176, 178
Freezing vegetables, 81
Frost dates, 44
Frost protection, 40, 44
Fruit-producing vegetables, 9
Fungicides, 69
Fusarium wilt, 32, 69

G

Galium odoratum, 189
Garbanzo bean, 48-51, 91
Garden huckleberry, 48-51, 129
   harvesting, 78
Garden planning, 9-17
Garden size, 10
Garden vegetables, encyclopedia, 83-191
Garlic, 48-51, **126,** 137
   harvesting, 78
Garlic-pepper spray for pest control, 64
General-purpose fertilizer, 27
Germination, 31
   days required, 49, 51
   requirements for, 31
   testing, 34
Gherkin, 121, 123
Giant cucumbers, 122
Giant-fruited tomato, 169
Ginseng, 48-51, 127
Globe artichoke, 48-51
Gold sweet potato, 148
Golden beet, 173
Golden nugget, 161
Gourds, 48-51, 127
   illustrations of, 121
Grain amaranth, 84
Grass clippings, 24, 58, 59
Green manure, 29
Ground bark, 59
Ground limestone, 22
Growing seasons, 46

H

Hand fork, 16
Hand pollination, 157
Hanging baskets, 73, 74
Hardening-off, 40
Harlequin bug, 60, 67
Harvesting, 77-79
   days to, 49, 51
Hay, as mulch, 59
Heat, 10
Herbicidal weed killers, 57
Herbs, 10, 13, 72, 74, **177-190**
   in containers, 178
Hercules war club, 128

Heterosis, 32
Hoe, 16, 57
Honeydew melon, 104
Honeyloupe melon, 104
Horehound, 184
Hornworm, 61, 65
Horseradish, 129
Hose, for watering, 16
Hot caps, 103
Hot pepper, 146
Husk tomato, 48-51, 130
Hybrid vegetables, 31
Hyssop, 184,
Hyssopus officinalis, 184

I

Ice-box watermelon, 174
Iceburg lettuce, 134
Imported cabbage worm, 60, 66
Indeterminate tomatoes, 169
Insects, beneficial, 64
Intensive gardening, 75
Intercropping, 42
Interplanting, 75
Irish potatoes, 15, 147
Iron chlorosis, 27
Irrigation, furrow, 54
Irrigation, hand, 54
Italian parsley, 140

J

Japanese beetle, 60, 63, 66
   trap for, 63
Jerusalem artichoke, 48-51, **130,** 148
   harvesting, 78
Jicama, 48-51, **131,** 148

K

Kale, 48-51, 100, **131**
   harvesting, 78
Knot garden, 177
Kohlrabi, 48-51, 100, **132**
   harvesting, 78
   storage, 79

L

Labels, 17
Laboratory soil test, 20
Lacewings, 64
Ladybird beetle, 64
Landscaped vegetable garden, 4
Large-fruited red tomatoes, 169
Large garden plan, 13
Leaf blight, 69
Leaf chicory, 48-51, 111, 112
Leafhoppers, 66
Leaf lettuce, 133, 134
Leaf mold, 25, 59
Leaf spots, 69
Leeks, 48-51, 132
   harvesting, 78
Lemon balm, 185
Lemon cucumber, 121
Lettuce, 12, 13, 15, 31, 35, 48-51, 74, **133-135**
   butterhead, 134
   cos (romaine), 135
   crisp head, 135
   for greenhouses, 135
   harvesting, 78
   leaf, 134
Light, 10, 35
Lima beans, 13, 48-51, **91**
Lime, 22, 23
Limestone, 21
Liquid fertilizer, 28
Loam soil, 19, 20

Loopers, 60, 66
Looseleaf lettuce, 133
Luffa gourd, 121, 127, 128

M
Mail order sources, 32, 33,
Malabar spinach, 48-51, 155
Maneb, 69
Marjoram, 185
Marrubium vulgare, 184
Maturity dates, 42
Medium-size garden plan, 12
Melissa officinalis, 185
Melon squash, 162
Melons, 13, 103-105
Mentha piperita, 186
Mentha spicata, 188
Mexican bean beetle, 62, 66
Microclimates, 44
Mineral pest controls, 63
Minor elements, 26
Mites, 66
Moisture, 35
Moisture-holding capacity of
  soil, 54
Mounded row, 86
Mulching, 9, 14, 38, 53, 57,
  58-59, 168
  chart of materials, 59
Muskmelon, 35
  harvesting, 78
Mustard greens, 48-51, 100, **135**
  harvesting, 78
Myrrhis odorata, 189

N
Nantes carrot, 106
Natural fertilizer, 27, 28
Nematodes, 32, 66
Nepeta cataria, 181
Netting, 75
Neutral, 20
New Zealand spinach, 48-51, 155
Newspapers, 59
Nicotine sulfate, 63
Nitrogen, 21, 26
Novelty tomatoes, 170
Nutrient deficiencies, 27

O
Ocimum basilicum, 179
Okra, 35, 48-51, 136
  harvesting, 78
Onion, 12, 13, 35, 48-51, 74,
  136-139
  harvesting, 78
  illustration of varieties, 137
  storage, 80
Oregano, 185
Organic controls, 62
Organic fungicides, 69
Organic matter, 19, 43
Origanum majorana, 185
Origanum vulgare, 185
Ornamental corn, 116, 117

P
Pak choy, 102
Parsley, 35, 48-51, 139
  harvesting, 78
  parsnip-rooted, 140
Parsnips, 35, 48-51, **140,** 173
  harvesting, 78
  storage, 79
Parthenocarpic cucumber, 123
Paste tomatoes, 170
Peanut, 48-51, **141,** 148
  harvesting, 78

hulls as mulch, 59
Peas, 12, 13, 48-51, **142-143**
  edible-pod, 143
  English, 35, 143
  harvesting, 78
  snap pea, 143
  storage, 79
Peat moss, 59
Peat pellets, 36
Peat pots, 36
Peat trays, 36
Pelleted seeds, 32
Pepper cress, 48-51, 118
Peppermint, 186
Peppers, 12, 13, 15, 35, 48-51,
  74, **144-146**
  bell, 144
  harvesting, 78
  hot, 146
  sweet, 146
Pest control, 62, 65
Pest protection, 39
Pests, 16, 61
pH scale, 20
pH test kit, 20
Phosphorus, 21, 26
Photosynthesis, 9
Pickle cucumbers, 121, 122, 123
Pickling, 81
Pimpinella anisum, 179
Pine needles, 58, 59, 168
Plan on paper, 11
Planning, 9-17
Plant diseases, 68
Planting, 31, 41
  dates by regions, 44
  in squares, 13
  large seeds, 43
  small seeds, 39
  step by step, 43
Pole beans, 9, 13, 89, 90
Popcorn, 115, 117
Potassium, 21, 26
Potatoes, Irish, 15, 48-51, 74,
  147-148
  harvesting, 79
Poterium sanguisorba, 180
Potting soil, 36, 37
Powdery mildew, 69
Power tiller, 17, 23
Praying mantis, 64
Preplanters, 36
Preserving harvests, 80
Preserving herbs, 178
Protecting plants, 10
Pump-action sprayer, 17
Pumpkins, 35, 48-51, **149-150**
  storage, 80
Purple-top rutabaga, 173
Purple-top turnip, 173
Pyrethrum, 63

R
Radishes, 6, 12, 13, 35, 48-51,
  74, **150-151**
  harvesting, 79
  illustration of varieties, 151
Raised beds, 9, 11, 14, 72, **74**
Rake, 16
Recycled containers, 36
Recycled supports, 75
Red beet, 173
Red potato, 148
Repellent plants, 64
Rhubarb, 13, 48-51, 74, **152**
  harvesting, 79
Romaine lettuce, 133, 135

Romanesco broccoli, 97
Romano bean, 92
Root crops illustration, 173
Root maggots, 67
Rosemary, 186
Rosmarinus officinalis, 186
Rotating crops, 68
Rotenone, 62, 63
Rotenone-pyrethrum, 16
Rows, spacing, 11, 49, 51
Runner beans, 92
Rust, 69
Rutabagas, 48-51, **172-173**
  storage, 80

S
Sage, 187
Salsify, 48-51, 153, **173**
  harvesting, 79
Salvia officinalis, 187
Sample garden layouts, 12-13
Sandy soil, 19, 20
Satureja hortensis, 188
Satureja montana, 188
Savory, summer, 188
Savory, winter, 188
Scallions, 138
Scallop squash, 158
Scarlet runner bean, 48-51
Scatter seeding, 39
Scorzonera, 48-51, 153
Seed, depth to plant, 49, 51
Seed catalogs, list of, 33
Seed germination, soil
  temperature, 35
Seed packets, 32
Seed pellets, 32
Seed racks, 32
Seed starting, 14, 31, 35
  materials, 36
Seed storage, 34
Seed tapes, 32
Seeding tips, 39
Seedless watermelon, 175
Seeds, saving your own, 34
Self-fertile cucumbers, 123
Shade, 9
Shallot, 48-51, 154
Shelling bean, 48-51, 93
Shelter, 10
Side dress, 16
Single dig, 23
Single-row planting, 41
Sized seed, 172
Slicing cucumbers, 119, 121
Slugs, 60, 66
Small-fruited tomatoes, 170
Small garden plan, 12
Small spaces, 71
Snail and slug bait, 63
Snails, 60, 67
Snake cucumber, 121
Snap beans, 12, 13, 15, 48-51,
  88-89
Snap peas, 78, 81, 142, **143**
Soil, 19
  adjusting pH, 22
  drainage, 10, 53
  for containers, 71
  mixes, 36, 72
  preparation, 22, 43
  sample test report, 21
  structure, 22
  substitutes, 36
  test, 19
  types, 19
Soil-borne pests, 39

Soy beans, 48-51, 92, 93
Space-saving training, 75
Spacing plants, rows, 49, 51
Spade, 16
Spagnum peat moss, 74
Spearmint, 188
Spinach, 35, 48-51, 74, 79,
  154-155
  harvesting, 79
  hot weather substitutes, 155
Sprinklers, 55
Square-foot gardening, 41
Squash blossom, how to
  pollinate, 157
Squash bugs, 67
Squash, summer, 6, 12, 13, 35,
  48-51, 74, **156-158**
  harvesting, 79
  storage, 80
Squash vine borer, 67
Squash, winter, 159-162
  harvesting, 79
  storage, 80
Stakes and string, 17
Staking, 75
Standard vegetables, 31
Starting seeds indoors, 37
Starting sweet potatoes indoors,
  164
Stink bugs, 67
Stonehead cabbage, 100
Storage, 77, 79
Storage times for vegetables, 80
Straightneck squash, 158
Straw, 59
Strawberries, 15
Succession planting, 13, 42
Sugar pumpkins, 150
Sulfur, 22
Sulfur-containing fungicides, 69
Summer savory, 188
Summer squash, 6, 12, 13, 15,
  35, 48-51, **156-158**
  harvesting, 79
  storage, 80
Sunflower, 48-51, 163
Sunlight, 9
Sweet basil, 179
Sweet cicely, 189
Sweet corn, 13, 48-51, **113-117**
  harvesting, 79
Sweet marjoram, 185
Sweet peppers, 145-146
Sweet potatoes, 19, 48-51, **164**
  harvesting, 79
Sweet woodruff, 189
Swiss chard, 48-51, 74, 110
Symphytum officinale, 182

T
Tahiti squash, 162
Tampala, 84, 155
Tarragon, 190
Temperature, 35, 44
Thinning, 41, 42
Thyme, 190
Thymus vulgaris, 190
Tilling, 23
Timed-release fertilizer, 28
Tomato spray for pest control, 64
Tomatoes, 7, 12, 13, 15, 35, 40,
  48-51, 72, 74, 78, 83, **165-171**
  harvesting, 79
  illustration of anatomy, 166
  illustration of varieties, 167
Tools, 17
Toxic plants, 10

Trace elements, 21
Transplanting, 31, 40
  weeks to transplant size, 49, 51
Treated seeds, 38, 69
Trellis, 9
Trowel, 16
Tuberous vegetables,
  illustration, 148
Turk's turban, 159
Turnips, 13, 35, 48-51, 74,
  172-173
  harvesting, 79
  storage, 80

U
U.C. soil mix, 72
Upland cress, 48-51, 118

V
Vegetables, 83-175
  for containers, 73
Verticillium wilt, 32, 69
Vidalia onion, 138
Vine borer, 103
Vining varieties, 75
Virus-free plants, 68

W
Warm-dry storage, 79
Warm-season vegetables, 44
Watercress, 48-51, 118
  harvesting, 79
Watering, 53-55
  container plants, 73
  established plants, 54
  methods, 54
  newly planted seeds, 38, 54
  transplants, 54
Watermelon, 35, 48-51, 74,
  174-175
  harvesting, 79
Weeding, 56
Weeds, 24, 53
Welsh onion, 138
Wheelbarrow, 17
When to plant, 48-51
Whiteflies, 67
Wide-row planting, 41, 101, 140
Winged bean, 48-51, **93-94**
Winter squash, 13, 48-51, 80,
  159-162
  harvesting, 79
  storage, 80
Wire cage, for support, 75, 168
Wireworms, 67
Witloof chicory, 111, 112

Y
Yam, Chinese, 48-51, 175
Yard-long beans, 94
Yields, 10, 15, 49, 51

Z
Zineb, 69
Zucchini, 53, 157, 158

7.7318063890 2265